Study Guide

Study Guide

to accompany

KATHLEEN STASSEN BERGER

The Developing Person

Through Childhood and Adolescence

Fifth Edition

Richard O. Straub

University of Michigan, Dearborn

WORTH PUBLISHERS

Study Guide
by Richard O. Straub
to accompany
Berger: **The Developing Person Through Childhood and Adolescence**, Fifth Edition

ISBN: 1-57259-725-9

Printed in the United States of America

Printing: 5 4 3 2 1
Year: 03 02 01 00

Cover: Christian Pierre, *My Friend*, 1995. Acrylic on canvas, 14″ × 18″.

Worth Publishers
41 Madison Avenue
New York, New York 10010
www:worthpublishers.com

Contents

Preface

This Study Guide is designed for use with The *Developing Person Through Childhood and Adolescence*, Fifth Edition, by Kathleen Stassen Berger. It is intended to help you to evaluate your understanding of that material, and then to review any problem areas. "How to Manage Your Time Efficiently, Study More Effectively, and Think Critically" provides detailed instructions on how to use the textbook and this Study Guide for maximum benefit. It also offers additional study suggestions based on principles of time management, effective note-taking, evaluation of exam performance, and an effective program for improving your comprehension while studying from textbooks.

Each chapter of the Study Guide includes a Chapter Overview, a set of Guided Study questions to pace your reading of the text chapter, a Chapter Review section to be completed after you have read the text chapter, three review tests, a list of the key terms in the chapter, and in several chapters a crossword puzzle that provides an alternative method of testing your knowledge of the key terms. The review tests are of two types: Progress Tests that consist of questions focusing on facts and definitions and a Thinking Critically Test that evaluates your understanding of the text chapter's broader conceptual material and its application to real-world situations. For all three review tests, the correct answers are given, followed by textbook page references (so you can easily go back and reread the material), and complete explanations not only of why the answer is correct but also of why the other choices are incorrect.

I would like to offer a special thanks to Betty Probert of The Special Projects Group for her exceptional work in all phases of this project. Having worked with Betty for many years now, I continue to marvel at the depth of her knowledge of the field of psychology, as well as her abundant skills as an editor and writer. Betty deserves an equal share in the credit for this book's success in helping students study developmental psychology. Thanks also to Don Probert for keyboarding most of the text and for designing the beautiful new style, Laura Rubin for her proofreading skills, and Stacey Alexander at Worth for her outstanding production work.

Most important, I want to thank Pamela for her love and continued support, and our children—Jeremy, Rebecca, and Melissa—for developing into the wonderful people they have become.

Those at Worth Publishers who assisted in the preparation of this Study Guide join me in hoping that our work will help you to achieve your highest level of academic performance in this course and to acquire a keen appreciation of human development.

Richard O. Straub
June 1999

How to Manage Your Time Efficiently, Study More Effectively, and Think Critically

How effectively do you study? Good study habits make the job of being a college student much easier. Many students, who *could* succeed in college, fail or drop out because they have never learned to manage their time efficiently. Even the best students can usually benefit from an in-depth evaluation of their current study habits.

There are many ways to achieve academic success, of course, but your approach may not be the most effective or efficient. Are you sacrificing your social life or your physical or mental health in order to get A's on your exams? Good study habits result in better grades *and* more time for other activities.

Evaluate Your Current Study Habits

To improve your study habits, you must first have an accurate picture of how you currently spend your time. Begin by putting together a profile of your present living and studying habits. Answer the following questions by writing *yes* or *no* on each line.

______ **1.** Do you usually set up a schedule to budget your time for studying, recreation, and other activities?

______ **2.** Do you often put off studying until time pressures force you to cram?

______ **3.** Do other students seem to study less than you do, but get better grades?

______ **4.** Do you usually spend hours at a time studying one subject, rather than dividing that time between several subjects?

______ **5.** Do you often have trouble remembering what you have just read in a textbook?

______ **6.** Before reading a chapter in a textbook, do you skim through it and read the section headings?

______ **7.** Do you try to predict exam questions from your lecture notes and reading?

______ **8.** Do you usually attempt to paraphrase or summarize what you have just finished reading?

______ **9.** Do you find it difficult to concentrate very long when you study?

______ **10.** Do you often feel that you studied the wrong material for an exam?

Thousands of college students have participated in similar surveys. Students who are fully realizing their academic potential usually respond as follows: (1) yes, (2) no, (3) no, (4) no, (5) no, (6) yes, (7) yes, (8) yes, (9) no, (10) no.

Compare your responses to those of successful students. The greater the discrepancy, the more you could benefit from a program to improve your study habits. The questions are designed to identify areas of weakness. Once you have identified your weaknesses, you will be able to set specific goals for improvement and implement a program for reaching them.

Manage Your Time

Do you often feel frustrated because there isn't enough time to do all the things you must and want to do? Take heart. Even the most productive and successful people feel this way at times. But they establish priorities for their activities and they learn to budget time for each of them. There's much in the saying "If you want something done, ask a busy person to do it." A busy person knows how to get things done.

If you don't now have a system for budgeting your time, develop one. Not only will your academic accomplishments increase, but you will actually find more time in your schedule for other activities. And you won't have to feel guilty about "taking time off," because all your obligations will be covered.

Establish a Baseline

As a first step in preparing to budget your time, keep a diary for a few days to establish a summary, or baseline, of the time you spend in studying, socializing, working, and so on. If you are like many students, much of your "study" time is nonproductive; you may sit at your desk and leaf through a book, but the time is actually wasted. Or you may procrastinate. You are always getting ready to study, but you rarely do.

Besides revealing where you waste time, your diary will give you a realistic picture of how much time you need to allot for meals, commuting, and other fixed activities. In addition, careful records should indicate the times of the day when you are consistently most productive. A sample time-management diary is shown in Table 1.

Table 1 Sample Time-Management Diary

Monday		
Activity	Time Completed	Duration Hours: Minutes
Sleep	7:00	7:30
Dressing	7:25	:25
Breakfast	7:45	:20
Commute	8:20	:35
Coffee	9:00	:40
French	10:00	1:00
Socialize	10:15	:15
Videogame	10:35	:20
Coffee	11:00	:25
Psychology	12:00	1:00
Lunch	12:25	:25
Study Lab	1:00	:35
Psych. Lab	4:00	3:00
Work	5:30	1:30
Commute	6:10	:40
Dinner	6:45	:35
TV	7:30	:45
Study Psych.	10:00	2:30
Socialize	11:30	1:30
Sleep		

Prepare a similar chart for each day of the week. When you finish an activity, note it on the chart and write down the time it was completed. Then determine its duration by subtracting the time the previous activity was finished from the newly entered time.

Plan the Term

Having established and evaluated your baseline, you are ready to devise a more efficient schedule. Buy a calendar that covers the entire school term and has ample space for each day. Using the course outlines provided by your instructors, enter the dates of all exams, term paper deadlines, and other important academic obligations. If you have any long-range personal plans (concerts, weekend trips, etc.), enter the dates on the calendar as well. Keep your calendar up to date and refer to it often. I recommend carrying it with you at all times.

Develop a Weekly Calendar

Now that you have a general picture of the school term, develop a weekly schedule that includes all of your activities. Aim for a schedule that you can live with for the entire school term. A sample weekly schedule, incorporating the following guidelines, is shown in Table 2.

1. Enter your class times, work hours, and any other fixed obligations first. *Be thorough.* Using information from your time-management diary, allow plenty of time for such things as commuting, meals, laundry, and the like.

2. Set up a study schedule for each of your courses. The study habits survey and your time-management diary will direct you. The following guidelines should also be useful.

(a) Establish regular study times for each course. The 4 hours needed to study one subject, for example, are most profitable when divided into shorter periods spaced over several days. If you cram your studying into one 4-hour block, what you attempt to learn in the third or fourth hour will interfere with what you studied in the first 2 hours. Newly acquired knowledge is like wet cement. It needs some time to "harden" to become memory.

(b) Alternate subjects. The type of interference just mentioned is greatest between similar topics. Set up a schedule in which you spend time on several *different* courses during each study session. Besides reducing the potential for interference, alternating subjects will help to prevent mental fatigue with one topic.

(c) Set weekly goals to determine the amount of study time you need to do well in each course. This will

Table 2 Sample Weekly Schedule

Time	Mon.	Tues.	Wed.	Thurs.	Fri.	Sat.
7–8	Dress Eat	Dress Eat	Dress Eat	Dress Eat	Dress Eat	
8–9	Psych.	Study Psych.	Psych.	Study Psych.	Psych.	Dress Eat
9–10	Eng.	Study Eng.	Eng.	Study Eng.	Eng.	Study Eng.
10–11	Study French	Free	Study French	Open Study	Study French	Study Stats.
11–12	French	Study Psych. Lab	French	Open Study	French	Study Stats.
12–1	Lunch	Lunch	Lunch	Lunch	Lunch	Lunch
1–2	Stats.	Psych. Lab	Stats.	Study or Free	Stats.	Free
2–3	Bio.	Psych. Lab	Bio.	Free	Bio.	Free
3–4	Free	Psych.	Free	Free	Free	Free
4–5	Job	Job	Job	Job	Job	Free
5–6	Job	Job	Job	Job	Job	Free
6–7	Dinner	Dinner	Dinner	Dinner	Dinner	Dinner
7–8	Study Bio.	Study Bio.	Study Bio.	Study Bio.	Free	Free
8–9	Study Eng.	Study Stats.	Study Psych.	Open Study	Open Study	Free
9–10	Open Study	Open Study	Open Study	Open Study	Free	Free

This is a sample schedule for a student with a 16-credit load and a 10-hour-per-week part-time job. Using this chart as an illustration, make up a weekly schedule, following the guidelines outlined here.

depend on, among other things, the difficulty of your courses and the effectiveness of your methods. Many professors recommend studying at least 1 to 2 hours for each hour in class. If your time-management diary indicates that you presently study less time than that, do not plan to jump immediately to a much higher level. Increase study time from your baseline by setting weekly goals [see (4)] that will gradually bring you up to the desired level. As an initial schedule, for example, you might set aside an amount of study time for each course that matches class time.

(d) Schedule for maximum effectiveness. Tailor your schedule to meet the demands of each course. For the course that emphasizes lecture notes, schedule time for a daily review soon after the class. This will give you a chance to revise your notes and clean up any hard-to-decipher shorthand while the material is still fresh in your mind. If you are evaluated for class participation (for example, in a language course), allow time for a review just before the class meets. Schedule study time for your most difficult (or least motivating) courses during hours when you are the most alert and distractions are fewest.

(e) Schedule open study time. Emergencies, additional obligations, and the like could throw off your schedule. And you may simply need some extra time periodically for a project or for review in one of your courses. Schedule several hours each week for such purposes.

3. After you have budgeted time for studying, fill in slots for recreation, hobbies, relaxation, household errands, and the like.

4. Set specific goals. Before each study session, make a list of specific goals. The simple note "7–8 PM: study psychology" is too broad to ensure the most effective use of the time. Formulate your daily goals according to what you know you must accomplish during the term. If you have course outlines with advance assignments, set systematic daily goals that will allow you, for example, to cover fifteen chapters before the exam. And be realistic: Can you actually expect to cover a 78-page chapter in one session? Divide large tasks into smaller units; stop at the most logical resting points. When you complete a specific goal, take a 5- or 10-minute break before tackling the next goal.

5. Evaluate how successful or unsuccessful your studying has been on a daily or weekly basis. Did you reach most of your goals? If so, reward yourself immediately. You might even make a list of five to ten rewards to choose from. If you have trouble studying regularly, you may be able to motivate yourself by making such rewards contingent on completing specific goals.

6. Finally, until you have lived with your schedule for several weeks, don't hesitate to revise it. You may need to allow more time for chemistry, for example, and less for some other course. If you are trying to study regularly for the first time and are feeling burned out, you probably have set your initial goals too high. Don't let failure cause you to despair and abandon the program. Accept your limitations and revise your schedule so that you are studying only 15 to 20 minutes more each evening than you are used to. The point is to identify a regular schedule with which you can achieve some success. Time management, like any skill, must be practiced to become effective.

Techniques for Effective Study

Knowing how to put study time to best use is, of course, as important as finding a place for it in your schedule. Here are some suggestions that should enable you to increase your reading comprehension and improve your note-taking. A few study tips are included as well.

Using SQ3R to Increase Reading Comprehension

How do you study from a textbook? If you are like many students, you simply read and reread in a *passive* manner. Studies have shown, however, that most students who simply read a textbook cannot remember more than half the material ten minutes after they have finished. Often, what is retained is the unessential material rather than the important points upon which exam questions will be based.

This *Study Guide* employs a program known as SQ3R (Survey, Question, Read, *Recite, and* Review) to facilitate, and allow you to assess, your comprehension of the important facts and concepts in *The Developing Person Through Childhood and Adolescence*, Fifth Edition, by Kathleen Stassen Berger.

Research has shown that students using SQ3R achieve significantly greater comprehension of textbooks than students reading in the more traditional passive manner. Once you have learned this program, you can improve your comprehension of any textbook.

Survey Before reading a chapter, determine whether the text or the study guide has an outline or list of objectives. Read this material and the summary at the end of the chapter. Next, read the textbook chapter fairly quickly, paying special attention to the major headings and subheadings. This survey will give you an idea of the chapter's contents and organization. You will then be able to divide the chapter into logical sections in order to formulate specific goals for a more careful reading of the chapter.

In this Study Guide, the *Chapter Overview* summarizes the major topics of the textbook chapter. This section also provides a few suggestions for approaching topics you may find difficult.

Question You will retain material longer when you have a use for it. If you look up a word's definition in order to solve a crossword puzzle, for example, you will remember it longer than if you merely fill in the letters as a result of putting other words in. Surveying the chapter will allow you to generate important questions that the chapter will proceed to answer. These question correspond to "mental files" into which knowledge will be sorted for easy access.

As you survey, jot down several questions for each chapter section. One simple technique is to generate questions by rephrasing a section heading. For example, the "Preoperational Thought" head could be turned into "What is preoperational thought?" Good questions will allow you to focus on the important points in the text. Examples of good questions are those that begin as follows: "List two examples of . . .." "What is the function of . . .?" "What is the significance of . . .?" Such questions give a purpose to your reading. Similarly, you can formulate questions based on the chapter outline.

The *Guided Study* section of this Study Guide provides the types of questions you might formulate while surveying each chapter. This section is a detailed set of objectives covering the points made in the text.

Read When you have established "files" for each section of the chapter, review your first question, begin reading, and continue until you have discovered its answer. If you come to material that seems to answer an important question you don't have a file for, stop and write down the question.

Using this Study Guide, read the chapter one section at a time. First, preview the section by skimming it, noting headings and boldface items. Next, study the appropriate section objectives in the *Guided Study*. Then, as you read the chapter section, search for the answer to each objective.

Be sure to read everything. Don't skip photo or art captions, graphs, marginal notes. In some cases, what may seem vague in reading will be made clear by a simple graph. Keep in mind that test questions are sometimes drawn from illustrations and charts.

Recite When you have found the answer to a question, close your eyes and mentally recite the question and its answer. Then *write* the answer next to the question. It is important that you recite an answer in your own words rather than the author's. Don't rely on your short-term memory to repeat the author's words verbatim.

In responding to the objectives, pay close attention to what is called for. If you are asked to identify or list, do just that. If asked to compare, contrast, or do both, you should focus on the similarities (compare) and differences (contrast) between the concepts or theories. Answering the objectives carefully will not only help you to focus your attention on the important concepts of the text, but it will also provide excellent practice for essay exams.

Recitation is an extremely effective study technique, recommended by many learning experts. In addition to increasing reading comprehension, it is useful for review. Trying to explain something in your own words clarifies your knowledge, often by revealing aspects of your answer that are vague or incomplete. If you repeatedly rely upon "I know" in recitation, you really may not know.

Recitation has the additional advantage of simulating an exam, especially an essay exam; the same skills are required in both cases. Too often students study without ever putting the book and notes aside, which makes it easy for them to develop false confidence in their knowledge. When the material is in front of you, you may be able to recognize an answer, but will you be able to recall it later, when you take an exam that does not provide these retrieval cues?

After you have recited and written your answer, continue with your next question. Read, recite, and so on.

Review When you have answered the last question on the material you have designated as a study goal, go back and review. Read over each question and your written answer to it. Your review might also include a brief written summary that integrates all of your questions and answers. This review need not take longer than a few minutes, but it is important. It will help you retain the material longer and will greatly facilitate a final review of each chapter before the exam.

In this Study Guide, the *Chapter Review* section contains fill-in and one- or two-sentence essay questions for you to complete after you have finished reading the text and have written answers to the objectives. The correct answers are given at the end of the chapter. Generally, your answer to a fill-in question should match exactly (as in the case of important terms, theories, or people). In some cases, the answer is not a term or name, so a word close in meaning will suffice. You should go through the *Chapter Review* several times before taking an exam, so it is a good idea to mentally fill in the answers until you are ready for a final pretest review. Textbook page references are provided with each section title, in case you need to reread any of the material.

Also provided to facilitate your review are two *Progress Tests* that include multiple-choice questions and, where appropriate, matching or true–false questions. These tests are not to be taken until you have read the chapter, written answers to the objectives, and completed the *Chapter Review*. Correct answers, along with explanations of why each alternative is correct or incorrect, are provided at the end of the chapter. The relevant text page numbers for each question are also given. If you miss a question, read these explanations and, if necessary, review the text pages to further understand why. The *Progress Tests* do not test every aspect of a concept, so you should treat an incorrect answer as an indication that you need to review the concept.

Following the two Progress Tests is a *Thinking Critically Test*, which should be taken just prior to an exam. It includes questions that test your ability to analyze, integrate, and apply the concepts in the chapter. As with the *Progress Tests*, answers for the *Thinking Critically Test* are provided at the end of each chapter, along with relevant page numbers.

The chapter concludes with a list of *Key Terms* and in some cases a crossword puzzle. Definitions of the terms in the list are to be written on a separate piece of paper. As with the *Guided Study* objectives, it is important that these answers be written from memory, and in your own words. The *Answers* section at the end of the chapter gives a definition of each term, sometimes along with an example of its usage and/or a tip to help you remember its meaning. Answers to the crossword puzzle are also provided.

One final suggestion: Incorporate SQ3R into your time-management calendar. Set specific goals for completing SQ3R with each assigned chapter. Keep a record of chapters completed, and reward yourself for being conscientious. Initially, it takes more time and effort to "read" using SQ3R, but with practice, the steps will become automatic. More important, you will comprehend significantly more material and retain what you have learned longer than passive readers do.

Taking Lecture Notes

Are your class notes as useful as they might be? One way to determine their worth is to compare them with those taken by other good students. Are yours as thorough? Do they provide you with a comprehensible outline of each lecture? If not, then the following suggestions might increase the effectiveness of your note-taking.

1. Keep a separate notebook for each course. Use 8 1/2 × 11-inch pages. Consider using a ring binder, which would allow you to revise and insert notes while still preserving lecture order.

2. Take notes in the format of a lecture outline. Use roman numerals for major points, letters for supporting arguments, and so on. Some instructors will make this easy by delivering organized lectures and, in some cases, by outlining their lectures on the board. If a lecture is disorganized, you will probably want to reorganize your notes soon after the class.

3. As you take notes in class, leave a wide margin on one side of each page. After the lecture, expand or clarify any shorthand notes while the material is fresh in your mind. Use this time to write important questions in the margin next to notes that answer them. This will facilitate later review and will allow you to anticipate similar exam questions.

Evaluate Your Exam Performance

How often have you received a grade on an exam that did not do justice to the effort you spent preparing for the exam? This is a common experience that can leave one feeling bewildered and abused. "What do I have to do to get an A?" "The test was unfair!" "I studied the wrong material!"

The chances of this happening are greatly reduced if you have an effective time-management schedule and use the study techniques described here. But it can happen to the best-prepared student and is most likely to occur on your first exam with a new professor.

Remember that there are two main reasons for studying. One is to learn for your own general academic development. Many people believe that such knowledge is all that really matters. Of course, it is possible, though unlikely, to be an expert on a topic without achieving commensurate grades, just as one can, occasionally, earn an excellent grade without truly mastering the course material. During a job interview or in the workplace, however, your A in Computer Science won't mean much if you can't actually program a computer.

In order to keep career options open after you graduate, you must know the material and maintain competitive grades. In the short run, this means performing well on exams, which is the second main objective in studying.

Probably the single best piece of advice to keep in mind when studying for exams is to *try to predict exam questions.* This means ignoring the trivia and focusing on the important questions and their answers (with your instructor's emphasis in mind).

A second point is obvious. How well you do on exams is determined by your mastery of both lecture and textbook material. Many students (partly because of poor time management) concentrate too much on one at the expense of the other.

To evaluate how well you are learning lecture and textbook material, analyze the questions you missed on the first exam. If your instructor does not review exams during class, you can easily do it yourself. Divide the questions into two categories: those drawn primarily from lectures and those drawn primarily from the textbook. Determine the percentage of questions you missed in each category. If your errors are evenly distributed and you are satisfied with your grade, you have no problem. If you are weaker in one area, you will need to set future goals for increasing and/or improving your study of that area.

Similarly, note the percentage of test questions drawn from each category. Although exams in most courses cover both lecture notes and the textbook, the relative emphasis of each may vary from instructor to instructor. While your instructors may not be entirely consistent in making up future exams, you may be able to tailor your studying for each course by placing additional emphasis on the appropriate area.

Exam evaluation will also point out the types of questions your instructor prefers. Does the exam consist primarily of multiple-choice, true–false, or essay questions? You may also discover that an instructor is fond of wording questions in certain ways. For example, an instructor may rely heavily on questions that require you to draw an analogy between a theory or concept and a real-world example. Evaluate both your instructor's style and how well you do with each format. Use this information to guide your future exam preparation.

Important aids, not only in studying for exams but also in determining how well prepared you are, are the Progress and Thinking Critically Tests provided in this Study Guide. If these tests don't include all of the types of questions your instructor typically writes, make up your own practice exam questions. Spend extra time testing yourself with question formats that are most difficult for you. There is no better way to evaluate your preparation for an upcoming exam than by testing yourself under the conditions most likely to be in effect during the actual test.

A Few Practical Tips

Even the best intentions for studying sometimes fail. Some of these failures occur because students attempt to work under conditions that are simply not conducive to concentrated study. To help ensure the success of your time-management program, here are a few suggestions that should assist you in reducing the possibility of procrastination or distraction.

1. If you have set up a schedule for studying, make your roommate, family, and friends aware of this commitment, and ask them to honor your quiet study time. Close your door and post a "Do Not Disturb" sign.

2. Set up a place to study that minimizes potential distractions. Use a desk or table, not your bed or an extremely comfortable chair. Keep your desk and the walls around it free from clutter. If you need a place other than your room, find one that meets as many of the above requirements as possible—for example, in the library stacks.

3. Do nothing but study in this place. It should become associated with studying so that it "triggers" this activity, just as a mouth-watering aroma elicits an appetite.

4. Never study with the television on or with other distracting noises present. If you must have music in the background in order to mask outside noise, for example, play soft instrumental music. Don't pick vocal selections; your mind will be drawn to the lyrics.

5. Study by yourself. Other students can be distracting or can break the pace at which your learning is most efficient. In addition, there is always the possibility that group studying will become a social gathering. Reserve that for its own place in your schedule.

If you continue to have difficulty concentrating for very long, try the following suggestions.

6. Study your most difficult or most challenging subjects first, when you are most alert.

7. Start with relatively short periods of concentrated study, with breaks in between. If your attention starts to wander, get up immediately and take a break. It is better to study effectively for 15 minutes and then take a break than to fritter away 45 minutes out of an hour. Gradually increase the length of study periods, using your attention span as an indicator of successful pacing.

Critical Thinking

Having discussed a number of specific techniques for managing your time efficiently and studying effectively, let us now turn to a much broader topic: What exactly should you expect to learn as a student of developmental psychology?

Most developmental psychology courses have two major goals: (1) to help you acquire a basic understanding of the discipline's knowledge base, and (2) to help you learn to think like a psychologist. Many students devote all of their efforts to the first of these goals, concentrating on memorizing as much of the course's material as possible.

The second goal—learning to think like a psychologist—has to do with critical thinking. Critical thinking has many meanings. On one level, it refers to an attitude of healthy skepticism that should guide your study of psychology. As a critical thinker, you learn not to accept any explanation or conclusion about behavior as true until you have evaluated the evidence. On another level, critical thinking refers to a systematic process for examining the conclusions and arguments presented by others. In this regard, many of the features of the SQ3R technique for improving reading comprehension can be incorporated into an effective critical thinking system.

To learn to think critically, you must first recognize that psychological information is transmitted through the construction of persuasive arguments. An argument consists of three parts: an assertion, evidence, and an explanation (Mayer and Goodchild, 1990).

An assertion is a statement of relationship between some aspect of behavior, such as intelligence, and another factor, such as age. Learn to identify and evaluate the assertions about behavior and mental processes that you encounter as you read your textbook, listen to lectures, and engage in discussions with classmates. A good test of your understanding of an assertion is to try to restate it in your own words. As you do so, pay close attention to how important terms and concepts are defined. When a researcher asserts that "intelligence declines with age," for example, what does he or she mean by "intelligence"? Assertions such as this one may be true when a critical term ("intelligence") is defined one way (for example, "speed of thinking"), but not when defined in another way (for example, "general knowledge"). One of the strengths of psychology is the use of *operational* definitions that specify how key terms and concepts are measured, thus eliminating any ambiguity about their meaning. "Intelligence," for example, is often operationally defined as performance on a test measuring various cognitive skills. Whenever you encounter an assertion that is ambiguous, be skeptical of its accuracy.

When you have a clear understanding of an argument's assertion, evaluate its supporting evidence, the second component of an argument. Is it *empirical*? Does it, in fact, support the assertion? Psychologists accept only *empirical (observable) evidence* that is based on direct measurement of behavior. Hearsay, intuition, and personal experiences are not acceptable evidence. Chapter 1 discusses the various research methods used by developmental psychologists to gather empirical evidence. Some examples include surveys, observations of behavior in natural settings, and experiments.

As you study developmental psychology, you will become aware of another important issue in evaluating evidence—determining whether or not the research on which it is based is faulty. Research can be faulty for many reasons, including the use of an unrepresentative sample of subjects, experimenter bias, and inadequate control of unanticipated factors that might influence results. Evidence based on faulty research should be discounted.

The third component of an argument is the explanation provided for an assertion, which is based on the evidence that has been presented. While the argument's assertion merely *describes* how two things (such as intelligence and age) are related, the explanation tells *why*, often by proposing some theoretical mechanism that causes the relationship. Empirical evidence that thinking speed slows with age (the assertion), for example, may be explained as being caused by age-related changes in the activity of brain cells (a physiological explanation).

Be cautious in accepting explanations. In order to think critically about an argument's explanation, ask yourself three questions: (1) Can I restate the explanation in my own words?; (2) Does the explanation make sense based on the stated evidence?; and (3) Are there alternative explanations that adequately explain the assertion? Consider this last point in relation to our sample assertion: It is possible that the slower thinking speed of older adults is due to their having less recent experience than younger people with tasks that require quick thinking (a disuse explanation).

Because psychology is a relatively young science, its theoretical explanations are still emerging, and often change. For this reason, not all psychological arguments will offer explanations. Many arguments will only raise additional questions for further research to address.

Some Suggestions for Becoming a Critical Thinker

1. Adopt an attitude of healthy skepticism in evaluating psychological arguments.

2. Insist on unambiguous operational definitions of an argument's important concepts and terms.

3. Be cautious in accepting supporting evidence for an argument's assertion.

4. Refuse to accept evidence for an argument if it is based on faulty research.

5. Ask yourself if the theoretical explanation provided for an argument "makes sense" based on the empirical evidence.

6. Determine whether there are alternative explanations that adequately explain an assertion.

7. Use critical thinking to construct your own effective arguments when writing term papers, answering essay questions, and speaking.

8. Polish your critical-thinking skills by applying them to each of your college courses, and to other areas of life as well. Learn to think critically about advertising, political speeches, and the material presented in popular periodicals.

Some Closing Thoughts

I hope that these suggestions help make you more successful academically, and that they enhance the quality of your college life in general. Having the necessary skills makes any job a lot easier and more pleasant. Let me repeat my warning not to attempt to make too drastic a change in your life-style immediately. Good habits require time and self-discipline to develop. Once established they can last a lifetime.

Study Guide

CHAPTER 1

Introduction

Chapter Overview

The first chapter introduces the study of human development. The first section defines development and describes the three domains into which it is often divided.

The second section makes clear that development is influenced as much by external factors as by internal factors. Beginning with a discussion of the ecological perspective—Bronfenbrenner's model of how the individual is affected by, and affects, many other individuals, groups of individuals, and larger systems in the environment—this section describes different aspects of the social context in which people develop. The story of David illustrates the effects of this context.

The next two sections discuss the strategies developmentalists use in their research, beginning with the scientific method and including scientific observation, experiments, interviews or surveys, and case studies. To study people over time, developmentalists have created several research designs: cross-sectional, longitudinal, and cross-sequential.

The final section discusses the ethics of research with children. In addition to ensuring confidentiality and safety, developmentalists who study children are especially concerned that the benefits of research with children outweigh the risks.

NOTE: Answer guidelines for all Chapter 1 questions begin on page 11.

Guided Study

The text chapter should be studied one section at a time. Before you read, preview each section by skimming it, noting headings and boldface items. Then read the appropriate section objectives from the following outline. Keep these objectives in mind and, as you read the chapter section, search for the information that will enable you to meet each objective. Once you have finished a section, write out answers for its objectives.

The Study of Human Development (pp. 1–4)

1. Define the study of human development.

2. Identify and describe the three domains into which human development is often separated.

The Many Contexts of Development (pp. 4–18)

3. Describe the ecological approach to human development, and explain how this approach leads to an understanding of contextual influences on development.

4. Briefly describe how the social context is used to encompass Bronfenbrenner's social ecosystems.

5. Discuss the three broad, overlapping contexts that affect development throughout the life span.

Developmental Study as a Science (pp. 18–19)

6. List and describe the basic steps of the scientific method.

Research Methods (pp. 19–31)

7. Describe observation and correlation as research strategies, noting at least one advantage (or strength) and one disadvantage (or weakness) of each.

8. Describe experiments, surveys, and case studies, noting at least one advantage (or strength) and one disadvantage (or weakness) of each.

9. (Research Report) Describe the six techniques used by psychologists to ensure the validity of their research.

10. Explain why correlation does not identify causation.

11. Describe three basic research designs used by developmental psychologists.

Ethics of Research With Children (pp. 31–34)

12. Briefly summarize some of the ethical issues involved in conducting research with children.

Chapter Review

When you have finished reading the chapter, work through the material that follows to review it. Complete the sentences and answer the questions. As you proceed, evaluate your performance for each section by consulting the answers on page 11. Do not continue with the next section until you understand each answer. If you need to, review or reread the appropriate section in the textbook before continuing.

The Study of Human Development (pp. 1–4)

1. The scientific study of human development can be defined as the science that seeks to understand ______________________________ ______________________________.

2. The study of human development involves many academic disciplines, especially ______________, ______________, and ______________.

3. The study of human development can be separated into three domains: ______________, ______________, and ______________.

4. The study of brain and body changes and the social influences that guide them falls within the ______________ domain.

5. Thinking, perception, and language learning fall mainly in the ______________ domain of development.

6. The study of emotions, personality, and interpersonal relationships falls within the ______________ domain.

7. All three domains ______________ (are/are not) important at every age. Each of the domains ______________ (is/is not) affected by the other two. While development is organized into domains, each person is an integrated whole; that is, development is ______________.

The Many Contexts of Development (pp. 4–18)

8. Forces outside the individual that influence development make up the ______________ of development.

9. The approach that emphasizes the influence of the systems, or contexts, that support the developing person is called the ______________ approach to development. This approach was first emphasized 25 years ago by ______________.

10. According to this model, the family, the peer group, and other aspects of the immediate social setting constitute the ______________.

11. Systems that link one microsystem to another constitute the ______________.

12. Economic, political, educational, and cultural institutions and practices make up the ______________.

13. The overarching traditions, beliefs, and values of the society make up the ______________.

14. The ecological perspective emphasizes the ______________ (unidirectional/multidirectional) and ______________ nature of social influences.

Give an example of the above.

15. Using Bronfenbrenner's approach, it is important to remember that the ecosystems ______________ (are/are not) discrete entities.

16. Taken together, all the ecosystems that influence development make up the ______________ ______________ of the individual.

17. Some researchers have suggested that only children and ______________ children benefit from greater ______________ resources than do middle children in a large family. This hypothesis ______________ (has/has not) been accepted by all scientists.

18. The ecological approach emphasizes that human development must be understood not only in the context of the family, but also in its ______________, ______________, and ______________–______________ contexts.

19. A group of people born within a few years of each other is called a ______________. These people tend to be affected by history in ______________ (the same way/different ways).

20. In addition to being influenced by the particular social contexts in which they develop, cohorts can be affected by differences in their relative ______________.

21. The idea that women should be docile housewives while men should be strong and independent is an example of a ______________ ______________. An important point about such ideas is that they ______________ (often change/are very stable) over time.

22. The life stage of ______________ is also an example of a social construction.

23. A contextual influence that is determined by a person's income, education, place of residence, and occupation, is called ______________ ______________, which is often abbreviated ______________.

24. Among the hazards and pressures of poverty are higher rates of ______________ ______________, ______________ ______________, inadequate ______________, and ______________.

25. Today, poverty rates are highest in the ______________ age group.

26. The values, assumptions, and customs as well as the physical objects that a group of people have adopted as a design for living constitute a ______________.

27. One example of the impact of cultural values on development is the greater tendency for children to be viewed as an economic asset in ______________ ______________ communities. In such communities infant care is designed to maximize ______________ ______________. By contrast, middle-class parents in ______________ nations are less worried about infant mortality and thus focus care on fostering ______________.

28. A collection of people who share certain attributes, such as ancestry, national origin, religion, and language and, as a result, tend to have similar beliefs, values, and experiences is called a(n) ______________ ______________.

In distinguishing racial identity, ______________ traits are less important than are the ______________ that arise from ethnic or racial consciousness.

29. Because his mother contracted the disease ______________ during her pregnancy, David was born with a heart defect and cataracts over both eyes. Thus, his immediate problems centered on the ______________ domain. However, because he was born at a particular time, he was already influenced by the larger ______________ context. His physical handicaps later produced ______________ and ______________ handicaps.

Developmental Study as a Science (pp. 18–19)

30. In order, the basic steps of the scientific method are:

a. ______________

b. ______________

c. ______________

d. ______________

e. ______________

31. To repeat an experimental test procedure and obtain the same results is to ______________ the test of the hypothesis.

32. Age, sex, education, and other quantities that may differ during an investigation are called ______________. Developmental researchers deal with both ______________ variation, which occurs from day to day in each person, and ______________ variation, which occurs between people or groups.

Research Methods (pp. 19–31)

33. In designing research studies, scientists are concerned with four issues: ______________, or whether a study measures what it purports to measure; ______________, or whether its measurements are correct; ______________, or whether the study applies to other populations and situations; and ______________, or whether it solves real-life problems.

34. Using ______________ ______________, researchers observe and record what people, the

______________ ______________,
do in a systematic and unbiased manner. People may be observed in a ______________ setting, or in a ______________.

35. (Research Report) To make statements about people in general, called ______________, scientists study a subset, or ______________. An important factor in selecting this group is ______________ ______________, that is, the group must be large enough to be representative.

36. (Research Report) When a sample is typical of the group under study—in gender, ethnic background, and other important variables—the sample is called a(n) ______________ ______________.

37. (Research Report) When the person carrying out research is unaware of the purpose of the research, that person is said to be a "______________" ______________.

38. (Research Report) Researchers use ______________ ______________ to define variables in terms of specific, observable behavior that can be measured precisely.

39. (Research Report) To test a hypothesis, researchers often compare a(n) ______________ group, which receives some special treatment, with a(n) ______________ group, which does not.

40. (Research Report) To determine whether or not experimental results are merely the result of chance, researchers use a statistical test, called a test of statistical ______________.

Identify the chief limitation of observation in terms of the variable affecting behavior.

41. A statistic that indicates whether two variables are related to each other is ______________. To say that two variables are related in this way ______________ (does/does not) necessarily imply that one caused the other.

42. The method that allows a scientist to test a hypothesis in a controlled environment, in which the variables can be manipulated, is the ______________. In this method, researchers manipulate a(n) ______________ variable to determine its effect on a(n) ______________ variable.

43. Although this research method enables researchers to uncover the links between ______________ and ______________, it is sometimes criticized for studying behavior in a situation that is ______________.

44. Another limitation is that participants in this research technique (except very young children) ______________.

45. In a(n) ______________, scientists collect information from a large group of people by personal interview, written questionnaire, or by some other means.

46. One potential problem with this research method is that the ______________ of questions can influence the answers. In addition, many respondents give answers they think the researcher ______________.

47. An intensive study of one individual is called a(n) ______________ ______________.

48. Research that involves the comparison of people of different ages is called a ______________-______________ research design.

49. With cross-sectional research it is very difficult to ensure that ______________ ______________.

In addition, every cross-sectional study will, to some degree, reflect ______________ ______________.

50. Research that follows the same people over a relatively long period of time is called a ______________ research design.

State three drawbacks of this type of research design.

51. The research method that combines the longitudinal and cross-sectional methods is the

________________-________________

research method.

Ethics of Research With Children (pp. 31–34)

52. The most complex matter in research with children is ensuring that the ________________

________________.

Progress Test 1

Multiple-Choice Questions

Circle your answers to the following questions and check them against the answers on page 11. If your answer is incorrect, read the explanation for why it is incorrect and then consult the appropriate pages of the text (in parentheses following the correct answer).

1. The scientific study of human development is defined as the study of:
   a. how and why people change or remain the same over time.
   b. psychosocial influences on aging.
   c. individual differences in learning over the life span.
   d. all of the above.

2. The cognitive domain of development includes:
   a. perception.
   b. thinking.
   c. language.
   d. all of the above.

3. Changes in height, weight, and bone thickness are part of the ________ domain.
   a. cognitive
   b. biosocial
   c. psychosocial
   d. physical

4. Psychosocial development focuses primarily on personality, emotions, and:
   a. intellectual development.
   b. sexual maturation.
   c. relationships with others.
   d. perception.

5. The ecological approach to developmental psychology focuses on the:
   a. biochemistry of the body systems.
   b. cognitive domain only.
   c. internal thinking processes
   d. overall environment of development.

6. The control group in an experiment:
   a. receives the treatment of interest.
   b. does not receive the treatment of interest.
   c. is always drawn from a population different from the experimental group.
   d. must be larger in size than the experimental group.

7. During the 1960s, American society tilted toward a youth culture. This is a vivid example of the effect of ________ on society.
   a. the "baby boom" cohort
   b. the biosocial domain
   c. the cognitive domain
   d. the microsystem

8. A hypothesis is a:
   a. conclusion.
   b. prediction to be tested.
   c. statistical test.
   d. correlation.

9. A developmentalist who is interested in studying the influences of a person's immediate environment on his or her behavior is focusing on which system?
   a. mesosystem
   b. macrosystem
   c. microsystem
   d. exosystem

10. Socioeconomic status is determined by a combination of variables, including:
    a. age, education, and income.
    b. income, ethnicity, and occupation.
    c. income, education, and occupation.
    d. age, ethnicity, and occupation.

11. A disadvantage of experiments is that:
    a. people may behave differently in the artificial environment of the laboratory.
    b. control groups are too large to be accommodated in most laboratories.
    c. it is the method most vulnerable to bias on the part of the researcher.
    d. proponents of the ecological approach overuse them.

True or False Items

Write *true* or *false* on the line in front of each statement.

_______ 1. Psychologists separate human development into three domains, or areas of study.

_______ 2. The case study of David clearly demonstrates that for some children only nature (or heredity) is important.

_______ 3. Observation usually indicates a clear relationship between cause and effect.

_______ 4. Each developmental domain influences development independently.

_______ 5. Cohort differences are an example of the impact of the social context on development.

_______ 6. A study of history suggests that particular well-defined periods of child and adult development have always existed.

_______ 7. Socioeconomic status is rarely measured solely by family income.

_______ 8. The influences between and within Bronfenbrenner's systems are unidirectional and independent.

_______ 9. People of different ethnic groups can all share one culture.

_______ 10. Longitudinal research is the design used by most psychologists working from the developmental perspective.

Progress Test 2

Progress Test 2 should be completed during a final chapter review. Answer the following questions after you thoroughly understand the correct answers for the Chapter Review and Progress Test 1.

Multiple-Choice Questions

1. An individual's social context refers to his or her:

a. microsystem and mesosystem.
b. exosystem.
c. macrosystem.
d. microsystem, mesosystem, exosystem, and macrosystem.

2. The three domains of developmental psychology are:

a. physical, cognitive, psychosocial.
b. physical, biosocial, cognitive.
c. biosocial, cognitive, psychosocial.
d. biosocial, cognitive, emotional.

3. Which of the following is true of the three domains of development?

a. They are important at every age.
b. They interact in influencing development.
c. They are more influential in some cultures than in others.
d. a. and b. are true.

4. People often mistakenly believe that most developmental changes:

a. originate within each individual.
b. take place in a larger social context.
c. are temporary.
d. occur in the same way in all people.

5. According to the ecological perspective, the macrosystem would include:

a. the peer group.
b. the community.
c. values.
d. the family.

6. The effects of a person's family life on his or her development would be classified as part of the:

a. microsystem.
b. mesosystem.
c. exosystem.
d. macrosystem.

7. According to the ecological perspective:

a. the influences of developmental factors are multidirectional.
b. actions in any one part of the system affect all the other parts.
c. human development must be understood in terms of its cultural, historical, ethnic, and socioeconomic context.
d. all of the above are true.

8. A cohort is defined as a group of people:

a. of similar national origin.
b. who share a common language.
c. born within a few years of each other.
d. who share the same religion.

9. Four decades ago, __________ people were the poorest age group in the United States. Today, __________ people are poorest.

a. young; old
b. old; young
c. young; young
d. old; old

10. In differentiating ethnicity and culture, we note that:
   a. ethnicity is an exclusively biological phenomenon.
   b. an ethnic group is a group of people who were born within a few years of each other.
   c. people of many ethnic groups can share one culture, yet maintain their ethnic identities.
   d. racial identity is always an element of culture.

11. For a psychologist's generalizations to be valid, the sample must be representative of the population under study. The sample must also be:
   a. significant.
   b. large enough.
   c. all the same age.
   d. none of the above.

Matching Items

Match each definition or description with its corresponding term.

Terms

_______ 1. independent variable
_______ 2. dependent variable
_______ 3. culture
_______ 4. replicate
_______ 5. biosocial domain
_______ 6. cognitive domain
_______ 7. psychosocial domain
_______ 8. socioeconomic status
_______ 9. cohort
_______ 10. ethnic group
_______ 11. experimental group
_______ 12. control group

Definitions or Descriptions

a. group of people born within a few years of each other
b. determined by a person's income, education, and occupation
c. the "treatment absent" group in an experiment
d. concerned with physical growth and development
e. collection of people who share certain attributes, such as national origin
f. shared values, attitudes, and customs maintained by people in a specific setting
g. concerned with thought processes
h. the variable manipulated in an experiment
i. concerned with emotions, personality traits, and relationships
j. to repeat a study and obtain the same findings
k. the variable measured in an experiment
l. the "treatmen present" group in an experiment

Thinking Critically About Chapter 1

Answer these questions the day before an exam as a final check on your understanding of the chapter's terms and concepts.

1. Dr. Wong conducts research on the psychosocial domain of development. She is *most* likely to be interested in a child's:
   a. perceptual abilities.
   b. brain wave patterns.
   c. emotions.
   d. use of language.

2. A psychologist who focuses on the connections between a child's home and school environments is interested primarily in the child's:
   a. microsystem.
   b. mesosystem.
   c. exosystem.
   d. macrosystem.

3. Jahmal is writing a paper on the role of the social context in development. He would do well to consult the writings of:
   a. Piaget.
   b. Freud.
   c. Bronfenbrenner.
   d. Skinner.

4. Dr. Ramirez looks at human development in terms of the individual's supporting ecosystems. Evidently, Dr. Ramirez subscribes to the ______ perspective.
   a. psychosocial
   b. ecological
   c. biosocial
   d. cognitive

5. For her class project, Shelly decides to write a paper on how neighborhood and community structures influence the family. She cleverly titles her paper:
   a. "The Microsystem in Action."
   b. "The Mesosystem in Action."
   c. "The Exosystem in Action."
   d. "The Macrosystem in Action."

6. (Research Report) When researchers find that the results of a study are significant, this means that:
   a. they may have been caused purely by chance.
   b. it is unlikely they could be replicated.
   c. it is unlikely they could have occurred by chance.
   d. the sample population was representative of the general population.

7. When we say that the idea of old age as we know it is a "social construction," we are saying that:
   a. the idea is built on the shared perceptions of members of society.
   b. old age has only recently been regarded as a distinct period of life.
   c. old age cannot be defined.
   d. the idea is based on a well-tested hypothesis.

8. According to Robert LeVine, as compared with parents in developing countries, middle-class American parents emphasize cognitive and social stimulation in their child-rearing efforts because:
   a. they are more likely to regard children as an economic asset.
   b. their families are smaller.
   c. they do not have to be as concerned about infant mortality.
   d. of all the above reasons.

9. Karen's mother is puzzled by the numerous discrepancies between the developmental psychology textbook she used in 1976 and her daughter's contemporary text. Karen explains that the differences are the result of:
   a. the lack of regard by earlier researchers for the scientific method.
   b. changing social conditions and cohort effects.
   c. the widespread use of cross-sectional research today.
   d. the widespread use of longitudinal research today.

10. If height and body weight are positively correlated, which of the following is true?
    a. There is a cause-and-effect relationship between height and weight.
    b. Knowing a person's height, one can predict his or her weight.
    c. As height increases, weight decreases.
    d. All of the above are true.

11. Which of the following is an example of longitudinal research?
    a. an investigator compares the performance of several different age groups on a test of memory.
    b. an investigator compares the performance of the same group of people, at different ages, on a test of memory.
    c. an investigator compares the performance of an experimental group and a control group of subjects on a test of memory.
    d. an investigator compares the performance of several different age groups on a test of memory as each group is tested repeatedly over a period of years.

Key Terms

Writing Definitions

Using your own words, write a brief definition or explanation of each of the following terms on a separate piece of paper.

1. scientific study of human development
2. biosocial domain
3. cognitive domain
4. psychosocial domain
5. ecological approach
6. social context
7. cohort
8. social construction
9. socioeconomic status (SES)
10. culture
11. ethnic group
12. scientific method

13. hypothesis
14. replicate
15. variable
16. scientific observation
17. population
18. sample
19. sample size
20. representative sample
21. blind
22. experimental group
23. control group
24. statistical significance
25. correlation
26. experiment
27. independent variable
28. dependent variable
29. scientific survey
30. case study
31. cross-sectional research
32. longitudinal research
33. cross-sequential research

Cross Check

After you have written the definitions of the key terms in this chapter, you should complete the crossword puzzle to ensure that you can reverse the process—recognize the term, given the definition.

ACROSS

1. To prevent bias, the experiment should be "_________ ."
2. Domain concerned with thinking.
7. Group of people born at about the same time.
9. A subset of a population.
11. A measure of status.
13. Research design involving the study of different age groups over time.
14. Set of values shared by a group.
15. Treatment-absent comparison group.

DOWN

1. Domain concerned with physical growth.
3. An _______ _______ shares certain characteristics such as national origin.
4. The treatment-present group.
5. A testable prediction.
6. Research design in which people in different age groups are compared.
7. A measure of a statistical relationship.
8. Research design that follows a group of people over time.
10. All the members of a certain group.
12. An in-depth study of one person.

ANSWERS

CHAPTER REVIEW

1. how and why people change as they grow older, as well as how and why they remain the same
2. biology; education; psychology
3. biosocial; cognitive; psychosocial
4. biosocial
5. cognitive
6. psychosocial
7. are; is; holistic
8. context (or systems or environments)
9. ecological; Urie Bronfenbrenner
10. microsystem
11. mesosystem
12. exosystem
13. macrosystem
14. multidirectional; interactive

Research has shown that the quality of life in the family microsystem directly affects a worker's productivity on the job. At the same time, the microsystem of the workplace affects the quality of life at home.

15. are not
16. social context
17. firstborn; cognitive; has not
18. historical; socioeconomic; cultural-ethnic
19. cohort; the same way
20. sizes
21. social construction; often change
22. childhood
23. socioeconomic status; SES
24. child neglect; infant mortality; schools; adolescent violence
25. youngest
26. culture
27. developing agricultural; survival and emphasize family cooperation; postindustrial; cognitive growth and emotional independence
28. ethnic group; biological; attitudes and experiences
29. rubella; biosocial; social; cognitive; psychosocial
30. a. formulate a research question;
    b. develop a hypothesis;
    c. test the hypothesis;
    d. draw conclusions;
    e. make the findings available
31. replicate
32. variables; intrapersonal; interpersonal
33. validity; accuracy; generalizability; usefulness
34. scientific observation; research subjects; naturalistic; laboratory
35. populations; sample; sample size
36. representative sample
37. "blind" experimenter
38. operational definitions
39. experimental; control
40. significance

Behavior may be affected by any number of variables, and observation does not pinpoint the direct cause of the behaviors being observed.

41. correlation; does not
42. experiment; independent; dependent
43. cause; effect; artificial
44. know they are in an experiment
45. scientific survey
46. phrasing; expects
47. case study
48. cross-sectional
49. comparison groups are similar in background variables; cohort differences
50. longitudinal

Over time, some subjects may leave the study. Some people may change simply because they are part of the study. Longitudinal studies are time-consuming and expensive.

51. cross-sequential
52. benefits outweigh the costs

PROGRESS TEST 1

Multiple-Choice Questions

1. **a.** is the answer. (p. 2)

   b. & c. The study of development is concerned with a broader range of phenomena, including biosocial aspects of development, than these answers specify.

2. **d.** is the answer. (p. 2)
3. **b.** is the answer. (p. 2)

   a. This domain is concerned with thought processes.

   c. This domain is concerned with emotions, personality, and interpersonal relationships.

d. This is not a domain of development.

4. **c.** is the answer. (p. 2)

   a. This falls within the cognitive and biosocial domains.

   b. This falls within the biosocial domain.

   d. This falls within the cognitive domain.

5. **d.** is the answer. This approach sees development as occurring within four interacting levels, or environments. (p. 4)

6. **b.** is the answer. (p. 23)

   a. This is true of the experimental group.

   c. The control group must be similar to the experimental group (and therefore drawn from the same population).

   d. The control group is usually the same size as the experimental group.

7. **a.** is the answer. (p. 9)

   b. The biosocial domain is concerned with brain and body changes.

   c. The cognitive domain is concerned with thought processes in individuals and the factors that influence them.

   d. The microsystem is the immediate social setting that surrounds an individual.

8. **b.** is the answer. (p. 19)

9. **c.** is the answer. (p.5)

   a. This refers to systems that link one microsystem to another.

   b. This refers to the overarching traditions, beliefs, and values of the society.

   d. This includes the community structures that affect the functioning of smaller systems.

10. **c.** is the answer. (p. 11)

11. **a.** is the answer. (p. 23)

True or False Items

1. T (p. 2)
2. F The case study of David shows that both nature and nurture are important in affecting outcome. (pp. 15–18)
3. F A disadvantage of observation is that the variables are numerous and uncontrolled, and therefore cause-and-effect relationships are difficult to pinpoint. (p. 20)
4. F Each domain is affected by the other two. (p. 3)
5. T (p. 9)
6. F Our ideas about the stages of childhood and adulthood are historical creations that have varied over the centuries. (p. 10)
7. F In government statistics it often is. (p. 11)
8. F Quite the reverse is true. (p. 5)
9. T (p. 14)
10. T (p. 29)

PROGRESS TEST 2

Multiple-Choice Questions

1. **d.** is the answer. (p. 6)

2. **c.** is the answer. (p. 2)

3. **d.** is the answer. (p. 3)

   c. Research has not revealed cultural variations in the overall developmental influence of the three domains.

4. **a.** is the answer. (pp. 5–6)

   b. This is the emphasis of the newer, ecological perspective.

   c. & d. The text does not suggest that people commonly make these assumptions.

5. **c.** is the answer. (p. 5)

   a. & d. These are part of the microsystem.

   b. This is part of the exosystem.

6. **a.** is the answer. (p. 5)

   b. This refers to systems that link one microsystem to another.

   c. This refers to the community structures that affect the functioning of smaller systems.

   d. This refers to the overarching traditions, beliefs, and values of the society.

7. **d.** is the answer. (pp. 4–6)

8. **c.** is the answer. (p. 9)

   a., b., & d. These are attributes of an ethnic group.

9. **b.** is the answer. (pp. 11–12)

10. **c.** is the answer. (p. 14)

    a. & d. Ethnicity refers to shared attributes, such as ancestry, national origin, religion, and language.

    b. This describes a cohort.

11. **b.** is the answer. (p. 22)

    a. Significance refers to whether or not research results are due to chance factors.

    c. This is not a requirement of a valid sample.

Matching Items

1. h (p. 25)
2. k (p. 25)
3. f (p. 12)
4. j (p. 18)
5. d (p. 2)
6. g (p. 2)
7. i (p. 2)
8. b (p. 11)
9. a (p. 9)
10. e (p. 14)
11. l (p. 23)
12. c (p. 23)

THINKING CRITICALLY ABOUT CHAPTER 1

1. **c.** is the answer. (p. 2)

   a. & d. These pertain to the cognitive domain.

   b. This pertains to the biosocial domain.
2. **b.** is the answer. (p. 5)
3. **c.** is the answer. (pp. 4–5)

   a. Piaget is notable in the area of cognitive development.

   b. Freud was a pioneer of psychoanalysis.

   b. Skinner is notable in the history of learning theory.
4. **b.** is the answer. (p. 5)

   a., c., & d. These are the three domains of development.
5. **c.** is the answer. (p. 5)
6. **c.** is the answer. (p. 23
7. **a.** is the answer. (p. 10)
8. **c.** is the answer. (p. 13)
9. **b.** is the answer. (p. 9)

   a. Earlier developmentalists had no less regard for the scientific method.

   c. & d. Both cross-sectional and longitudinal research were widely used in the 1970s.
10. **b.** is the answer. (p. 23)

    a. correlation does not imply

    c. if height and body weight are positively correlated, as one increases so does the other.
11. **b.** is the answer. (p. 28)

    a. This is an example of cross-sectional research.

    c. This is an example of an experiment.

    d. This type of study is not described in the text.

KEY TERMS

Writing Definitions

1. The **scientific study of human development** is the science that seeks to understand how and why people change, and how and why they remain the same, as they grow older. (p. 2)
2. The **biosocial domain** is concerned with brain and body changes and the social influences that guide them. (p. 2)
3. The **cognitive domain** is concerned with thought processes, perceptual abilities, and language mastery, and the educational institutions that encourage these aspects of development. (p. 2)
4. The **psychosocial domain** is concerned with emotions, personality, interpersonal relationships with family, friends, and the wider community. (p. 2)
5. Developmentalists who take the **ecological approach** take into account the various physical and social settings in which human development occurs. (p. 4)
6. The **social context** is all the means—including the people, the customs, the institutions, and the beliefs—by which society influences the developing person. (p. 6)
7. A **cohort** is a group of people who, because they were born within a few years of each other, experience many of the same historical and social emotions. (p. 9)
8. A **social construction** is an idea about the way things are, or should be, that is built more on the shared perceptions of members of a society than on objective reality. (p. 10)
9. An individual's **socioeconomic status (SES)** is determined by his or her income, education, place of residence, and occupation. (p. 11)
10. **Culture** refers to the set of shared values, assumptions, customs, and physical objects that a group of people have developed over the years as a design for living to structure their life together. (p. 12)
11. An **ethnic group** is a collection of people who share certain attributes, such as national origin, religion, ancestry, and/or language and who, as a result, tend to identify with each other and have similar daily encounters with the social world. (p. 14)
12. The **scientific method** is a general procedural model that helps researchers remain objective as they study behavior. The five basic steps of the scientific method are: (1) formulate a research question; (2) develop a hypothesis; (3) test the hypothesis; (4) draw conclusions; and (5) make the findings available. (p. 18)
13. A **hypothesis** is a specific prediction that is stated in such a way that it can be tested and either proved or disproved. (p. 19)
14. To **replicate** a test of a research hypothesis is to repeat it and obtain the same results using a different but related set of subjects or procedures in order to test its validity. (p. 19)
15. A **variable** is any quantity, characteristic, or

action that can take on different values within a group of individuals or a single individual. (p. 19)

16. **Scientific observation** is the unobtrusive watching and recording of subjects' behavior in a situation that is being studied, either in the laboratory or in a natural setting. (p. 20)

17. A **population** consists of the entire group of individuals who are of concern in a particular study. (p. 22)

18. A **sample** is a group of individuals drawn from a specified population. (p.22)

19. In order to make research more valid, scientists ensure that **sample size** is sufficiently large so that a few extreme cases will not distort the picture of the group as a whole. (p. 22)

20. A **representative sample** is a group of subjects who are typical of the general population the researchers wish to learn about. (p. 22)

21. A **blind** experimenter is one who is unaware of the purpose of the research and can therefore remain objective in gathering data. (p. 22)

22. In an experiment, the **experimental group** receives some special treatment that the control group does not receive. (p.23)

    Example: In a study of the effects of a new drug on reaction time, subjects in the **experimental group** would actually receive the drug being tested.

23. The **control group** in an experiment is the one from which the treatment of interest is withheld so that comparison to the experimental group can be made. (p. 23)

24. **Statistical significance** means that an obtained result, such as a difference between two groups, very likely reflects a real difference rather than chance factors. (p. 23)

25. **Correlation** is a statistical term that merely indicates whether two variables are related to each other such that one is likely (or unlikely) to occur when the other occurs or one is likely to increase (or decrease) when the other increases (or decreases). (p. 24)

26. The **experiment** is the research method in which an investigator tests a hypothesis in a controlled situation in which the relevant variables are limited and can be manipulated by the experimenter. (p. 25)

27. The **independent variable** is the variable that is manipulated in an experiment. (p. 25)

28. The **dependent variable** is the variable that is being studied in an experiment. (p. 25)

    Example: In the study of the effects of a new drug on memory, the subjects' memory is the dependent variable.

29. The **scientific survey** is the research method in which information is collected from a large number of people, either through written questionnaires or through interviews. (p. 27)

30. The **case study** is the research method involving the intensive study of one person. (p. 28)

31. In **cross-sectional research**, groups of people who differ in age but share other important characteristics are compared with regard to the variable under investigation. (p. 29)

32. In **longitudinal research**, the same group of individuals is studied over a period of time to measure both change and stability as they age. (p. 30)

33. **Cross-sequential research** follows a group of people of different ages over time, thus combining the strengths of the cross-sectional and longitudinal methods. (p. 30)

Cross-Check

ACROSS

1. blind
2. cognitive
7. cohort
9. sample
11. SES
13. cross-sequential
14. culture
15. control

DOWN

1. biosocial
3. ethnic group
4. experimental
5. hypothesis
6. cross-sectional
7. correlation
8. longitudinal
10. population
12. case study

CHAPTER 2

Theories

Chapter Overview

Developmental theories are systematic statements of principles and generalizations that explain behavior and development and provide a framework for future research. Many such theories have influenced our understanding of human development. This chapter describes and evaluates five broad theories—psychoanalytic, learning, cognitive, sociocultural, and epigenetic systems—that will be used throughout the book to present information and to provide a framework for interpreting events and issues in human development. Each of the theories has developed a unique vocabulary with which to describe and explain events as well as to organize ideas into a cohesive system of thought.

Three of the theories presented—psychoanalytic, cognitive, and learning theory—are "grand theories" that are comprehensive in scope but inadequate in the face of recent research findings. Two of the theories—sociocultural and epigenetic systems—are considered "emergent theories" because they may become the comprehensive theories of the future. Rather than adopt any one theory exclusively, most developmentalists take an eclectic perspective and use many or all of them.

As you study this part of the chapter, consider what each of the theories has to say about your own development, as well as that of friends and relatives in other age groups. It is also a good idea to keep the following questions in mind as you study each theory: Which of the theory's principles are generally accepted by contemporary developmentalists? How has the theory been criticized? In what ways does this theory agree with the other theories? In what ways does it disagree?

NOTE: Answer guidelines for all Chapter 2 questions begin on page 28.

Guided Study

The text chapter should be studied one section at a time. Before you read, preview each section by skimming it, noting headings and boldface items. Then read the appropriate section objectives from the following outline. Keep these objectives in mind and, as you read the chapter section, search for the information that will enable you to meet each objective. Once you have finished a section, write out answers for its objectives.

What Theories Do (pp. 37–38)

1. Define developmental theory, and describe how developmental theories help explain human behavior and development. In your answer, be sure to differentiate grand theories, minitheories, and emergent theories.

Grand Theories (pp. 38–50)

2. Discuss the major focus of psychoanalytic theories, and describe the conflicts that occur during Freud's stages of psychosexual development.

3. Describe the crises of Erikson's theory of psychosocial development, and contrast them with Freud's stages.

4. Discuss the major focus of learning theories, and explain the basic principles of classical and operant conditioning.

5. Discuss social learning theory as an extension of learning theory.

6. Identify the primary focus of cognitive theory, and briefly describe Piaget's stages of cognitive development.

7. Discuss the process that, according to Piaget, guides cognitive development.

8. Identify the major criticisms and contributions of each of the grand theories of development.

Emergent Theories (pp. 50–58)

9. Discuss the basic ideas of Vygotsky and the sociocultural theory of development.

10. (Changing Policy) Explain the nature–nurture controversy, particularly as it pertains to math aptitude and homosexuality.

11. Discuss the basic ideas of epigenetic systems theory.

The Theories Compared (pp. 59–62)

12. Summarize the contributions and criticisms of the major developmental theories, and explain the eclectic perspective of contemporary developmentalists.

13. (Children Up Close) Discuss the ethology of infant social instincts and adult caregiving impulses.

Chapter Review

When you have finished reading the chapter, work through the material that follows to review it. Complete the sentences and answer the questions. As you proceed, evaluate your performance for each section by consulting the answers on page 28. Do not continue with the next section until you understand each answer. If you need to, review or reread the appropriate section in the textbook before continuing.

What Theories Do (pp. 37–38)

1. A systematic set of principles and generalizations that explains behavior and development is called a(n) ______________ ______________.

2. Developmental theories provide a broad and ______________ view of the influences on development; they form the basis for educated guesses, or ______________, about behavior; and they provide a framework for future research.

3. Developmental theories fall into three categories: ______________ theories, which offer a comprehensive view of development but have proven to be outdated; ______________ theories, which explain a specific area of development; and ______________ theories, which may be the comprehensive theories of the future.

Grand Theories (pp. 38–50)

4. Psychoanalytic theories interpret human development in terms of intrinsic ______________ and ______________, many of which are ______________ (conscious/unconscious) and ______________.

5. According to Freud's ______________ theory, children experience sexual pleasures and desires during the first six years as they pass through three ______________ ______________. From infancy to early childhood to the preschool years, these stages are the ______________ stage, the ______________ stage, and the ______________ stage. Finally, after a period of sexual ______________, which lasts for about ______________ years, the individual enters the ______________ stage, which begins at about age ______________ and lasts throughout adulthood.

Specify the focus of sexual pleasure and the major developmental need associated with each of Freud's stages.

oral ______________

____

anal ______________

____

phallic ______________________________

____

genital ______________________________

____

6. Erik Erikson's theory of development, which focuses on social and cultural influences, is called a(n) ______________ theory. In this theory, there are ______________ (number) developmental stages, each characterized by a particular developmental ______________ related to the person's relationship to the social environment. Unlike Freud, Erikson proposed stages of development that ______________ (span/do not span) a person's lifetime.

Complete the following chart regarding Erikson's stages of psychosocial development.

Age Period	Stage
Birth to 1 yr.	trust vs. ______________
1–3 yrs.	autonomy vs. ______________
3–6 yrs.	initiative vs. ______________
7–11 yrs.	______________ vs. inferiority
Adolescence	identity vs. ______________
Young adulthood	______________ vs. isolation
Middle adulthood	______________ vs. stagnation
Older adulthood	______________ vs. despair

7. A major theory in American psychology is ______________, which forms the basis for contemporary ______________ theory because of its emphasis on how we learn specific behaviors. This theory emerged early in the present century under the influence of ______________.

8. Learning theorists have formulated laws of behavior that are believed to apply ______________ (only at certain ages/at all ages). The basic principles of learning theory explore the relationship between an experience or event (called the ______________) and the behavioral reaction associated with it (called the ______________). The learning process, which is called ______________, takes two forms: ______________ and ______________ ______________.

9. In classical conditioning, which was discovered by the Russian scientist ______________ and is also called ______________ conditioning, a person or an animal learns to associate a(n) ______________ stimulus with a meaningful one. Many human ______________ responses are susceptible to classical conditioning, particularly in childhood.

10. According to ______________, the learning of more complex responses is the result of ______________ conditioning, in which a person learns that a particular behavior produces a particular ______________, such as a reward. This type of learning is also called ______________ conditioning.

11. The process of repeating a consequence to make it more likely that the behavior in question will recur is called ______________. The consequence that increases the likelihood that a behavior will be repeated is called the ______________.

12. The extension of learning theory that emphasizes the ways that people learn new behaviors by observing others is called ______________ ______________ theory. The process whereby a child patterns his or her behavior after a parent or teacher, for example, is called ______________.

13. Children's susceptibility to modeling ______________ (does/does not) change as they mature. This indicates that cognitive and motivational processes ______________ (are/are not) important factors in modeling.

14. The structure and development of the individual's thought processes and the way those thought processes affect the person's understanding of the world are the focus of ______________ theory. A major pioneer of this theory is ______________.

15. In Piaget's first stage of development, the ________ stage, children experience the world through their senses and motor abilities. This stage occurs between birth and age ________.

16. According to Piaget, during the preschool years (up to age ________), children are in the ________ stage. A hallmark of this stage is that children begin to think ________.

17. Piaget believed that children begin to think logically in a consistent way at about ________ years of age. At this time, they enter the ________ stage.

18. In Piaget's final stage, the ________ ________ stage, reasoning expands from the purely concrete to encompass ________ thinking. Piaget believed most children enter this stage by age ________.

19. According to Piaget, cognitive development is guided by the need to maintain a state of mental balance, called ________ ________.

20. When new experiences challenge existing schemes, creating a kind of imbalance, the individual experiences ________ ________, which eventually leads to mental growth.

21. According to Piaget, people adapt to new experiences either by reinterpreting them to fit into, or ________ with, old ideas. Some new experiences force people to revamp old ideas so that they can ________ new experiences.

22. Two of the grand theories focus on the powerful influences parents have on children. These are ________ theory and ________ theory.

Identify one common criticism of learning theory.

23. Psychoanalytic theory's emphasis on ________ has been criticized for being ________-specific and ________-bound.

24. Critics of cognitive theory complain that Piaget ignored individual differences in ________, ________, or ________.

25. Each of the grand theories has been faulted for focusing too much on the ________ ________, too little on the ________ ________, and for underestimating the role of ________ and ________ influences.

Identify two psychoanalytic ideas that *are* widely accepted.

Identify one way in which the study of human development has benefited from learning theory. From cognitive theory.

26. The debate over the relative influence of heredity and environment in shaping personal traits and characteristics is called the ________________-________________ controversy. Traits inherited at the moment of conception give evidence of the influence of ________________; those that emerge in response to learning and environmental influences give evidence of the effect of ________________.

27. (Changing Policy) Developmentalists agree that, at every point, the ________________ between nature and nurture is the crucial influence on any particular aspect of development.

28 (Changing Policy) In elementary school, boys and girls show similar mathematics ________________; by the teenage years, however, the mathematical ________________ of the average boy is higher than that of the average girl.

29. (Changing Policy) Research suggests that ________________ (nature/nurture) plays the larger role in the development of sexual orientation.

(Changing Policy) Briefly summarize two research findings concerning homosexuality and the nature-nurture controversy.

Emergent Theories (pp. 50–58)

30. In contrast to the grand theories, which were each set forth by ________________ (one/many) person(s), the two emerging theories draw from the findings of ________________ (one/many) discipline(s).

31. Sociocultural theory sees human development as the result of ________________ ________________ between developing persons and their surrounding ________________.

32. A major pioneer of this perspective was ________________, who was primarily interested in the development of ________________ competencies.

33. Vygotsky believed that these competencies result from the interaction between children and ________________, in what has been called an ________________ ________________.

34. In Vygotsky's view, the best way to accomplish the goals of apprenticeship is through ________________ ________________, in which the tutor engages the learner in ________________ ________________.

35. Vygotsky believed that the specific ________________ of a society is the most important of all learning tools.

36. According to Vygotsky, a mentor draws a child into the ________________ ________________ ________________, which is defined as the range of skills that the child can exercise with ________________ but cannot perform independently.

Cite several contributions, and several criticisms, of sociocultural theory.

37. The newest of the theories, epigenetic systems theory emphasizes the interaction between ________________ and the ________________ .

38. In using the word *genetic*, this theory emphasizes that we have powerful ________________ and abilities that arise from our ________________ heritage.

39. The prefix "epi" refers to the various ________________ factors that affect the expression of ________________ ________________ . These include the presence or absence of chemical factors such as ________________ , ________________ , and ________________ ; and stress factors such as ________________ , ________________ , or ________________ .

40. Some epigenetic factors are the result of the evolutionary process called ________________ ________________ , in which, over generations, genes for useful traits that promote survival become more prevalent.

41. "Everything that seems to be genetic is actually epigenetic." This statement highlights the fact that ________________ (some/most/all) genetic instructions are affected by the environment.

42. The "systems" aspect of this theory points out that changes in one part of the individual's system ________________ .

The Theories Compared (pp. 59–62)

43. Which major theory of development emphasizes:
    a. the importance of culture in fostering development? ________________
    b. the ways in which thought processes affect actions? ________________
    c. environmental influences? ________________
    d. the impact of "hidden dramas" on development? ________________ ________________
    e. the interaction of genes and environment ________________ ________________

44. Which major theory of development has been criticized for:
    a. being too mechanistic? ________________
    b. undervaluing genetic differences? ________________
    c. being too subjective? ________________
    d. neglecting society? ________________
    e. neglecting individuals? ________________

45. Because no one theory can encompass all of human behavior, most developmentalists have a(n) ________________ perspective, which capitalizes on the strengths of all the theories.

46. (Children Up Close) The study of the evolutionary origins and adaptive value of patterns of animal behavior is called ________________ . Newborn animals and human infants are genetically programmed for ________________ ________________ as a means of survival. Similarly, adult animals and humans are genetically programmed for ________________ .

Progress Test 1

Multiple-Choice Questions

Circle your answers to the following questions and check them with the answers on page 29. If your answer is incorrect, read the explanation for why it is incorrect and then consult the appropriate pages of the text (in parentheses following the correct answer).

1. The purpose of a developmental theory is to:
   a. provide a broad and coherent view of the complex influences on human development.
   b. offer guidance for practical issues encountered by parents, teachers, and therapists.
   c. generate testable hypotheses about development.
   d. do all of the above.

2. Which developmental theory emphasizes the influence of unconscious drives and motives on behavior?
   a. psychoanalytic
   b. learning
   c. cognitive
   d. sociocultural

3. Which of the following is the correct order of the psychosexual stages proposed by Freud?
   a. oral stage; anal stage; phallic stage; latency; genital stage
   b. anal stage; oral stage; phallic stage; latency; genital stage
   c. oral stage; anal stage; genital stage; latency; phallic stage
   d. anal stage; oral stage; genital stage; latency; phallic stage

4. Erikson's psychosocial theory of human development describes:
   a. eight crises all people are thought to face.
   b. four psychosocial stages and a latency period.
   c. the same number of stages as Freud's, but with different names.
   d. a stage theory that is not psychoanalytic.

5. Which of the following theories does *not* belong with the others?
   a. psychoanalytic
   b. learning
   c. sociocultural
   d. cognitive

6. An American psychologist who explained complex human behaviors in terms of operant conditioning was:
   a. Lev Vygotsky.
   b. Ivan Pavlov.
   c. B. F. Skinner.
   d. Jean Piaget.

7. Pavlov's dogs learned to salivate at the sound of a bell because they associated the bell with food. Pavlov's experiment with dogs was an early demonstration of:
   a. classical conditioning.
   b. operant conditioning.
   c. positive reinforcement.
   d. social learning.

8. (Changing Policy) The nature-nurture controversy considers the degree to which traits, characteristics, and behaviors are the result of:
   a. early or lifelong learning.
   b. genes or heredity.
   c. heredity or experience.
   d. different historical concepts of childhood.

9. Social learning is sometimes called modeling because it:
   a. follows the scientific model of learning.
   b. molds character.
   c. follows the immediate reinforcement model developed by Bandura.
   d. involves people's patterning their behavior after that of others.

10. Which developmental theory suggests that each person is born with genetic possibilities that must be nurtured in order to grow?
    a. sociocultural
    b. cognitive
    c. learning
    d. epigenetic systems

11. Which developmental theories place the *greatest* emphasis on parental influence on children?
    a. psychoanalytic and learning
    b. learning and cognitive
    c. sociocultural and epigenetic systems
    d. cognitive and epigenetic systems

12. Which is the correct sequence of stages in Piaget's theory of cognitive development?
    a. sensorimotor, preoperational, concrete operational, formal operational
    b. sensorimotor, preoperational, formal operational, concrete operational
    c. preoperational, sensorimotor, concrete operational, formal operational
    d. preoperational, sensorimotor, formal operational, concrete operational

13. When an individual's existing understanding no longer fits his or her present experiences, the result is called:
    a. a psychosocial crisis.
    b. equilibrium.
    c. disequilibrium.
    d. negative reinforcement.

14. The fact that nations differ dramatically in how many of their university professors of math are women suggests:
    a. that nature is more important than nurture in determining math ability.
    b. that nurture is more important than nature in determining math ability.
    c. that nature and nurture are equally important.
    d. nothing, because of the cultural diversity among nations.

15. The zone of proximal development refers to:
    a. the control process by which information is transferred from the sensory register to working memory.
    b. the influence of a pleasurable stimulus on behavior.
    c. the range of skills that a child can exercise with assistance but cannot perform independently.
    d. the mutual interaction of a person's internal characteristics, the environment, and the person's behavior.

True or False Items

Write *true* or *false* on the line in front of each statement.

______ 1. Learning theorists study what people actually do, not what they might be thinking.

______ 2. Erikson's eight developmental stages are centered not on a body part but on each person's relationship to the social environment.

______ 3. Most developmentalists agree that the nature-nurture controversy has been laid to rest.

______ 4. Few developmental theorists today believe that humans have instincts or abilities that arise from our species' biological heritage.

______ 5. Of the major developmental theories, cognitive theory gives the most emphasis to the interaction of genes and experience in shaping development.

______ 6. Piaget was so absorbed in the individual's active search for knowledge that he neglected the importance of instruction.

______ 7. According to Piaget, a state of cognitive equilibrium must be attained before cognitive growth can occur.

______ 8. In part, cognitive theory examines how an individual's understandings and expectations affect his or her behavior.

______ 9. According to Piaget, children begin to think only when they reach preschool age.

______ 10. Most contemporary researchers have adopted an eclectic perspective on development.

Progress Test 2

Progress Test 2 should be completed during a final chapter review. Answer the following questions after you thoroughly understand the correct answers for the Chapter Review and Progress Test 1.

Multiple-Choice Questions

1. Which developmental theorist has been criticized for suggesting that every child, in every culture, in every nation, passes through certain fixed stages?

   a. Freud
   b. Erikson
   c. Piaget
   d. all of the above.

2. Of the following terms, the one that does *not* describe a stage of Freud's theory of childhood sexuality is:

   a. phallic.
   b. oral.
   c. anal.
   d. sensorimotor.

3. We are more likely to imitate the behavior of others if we particularly admire and identify with them. This belief finds expression in:

   a. stage theory.
   b. sociocultural theory.
   c. social learning theory.
   d. Pavlov's experiments.

4. How do minitheories differ from grand theories of development?

   a. Unlike the more comprehensive grand theories, minitheories explain only a part of development.
   b. Unlike grand theories, which usually reflect the thinking of many researchers, minitheories tend to stem from one person.
   c. Only the recency of the research on which they are based keeps minitheories from having the sweeping influence of grand theories.
   d. They differ in all of the above ways.

5. According to Erikson, an adult who has difficulty establishing a secure, mutual relationship with a life partner might never have resolved the crisis of:

   a. initiative versus guilt
   b. autonomy versus shame
   c. intimacy versus isolation
   d. trust versus mistrust

6. Who would be most likely to agree with the statement, "anything can be learned"?

   a. Jean Piaget
   b. Lev Vygotsky
   c. John Watson
   d. Erik Erikson

7. Classical conditioning is to ____________ as operant conditioning is to ____________.

   a. Skinner; Pavlov
   b. Watson; Vygotsky
   c. Pavlov: Skinner
   d. Vygotsky; Watson

8. Learning theorists have found that they can often solve a person's seemingly complex psychological problem by:

   a. analyzing the patient.
   b. admitting the existence of the unconscious.
   c. altering the environment.
   d. administering well-designed punishments.

9. According to Piaget, an infant first comes to know the world through:
   a. sucking and grasping.
   b. naming and counting.
   c. preoperational thought.
   d. instruction from parents.

10. According to Piaget, the stage of cognitive development that generally characterizes preschool children (2 to 6 years old) is the:
    a. preoperational stage.
    b. sensorimotor stage.
    c. oral stage.
    d. psychosocial stage.

11. In Piaget's theory, equilibrium refers to:
    a. a state of mental balance.
    b. a kind of imbalance that leads to cognitive growth.
    c. the ultimate stage of cognitive development.
    d. the first stage in the processing of information.

12. You teach your dog to "speak" by giving her a treat each time she does so. This is an example of:
    a. classical conditioning.
    b. respondent conditioning.
    c. reinforcement.
    d. modeling.

13. A child who must modify an old idea in order to incorporate a new experience is using the process of:
    a. assimilation.
    b. accommodation.
    c. cognitive equilibrium.
    d. guided participation.

14. Which of the following is a common criticism of sociocultural theory?
    a. It places too great an emphasis on unconscious motives and childhood sexuality.
    b. Its mechanistic approach fails to explain many complex human behaviors.
    c. Development is more gradual than its stages imply.
    d. It neglects developmental processes that are not primarily social.

15. A major pioneer of the sociocultural perspective was:
    a. Jean Piaget.
    b. Albert Bandura.
    c. Lev Vygotsky.
    d. Ivan Pavlov.

Matching Items

Match each theory or term with its corresponding description or definition.

Theories or Terms

_______ 1. psychoanalytic theory
_______ 2. response
_______ 3. learning theory
_______ 4. social learning theory
_______ 5. cognitive theory
_______ 6. stimulus
_______ 7. sociocultural theory
_______ 8. conditioning
_______ 9. emergent theories
_______ 10. modeling
_______ 11. epigenetic systems theory

Descriptions or Definitions

a. emphasizes the impact of the immediate environment on behavior
b. relatively new, comprehensive theories
c. emphasizes that people learn by observing others
d. an action or event that triggers a behavioral response
e. a process of learning, as described by Pavlov or Skinner
f. emphasizes the "hidden dramas" that influence behavior
g. emphasizes the cultural context in development
h. emphasizes how our thoughts shape our actions
i. the process whereby a person learns by imitating someone else's behavior
j. emphasizes the interaction of genes and environmental forces
k. a behavior triggered by an action or event

Thinking Critically About Chapter 2

Answer these questions the day before an exam as a final check on your understanding of the chapter's terms and concepts.

1. Many songbirds inherit a genetically programmed species song that enhances their ability to mate and establish a territory. The evolution of such a trait is an example of:
   a. selective adaptation.
   b. epigenetic development.
   c. accommodation.
   d. assimilation.

2. When a pigeon is rewarded for producing a particular response, and so learns to produce that response to obtain rewards, psychologists describe this chain of events as:
   a. operant conditioning.
   b. classical conditioning.
   c. modeling.
   d. reflexive actions.

3. Research studies have shown that human handling of rat pups makes them smarter as adults. This is because handling:
   a. increases the mother's grooming of her pup.
   b. indirectly increases the release of stress hormones.
   c. leads to less brain degeneration in the face of adult stresses.
   d. does all of the above.

4. Dr. Ivey's research focuses on the biological forces that shape each child's characteristic way of reacting to environmental experiences. Evidently, Dr. Ivey is working from a(n) ________________ perspective.
   a. psychoanalytic
   b. cognitive
   c. sociocultural
   d. epigenetic systems

5. Which of the following is the best example of guided participation?
   a. After watching her mother change her baby sister's diaper, 4-year-old Brandy changes her doll's diaper.
   b. To help her son learn to pour liquids, Sandra engages him in a bathtub game involving pouring water from cups of different sizes.
   c. Seeing his father light a cigarette, 3-year-old Kyle pretends to "smoke" his drinking straw.
   d. After reading a recipe in a magazine, Jack gathers ingredients from the cupboard.

6. A child who calls all furry animals "doggie" will experience cognitive ________________ when she encounters a hairless breed for the first time. This may cause her to revamp her concept of "dog" in order to ________________ the new experience.
   a. disequilibrium; accommodate
   b. disequilibrium; assimilate
   c. equilibrium; accommodate
   d. equilibrium; assimilate

7. Which of Freud's ideas would *not* be accepted by most psychologists today?
   a. Sexuality is a potent drive in humans.
   b. People are often unaware of their deep needs, wishes, and fears.
   c. The child's experiences during the first two psychosexual stages form the basis for character structure and personality problems in adulthood.
   d. Human thoughts and actions are probably far more complicated than is at first apparent.

8. After watching several older children climbing around a new junglegym, 5-year-old Jennie decides to try it herself. Which of the following best accounts for her behavior?
   a. classical conditioning
   b. modeling
   c. guided participation
   d. reinforcement

9. I am 8 years old, and, although I understand some logical principles, I have trouble thinking about hypothetical concepts. According to Piaget, I am in the ________________ stage of development.
   a. sensorimotor
   b. preoperational
   c. concrete operational
   d. formal operational

10. Two-year-old Jamail has a simple understanding for "dad," and so each time he encounters a man with a child, he calls him "dad." When he learns that these other men are not "dad," Jamail experiences:
    a. conservation.
    b. cognition.
    c. equilibrium.
    d. disequilibrium.

11. (Children Up Close) Most adults become physiologically aroused by the sound of an infant's laughter. These interactive reactions, in which caregivers and babies elicit responses in each other:
    a. help ensure the survival of the next generation.
    b. do not occur in all human cultures.
    c. are the result of conditioning very early in life.
    d. are more often found in females than in males.

12. The school psychologist believes that each child's developmental needs can be understood only by taking into consideration the child's broader social and cultural background. Evidently, the school psychologist is working within the ______________ perspective.
    a. psychoanalytic
    b. epigenetic systems
    c. social learning
    d. sociocultural

13. Four-year-old Bjorn takes great pride in successfully undertaking new activities. Erikson would probably say that Bjorn is capably meeting the psychosocial challenge of:
    a. trust vs. mistrust.
    b. initiative vs. guilt.
    c. industry vs. inferiority.
    d. identity vs. role confusion.

14. Dr. Cleaver's developmental research draws upon insights from several theoretical perspectives. Evidently, Dr. Cleaver is working from a(n) ______________ perspective.
    a. cognitive
    b. learning
    c. eclectic
    d. sociocultural

15. Dr. Bazzi believes that development is a lifelong process of gradual and continuous growth. Based on this information, with which of the following theories would Dr. Bazzi most likely agree?
    a. Piaget's cognitive theory
    b. Erikson's psychosocial theory
    c. Freud's psychoanalytic theory
    d. learning theory

Key Terms

Writing Definitions

Using your own words, write a brief definition or explanation of each of the following terms on a separate piece of paper.

1. developmental theory
2. grand theories
3. minitheories
4. emergent theories
5. psychoanalytic theory
6. learning theory
7. stimulus
8. response
9. conditioning
10. reinforcement
11. social learning
12. modeling
13. cognitive theory
14. cognitive equilibrium
15. sociocultural theory
16. guided participation
17. zone of proximal development
18. epigenetic systems theory
19. selective adaptation
20. ethology
21. eclectic perspective

Cross Check

After you have written the definitions of the key terms in this chapter, you should complete the crossword puzzle to ensure that you can reverse the process—recognize the term, given the definition.

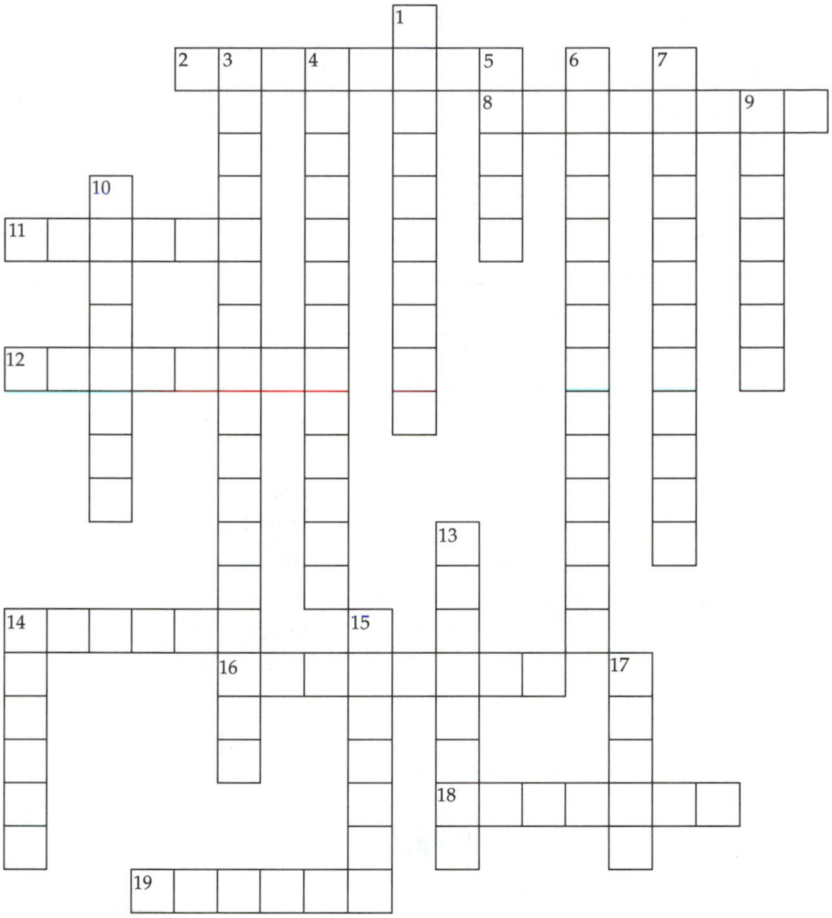

ACROSS

2. Theory that emphasizes the sequences and processes of conditioning.
8. An instinctive or learned behavior that is elicited by a specific stimulus.
11. All the genetic influences on development.
12. Developmental perspective that accepts elements from several theories.
14. Influential theorist who developed a stage theory of cognitive development.
16. Type of theory that brings together information from many disciplines into a comprehensive model of development.
18. All the environmental (nongenetic) influences on development.
19. An early and especially strong proponent of learning theory in America.

DOWN

1. Theory that focuses on some specific area of development.
3. Theory that emphasizes the interaction of genetic and environmental factors in development.
4. The process by which the consequences of a behavior make the behavior more likely to occur.
5. Comprehensive theory of development that has proven to be inadequate in explaining the full range of human development.
6. Theory of personality and development that emphasizes unconscious forces.
7. Learning process that occurs through the association of two stimuli or through the use of reinforcement.
9. Influential theorist who outlined the principles of operant conditioning.
10. The study of behavior as it relates to the evolution and survival of a species.
13. The process of learning by imitating another person's behavior.
14. Russian scientist who outlined the principles of classical conditioning.
15. Psychoanalytic theorist who viewed development as a series of psychosocial crises.
17. The developer of psychoanalytic theory.

ANSWERS

CHAPTER REVIEW

1. developmental theory
2. coherent; hypotheses
3. grand; mini; emergent
4. motives; drives; unconscious; irrational
5. psychoanalytic; psychosexual stages; oral; anal; phallic; latency; 5 or 6; genital; 12

Oral stage: The mouth is the focus of pleasurable sensations as the baby becomes emotionally attached to the person who provides the oral gratifications derived from sucking.

Anal stage: Pleasures related to control and self-control, initially in connection with defecation and toilet training, are paramount.

Phallic stage: Pleasure is derived from genital stimulation; interest in physical differences between the sexes leads to the development of gender identity, sexual orientation, and the child's development of moral standards.

Genital stage: Mature sexual interests that last throughout adulthood emerge.

6. psychosocial; 8; crisis (challenge); span

Age Period	Stage
Birth to 1 yr.	trust vs. **mistrust**
1–3 yrs.	autonomy vs. **shame and doubt**
3–6 yrs.	initiative vs. **guilt**
7–11 yrs.	**industry** vs. inferiority
Adolescence	identity vs. **role confusion**
Young adulthood	**intimacy** vs. isolation
Middle adulthood	**generativity** vs. stagnation
Older adulthood	**integrity** vs. despair

7. behaviorism; learning; John B. Watson
8. at all ages; stimulus; response; conditioning; classical conditioning; operant conditioning
9. Ivan Pavlov; respondent; neutral; emotional
10. B. F. Skinner; operant; consequence; instrumental
11. reinforcement; reinforcer
12. social learning; modeling
13. does; are
14. cognitive; Jean Piaget
15. sensorimotor; 2
16. 6; preoperational; symbolically
17. 7; concrete operational
18. formal operational; abstract (hypothetical); 12
19. cognitive equilibrium
20. cognitive disequilibrium
21. assimilate; accommodate
22. learning; psychoanalytic

Learning theory has been faulted for being unable to explain complex cognitive, emotional, and perceptual dimensions of human development.

23. unconscious and uncontrollable sexual longings; culture; time
24. ability; heredity; motivation
25. individual child; social context; biological; genetic

Two widely accepted psychoanalytic ideas are that (1) unconscious motives affect our behavior, and (2) the early years are a formative period of personality development.

Learning theory's emphasis on the causes and consequences of behavior has led researchers to see that many seemingly inborn problem behaviors may actually be the result of learning.

By focusing attention on active mental processes, cognitive theory has led to a greater understanding of the different types of thinking that are possible at various ages.

26. nature-nurture; nature; nurture
27. interaction
28. aptitude; achievement
29. nature

A man is more likely to be gay if his mother's brother or his own brother is gay. Most children who were raised by lesbian mothers are heterosexual.

30. one; many
31. dynamic interaction; culture
32. Lev Vygotsky; cognitive
33. more mature members of the society; apprenticeship in thinking
34. guided participation; joint activities
35. language
36. zone of proximal development; assistance

Sociocultural theory has deepened our understanding of the diversity in the pathways of development. It has also emphasized the need to study development in the specific cultural context in which it occurs. The theory has been criticized for neglecting the importance of developmental processes that are not primarily social, such as the role of biological maturation in development.

37. genes; environment
38. instincts; biological
39. environmental; genetic instructions; nutrients; hormones; toxins; injury; temperature; crowding
40. selective adaptation
41. all
42. cause corresponding changes and adjustments in every other part
43. **a.** sociocultural
    b. cognitive
    c. learning
    d. psychoanalytic
    e. epigenetic systems
44. **a.** learning
    b. cognitive
    c. psychoanalytic
    d. epigenetic systems
    e. sociocultural
45. eclectic
46. ethology; social contact; infant caregiving

PROGRESS TEST 1

Multiple-Choice Questions

1. **d.** is the answer (p. 37)
2. **a.** is the answer. (p. 38)

   b. Learning theory emphasizes the influence of the immediate environment on behavior.

   c. Cognitive theory emphasizes the impact of *conscious* thought processes on behavior.

   d. Sociocultural theory emphasizes the influence on development of social interaction in a specific cultural context.
3. **a.** is the answer. (p. 39)
4. **a.** is the answer. (p. 40)

   b. & c. Whereas Freud identified four stages of psychosexual development, Erikson proposed eight psychosocial stages.

   d. Although his theory places greater emphasis on social and cultural forces than Freud's, Erikson's theory is nevertheless classified as a psychoanalytic theory.
5. **c.** is the answer. Sociocultural theory is an emergent theory. (p. 38)

   a., b., & d. Each of these is an example of a grand theory.
6. **c.** is the answer. (p. 43)
7. **a.** is the answer. In classical conditioning, a neutral stimulus—in this case, the bell—is associated with a meaningful stimulus—in this case, food. (p. 42)

   b. In operant conditioning, the consequences of a voluntary response determine the likelihood of its being repeated. Salivation is an involuntary response.

   c. & d. Positive reinforcement and social learning pertain to voluntary, or operant, responses.
8. **c.** is the answer. (p. 52)

   a. These are both examples of nurture.

   b. Both of these refer to nature.

   d. The impact of changing historical concepts of childhood on development is an example of how environmental forces (nurture) shape development.
9. **d.** is the answer. (p. 44)

   a. & c. These can be true in all types of learning.

   b. This was not discussed as an aspect of developmental theory.
10. **d.** is the answer. (p. 55)

    a. & c. Sociocultural and learning theories focus almost entirely on environmental factors (nurture) in development.

    b. Cognitive theory emphasizes the developing person's own mental activity but ignores genetic differences in individuals.
11. **a.** is the answer. (p. 48)

    b, c, & d. These theories place less emphasis on the all-powerful role of parents in shaping development.
12. **a.** is the answer. (pp. 46–47)
13. **c.** is the answer. (p. 47)

    a. This refers to the core of Erikson's psychosocial stages, which deals with people's interactions with the environment.

    b. Equilibrium occurs when existing schemes *do* fit a person's current experiences.

    d. Negative reinforcement is the removal of a stimulus as a consequence of a desired behavior.
14. **b.** is the answer. (p. 52)

    a. Nature refers to genetic influences on development.
15. **c.** is the answer. (p. 54)

    a. This describes attention.

    b. This describes positive reinforcement.

    d. This describes reciprocal determinism.

True or False Items

1. T (p. 41)
2. T (p. 40)
3. F Although most developmentalists believe that nature and nurture interact in shaping development, the practical implicating of whether nature or nurture play a greater role in certain abilities keep the controversy alive. (p. 52)
4. F This assumption lies at the heart of epigenetic systems theory. (p. 55)
5. F Epigenetic systems theory emphasizes the interaction of genes and experience. (p. 55)
6. T (p. 49)
7. F On the contrary, *dis*equilibrium often fosters greater growth. (p. 47)
8. T (p. 45)
9. F The hallmark of Piaget's theory is that, at every age, individuals think about the world in unique ways. (p. 46)
10. T (p. 62)

PROGRESS TEST 2

Multiple-Choice Questions

1. **d.** is the answer. (p. 49)
2. **d.** is the answer. This is one of Piaget's stages of cognitive development. (pp. 39, 46)
3. **c.** is the answer. (p. 44)
4. **a.** is the answer. (p. 38)

   b. *Grand* theories, rather than minitheories, usually stem from one person.

   c. Minitheories focus on a specific area of development.
5. **d.** is the answer. (p. 40)
6. **c.** is the answer. (p. 41)

   a. Piaget formulated a cognitive theory of development.

   b. Vygotsky formulated a sociocultural theory of development.

   d. Erikson formulated a psychoanalytic theory of development.
7. **c.** is the answer. (pp. 42–43)
8. **c.** is the answer. (p. 42)

   a. & b. These are psychoanalytic approaches to treating psychological problems.

   d. Learning theorists generally do not recommend the use of punishment.
9. **a.** is the answer. These behaviors are typical of infants in the sensorimotor stage. (p. 46)

   b., c., & d. These are typical of older children.
10. **a.** is the answer. (pp. 46–47)

    b. The sensorimotor stage describes development from birth until 2 years of age.

    c. This is a psychoanalytic stage described by Freud.

    d. This is not the name of a stage; "psychosocial" refers to Erikson's stage theory.
11. **a.** is the answer. (p. 47)

    b. This describes *dis*equilibrium.

    c. This is formal operational thinking.

    d. Piaget's theory does not propose stages of information processing.
12. **c.** is the answer. (p. 43)

    a. & b. Teaching your dog in this way is an example of operant, rather than classical (respondent), conditioning.

    d. Modeling involves learning by imitating others.
13. **b.** is the answer. (p. 47)

    a. Assimilation occurs when new experiences do *not* clash with existing ideas.

    c. Cognitive equilibrium is mental balance, which occurs when ideas and experiences do *not* clash.

    d. This is Vygotsky's term for the process by which a mentor engages a child in shared learning activities.
14. **d.** is the answer. (p. 55)

    a. This is a common criticism of psychoanalytic theory.

    b. This is a common criticism of learning theory.

    c. This is a common criticism of psychoanalytic and cognitive theories that describe development as occurring in a sequence of stages.
15. **c.** is the answer. (p. 51)

Matching Items

1. f (p. 38)	**5.** h (p. 45)	**9.** b (p. 38)
2. k (p. 42)	**6.** d (p. 42)	**10.** i (p. 44)
3. a (p. 42)	**7.** g (p. 50)	**11.** j (p. 55)
4. c (p. 44)	**8.** e (p. 42)	

THINKING CRITICALLY ABOUT CHAPTER 2

1. **a.** is the answer. (p.56)

   b. This term was not used to describe development.

   c. & d. These terms describe the processes by which cognitive concepts incorporate (assimilate) new experiences, or are revamped (accommodate) by them.

2. **a.** is the answer. This is an example of operant conditioning because a response recurs because of its consequences. (p. 43)

   b. & d. In classical conditioning, the individual learns to associate a neutral stimulus with a meaningful stimulus.

   c. In modeling, learning occurs through the observation of others, rather than through direct exposure to reinforcing consequences, as in this example.

3. **d.** is the answer. (p. 57)

4. **d.** is the answer. (p. 55)

   a. Psychoanalytic theorists focus on the role of unconscious forces in development.

   b. Cognitive theorists emphasize how the developing person actively seeks to understand experiences.

   c. Sociocultural theorists focus on the social context, as expressed through people, language, and customs.

5. **b.** is the answer. (p. 51)

   a. & c. These are both examples of modeling.

   d. Guided participation involves the coaching of a mentor. In this example, Jack is simply following written directions.

6. **a.** is the answer. (p. 47)

   b. Because the dog is not furry, the child's concept of dog cannot incorporate (assimilate) the discrepant experience without being revamped.

   c. & d. Equilibrium exists when ideas (such as what a dog is) and experiences (such as seeing a hairless dog) do *not* clash.

7. **c.** is the answer. Although the early years are an important formative age, most developmentalists agree that development is lifelong. (p. 49)

8. **b.** is the answer. Evidently, Jennie has learned by observing the other children at play. (p. 44)

   a. Classical conditioning is concerned with the association of stimuli, not with complex responses, as in this example.

   c. Guided participation involves the interaction of a mentor and a child.

   d. Reinforcement is a process for getting a response to recur.

9. **c.** is the answer. (p. 45)

10. **d.** is the answer. When Jamail experiences something that conflicts with his existing understanding, he experiences disequilibrium. (p. 47)

    a. Conservation is the ability to recognize that objects do not change when their appearances change.

    b. Cognition refers to all mental activities associated with thinking.

    c. If Jamail's thinking were in equilibrium, all men would be "dad"!

11. **a.** is the answer. (p. 60)

    b. & c. Infant social reflexes and adult caregiving impulses occur in all cultures (b), which indicates that they are the product of nature rather than nurture (c).

    d. The text does not address the issue of gender differences in infant reflexes or caregiving impulses.

12. **d.** is the answer. (p. 50)

13. **b.** is the answer. (p. 41)

    a. According to Erikson, this crisis concerns younger children.

    c. & d. In Erikson's theory, these crises concern older children.

14. **c.** is the answer. (p. 62)

    a., b., & d. These are three of the many theoretical perspectives upon which someone working from an eclectic perspective might draw.

15. **d.** is the answer. (p. 42)

    a., b., & c. Each of these theories emphasizes that development is a discontinuous process that occurs in stages.

KEY TERMS

Writing Definitions

1. A **developmental theory** is a systematic statement of principles that explains behavior and development and provides a framework for future research. (p. 37)

2. **Grand theories** are comprehensive theories of human development that have proven to be inadequate in the face of research evidence that devel-

opment is more diverse than the theories proposed. Examples of grand theories are psychoanalytic, cognitive, and learning theory. (p. 38)

3. **Minitheories** are less general and comprehensive than grand theories focusing instead on some specific area of development. (p. 38)
4. **Emergent theories**, such as sociocultural theory and epigenetic systems theory, are newer comprehensive theories that bring together information from many disciplines but are not yet a coherent, comprehensive whole. (p. 38)
5. **Psychoanalytic theory**, a grand theory, interprets human development in terms of intrinsic drives and motives, many of which are irrational and unconscious. (p. 38)
6. **Learning theory,** a grand theory based on behaviorism, emphasizes the sequences and processes of conditioning that underlie most of human and animal behavior. (p. 42)
7. In learning theory, a **stimulus** is an action or event that elicits a behavioral response. (p. 42)
8. In learning theory, a **response** is an instinctual, or learned, behavior that is elicited by a certain stimulus. (p. 42)
9. **Conditioning** is the learning process that occurs either through the association of two stimuli (classical conditioning) or through the use of positive or negative reinforcement or punishment (operant conditioning). (p. 42)
10. **Reinforcement** is the process by which the consequences of a particular behavior strengthen it, making it more likely that the behavior will be repeated. (p. 43)
11. An extension of learning theory, **social learning theory** emphasizes that people often learn new behaviors through observation and imitation of other people. (p. 44)
12. **Modeling** refers to the process by which we observe other people's behavior and then pattern our own after it. (p. 44)
13. **Cognitive theory** emphasizes that the way people think and understand the world shapes their perceptions, attitudes, and actions. (p. 45)
14. In Piaget's theory, **cognitive equilibrium** is a state of mental balance, in which a person's thoughts about the world seem not to clash with each other or with his or her experiences. (p. 47)
15. **Sociocultural theory** seeks to explain development as the result of a dynamic interaction between developing persons and their surrounding culture. (p. 46)
16. **Guided participation** is a learning process in which the learner is tutored through social interaction with a skilled teacher. (p. 51)
17. According to Vygotsky, developmental growth occurs when mentors draw children into the **zone of proximal development**, which is the range of skills the child can exercise with assistance but cannot perform independently. (p. 54)
18. The **epigenetic systems theory** emphasizes the genetic origins of behavior but also stresses that genes, over time, are directly and systematically affected by environmental forces. (p. 55)
19. **Selective adaptation** is the evolutionary process through which useful genes that enhance survival become more frequent within individuals. (p. 56)
20. **Ethology** is the study of behavior as it relates to the evolution and survival of a species. (p. 61)
21. Developmentalists who work from an **eclectic perspective** accept elements from several theories, instead of adhering to only a single perspective. (p. 62)

Cross-Check

ACROSS

2. learning
8. response
11. nature
12. eclectic
14. Piaget
16. emergent
18. nurture
19. Watson

DOWN

1. minitheory
3. epigenetic systems
4. reinforcement
5. grand
6. psychoanalytic
7. conditioning
9. Skinner
10. ethology
13. modeling
14. Pavlov
15. Erikson
17. Freud

CHAPTER 3

Heredity and Environment

Chapter Overview

Conception occurs when the male and female reproductive cells—the sperm and ovum, respectively—come together to create a new, one-celled zygote with its own unique combination of genetic material. The genetic material furnishes the instructions for development—not only for obvious physical characteristics, such as sex, coloring, and body shape, but also for certain psychological characteristics, such as bashfulness, moodiness, and vocational aptitude.

Every year scientists make new discoveries and reach new understandings about genes and their effects on the development of individuals. This chapter presents some of their findings, including that most human characteristics are polygenic and multifactorial, the result of the interaction of many genetic and environmental influences. Perhaps the most important findings have come from research into the causes of genetic and chromosomal abnormalities. The chapter discusses the most common of these abnormalities and concludes with a section on genetic counseling. Genetic testing before and after conception can help predict whether a couple will have a child with a genetic problem.

Many students find the technical material in this chapter difficult to master, but it *can* be done with a great deal of rehearsal. Working through the Chapter Review several times and mentally reciting terms are both useful techniques for rehearsing this type of material.

NOTE: Answer guidelines for all Chapter 3 questions begin on page 44.

Guided Study

The text chapter should be studied one section at a time. Before you read, preview each section by skimming it, noting headings and boldface items. Then read the appropriate section objectives from the following outline. Keep these objectives in mind and, as you read the chapter section, search for the information that will enable you to meet each objective. Once you have finished a section, write out answers for its objectives.

The Beginning of Development (pp. 67–75)

1. Describe the process of conception and the first hours of development of the zygote.

2. Identify the mechanisms of heredity, and explain how sex is determined.

3. Discuss genetic continuity and diversity, and distinguish between monozygotic and dizygotic twins.

4. (Text and Children Up Close) Explain several alternative methods of conception and several personal and ethical questions raised by these methods.

From Genotype to Phenotype (pp. 75–85)

5. Differentiate genotype from phenotype, and explain the polygenic and multifactorial nature of human traits.

6. Explain the additive and nonadditive patterns of genetic interaction. Give examples of the traits that result from each type of interaction.

7. Discuss X-linked genes in terms of genotype and phenotype, and explain the concept of genetic imprinting.

8. Explain how scientists distinguish the effects of genes and environment on development.

9. Identify some environmental variables that affect genetic inheritance, and describe how a particular trait, such as susceptibility to shyness (inhibition) or alcoholism, might be affected.

Genetic and Chromosomal Abnormalities (pp. 85–89, 90–91)

10. Describe the most common chromosomal abnormalities, focusing on abnormalities involving the sex chromosomes.

11. Identify two common genetic disorders, and discuss reasons for their relatively low incidence of occurrence.

Choices to Make (pp. 89, 92–95)

12. Describe four situations in which couples should seek genetic testing and counseling.

13. (Changing Policy) Explain the major methods of prenatal diagnosis, noting the advantages of each.

Chapter Review

When you have finished reading the chapter, work through the material that follows to review it. Complete the sentences and answer the questions. As you proceed, evaluate your performance for each section by consulting the answers on page 44. Do not continue with the next section until you understand each answer. If you need to, review or reread the appropriate section in the textbook before continuing.

The Beginning of Development (pp. 67–75)

1. The human reproductive cells, which are called ______________, include the male's ______________ and the female's ______________.

2. When the gametes' genetic material combine, a living cell called a ______________ is formed.

3. Before the zygote begins the process of cellular division that starts human development, the combined genetic material from both gametes is ______________ to form two complete sets of genetic instructions. Soon after, following a genetic timetable, the cells start to ______________, with various cells beginning to specialize and reproduce at different rates.

4. A complete copy of the genetic instructions inherited by the zygote at the moment of conception is found in ______________ (every/most/only a few) cell(s) of the body.

5. The basic units of heredity are the ______________, which are discrete segments of a ______________, which is a molecule of ______________.

6. Genetic instructions are "written" in a chemical code, made up of four pairs of bases: ______________, ______________, ______________, and ______________. The precise nature of a gene's instructions is determined by this ______________ ______________, that is, by the overall ______________ in which base pairs appear along each segment of the DNA molecule.

7. These genetic instructions direct the synthesis of hundreds of different kinds of ______________, including ______________, which are the body's building blocks and regulators. Genes direct not only the form and location of cells, but also life itself, instructing cells to ______________.

8. Each normal person inherits ______________ chromosomes, ______________ from each parent.

9. During cell division, the gametes each receive ______________ (one/both) member(s) of

each chromosome pair. Thus, in number each gamete has ______________ chromosomes.

10. The developing person's sex is determined by the ______________ pair of chromosomes. In the female, this pair is composed of two ______________-shaped chromosomes and is designated ______________. In the male, this pair includes one ______________ and one ______________ chromosome and is therefore designated ______________.

11. The critical factor in the determination of a zygote's sex is which ______________ (sperm/ovum) reaches the other gamete first.

12. Genes ensure both genetic ______________ across the species and genetic ______________ within it.

13. When the twenty-three chromosome pairs divide up during the formation of gametes, which of the two pair members will end up in a particular gamete is determined by ______________. Genetic variability is also affected by the ______________-______________ of genes, and by the interaction of genetic instructions in ways unique to the individual. This means that any given mother and father can form approximately ______________ genetically different offspring.

14. Identical twins, which occur about once in every ______________ pregnancies, are called ______________ twins because they come from one zygote. Such twins ______________ (are/are not) genetically identical.

15. Twins who begin life as two separate zygotes created by the fertilization of two ova, are called ______________ twins. Such twins have approximately ______________ percent of their genes in common.

16. The number of multiple births has ______________ (increased/decreased/remained unchanged) in many nations, because of the increased use of ______________ ______________.

17. The timing of puberty is partly ______________ and partly ______________. Today, genes cause peak fertility at ______________ (older/younger) ages than in the past. Reproduction begins to become more difficult at about age ______________, reducing ______________ in men and impeding ______________ and ______________ in women. About one couple in every six is considered ______________, because they have been unable to conceive a child after ______________ (how long?).

18. Personal habits, such as ______________ ______________ may affect fertility. In the procedure called ______________ ______________ ______________, ova are surgically removed from the ovaries and fertilized by sperm in the laboratory. Other techniques include GIFT and ZIFT, which involve inserting either ______________ or ______________ into the ______________ ______________.

19. In the United States, twice as many babies are conceived through ______________ ______________ ______________ than are adopted each year. Ovum donation, such as when a woman volunteers to become a ______________ ______________, generally is ______________ (easier/more complicated).

From Genotype to Phenotype (pp. 754–85)

20. Most human characteristics are affected by many genes, and so are ______________; and by many factors, and so are ______________.

21. The sum total of all the genes a person inherits is called the ______________. The sum total of all the genes that are actually expressed is called the ______________.

22. A person who has a gene in his or her genotype that is not expressed in the phenotype is said to be a ______________ of that gene.

23. For any given trait, the phenotype arises from the interaction of the proteins synthesized from the specific ______________ that make up the genotype, and from the interaction between the genotype and the ______________ .

24. A phenotype that reflects the sum of the contributions of all the genes involved in its determination illustrates the ______________ pattern of genetic interaction. Genes that affect ______________ and ______________ ______________ are of this type.

25. Less often, genes interact in a ______________ fashion. In one example of this pattern, some genes are more influential than others; this is called the ______________-______________ pattern. In this pattern, the more influential gene is called ______________, and the weaker gene is called ______________ . In one variation of this pattern, the phenotype is influenced primarily, but not exclusively, by the dominant gene; this is the ______________ ______________ pattern. Hundreds of ______________ characteristics follow this basic pattern.

Explain how it is possible for two brown-eyed parents to have a blue-eyed child.

26. Some recessive genes are located only on the *X* chromosome and so are called ______________-______________ . Examples of such genes are the ones that determine ______________ ______________ .

Because they have only one *X* chromosome, ______________ (females/males) are more likely to have these characteristics in their phenotype.

27. Whether a gene is inherited from the mother or the father ______________ (does/does not) influence its behavior. This tendency of genes is called ______________ ______________, or tagging.

28. The complexity of genetic interaction is particularly apparent in ______________ characteristics.

Explain how social scientists define environment.

29. To identify genetic influences on development, researchers must distinguish genetic effects from ______________ effects. To this end, researchers study ______________ and ______________ children.

30. If ______________ (monozygotic/dizygotic) twins are found to be much more similar on a particular trait than ______________ (monozygotic/dizygotic) twins are, it is likely that genes play a significant role in the appearance of that trait.

31. Traits that show a strong correlation between adopted children and their ______________ (adoptive/biological) parents suggest a genetic basis for those characteristics.

32. The best way to try to separate the effects of genes and environments is to study ______________ twins who have been raised in ______________ (the same/different) environments.

33. Environment, as broadly defined in the text, affects ______________ (most/every/few) human characteristic(s).

34. Researchers can now directly compare a pattern of genes shared by two individuals with a promising new statistical technique called ______________ ______________ ______________ .

35. Throughout the twentieth century, as

__________ and __________ __________ improved, each generation grew slightly taller than the previous one. Over the past several decades, this trend has __________ (continued/stopped) because the majority of the population __________ (has/has not) reached its full genetic height.

Briefly explain how shyness (or inhibition), which is influenced by genes, is also affected by the social environment.

36. Other psychological traits that have strong genetic influences but may be affected by environment include __________, __________, __________, __________, and __________.

37. If one monozygotic twin develops schizophrenia, the chances are about __________ percent that the other will, too. Environmental influences __________ (do/do not) play an important role in the appearance of schizophrenia.

38. Alcoholism __________ (is/is not) partly genetic; furthermore, its expression __________ (is/is not) affected by the environment. Certain temperamental traits correlate with abusive drinking, including __________ __________.

Genetic and Chromosomal Abnormalities
(pp. 85–89, 90–91)

Researchers study genetic and chromosomal abnormalities for three major reasons. They are:

39. Chromosomal abnormalities occur during the formation of the __________, producing a sperm or ovum that does not have the normal complement of chromosomes.

40. An estimated __________ of all zygotes have too few or too many chromosomes. Most of these __________ (do/do not) begin to develop. Nevertheless, about 1 in every __________ newborns has one chromosome too few or one too many, leading to a cluster of characteristics called a __________.

41. The most common extra-chromosome syndrome is __________ __________, which is also called __________-__________.

List several of the physical and psychological characteristics associated with Down syndrome.

42. About 1 in every 500 infants has either a missing __________ chromosome or three or more such chromosomes.

Look at Table 3.1 on page 87, which lists the most common sex-linked chromosomal abnormalities. List at least two characteristics associated with each of the following syndromes.

Kleinfelter syndrome: __________

XYY: __________

XXX: __________

Turner syndrome: __________

43. In some individuals, part of the *X* chromosome is attached by such a thin string of molecules that it seems about to break off; this abnormality is called __________-__________ syndrome.

44. Chromosomal abnormalities such as Down syndrome __________ (occur/do not occur) more frequently when the parents are middle aged.

45. The variable that most often correlates with chromosomal abnormalities is ______________________ ______________________.

46. It is much ______________________ (more/less) likely that a person is a carrier of one or more harmful genes than that he or she has abnormal chromosomes.

47. Most of the known genetic disorders are ______________________ (dominant/recessive). Genetic disorders usually ______________________ (are/are not) seriously disabling.

48. Two exceptions are the central nervous system disease called ______________________ ______________________ and the disorder that causes its victims to exhibit uncontrollable tics and explosive outbursts, called ______________________ ______________________.

49. Genetic disorders that are ______________________ and ______________________ claim more victims than dominant ones. Three common recessive disorders are ______________________ ______________________, ______________________, and ______________________-______________________ ______________________.

Study Table 3.2 (pp. 90–91). Name two common genetic diseases or conditions that are multifactorial.

____

____

Choices to Make (pp. 89, 92–95)

50. Through ______________________ ______________________ and ______________________, couples today can learn more about their genes and about their chances of conceiving a child with chromosomal or other genetic abnormalities.

51. List four situations in which genetic counseling is strongly recommended.

a. ______________________________________

b. ______________________________________

c. ______________________________________

d. ______________________________________

52. A simple blood test is all that is needed for carrier detection of the genes for certain disorders: ______________________________________ ______________________________________.

For disorders for which the harmful genes have yet to be located, screening involves identifying the presence of ______________________ in the person's phenotype or genotype.

53. If one parent has a gene for a dominant disorder, the chances are about ______________________ that a child will inherit the condition. When two carriers of the same recessive gene for a particular disorder procreate, each of their children has a ______________________ chance of having the disease.

54. (Changing Policy) One test for neural-tube defects and Down syndrome analyzes the level of ______________________ in the mother's blood. An ultrasound, or ______________________, uses high-frequency sound waves to produce an image of the fetus. Physicians use a device called a ______________________ to directly observe the fetus and the inside of the placenta. The "mainstay" of prenatal diagnosis is ______________________, in which a small amount of fluid surrounding the fetus, inside the placenta, is analyzed for chromosomal or genetic abnormalities. A test that provides the same information but can be performed much earlier during the pregnancy is called ______________________ ______________________ ______________________.

55. Altering an organism's genetic instructions through the insertion of normal genes is called ______________________ ______________________ ______________________.

Progress Test 1

Circle your answers to the following questions and check them against the answers on page 46. If your answer is incorrect, read the explanation for why it is incorrect and then consult the appropriate pages of the text (in parentheses following the correct answer).

Multiple-Choice Questions

1. When a sperm and an ovum merge, a one-celled ________ is formed.
   a. zygote
   b. reproductive cell
   c. gamete
   d. monozygote

2. Genes are discrete segments that provide the biochemical instructions that each cell needs to become:
   a. a zygote.
   b. a chromosome.
   c. a specific part of a functioning human body.
   d. deoxyribonucleic acid.

3. In the male, the twenty-third pair of chromosomes is designated ________; in the female, this pair is designated ________.
   a. *XX*; *XY*
   b. *XY*; *XX*
   c. *XO*; *XXY*
   d. *XXY*; *XO*

4. Since the twenty-third pair of chromosomes in females is *XX*, each ovum carries an:
   a. *XX* zygote.
   b. *X* zygote.
   c. *XY* zygote.
   d. *X* chromosome.

5. When a zygote splits, the two identical, independent clusters that develop become:
   a. dizygotic twins.
   b. monozygotic twins.
   c. fraternal twins.
   d. trizygotic twins.

6. In scientific research, the *best* way to separate the effects of genes and the environment is to study:
   a. dizygotic twins.
   b. adopted children and their biological parents.
   c. adopted children and their adoptive parents.
   d. monozygotic twins raised in different environments.

7. Most of the known genetic disorders are:
   a. dominant.
   b. recessive.
   c. seriously disabling.
   d. sex-linked.

8. When we say that a characteristic is multifactorial, we mean that:
   a. many genes are involved.
   b. many environmental factors are involved.
   c. many genetic and environmental factors are involved.
   d. the characteristic is polygenic.

9. Genes are segments of molecules of:
   a. genotype.
   b. deoxyribonucleic acid (DNA).
   c. karyotype.
   d. phenotype.

10. The potential for genetic diversity in humans is so great because:
    a. there are approximately 8 million possible combinations of chromosomes.
    b. when the sperm and ovum unite, genetic combinations not present in either parent can be formed.
    c. just before a chromosome pair divides during the formation of gametes, genes cross over, producing recombinations.
    d. of all the above reasons.

11. A chromosomal abnormality that affects males only involves a(n):
    a. *XO* chromosomal pattern.
    b. *XXX* chromosomal pattern.
    c. *YY* chromosomal pattern.
    d. *XXY* chromosomal pattern.

12. Polygenic complexity is most apparent in ________ characteristics.
    a. physical
    b. psychological
    c. recessive gene
    d. dominant gene

13. Babies born with trisomy-21 (Down syndrome) are often:
    a. born to older parents.
    b. unusually aggressive.
    c. abnormally tall by adolescence.
    d. blind.

14. To say that a trait is polygenic means that:
    a. many genes make it more likely that the individual will inherit the trait.
    b. several genes must be present in order for the individual to inherit the trait.
    c. the trait is multifactorial.
    d. most people carry genes for the trait.

15. Some genetic diseases are recessive, so the child cannot inherit the condition unless both parents:
    a. have Kleinfelter syndrome.
    b. carry the same recessive gene.
    c. have *XO* chromosomes.
    d. have the disease.

Matching Items

Match each term with its corresponding description or definition.

Terms

_____ 1. gametes
_____ 2. chromosome
_____ 3. genotype
_____ 4. phenotype
_____ 5. markers
_____ 6. monozygotic
_____ 7. dizygotic
_____ 8. additive
_____ 9. fragile-*X* syndrome
_____ 10. carrier
_____ 11. zygote

Descriptions or Definitions

a. a person's entire genetic inheritance
b. identical twins
c. sperm and ovum
d. the first cell of the developing person
e. a person who has a recessive gene in his or her genotype that is not expressed in the phenotype
f. fraternal twins
g. a pattern in which each gene in question makes an active contribution to the final outcome
h. a DNA molecule
i. the behavioral or physical expression of genetic potential
j. indicators of harmful genes
k. a chromosomal abnormality

Progress Test 2

Progress Test 2 should be completed during a final chapter review. Answer the following questions after you thoroughly understand the correct answers for the Chapter Review and Progress Test 1.

1. Which of the following provides the best broad description of the relationship between heredity and environment in determining height?
   a. Heredity is the primary influence, with environment affecting development only in severe situations.
   b. Heredity and environment contribute equally to development.
   c. Environment is the major influence on physical characteristics.
   d. Heredity directs the individual's potential and environment determines whether and to what degree the individual reaches that potential.

2. Research studies of monozygotic twins who were raised apart suggest that:
   a. virtually every human trait is affected by both genes and environment.
   b. only a few psychological traits, such as emotional reactivity, are affected by genes.
   c. most traits are determined by environmental influences.
   d. most traits are determined by genes.

3. Males with fragile-*X* syndrome are:
   a. feminine in appearance.
   b. less severely affected than females.
   c. frequently retarded intellectually.
   d. unusually tall and aggressive.

4. Disorders that are _______________ are most likely to pass undetected from generation to generation.
   a. dominant
   b. dominant and polygenic
   c. recessive
   d. recessive and multifactorial

5. The incidences of sickle-cell anemia, phenylketonuria, thalassemia, and Tay-Sachs disease indicate that:
   a. these disorders are more common today than 50 years ago.
   b. these disorders are less common today than 50 years ago.
   c. certain genetic disorders are more common in certain ethnic groups.
   d. both a. and c. are true.

6. Dizygotic twins result when:
   a. a single egg is fertilized by a sperm and then splits.
   b. a single egg is fertilized by two different sperm.
   c. two eggs are fertilized by two different sperm.
   d. either a single egg is fertilized by one sperm or two eggs are fertilized by two different sperm.

7. Molecules of DNA that in humans are organized into twenty-three complementary pairs are called:
   a. zygotes.
   b. genes.
   c. chromosomes.
   d. ova.

8. Shortly after the zygote is formed, it begins the processes of duplication and division. Each resulting new cell has:
   a. the same number of chromosomes as was contained in the zygote.
   b. half the number of chromosomes as was contained in the zygote.
   c. twice, then four times, then eight times the number of chromosomes as was contained in the zygote.
   d. all the chromosomes except those that determine sex.

9. If an ovum is fertilized by a sperm bearing a *Y* chromosome:
   a. a female will develop.
   b. cell division will result.
   c. a male will develop.
   d. spontaneous abortion will occur.

10. When the male cells in the testes and the female cells in the ovaries divide to produce gametes, the process differs from that in the production of all other cells. As a result of the different process, the gametes have:
   a. one rather than both members of each chromosome pair.
   b. twenty-three chromosome pairs.
   c. *X* but not *Y* chromosomes.
   d. chromosomes from both parents.

11. Most human traits are:
   a. polygenic.
   b. multifactorial.
   c. determined by dominant-recessive patterns.
   d. both a. and b.

12. Genotype is to phenotype as ________________ is to ________________ .
   a. genetic potential; physical expression
   b. physical expression; genetic potential
   c. sperm; ovum
   d. gamete; zygote

13. The genes that influence height and skin color interact according to the ________________ pattern.
   a. dominant-recessive
   b. *X*-linked
   c. additive
   d. nonadditive

14. *X*-linked recessive genes explain why some traits seem to be passed from:
   a. father to son.
   b. father to daughter.
   c. mother to daughter.
   d. mother to son.

15. According to the text, the effects of environment on genetic inheritance include:
   a. direct effects, such as nutrition, climate, and medical care.
   b. indirect effects, such as the individual's broad economic, political, and cultural context.
   c. irreversible effects, such as those due to brain injury.
   d. everything that can interact with the person's genetic inheritance at every point of life.

True or False Items

Write *true* or *false* on the line in front of each statement.

________ 1. Most human characteristics are multifactorial, caused by the interaction of genetic and environmental factors.

________ 2. Less than 10 percent of all zygotes have harmful genes or an abnormal chromosomal makeup.

________ 3. Research suggests that susceptibility to alcoholism is at least partly the result of genetic inheritance.

________ 4. The human reproductive cells (ova and sperm) are called gametes.

________ 5. Only a very few human traits are polygenic.

________ 6. The zygote contains all the biologically inherited information—the genes and chromosomes—that a person will have during his or her life.

________ 7. A couple should probably seek genetic counseling if several earlier pregnancies ended in spontaneous abortion.

________ 8. Many genetic conditions are recessive; thus, a child will have the condition even if only the mother carries the gene.

________ 9. Two people who have the same phenotype may have a different genotype for a trait such as eye color.

________ 10. When cells divide to produce reproductive cells (gametes), each sperm or ovum receives only twenty-three chromosomes, half as many as the original cell.

Thinking Critically About Chapter 3

Answer these questions the day before an exam as a final check on your understanding of the chapter's terms and concepts.

1. Each person has two eye-color genes, one from each parent. If one gene is for brown eyes and the other for blue, the person's eye color is:
   a. blue.
   b. recessively produced.
   c. brown.
   d. impossible to predict.

2. If two people have brown eyes, they have the same phenotype with regard to eye color. Their brown eyes may be caused by:
   a. different genotypes.
   b. one brown-eye gene and one blue-eye gene.
   c. two brown-eye genes.
   d. all of the above.

3. Eye color can be hundreds of shades and tones, depending on the genes inherited. This is a result of:
   a. sex-linked chromosomal inheritance.
   b. the influence of the dominant genes only.
   c. the action of the twenty-third chromosome pair.
   d. incomplete dominance.

4. Some men are color-blind because they inherit a particular recessive gene from their mother. That recessive gene is carried on the:
   a. *X* chromosome.
   b. *XX* chromosome pair.
   c. *Y* chromosome.
   d. *X* or *Y* chromosome.

5. If your parents are much taller than your grandparents, the explanation probably lies in:
   a. genetics.
   b. environmental factors.
   c. better family planning.
   d. good genetic counseling.

6. If a dizygotic twin develops schizophrenia, the likelihood of the other twin experiencing serious mental illness is much lower than is the case with monozygotic twins. This suggests that:
   a. schizophrenia is caused by genes.
   b. schizophrenia is influenced by genes.
   c. environment is unimportant in the development of schizophrenia.
   d. monozygotic twins are especially vulnerable to schizophrenia.

7. A person's skin turns yellow-orange as a result of a carrot-juice diet regimen. This is an example of:
   a. an environmental influence.
   b. an alteration in genotype.
   c. polygenic inheritance.
   d. incomplete dominance.

8. The personality trait of inhibition (shyness) seems to be partly genetic. A child who inherits the genes for shyness will be shy:
   a. under most circumstances.
   b. only if shyness is the dominant gene.
   c. if the environment does not encourage greater sociability.
   d. if he or she is raised by biological rather than adoptive parents.

9. If a man carries the recessive gene for Tay-Sachs disease and his wife does not, the chances of their having a child with Tay-Sachs disease is:
   a. one in four.
   b. fifty-fifty.
   c. zero.
   d. dependent upon the wife's ethnic background.

10. One of the best ways to distinguish the relative influence of genetic and environmental factors on behavior is to compare children who have:
    a. the same genes and environments.
    b. different genes and environments.
    c. similar genes and environments.
    d. the same genes but different environments.

11. (Research Report) When identical twins have been reared apart, researchers have generally found:
    a. strong behavioral and psychological similarities.
    b. strong behavioral, but not necessarily psychological, similarities.
    c. striking behavioral and psychological differences.
    d. that it is impossible to predict how such twins will develop.

12. Laurie and Brad, who both have a history of alcoholism in their families, are concerned that the child they hope to have will inherit a genetic predisposition to alcoholism. Based on information presented in the text, what advice should you offer them?
   a. "Stop worrying, alcoholism is only weakly genetic."
   b. "It is almost certain that your child will become alcoholic."
   c. "Social influences, such as the family and peer environment, play a critical role in determining whether alcoholism is expressed."
   d. "Wait to have children until you are both middle aged, in order to see if the two of you become alcoholic."

13. Sixteen-year-old Joey experiences some mental slowness and hearing and heart problems, yet he is able to care for himself and is unusually sweet-tempered. Joey probably:
   a. is mentally retarded.
   b. has Alzheimer's disease.
   c. has Kleinfelter syndrome.
   d. has Down syndrome.

14. Genetically, Claude's potential height is 6′0. Because he did not receive a balanced diet, however, he grew to only 5'9". Claude's actual height is an example of a:
   a. recessive gene.
   b. dominant gene.
   c. genotype.
   d. phenotype.

15. Winona inherited a gene from her mother that, regardless of her father's contribution to her genotype, will be expressed in her phenotype. Evidently, the gene Winona received from her mother is a(n) ______________ gene.
   a. polygenic
   b. recessive
   c. dominant
   d. *X*-linked

Key Terms

Using your own words, write on a separate piece of paper a brief definition or explanation of each of the following terms.

1. sperm
2. ovum
3. gamete
4. zygote
5. genes
6. chromosome
7. genetic code
8. twenty-third pair
9. monozygotic twins
10. dizygotic twins
11. infertile
12. in vitro fertilization (IVF)
13. polygenic traits
14. multifactorial traits
15. genotype
16. phenotype
17. carrier
18. additive pattern
19. nonadditive pattern
20. dominant-recessive pattern
21. *X*-linked gene
22. genetic imprinting
23. environment
24. syndrome
25. Trisomy-21 (Down syndrome)
26. fragile-*X* syndrome
27. genetic counseling
28. markers

ANSWERS

CHAPTER REVIEW

1. gametes; sperm; ovum
2. zygote
3. duplicated; differentiate
4. every
5. genes; chromosome; DNA
6. adenine; guanine; cytosine; thymine; genetic code; sequence
7. proteins; enzymes; grow, to repair damage, to take in nourishment, to multiply, to atrophy, and so forth
8. 46; 23
9. one; 23
10. twenty-third; *X*; *XX*; *X*; *Y*; *XY*
11. sperm
12. continuity; diversity
13. chance; crossing-over; 64 trillion
14. 270; monozygotic; are
15. dizygotic (fraternal); 50

16. increased; fertility drugs
17. genetic; nutritional; younger; 30; sperm; ovulation; implantation; infertile; one year
18. diet, drug use, and levels of stress; in vitro fertilization; gametes; zygotes; fallopian tube
19. artificial insemination by donor; surrogate mother; more complicated
20. polygenic; multifactorial
21. genotype; phenotype
22. carrier
23. genes; environment
24. additive; height; skin color
25. nonadditive; dominant-recessive; dominant; recessive; incomplete dominance; physical

Eye color follows the dominant-recessive pattern of genetic interaction. Thus, a person with brown eyes (phenotype) may have two dominant genes for brown eyes (genotype)—or one dominant gene for brown eyes and a recessive gene for blue eyes (genotype). In order for a child to inherit blue eyes from brown-eyed parents, both parents have to be carriers, of the blue-eyed gene, with each contributing the recessive gene for blue eyes.

26. *X*-linked; color blindness, many allergies, several diseases, and some learning disabilities; males
27. does; genetic imprinting
28. psychological

Social scientists define *environment* broadly to refer to the multitude of variables that can interact with the person's genetic inheritance at every point of life. These variables include direct effects, such as the impact of the immediate cell environment on the genes, nutrition, climate, medical care, and family interaction; indirect effects, such as those of the broad economic, political, and cultural contexts; irreversible effects, such as the impact of brain injury; and less permanent effects, such as the impact of stress on mood.

29. environmental; twins; adopted
30. monozygotic; dizygotic
31. biological
32. identical (or monozygotic); different
33. every
34. quantitative trait loci
35. nutrition; medical care; stopped; has

A genetically shy child whose parents are outgoing, for example, would have many more contacts with other people and would observe his or her parents socializing more freely than if this same child's parents were also shy. In growing up, the child might learn to relax in social settings and would become less observably shy than he or she would have been with more introverted parents, despite the genetic predisposition toward shyness. Culture plays a role in the expression of shyness.

36. intelligence; emotionality; activity level; religiosity
37. 50; do
38. is; is; a quick temper, a willingness to take risks, and a high level of anxiety

By studying genetic disruptions of normal development, researchers (a) gain a fuller appreciation of the complexities of genetic interaction, (b) reduce misinformation and prejudice directed toward those afflicted by such disorders, and (c) help individuals understand the likelihood of occurrence and to become better prepared to limit their harmful effects.

39. gametes
40. half; do not; 200; syndrome
41. Down syndrome; trisomy-21

Most people with Down syndrome have certain facial characteristics—a thick tongue, round face, slanted eyes—as well as distinctive hands, feet, and fingerprints. Many also have hearing problems, heart abnormalities, muscle weakness, and short stature. Almost all experience some mental slowness.

42. sex

Kleinfelter syndrome (*XXY*): undeveloped secondary sex characteristics; learning disabled

XYY: prone to acne, unusually tall; aggressive, mildly retarded

XXX: normal female appearance; retarded in most intellectual skills

Turner syndrome (*XO*): short in stature, undeveloped secondary sex characteristics; learning disabled

43. fragile-*X*
44. occur
45. maternal age
46. more
47. dominant; are not
48. Huntington's chorea; Tourette syndrome
49. recessive; multifactorial; cystic fibrosis, thalassemia, sickle-cell anemia

Multifactorial diseases: cleft palate, cleft lip, club foot, diabetes, hydrocephalus, some forms of muscular dystrophy, neural tube defects, pyloric stenosis

50. genetic counseling; testing

51. Genetic counseling is recommended for (a) those who have a parent, sibling, or child with a serious genetic condition; (b) those who have a history of spontaneous abortions, stillbirths, or infertility; (c) couples who are from the same ethnic group or subgroup; and (d) women over age 34.
52. sickle-cell anemia, Tay-Sachs, PKU, hemophilia, and thalassemia; markers
53. 50-50; 25 percent
54. alphafetoprotein; sonogram; fetoscope; amniocentesis; chorionic villi sampling
55. genetic engineering

PROGRESS TEST 1

Multiple-Choice Questions

1. **a.** is the answer. (p. 67)

   b. & c. The reproductive cells (sperm and ova), which are also called gametes, are individual entities.

   d. *Monozygote* refers to one member of a pair of identical twins.
2. **c.** is the answer. (p. 68)

   a. The zygote is the first cell of the developing person.

   b. Chromosomes are molecules of DNA that *carry* genes.

   d. DNA molecules contain genetic information.
3. **b.** is the answer. (p. 69)
4. **d.** is the answer. When the gametes are formed, one member of each chromosome pair splits off; because in females both are *X* chromosomes, each ovum must carry an *X* chromosome. (p. 69)

   a., b., & c. The zygote refers to the merged sperm and ovum that is the first new cell of the developing individual.
5. **b.** is the answer. *Mono* means "one." Thus, monozygotic twins develop from one zygote. (p. 71)

   a. & c. Dizygotic, or fraternal, twins develop from two (*di*) zygotes.

   d. A trizygotic birth would result in triplets (*tri*), rather than twins.
6. **d.** is the answer. In this situation, one factor (genetic similarity) is held constant while the other factor (environment) is varied. Therefore, any similarity in traits is strong evidence of genetic inheritance. (p. 80)
7. **a.** is the answer. (p. 81)

   c. & d. Most dominant disorders are neither seriously disabling, nor sex-linked.
8. **c.** is the answer. (p. 75)

   a., b., & d. *Polygenic* means "many genes"; *multifactorial* means "many factors," which are not limited to either genetic or environmental ones.
9. **b.** is the answer. (p. 68)

   a. Genotype is a person's genetic potential.

   c. A karyotype is a picture of a person's chromosomes.

   d. Phenotype is the actual expression of a genotype.
10. **d.** is the answer. (p. 71)
11. **d.** is the answer. (p. 87)

    a. & b. These chromosomal abnormalities affect females.

    c. There is no such abnormality.
12. **b.** is the answer. (p. 79)

    c. & d. The text does not equate polygenic complexity with either recessive or dominant genes.
13. **a.** is the answer. (p. 88)
14. **b.** is the answer. (p. 75)
15. **b.** is the answer. (pp. 88–89)

    a. & c. These abnormalities involve the sex chromosomes, not genes.

    d. In order for an offspring to inherit a recessive condition, the parents need only be carriers of the recessive gene in their genotypes; they need not actually have the disease.

Matching Items

1. c (p. 67)	**5.** j (p. 92)	**9.** k (p. 87)
2. h (p. 68)	**6.** b (p. 71)	**10.** e (p. 76)
3. a (p. 76)	**7.** f (p. 71)	**11.** d (p. 67)
4. i (p. 76)	**8.** g (p. 76)	

PROGRESS TEST 2

Multiple-Choice Questions

1. **d.** is the answer. (p. 84)
2. **a.** is the answer. (p. 82)
3. **c.** is the answer. (p. 87)

   a. Physical appearance is usually normal in this syndrome.

   b. Males are more frequently and more severely affected.

   d. This is true of the *XYY* chromosomal abnormality, but not the fragile-X syndrome.
4. **d.** is the answer. (p. 88)

5. **c.** is the answer. Sickle-cell anemia is more common among African-Americans; phenylketonuria, among those of Norwegian and Irish ancestry; thalassemia, among Greek-, Italian-, Thai-, and Indian-Americans; and Tay-Sachs, among Jews as well as certain French-Canadians. (pp. 89–91)

   a. & b. The text does not present evidence indicating that the incidence of these disorders has changed.

6. **c.** is the answer. (p. 71)

   a. This would result in monozygotic twins.

   b. Only one sperm can fertilize an ovum.

   d. A single egg fertilized by one sperm would produce a single offspring or monozygotic twins.

7. **c.** is the answer. (p. 68)

   a. Zygotes are fertilized ova.

   b. Genes are the smaller units of heredity that are organized into sequences on chromosomes.

   d. Ova are female reproductive cells.

8. **a.** is the answer. (p. 68)

9. **c.** is the answer. The ovum will contain an *X* chromosome, and with the sperm's *Y* chromosome, will produce the male *XY* pattern. (p. 69)

   a. Only if the ovum is fertilized by an *X* chromosome from the sperm will a female develop.

   b. Cell division will occur regardless of whether the sperm contributes an *X* or a *Y* chromosome.

   d. Spontaneous abortions are likely to occur when there are chromosomal or genetic abnormalities; the situation described is perfectly normal.

10. **a.** is the answer. (p. 69)

    b. & d. These are true of all body cells *except* the gametes.

    c. Gametes have either *X* or *Y* chromosomes.

11. **a.** is the answer. (p. 75)

12. **a.** is the answer. Genotype refers to the sum total of all the genes a person inherits; phenotype refers to the actual expression of the individual's characteristics. (p. 76)

13. **c.** is the answer. (p. 76)

14. **d.** is the answer. *X*-linked genes are located only on the *X* chromosome. Because males inherit only one *X* chromosome, they are more likely than females to have these characteristics in their phenotype. (pp. 77–78)

15. **d.** is the answer. (p. 79)

True or False Items

1. T (p. 75)
2. F An estimated half of all zygotes have an odd number of chromosomes. (p. 86)
3. T (p. 84)
4. T (p.67)
5. F Most traits are polygenic. (p. 75)
6. T (p. 68)
7. T (p. 89)
8. F A trait from a recessive gene will be part of the phenotype only when the person has two recessive genes for that trait. (pp. 88–89)
9. T (pp. 76)
10. T (p. 69)

THINKING CRITICALLY ABOUT CHAPTER 3

1. **c.** is the answer. If one gene is for brown eyes and the other for blue, the person's eyes will be brown, since the brown-eye gene is dominant. (p. 77)

   b. In this eye-color example, the dominant gene will determine the phenotype.

2. **d.** is the answer. (p. 77)

3. **d.** is the answer. (p. 77)

   a. & c. Eye color is not a sex-linked trait.

   b. Recessive genes are not always completely suppressed by dominant genes.

4. **a.** is the answer. (p. 77)

   b. The male genotype is *XY*, not *XX*.

   c. & d. The mother contributes only an *X* chromosome.

5. **b.** is the answer. This trend in increased height has been attributed to improved nutrition and medical care. (p. 82)

   a., c., & d. It is unlikely that these factors account for height differences from one generation to the next.

6. **b.** is the answer. Since monozygotic twins are genetically identical, while dizygotic twins share only 50 percent of their genes, greater similarity of traits between monozygotic twins suggests that genes are an important influence. (p. 84)

   a. & c. Even though schizophrenia has a strong genetic component, it is not the case that if one twin has schizophrenia the other also automatically does. Therefore, the environment, too, is an important influence.

   d. This does not necessarily follow.

7. **a.** is the answer. (p. 79)

 b. Genotype is a person's genetic potential, established at conception.

 c. Polygenic inheritance refers to the influence of many genes on a particular trait.

 d. Incomplete dominance refers to the phenotype being influenced primarily, but not exclusively, by the dominant gene.

8. **c.** is the answer. (p. 83)

 a. & b. Research on adopted children shows that shyness is affected by both genetic inheritance and the social environment. Therefore, if a child's environment promotes socializing outside the immediate family, a genetically shy child might grow up much less timid socially than he or she would have been with less outgoing parents.

 d. Either biological or adoptive parents are capable of nurturing, or not nurturing, shyness in their children.

9. **c.** is the answer. Tay-Sachs is a recessive gene disorder; therefore, in order for a child to inherit this disease, he or she must receive the recessive gene from both parents. (pp. 88, 91)

10. **d.** is the answer. To separate the influences of genes and environment, one of the two must be held constant. (p. 80)

 a., b., & c. These situations would not allow a researcher to separate the contributions of heredity and environment.

11. **d.** is the answer. (p. 81)

12. **c.** is the answer. (p. 85)

 a. Some people's inherited biochemistry makes them highly susceptible to alcoholism.

 b. Despite a strong genetic influence, the environment plays a critical role in the expression of alcoholism.

 d. Not only is this advice unreasonable, but it might increase the likelihood of chromosomal abnormalities in the parents' sperm and ova.

13. **d.** is the answer. (p. 86)

14. **d.** is the answer. (p. 76)

 a. & b. Genes are discrete segments of a chromosome.

 c. Genotype refers to genetic potential.

15. **c.** is the answer. (pp. 76–77)

 a. There is no such thing as a "polygenic gene." *Polygenic* means "many genes."

 b. A recessive gene paired with a dominant gene will not be expressed in the phenotype.

 d. X-linked genes may be dominant or recessive.

KEY TERMS

1. Male gametes are called **sperm**. (p. 67)
2. **Ovum** (the Latin word for "egg") refers to the female reproductive cell, which, if united with a sperm, develops into a new individual. (p. 67)
3. **Gametes** are the human reproductive cells. (p. 67)
4. The **zygote** (a term derived from the Greek word for "joint") is the fertilized egg, that is, the one-celled organism formed during conception by the fusion of sperm and ovum. (p. 67)
5. **Genes** are discrete segments of a chromosome, which is a DNA molecule, that are the basic units of heredity. (p. 68)
6. **Chromosomes** are molecules of DNA that contain the genes organized in precise sequences. (p. 68)
7. The precise nature of a gene's instructions, called the **genetic code**, is determined by the overall sequence of the four chemical bases along a segment of DNA. (p. 68)
8. The **twenty-third pair** of chromosomes determines the individual's sex, among other things. (p. 69)
9. **Monozygotic**, or identical, **twins** develop from one zygote that splits in two, producing two genetically identical zygotes. (p. 71)

 Memory aid: Mono means "one"; **monozygotic twins** develop from one fertilized ovum.

10. **Dizygotic**, or fraternal, **twins** develop from two separate ova fertilized by different sperm at roughly the same time, and therefore are no more genetically similar than ordinary siblings. (p. 71)

 Memory aid: A fraternity is a group of two (*di*) or more nonidentical individuals.

11. A couple, or person, is considered to be **infertile** if they have been unable to conceive a child despite a year of trying to do so. (p. 72)
12. **In vitro fertilization (IVF)** is an alternative method of conception in which ova are fertilized by sperm in the laboratory, and then inserted into the uterus. (p. 73)
13. Most human traits, especially psychological traits, are **polygenic traits**; that is, they are affected by many genes. (p. 75)
14. Most human traits are also **multifactorial traits**—that is, influenced by many factors, including genetic and environmental factors. (p. 75)

 Memory aid: The roots of the words **polygenic** and **multifactorial** give their meaning: *poly* means "many" and *genic* means "of the genes"; *multi* means "several" and *factorial* obviously refers to factors.

15. The sum total of all the genes a person inherits—his or her genetic potential—is called the **genotype**. (p. 76)

16. The actual physical or behavioral expression of a genotype, the result of the interaction of the genes with each other and with the environment, is called the **phenotype**. (p. 76)

17. A person who has a recessive gene in his or her genotype that is not expressed in his or her phenotype is called a **carrier** of that gene. (p. 76)

18. In the **additive pattern** of genetic interaction, the phenotype reflects the contributions of all the genes involved. The genes affecting height, for example, interact in this fashion. (p. 76)

19. When a gene pair acts in a **nonadditive pattern**, the outcome depends much more on the influence of one gene than by others that could also influence that pattern. (p. 76)

20. In the **dominant-recessive pattern**, a type of nonadditive pattern, some genes are dominant and act in a controlling manner as they hide the influence of the weaker (recessive) genes. (pp. 76–77)

21. ***X*-linked genes** are genes that are located only on the *X* chromosome. Since males have only one *X* chromosome, they are more likely than females to have the characteristics determined by these genes in their phenotype. (p. 77)

22. **Genetic imprinting** is the tendency of certain genes to be expressed differently when they are inherited from the mother than when they are inherited from the father. (p. 78)

23. When social scientists discuss the effects of the **environment** on genes, they are referring to everything—from the impact of the immediate cell environment on the genes to the multitude of ways elements in the outside world, such as nutrition, climate, family interactions, and the cultural context—that can interact with the person's genetic inheritance at every point of life. (p. 79)

24. A **syndrome** is a cluster of distinct characteristics that tend to occur together in a given disorder. (p. 86)

25. **Trisomy-21 (Down syndrome)** is a chromosomal disorder in which there is an extra chromosome at site 21. Most people with Down syndrome have distinctive physical and psychological characteristics, including rounded face, short stature, and mental slowness. (p. 86)

26. The **fragile-*X* syndrome** is a single-gene disorder in which part of the *X* chromosome is attached by such a thin string of molecules that it seems about to break off. Although the characteristics associated with this syndrome are quite varied, some mental deficiency is relatively common. (p. 87)

27. **Genetic counseling** involves a variety of tests through which couples can learn more about their genes, and can thus make informed decisions about their childbearing and child-rearing future. (p. 89)

28. **Markers** are genetic traits, physiological characteristics, or gene clusters, harmless in themselves, that suggest that an individual might be a carrier of a harmful gene. (p. 92)

CHAPTER 4

Prenatal Development and Birth

Chapter Overview

Prenatal development is complex and startlingly rapid—more rapid than any other period of the life span. During the prenatal period, the individual develops from a one-celled zygote to a complex human baby. This development is outlined in Chapter 4, along with some of the problems that can occur—among them prenatal exposure to disease, drugs, and other hazards—and the factors that moderate the risks of teratogenic exposure.

For the developing person, birth marks the most radical transition of the entire lifespan. No longer sheltered from the outside world, the fetus becomes a separate human being who begins life almost completely dependent upon its caregivers. Chapter 4 also examines the process of birth, its possible variations and problems, and the parent-newborn bonding process.

The chapter concludes with a discussion of the significance of the parent-newborn bond, including factors that affect its development.

NOTE: Answer guidelines for all Chapter 4 questions begin on page 63.

Guided Study

The text chapter should be studied one section at a time. Before you read, preview each section by skimming it, noting headings and boldface items. Then read the appropriate section objectives from the following outline. Keep these objectives in mind and, as you read the chapter section, search for the information that will enable you to meet each objective. Once you have finished a section, write out answers for its objectives.

From Zygote to Newborn (pp. 99–105)

1. Describe the significant developments of the germinal period.

2. Describe the significant developments of the period of the embryo.

3. Describe the significant developments of the period of the fetus, noting the importance of the age of viability.

4. (Children Up Close) Describe the fetus's various responses to its immediate environment (the womb).

Risk Reduction (pp. 105–116)

5. Define teratology, and discuss several factors that determine whether a specific teratogen will be harmful.

7. Identify at least five teratogens, and describe their effects on the developing embryo or fetus, focusing on the effects of psychoactive drugs; explain what can be done to prevent drug damage.

7. Discuss several protective steps that may moderate the risk of teratogenic exposure.

Low Birthweight and Its Causes (pp. 116–122)

8. Distinguish among low-birthweight, preterm, and small-for-gestational-age (SGA) infants, and identify the causes of low birthweight, focusing on the relationship of poverty to low birthweight.

9. (Changing Policy) Discuss several medical and legal issues raised by the question of when a developing embryo becomes a person.

The Normal Birth (pp. 122–127)

10. Describe the normal process of birth, specifying the events of each stage.

11. Describe the test used to assess the neonate's condition at birth.

12. Discuss the importance of medical attention and the question of medical intervention.

Birth Complications (pp. 128–129)

13. Explain the causes of cerebral palsy, and discuss the special needs of high-risk infants.

The Beginning of Bonding (pp. 129–131)

14. (text and Research Report) Explain the concept of parent-newborn bonding and the current view of most developmentalists regarding bonding in humans.

Chapter Review

When you have finished reading the chapter, work through the material that follows to review it. Complete the sentences and answer the questions. As you proceed, evaluate your performance for each section by consulting the answers on page 63. Do not continue with the next section until you understand each answer. If you need to, review or reread the appropriate section in the textbook before continuing.

From Zygote to Newborn (pp. 99–105)

1. Prenatal development is divided into ______________ main periods. The first two weeks of development are called the ______________ period; from the ______________ week through the ______________ week is known as the period of the ______________; and from this point until birth is the period of the ______________.

2. At least through the ______________ (how many?) doubling of cells following conception, each of the zygote's cells is identical. Soon after, clusters of cells begin to take on distinct traits. The first clear sign of this process, called ______________, occurs about ______________ week(s) after conception, when the multiplying cells separate into outer cells that will become the ______________, and inner cells that will become the ______________.

3. The next significant event is the burrowing of the outer cells of the organism into the lining of the uterus, a process called ______________. This process ______________ (is/is not) automatic.

4. One study of low-income mothers in the United States found a ______________ (higher/lower) rate of birth complications than the U.S. average, despite the fact that about half were ______________ and did not begin ______________ ______________ until after the first 3 months. This outcome was probably due to the fact that these women had more encouragement from their babies' ______________ and from their ______________.

5. At the beginning of the period of the embryo, a fold in the outer cells of the developing individual forms a structure that will become the ______________ ______________, which will develop into the ______________ ______________ ______________.

6. Growth then proceeds from the head downward, referred to as ____________-____________ ____________, and from the center outward, referred to as ____________-____________ ____________. Following this pattern, the ____________ system is the first organ system to begin to function.

Briefly describe the major features of development during the second month.

7. Eight weeks after conception, the embryo weighs about ____________ and is about ____________ in length. The organism now becomes known as the ____________.

8. The first stage of development of the sex organs is the appearance in the ____________ week of the ____________ ____________, a cluster of cells that can develop into male or female sex organs.

9. If the fetus has a(n) ____________ (X/Y) chromosome, a gene on this chromosome sends a biochemical signal that triggers the development of the ____________ (male/female) sex organs at about nine weeks. Without that gene, no signal is sent, and the fetus begins to develop ____________ (male/female) sex organs. Not until the ____________ week are the external male or female genital organs fully formed.

10. By the end of the ____________ month, the fetus is fully formed, weighs approximately ____________, and is about ____________ long. These figures ____________ (vary/do not vary) from fetus to fetus.

11. The placenta connects the mother's ____________ ____________ with that of her growing embryo. It also contains the liquid surrounding the embryo, which is called ____________ ____________.

12. During the middle trimester, the brain increases in size by a factor of ____________. This neurological maturation is essential to the regulation of such basic body functions as ____________ and ____________.

13. The age at which a fetus has at least some chance of surviving outside the uterus is called the ____________ ____________ ____________, which occurs ____________ weeks after conception.

14. At about ____________ weeks after conception, brain-wave patterns begin to resemble the ____________-____________ cycles of a newborn.

15. A 28-week-old fetus typically weighs about ____________ and has more than a ____________ percent chance of survival.

16. The normal due date is calculated at ____________ days after conception.

17. Two crucial aspects of development in the last months of prenatal life are maturation of the ____________ and ____________ systems.

18. The average newborn weighs ____________.

19. An important part of the fetus's weight gain is the formation of body ____________, which will provide a layer of insulation to keep the newborn warm.

20. This weight gain also provides the fetus with ____________ for use until the mother's breast milk is fully established.

Risk Reduction (pp. 105–116)

21. The scientific study of factors that contribute to birth defects is called ______________ . Harmful agents that can cause birth defects, called ______________ , include ______________ ______________ .

22. Substances that impair the child's action and intellect by harming the brain are called ______________ ______________ .

23. Teratology is a science of ______________ ______________ , which attempts to evaluate the factors that can make prenatal harm more or less likely to occur.

24. Three crucial factors that determine whether a specific teratogen will cause harm, and of what nature, are the ______________ of exposure, the ______________ of exposure, and the developing organism's ______________ ______________ to damage from the substance.

25. The time when a particular part of the body is most susceptible to teratogenic damage is called its ______________ ______________ . For physical defects, this is the entire period of the ______________ . However, for ______________ teratogens, which damage the ______________ and ______________ ______________ , the entire prenatal period is critical.

26. Two especially critical periods are at the beginning of pregnancy, when ______________ can impede ______________ , and during the final weeks, when the fetus is particularly vulnerable to damage that can cause ______________ ______________ .

27. Some teratogens have a ______________ effect—that is, the substances are harmless until exposure reaches a certain frequency or amount. However, the ______________ of some teratogens when taken together may make them more harmful at lower dosage levels than when taken separately.

28. Genetic susceptibilities to the prenatal effects of alcohol and to certain birth disorders, such as cleft palate, may involve defective ______________ .

29. When the mother-to-be's diet is deficient in ______________ ______________ , neural-tube defects such as ______________ ______________ or ______________ may result.

30. Because the ______________ chromosome carries fewer genes, ______________ (male/female) embryos and fetuses are more vulnerable to teratogens. This sex not only has a higher rate of teratogenic birth defects and later behavioral problems, but also a higher rate of ______________ ______________ and later ______________ ______________ .

31. When contracted during the critical period, German measles, also called ______________ , is known to cause structural damage to the heart, eyes, ears, and brain.

32. The most devastating viral teratogen is ______________ ______________ ______________ , which gradually overwhelms the body's natural immune responses and leads to a host of diseases that together constitute ______________ ______________ ______________ ______________ . The first American children with AIDS were ______________ , who were infected by ______________ ______________ . About one in every four infants born to women with this virus acquire it themselves during ______________ or ______________ . About one-third die during ______________ , another third

before ______________, and the rest by age ______________. This disease's long incubation period—up to ______________ years or more—complicates its prevention.

33. Some widely used medicinal drugs, including ______________, are teratogenic in some cases.

34. Psychoactive drugs such as ______________ ______________ slow fetal ______________ and can trigger premature ______________. The potential long-term teratogenic effects of such drugs include ______________ ______________.

35. Prenatal exposure to alcohol may lead to ______________ ______________ ______________, which includes such symptoms as abnormal facial characteristics, slowed physical growth, behavior problems, and mental retardation. Likely victims of this syndrome are those who are genetically vulnerable and whose mothers ingest more than ______________ drinks daily during pregnancy. Even more moderate alcohol consumption can be teratogenic, causing ______________ ______________ ______________.

(Table 4.3) List some of the effects of fetal exposure to tobacco.

36. The specific effects of illicit drugs ______________ (are/are not) difficult to document because users often use multiple drugs and have other problems, including ______________

37. (Table 4.3) Infants born to heavy users of marijuana often show impairment to their ______________ ______________ ______________ system.

(Table 4.3) List some of the effects of fetal exposure to cocaine.

List five protective steps pregnant women should take to prevent drug damage to their offspring.

38. Babies born to women who recently emigrated to the U.S. often weigh ______________ (more/less) than babies of native-born women of the same ethnicity. One likely reason is that these women are more often ______________-______________.

39. Teratogenic effects of psychoactive drugs ______________ (do/do not) accumulate throughout pregnancy.

Low Birthweight and Its Causes (pp. 116–122)

40. Newborns who weigh less than ______________ are classified as ______________ ______________ babies. Many factors can cause this condition, including ______________ and ______________. Babies who are born 3 or more weeks early are called ______________.

State several factors that increase the likelihood of early birth.

41. Infants who weigh substantially less than they should, given how much time has passed since conception, are called ______________ ______________ ______________ ______________.

42. About 25 percent of all low-birthweight births in the United States are linked to maternal use of ______________, which is responsible for about ______________ percent of LBW in many European nations.

43. Many of the causes of low birthweight are related to ______________. Mothers of low-birthweight babies are more likely to be ______________, ______________, ______________, and ______________.

Give some statistical evidence that low birthweight is most common among infants from impoverished areas.

44. Perhaps because LBW babies are more demanding and less responsive, the rates of child ______________ and ______________ are elevated for these children, especially if they are also ______________.

45. Low-birthweight infants born into families of lower socioeconomic status ______________ (are/are not) likely to continue to have intellectual disabilities.

The Normal Birth (pp. 122–127)

46. At about the 266th day, the fetal brain signals the release of certain ______________ into the mother's bloodstream, which trigger her ______________ ______________ to contract and relax. The normal birth process begins when these contractions become regular. Contractions push the fetus downward until the ______________ dilates to about ______________ in diameter.

47. The newborn is usually rated on the ______________ ______________, which assigns a score of 0, 1, or 2 to each of the following five characteristics: ______________ ______________. A score below ______________ indicates that the newborn is in critical condition and requires immediate attention; if the score is ______________ or better, all is well. This rating is made twice, at ______________ minute(s) after birth and again at ______________ minutes.

48. The mother's birth experience is influenced by several factors, including ______________ ______________.

49. When a normal vaginal delivery is likely to be hazardous, a doctor may recommend a surgical procedure called a ______________ ______________. Another common procedure, which involves a minor incision of the tissue at the opening of the vagina, is the the ______________.

50. In many nations, increasing numbers of trained ______________ preside over uncomplicated births. Even in hospital births, an increasing number of deliveries occur in the ______________ ______________. An even more family-oriented environment is the ______________ ______________.

Birth Complications (pp. 128–129)

51. The disorder ______________ ______________, which affects motor centers in the brain, often results from ______________ vulnerability, worsened by exposure to ______________ and episodes of ______________, a temporary lack of ______________ during birth.

52. Because they are often confined to an isolette or hooked up to medical machinery, low-birthweight infants may be deprived of normal kinds of ______________, such as ______________.

53. Providing extra soothing stimulation to vulnerable infants in the hospital ______________ (does/does not) aid weight gain and ______________ (does/does not) increase overall alertness.

54. Preterm infants are more likely to have long-term difficulties in ______________ development. High-risk infants are often more ______________ and slower to ______________.

55. The deficits related to low birthweight usually ______________ (can/cannot) be overcome.

The Beginning of Bonding (pp. 129–131)

56. The term used to describe the close relationship that begins within the first hours after birth is the ______________-______________ ______________.

57. (Research Report) The best evidence for such a relationship comes from studies of ______________.

58. (Research Report) Three factors that contribute to animal bonding are:

a. ______________

b. ______________

c. ______________

59 Research suggests that such a period ______________ (does/does not) exist in humans, leading some social scientists to conclude that bonding is a ______________ ______________.

60. Some new mothers experience a profound feeling of sadness called ______________ ______________.

Progress Test 1

Multiple-Choice Questions

Circle your answers to the following questions and check them with the answers on page 64. If your answer is incorrect, read the explanation for why it is incorrect and then consult the appropriate pages of the text (in parentheses following the correct answer).

1. The third through the eighth week after conception is called the:
   a. period of the embryo.
   b. period of the ovum.
   c. period of the fetus.
   d. germinal period.

2. The neural tube develops into the:
   a. respiratory system.
   b. umbilical cord.
   c. brain and spinal column.
   d. circulatory system.

3. The embryo's growth from the head downward is called:
   a. cephalo-caudal development.
   b. fetal development.
   c. proximo-distal development.
   d. teratogenic development.

4. By the eighth week after conception, the embryo has almost all the basic organs except the:
   a. skeleton.
   b. elbows and knees.
   c. sex organs.
   d. fingers and toes.

5. The most critical factor in attaining the age of viability is development of the:
   a. placenta.
   b. eyes.
   c. brain.
   d. skeleton.

6. An important nutrient that many women do not get in adequate amounts from the typical diet is:
   a. vitamin A.
   b. zinc.
   c. guanine.
   d. folic acid.

7. An embryo begins to develop male sex organs if ______________, and female sex organs if ______________.
   a. genes on the *Y* chromosome send a biochemical signal; no signal is sent from an *X* chromosome.
   b. genes on the *Y* chromosome send a biochemical signal; genes on the *X* chromosome send a signal.
   c. genes on the *X* chromosome send a biochemical signal; no signal is sent from an *X* chromosome.
   d. genes on the *X* chromosome send a biochemical signal; genes on the *Y* chromosome send a signal.

8. A teratogen:
   a. cannot cross the placenta during the period of the embryo.
   b. is usually inherited from the mother.
   c. can be counteracted by good nutrition most of the time.
   d. may be a virus, drug, chemical, radiation, or environmental pollutants.

9. Among the characteristics of babies born with fetal alcohol syndrome are:
   a. slowed physical growth and behavior problems.
   b. addiction to alcohol and methadone.
   c. deformed arms and legs.
   d. blindness.

10. The birth process begins:
   a. when the fetus moves into the right position.
   b. when the uterus begins to contract at regular intervals to push the fetus out.
   c. about eight hours (in the case of firstborns) after the uterus begins to contract at regular intervals.
   d. when the baby's head appears at the opening of the vagina.

11. The Apgar scale is administered:
   a. only if the newborn is in obvious distress.
   b. once, just after birth.
   c. twice, 1 minute and 5 minutes after birth.
   d. repeatedly during the newborn's first hours.

12. Most newborns weigh about:
   a. 5 pounds.
   b. 6 pounds.
   c. 7 1/2 pounds.
   d. 8 1/2 pounds.

13. Low-birthweight babies born near the due date but weighing substantially less than they should:
   a. are classified as preterm.
   b. are called small for gestational age.
   c. usually have no sex organs.
   d. show many signs of immaturity.

14. Approximately 1 out of every 4 low-birthweight births in the United States is caused by maternal use of:
   a. alcohol.
   b. tobacco.
   c. crack cocaine.
   d. household chemicals.

15. (Research Report) The idea of a parent-newborn bond in humans arose from:
   a. observations in the delivery room.
   b. data on adopted infants.
   c. animal studies.
   d. studies of disturbed mother-newborn pairs.

Matching Items

Match each definition or description with its corresponding term.

Terms

_______ 1. period of the embryo
_______ 2. period of the fetus
_______ 3. placenta
_______ 4. preterm
_______ 5. teratology
_______ 6. rubella
_______ 7. HIV
_______ 8. critical period
_______ 9. neural tube
_______ 10. fetal alcohol syndrome
_______ 11. germinal period

Definitions or Descriptions

a. term for the period during which a developing baby's body parts are most susceptible to damage
b. the scientific study of birth defects
c. the age when viability is attained
d. the precursor of the central nervous system
e. also called German measles
f. characterized by abnormal facial characteristics, slowed growth, behavior problems, and mental retardation
g. a virus that gradually overwhelms the body's immune responses
h. the life-giving organ that nourishes the embryo and fetus
i. when implantation occurs
j. the prenatal period when all major body structures begin to form
k. a baby born 3 or more weeks early

Progress Test 2

Progress Test 2 should be completed during a final chapter review. Answer the following questions after you thoroughly understand the correct answers for the Chapter Review and Progress Test 1.

Multiple-Choice Questions

1. During which period does cocaine use affect the fetus and/or newborn?
   a. throughout pregnancy
   b. before birth
   c. after birth
   d. during all of the above periods

2. In order, the correct sequence of prenatal stages of development is:
   a. embryo; germinal; fetus
   b. germinal; fetus; embryo
   c. germinal; embryo; fetus
   d. ovum; fetus; embryo

3. The embryo's growth from the spine outward is called:
   a. cephalo-caudal development.
   b. fetal development.
   c. proximo-distal development.
   d. teratogenic development.

4. Tetracycline, retinoic acid, and most hormones:
   a. can be harmful to the human fetus.
   b. have been proven safe for pregnant women after the period of the embryo.
   c. will prevent spontaneous abortions.
   d. are safe when used before the period of the fetus.

5. One of the first teratogens to be recognized, possibly causing deafness, blindness, and brain damage if the fetus is exposed early during the pregnancy, is:
   a. rubella (German measles).
   b. anoxia.
   c. acquired immune deficiency syndrome (AIDS).
   d. neural-tube defect.

6. The most realistic way for pregnant women to reduce the risk of birth defects in their unborn children is to avoid unnecessary drugs and:
   a. have a diagnostic x-ray or sonogram.
   b. improve their genetic predispositions.
   c. seek early and regular prenatal care.
   d. avoid exposure to any suspected pollutant.

7. Among the characteristics rated on the Apgar scale are:
   a. shape of the newborn's head and nose.
   b. presence of body hair.
   c. interactive behaviors.
   d. muscle tone and color.

8. A newborn is classified as low birthweight if he or she weighs less than:
   a. 7 pounds.
   b. 6 pounds.
   c. 5 1/2 pounds.
   d. 4 pounds.

9. The most critical problem for preterm babies is:
   a. the immaturity of the sex organs—for example, undescended testicles.
   b. spitting up or hiccupping.
   c. infection from intravenous feeding.
   d. breathing difficulties.

10. Which of the following was *not* cited as evidence that social-contextual factors are an underlying cause of low birthweight?
    a. In many developed countries, the rate of low birthweight is higher in inner cities than in suburbs.
    b. Developing countries in the same general region, with similar ethnic populations, typically have similar rates of low birthweight.
    c. The rate of low-birthweight infants is much higher in developing, than developed, countries.
    d. Ethnic-group variations in low-birthweight rates within nations tend to follow socioeconomic, rather than genetic, patterns.

11. Many low-birthweight infants experience brain damage as the result of:
    a. anoxia.
    b. cerebral hemorrhaging.
    c. anoxia or cerebral hemorrhaging.
    d. genetic defects.

12. Which Apgar score indicates that a newborn is in normal health?
    a. 4
    b. 5
    c. 6
    d. 7

13. Worldwide, the fastest growing HIV-positive group are:
    a. hemophiliacs.
    b. heterosexual women of childbearing age.
    c. children under 4 years of age.
    d. gay men.

14. Many of the factors that contribute to low birthweight are related to poverty; for example, women of lower socioeconomic status tend to:
    a. be less well nourished.
    b. have less education.
    c. be subjected to stressful living conditions.
    d. be all of the above.

15. The critical period for preventing physical defects appears to be the:
    a. period of the zygote.
    b. period of the embryo.
    c. period of the fetus.
    d. entire pregnancy.

True or False Items

Write *true* or *false* on the line in front of each statement.

_______ 1. Newborns can recognize some of what they heard while in the womb.

_______ 2. Eight weeks after conception, the embryo has formed almost all the basic organs.

_______ 3. The embryo develops from the head downward, and from the center outward.

_______ 4. In general, behavioral teratogens have the greatest effect during the period of the embryo.

_______ 5. The effects of cigarette smoking during pregnancy remain highly controversial.

_______ 6. The Apgar scale is used to measure vital signs such as heart rate, breathing, and reflexes.

_______ 7. Newborns usually cry on their own, moments after birth.

_______ 8. Research shows that immediate mother-newborn contact at birth is necessary for the normal emotional development of the child.

_______ 9. Low-birthweight babies are more likely than other children to experience developmental difficulties in early childhood.

_______ 10. Cesarean sections are rarely performed in the United States today because of the resulting danger to the fetus.

Thinking Critically About Chapter 4

Answer these questions the day before an exam as a final check on your understanding of the chapter's terms and concepts.

1. Babies born to mothers who are powerfully addicted to a psychoactive drug are *most* likely to suffer from:
   a. structural problems.
   b. behavioral problems.
   c. both a. and b.
   d. neither a. nor b.

2. I am about 1 inch long and 1 gram in weight. I have all of the basic organs (except sex organs) and features of a human being. What am I?
   a. a zygote
   b. an embryo
   c. a fetus
   d. an indifferent gonad

3. Karen and Brad report to their neighbors that, 5 weeks after conception, a sonogram of their child-to-be revealed female sex organs. The neighbors are skeptical of their statement because:
   a. sonograms are never administered before the ninth week.
   b. sonograms only reveal the presence or absence of male sex organs.
   c. the fetus does not begin to develop female sex organs until about the ninth week.
   d. it is impossible to determine that a woman is pregnant until six weeks after conception.

4. Five-year-old Benjamin can't sit quietly and concentrate on a task for more than a minute. Dr. Simmons, who is a teratologist, suspects that Benjamin may have been exposed to _______ during prenatal development.
   a. human immunodeficiency virus
   b. a behavioral teratogen
   c. rubella
   d. lead

5. Sylvia and Stan, who are of British descent, are hoping to have a child. Doctor Caruthers asks for a complete nutritional history and is particularly concerned when she discovers that Sylvia may have a deficiency of folic acid in her diet. Doctor Caruthers is probably worried about the risk of _______ in the couple's offspring.
   a. FAS
   b. brain damage
   c. neural-tube defects
   d. FAE

6. Three-year-old Kenny was born underweight and premature. Today, he is small for his age. His doctor suspects that:
   a. Kenny is a victim of fetal alcohol syndrome.
   b. Kenny suffers from fetal alcohol effects.
   c. Kenny's mother smoked heavily during her pregnancy.
   d. Kenny's mother used cocaine during her pregnancy.

7. Which of these fetuses is most likely to experience serious prenatal damage?
   a. a male whose 15-year-old mother has an unusually stressful home life
   b. a female whose mother did not begin to receive prenatal care until the second month of her pregnancy
   c. a female whose 30-year-old mother is on welfare
   d. a male whose mother was somewhat undernourished early in the pregnancy

8. Fetal alcohol syndrome is common in newborns whose mothers were heavy drinkers during pregnancy, whereas newborns whose mothers were moderate drinkers may suffer fetal alcohol effects. This finding shows that to assess and understand risk we must know:
   a. the kind of alcoholic beverage (for example, beer, wine, or whiskey).
   b. the level of exposure to the teratogen.
   c. whether the substance really is teratogenic.
   d. the timing of exposure to the teratogen.

9. Your sister and brother-in-law, who are about to adopt a 1-year-old, are worried that the child will never bond with them. What advice should you offer?
   a. Tell them that, unfortunately, this is true; they would be better off waiting for a younger child who has not yet bonded.
   b. Tell them that, although the first year is a biologically determined critical period for attachment, there is a fifty-fifty chance that the child will bond with them.
   c. Tell them that bonding is a long-term process between parent and child that is determined by the nature of interaction throughout infancy, childhood, and beyond.
   d. Tell them that if the child is female, there is a good chance that she will bond with them, even at this late stage.

10. Which of the following newborns would be most likely to have problems in body structure and functioning?
    a. Anton, whose Apgar score is 6
    b. Debora, whose Apgar score is 7
    c. Sheila, whose Apgar score is 3
    d. Simon, whose Apgar score is 5

11. At birth, Clarence was classified as small for gestational age. It is likely that Clarence:
    a. was born in a rural hospital.
    b. suffered several months of prenatal malnutrition.
    c. was born in a large city hospital.
    d. comes from a family with a history of such births.

12. Of the following, who is *most* likely to give birth to a low-birthweight child?
    a. twenty-one-year-old Janice, who lives in the North
    b. twenty-five-year-old May Ling, who lives in China
    c. sixteen-year-old Donna, who lives in a remote, rural part of the United States
    d. thirty-year-old Maria, who lives in southern California

13. An infant born 266 days after conception, weighing 4 pounds, would be designated a ______________ infant.
    a. preterm
    b. low-birthweight
    c. small-for-gestational-age
    d. b. & c.

14. An infant who was born at thirty-five weeks, weighing 6 pounds, would be called a ______________ infant.
    a. preterm
    b. low-birthweight
    c. small-for-gestational-age
    d. premature

15. The five characteristics evaluated by the Apgar scale are:
    a. heart rate, length, weight, muscle tone, and color.
    b. orientation, muscle tone, reflexes, interaction, and responses to stress.
    c. reflexes, breathing, muscle tone, heart rate, and color.
    d. pupillary response, heart rate, reflex irritability, alertness, and breathing.

Key Terms

Using your own words, write a brief definition or explanation of each of the following terms on a separate piece of paper .

1. germinal period
2. period of the embryo
3. period of the fetus
4. implantation
5. neural tube
6. cephalo-caudal development
7. proximo-distal development
8. placenta
9. age of viability
10. teratology
11. teratogens
12. behavioral teratogens
13. risk analysis
14. critical period
15. threshold effect
16. interaction effect
17. rubella
18. human immunodeficiency virus (HIV)
19. acquired immune deficiency syndrome (AIDS)
20. fetal alcohol syndrome (FAS)

21. low-birthweight (LBW) infant
22. preterm
23. small for gestational age (SGA)
24. Apgar scale
25. Cesarean section
26. cerebral palsy
27. anoxia
28. parent-newborn bond
29. postpartum depression

ANSWERS

CHAPTER REVIEW

1. three; germinal; third; eighth; embryo; fetus
2. third; differentiation; one; placenta; embryo
3. implantation; is not
4. lower; teenagers; prenatal care; fathers; culture
5. neural tube; central nervous system
6. cephalo-caudal development; proximo-distal development; cardiovascular

Following the proximo-distal sequence, the upper arms, then the forearms, palms, and webbed fingers appear. Legs, feet, and webbed toes follow. At eight weeks, the embryo's head is more rounded, and the facial features are fully formed. The fingers and toes are distinct and separate. The "tail" is no longer visible.

7. 1/30 of an ounce (1 gram); 1 inch (2.5 centimeters); fetus
8. sixth; indifferent gonad
9. *Y*; male; female; twelfth
10. third; 3 ounces (87 grams); 3 inches (7.5 centimeters); vary
11. circulatory system; amniotic fluid
12. six; breathing; sucking
13. age of viability; twenty-two
14. 28; sleep-wake
15. 1,300 grams (3 pounds); 90
16. 266
17. respiratory; cardiovascular
18. 3,400 grams (7 $^1/_2$ pounds)
19. fat
20. calories
21. teratology; teratogens; viruses, drugs, chemicals, pollutants, stressors, and malnutrition
22. behavioral teratogens
23. risk analysis
24. timing; amount; genetic vulnerability
25. critical period; embryo; behavioral; brain; nervous system
26. stress; implantation; learning disabilities
27. threshold; interaction
28. enzymes
29. folic acid; spina bifida; anencephaly
30. *Y*; male; spontaneous abortions; learning disabilities
31. rubella
32. human immunodeficiency virus (HIV); acquired immune deficiency syndrome (AIDS); hemophiliacs; blood transfusions; pregnancy; birth; infancy; kindergarten; 20; 10
33. tetracycline, anticoagulants, phenobarbital, bromides, retinoic acid, most hormones, aspirin, antacids, diet pills
34. beer, wine, liquor, cigarettes, smokeless tobacco, heroin, methadone, LSD, marijuana, and cocaine; growth; labor; learning difficulties, impaired self-control, poor concentration, overall irritability
35. fetal alcohol syndrome; three; fetal alcohol effects

Smoking increases risk of abnormalities, reduces birthweight and size. Babies born to regular smokers tend to have respiratory problems and, in adulthood, increased risk of becoming smokers themselves.

36. are; malnutrition, stress, sickness, poor family support and health care
37. central nervous

Cocaine use causes overall growth retardation, increases the risk of problems with the placenta, and often leads to learning problems in the first months of life.

The five protective steps are:

a. Abstain from drugs altogether, even before pregnancy.

b. Abstain from drugs after the first trimester.

c. Use drugs in moderation throughout pregnancy (if abstinence is impossible).

d. Seek out social support.

e. Keep up with postnatal care.

38. more; drug-free

39. do

40. 2,500 grams (5 1/2 pounds); low birthweight; malnutrition; poverty; preterm

The possible causes of early birth include infections, drugs, extreme stress, exhaustion, a placenta that becomes detached from the uterine wall, and a uterus that cannot accommodate further growth.

41. small for gestational age

42. tobacco; 50

43. poverty; ill, malnourished, teenaged, stressed

Worldwide, the vast majority of low-birthweight infants born each year are from developing countries. Within developing countries, the greatest number of low-birthweight infants is born where per-capita income is lowest. Within nations, differences in LBW rates among ethnic groups follow socioeconomic differences among those groups. In the United States, the rate of low birthweight is highest in the poorest states. Ethnic-group variations in low-birthweight births tend to follow socioeconomic patterns.

44. abuse; neglect; disabled

45. are

46. hormones; uterine muscles; cervix; 10 centimeters (4 inches)

47. Apgar scale; heart rate, breathing, muscle tone, color, and reflexes; 4; 7; 1; 5

48. the mother's preparation for birth, the physical and emotional support provided by birth attendants, the position of the fetus, the cultural context, the nature and degree of medical intervention

49. Cesarean section; episiotomy

50. midwives; labor room; birthing center

51. cerebral palsy; genetic; teratogens; anoxia; oxygen

52. stimulation; rocking (or regular handling)

53. does; does

54. cognitive; distractible; talk

55. can

56. parent-newborn bond

57. mammals

58. **a.** birth hormones that trigger maternal feelings

b. the mother's identification of her infant by its smell

c. the timing of first contact between mother and newborn

59. does not; social construction

60. postpartum depression

PROGRESS TEST 1

Multiple-Choice Questions

1. **a.** is the answer. (p. 99)

b. This term, which refers to the germinal period, is not used in the text.

c. The period of the fetus is from the ninth week until birth.

d. The germinal period covers the first two weeks.

2. **c.** is the answer. (p. 101)

3. **a.** is the answer. (p. 101)

b. This term refers to all development that occurs from the ninth week after conception until birth.

c. This describes development from the center outward.

d. There is no such thing as "teratogenic development"; teratogens are substances that can lead to prenatal abnormalities.

4. **c.** is the answer. The sex organs do not begin to take shape until the period of the fetus. (p. 102)

5. **c.** is the answer. (p. 104)

6. **d.** is the answer. (p. 109)

7. **a.** is the answer. (p. 102)

8. **d.** is the answer. (p. 105)

a. In general, teratogens can cross the placenta at any time.

b. Teratogens are agents in the environment, not heritable genes (although *susceptibility* to individual teratogens has a genetic component).

c. Although nutrition is an important factor in healthy prenatal development, the text does not suggest that nutrition alone can usually counteract the harmful effects of teratogens.

9. **a.** is the answer. (p. 113)

10. **b.** is the answer. (p. 122)

11. **c.** is the answer. (p. 123)
12. **c.** is the answer. (p. 105)
13. **b.** is the answer. (p. 117)
14. **b.** is the answer. (p. 117)
15. **c.** is the answer. (p. 130)

Matching Items

1. j (p. 99)	**5.** b (p. 105)	**9.** d (p. 101)
2. c (p. 99)	**6.** e (p. 110)	**10.** f (p. 113)
3. h (p. 103)	**7.** g (p. 111)	**11.** i (p. 99)
4. k (p. 116)	**8.** a (p. 108)	

PROGRESS TEST 2

Multiple-Choice Questions

1. **d.** is the answer. (pp. 108, 112)
2. **c.** is the answer. (p. 99)
3. **c.** is the answer. (p. 101)
4. **a.** is the answer. (p. 112)
5. **a.** is the answer. (p. 110)
6. **c.** is the answer. (p. 115)
7. **d.** is the answer. (p. 123)
8. **c.** is the answer. (p. 116)
9. **d.** is the answer. (p. 104–105)
10. **b.** is the answer. Developing countries in the same general region, with similar ethnic populations, often have *different* rates of low birthweight. (pp. 120–121)
11. **c.** is the answer. (p. 128)
12. **d.** is the answer. (p. 123)
13. **b.** is the answer. (p. 111)
14. **d.** is the answer. (p. 120)
15. **b.** is the answer. (p. 108)

True or False Items

1. T (p. 105)
2. T (p. 102)
3. T (p. 101)
4. F Behavioral teratogens can affect the fetus at any time during the prenatal period. (p. 106)
5. F There is no controversy about the damaging effects of smoking during pregnancy. (p. 115)
6. T (p. 123)
7. T (p. 123)
8. F Though highly desirable, mother-newborn contact at birth is not necessary for the child's normal development or for a good parent-child relationship. Many opportunities for bonding occur throughout childhood. (p. 131)
9. T (p. 122)
10. F Nearly one in four births in the United States are now Cesarean. (p. 125)

THINKING CRITICALLY ABOUT CHAPTER 4

1. **c.** is the answer. (p. 112)
2. **b.** is the answer. (pp. 101–102)

   a. The zygote is the fertilized ovum.

   c. The developing organism is designated a fetus starting at the ninth week.

   d. The indifferent gonad is the mass of cells that will eventually develop into female or male sex organs.
3. **c.** is the answer. (p. 102)
4. **b.** is the answer. (p. 106)

   a. This is the virus that causes AIDS.

   c. Rubella may cause blindness, deafness, and brain damage.

   d. The text does not discuss the effects of exposure to lead.
5. **c.** is the answer. (p. 109)

   a. FAS is caused in infants by the mother-to-be drinking three or more drinks daily during pregnancy.

   b. Brain damage is caused by the use of social drugs during pregnancy.

   d. FAE is caused in infants by the mother-to-be drinking 1 ounce of alcohol per day.
6. **c.** is the answer. (p. 113)
7. **a.** is the answer. (p. 120)
8. **b.** is the answer. (p. 109)
9. **c.** is the answer. (p. 131)

   a. & b. Bonding in humans is not a biologically determined event limited to a critical period, as it is in many other animal species.

   d. There is no evidence of any gender differences in the formation of the parent-newborn bond.
10. **c.** is the answer. If a neonate's Apgar score is

below 4, the infant is in critical condition and needs immediate medical attention. (p. 119)

11. **b.** is the answer. (p. 117)

    a., c., & d. Prenatal malnutrition is the most common cause of a small-for-dates neonate.

12. **c.** is the answer. (p. 121)

    a., b., & d. The incidence of low birthweight is higher among teenaged mothers.

13. **d.** is the answer. (pp. 117, 122)

    a. & c. At 266 days, this infant is full term.

14. **a.** is the answer. (pp. 116–117)

    b. Low birthweight is defined as weighing less than 5 1/2 pounds.

    c. Although an infant can be both preterm and small for gestational age, this baby's weight is within the normal range of healthy babies.

    d. This term is no longer used to describe early births.

15. **c.** is the answer. (p. 123)

KEY TERMS

1. The first two weeks of development, characterized by rapid cell division and the beginning of cell differentiation, are called the **germinal period**. (p. 99)

   Memory aid: A *germ cell* is one from which a new organism can develop. The ***germ*inal period** is the first stage in the development of the new organism.

2. The **period of the embryo** is the third through the eighth week of prenatal development, when the rudimentary forms of all anatomical structures develop. (p. 99)

3. From the ninth week until birth is the **period of the fetus**, when the organs grow in size and complexity. (p. 99)

4. **Implantation** is the process by which the outer cells of the organism burrow into the uterine lining and rupture its blood vessels to obtain nourishment and trigger the bodily changes that signify the beginning of pregnancy. (p. 100)

5. The **neural tube** forms from a fold of outer embryonic cells during the period of the embryo; it is the precursor of the central nervous system. (p. 101)

   Memory aid: Neural means "of the nervous system." The **neural tube** is the precursor of the central nervous system.

6. **Cephalo-caudal development** refers to growth and maturation that proceeds from the head downward. (p. 101)

   Memory aid: Cephalo-caudal literally means "of the head–of the tail." Think of *cephalic*, an adjective which also means "of the head."

7. **Proximo-distal development** refers to growth that proceeds from "near to far." According to this process, the most vital organs and body parts form first, before the extremities. (p. 101)

   Memory aid: Something that is *proximal* is situated very near. ***Proximo*-distal development** begins with the very near organs at the center of the body.

8. The **placenta** is the organ that connects the mother's circulatory system with that of her growing embryo, providing nourishment to the developing organism and removing wastes (p. 103).

9. About twenty-two weeks after conception, the fetus attains the **age of viability**, at which point it has at least some slight chance of survival outside the uterus if specialized medical care is available. (p. 104)

10. **Teratology** is the scientific study of the factors that can contribute to birth defects. (p. 105)

11. **Teratogens** are external agents and conditions, such as viruses, bacteria, drugs, chemicals, stressors, and malnutrition, that can cause damage to the developing organism. (p. 105)

12. **Behavioral teratogens** tend to damage the brain and nervous system, impairing the future child's intellectual and emotional functioning. (p. 106)

13. The science of teratology is a science of **risk analysis**, meaning that it attempts to evaluate what factors make prenatal harm more or less likely to occur. (p. 106)

14. The first eight weeks, as well as the last months, of pregnancy are often called **critical period**, because teratogenic exposure during these time periods can produce malformations of basic body organs and structure. (p. 108)

15. A **threshold effect** is the harmful effect of a substance that occurs when exposure to it reaches a certain level. (p. 109)

16. An **interaction effect** occurs when one teratogen intensifies the harmful effects of another. (p. 109)

17. **Rubella** (German measles) is a viral disease that, if contracted by the expectant mother early in pregnancy, is likely to cause birth handicaps, including blindness, deafness, heart abnormalities, and brain damage. (p. 110)

18. **Human immunodeficiency virus (HIV)** is the most devastating viral teratogen. HIV gradually overwhelms the body's immune system, making the individual vulnerable to the host of diseases and infections that constitute AIDS. (p. 111)

19. The **acquired immune deficiency syndrome (AIDS)** is the conglomerate of diseases and infections caused by the HIV virus. (p. 111)

20. Prenatal alcohol exposure may cause **fetal alcohol syndrome (FAS)**, which includes abnormal facial characteristics, slowed physical growth, behavior problems, and mental retardation. Likely victims are those who are genetically vulnerable and whose mothers drink three or more drinks daily during pregnancy. (p. 113)

21. Newborns who weigh less than 2,500 grams (5 1/2 pounds) are called **low-birthweight (LBW) infants**. Such infants are at risk for many immediate and long-term problems. (p. 116)

22. Infants who are born three or more weeks before the due date are called **preterm**. (p. 116)

23. Infants who weigh substantially less than they should, given how much time has passed since conception, are called **small for gestational age (SGA)**, or small-for-dates. (p. 117)

24. Newborns are rated at one and then at five minutes after birth according to the **Apgar scale**. This scale assigns a score of 0, 1, or 2 to each of five characteristics: heart rate, breathing, muscle tone, color, and reflexes. A score of 7 or better indicates that all is well. (p. 123)

25. In a **Cesarean section**, the fetus is removed from the mother surgically. (p. 125)

26. **Cerebral palsy** is a muscular control disorder caused by damage to the brain's motor centers during or before birth. (p. 128)

27. **Anoxia** is a temporary lack of fetal oxygen during the birth process that, if prolonged, can cause brain damage or even death. (p. 128)

28. The term **parent-newborn bond** describes the strong feelings of attachment between parent and child in the early moments of their relationship together. (p. 129)

29. **Postpartum depression** is a profound feeling of sadness and inadequacy sometimes experienced by new mothers. (p. 131)

CHAPTER 5

The First 2 Years: Biosocial Development

Chapter Overview

Chapter 5 is the first of a three-chapter unit that describes the developing person from birth to age 2 in terms of biosocial, cognitive, and psychosocial development. Physical development is the first to be examined.

The chapter begins with observations on the overall growth and health of infants, including their size and shape and the importance of immunizations during the first two years. Following is a discussion of brain growth and development, the importance of experience in brain development, and the role of the brain in regulating the infant's physiological states. The chapter then turns to a discussion of motor abilities, and the ages at which the average infant acquires them. Vision and hearing are discussed next, along with research on infant perception. The final section discusses the importance of nutrition during the first two years and the consequences of severe malnutrition and undernutrition.

NOTE: Answer guidelines for all Chapter 5 questions begin on page 82.

Guided Study

The text chapter should be studied one section at a time. Before you read, preview each section by skimming it, noting headings and boldface items. Then read the appropriate section objectives from the following outline. Keep these objectives in mind and, as you read the chapter section, search for the information that will enable you to meet each objective. Once you have finished a section, write out answers for its objectives.

Physical Growth and Health (pp. 137–143)

1. Describe the size and proportions of an infant's body, including how they change during the first two years and how they compare with those of an adult.

2. List several reasons for the twentieth-century improvement in the survival of young children.

3. Identify risk factors and possible explanations for sudden infant death syndrome.

Brain Growth and Development (pp. 143–148)

4. Describe the ways in which the brain changes or matures during infancy.

5. Discuss the role of experience in brain development.

6. Discuss the role of the brain in regulating the infant's physiological states, and name four normal physiological states of the infant.

Motor Skills (pp. 148–156)

7. Describe the basic reflexes of the newborn and distinguish between gross motor skills and fine motor skills.

8. Describe the basic pattern of motor-skill development, and discuss variations in the timing of motor-skill acquisition.

Sensory and Perceptual Capacities (pp. 156–163)

9. Distinguish between sensation and perception, and describe how and why habituation is used in research on infant perception.

10. Describe the extent and development of an infant's perceptual abilities in terms of the sense of vision.

11. (text and Research Report) Identify the cause of most mild hearing losses in infants, and discuss chronic otitis media, focusing on its potential developmental consequences and treatment.

12. Describe the extent and development of an infant's perceptual abilities in terms of the senses of taste, smell, and touch.

Nutrition (pp. 163–169)

13. Describe the nutritional needs of infants.

14. (text and Changing Policy) Discuss the causes and results of malnutrition and undernutrition in the first years, and explain ways of preventing undernutrition.

Chapter Review

When you have finished reading the chapter, work through the material that follows to review it. Complete the sentences and answer the questions. As you proceed, evaluate your performance for each section by consulting the answers on page 82. Do not continue with the next section until you understand each answer. If you need to, review or reread the appropriate section in the textbook before continuing.

Physical Growth and Health (pp. 137–143)

1. With the exception of ______________ development, infancy is the period of the fastest and most notable increases in ______________ and changes in ______________ .
2. The average North American newborn measures ______________ and weighs a little more than ______________ .
3. In the first days of life, most newborns ______________ (gain/lose) between 5 and 10 percent of their body weight.
4. By age 1, the typical baby weighs about ______________ and measures almost ______________ . The typical 2-year-old is almost ______________ (what proportion?) of his or her adult weight and ______________ (what proportion?) of his or her adult height.
5. Newborns often seem top-heavy because their heads are equivalent to about ______________ (what proportion?) of their total length, compared to about ______________ at one year and ______________ in adulthood.
6. Newborns' legs represent about ______________ (what proportion?) of their total length, whereas an adult's legs represent about ______________ of it.
7. The chance of infants dying from infectious disease within the first year in North America and most developed nations is less than 1 in ______________ . The single most important cause of the improvement in child survival is ______________ .
8. Among the childhood diseases that have either been completely eradicated, or nearly so, are ______________ , ______________ , and ______________ .

State two other reasons for the increased survival of young children.

9. Most infant deaths occur in the first ______________ of life, and are related to problems such as ______________ ______________ .
10. One common cause of infant death that is not related to any obvious problem is ______________ ______________ ______________ ______________ , which ranks as the ______________ leading cause of infant death in the United States.

Identify several SIDS risk factors.

List several potential causes of SIDS that have recently been identified.

11. There is less of a risk for SIDS when healthy infants sleep on their ________________ .

12. In terms of ethnicity, babies of ________________ descent are more likely, and babies of ________________ descent less likely, to succumb to SIDS than are babies of ________________ descent. Bangladeshi infants in England tend to be low in both ________________ and ________________ ________________ ; they also have ________________ (higher/lower) rates of SIDS than white British infants.

Explain why Chinese infants tend to have a low rate of SIDS.

Brain Growth and Development (pp. 143–148)

13. At birth, the brain has attained about ________________ percent of its adult weight; by age 2 the brain is about ________________ percent of its adult weight. In comparison, body weight at age 2 is about ________________ percent of what it will be in adulthood.

14. The brain's communication system consists primarily of nerve cells called ________________ and intricate networks of nerve fibers, called ________________ and ________________ , which interconnect them. Each neuron has many ________________ , but only a single ________________ .

15. Neurons communicate with one another at intersections called ________________ . After travelling down the length of the ________________ , electrical impulses trigger chemicals called ________________ that diffuse across the ________________ ________________ to the ________________ of a "receiving" neuron. Most of the nerve cells ________________ (are/are not) present at birth, whereas the fiber networks ________________ (are/are not) rudimentary.

16. During the first months of life, brain development is most noticeable in its outer layer, which is called the ________________ . This area of the brain controls ________________ and ________________ .

17. From birth until age 2, the density of dendrites in the cortex ________________ (increases/decreases) by a factor of ________________ . The phenomenal increase in neural connections over the first two years has been called ________________ ________________ .

The fibers that transmit impulses also become coated with the insulating substance called ________________ , which makes neural transmission more efficient. This coating process continues through ________________ .

18. The ________________ area of the cortex, which assists in ________________ and ________________ , becomes more mature during infancy, giving infants greater regulation of their ________________ - ________________ patterns and increasing control over their early ________________ .

19. Brain development ________________ (is/is not) influenced by the infant's experiences.

20. Kittens that are ________________ for the first several weeks of life never acquire normal vision. Kittens who are temporarily blinded in one eye never acquire ________________

______________, which is the ability to focus two eyes together on an object; these visual deficits occur because the ______________ ______________ of the brain fail to develop normally.

Explain why animal studies of sensory restriction provide evidence for epigenetic systems theory.

21. Because the areas of the brain dedicated to ______________ and ______________ mature rapidly in the first two years, the child's cognitive and emotional experiences during this time are probably critical in fine-tuning neural connections involved in these abilities.

22. The various conditions of sleep and waking in an infant are referred to as physiological ______________.

List and briefly describe the most distinctive of these conditions in the infant.

23. Patterns of electrical activity in the brain can be measured and recorded by the device called an ______________.

24. While the infant's total daily sleep ______________ (does/does not) change much between birth and age 1, the length and ______________ of sleep episodes more closely match the family pattern. Approximately ______________ (what proportion?) of all 3-month-olds and ______________ percent of all 1-year-olds sleep through the night. In comparison, preterm infants sleep ______________ (more/less) and ______________ (more/less) regularly than full-term infants.

Motor Skills (pp. 148–156)

25. The study of the maturation of movement skills is called ______________ ______________.

26. An involuntary physical response to a stimulus is called a ______________.

27. The involuntary response of breathing, which causes the newborn to take the first breath even before the umbilical cord is cut, is called the ______________ ______________.

Because breathing is irregular during the first few days, other reflexive behaviors, such as ______________, ______________, and ______________, are common.

28. Shivering, crying, and tucking the legs close to the body are examples of reflexes that help to maintain ______________ ______________.

29. A third set of reflexes fosters ______________. One of these is the tendency of the newborn to suck anything that touches the lips; this is the ______________ reflex. Another is the tendency of newborns to turn their heads and start to suck when something brushes against their cheek; this is the ______________ reflex.

30. The tendency of a baby's toes to fan upward when the feet are stroked is called the ______________ reflex.

31. The tendency of babies to move their feet as if to walk when the feet touch a flat surface is called the ______________ reflex.

32. The tendency of a baby's arms and legs to stretch out when he or she is held horizontally on the stomach is called the ______________ reflex.

33. The tendency of a baby's hands to close tightly when something touches the palm is called the ______________ ______________ reflex.

34. The tendency of newborns to fling their arms outward and then bring them together on the chest when someone bangs the table on which they are lying is called the ______________ reflex.

35. Large movements such as running and climbing are called ______________ ______________ skills; abilities that require more precise, small movements, such as picking up a coin, are called ______________ ______________ skills.

36. Most infants are able to crawl on all fours (sometimes called creeping) between ______________ and ______________ months of age.

List the major landmarks in children's mastery of walking.

37. Babies who have just begun to walk are given the name ______________ for the characteristic way they move their bodies from side to side.

38. The advent of crawling coincides with a wariness for ______________ things, which conveys some protection to the potential new dangers associated with self-mobility.

List several ways in which self-mobility fosters development.

39. By ______________ of age, most babies can reach for, grab, and hold onto almost any object of the right size.

Briefly describe the development of the ability to pick up and manipulate small objects.

40. The ability to use the thumb and forefinger together, a skill called the ______________ ______________, is generally mastered between ______________ and ______________ months.

41. Although the ______________ in which motor skills are mastered is the same in all healthy infants, the ______________ of acquisition of skills varies greatly.

42. The average ages at which most infants master major motor skills are known as ______________. These averages are based on a large sample of infants drawn from ______________ (a single/many) ethnic group(s).

43. Motor skill norms vary from one ______________ group to another.

List several factors that account for the variation in the acquisition of motor skills.

44. Motor skill acquisition in identical twins ______________ (is/is not) more similar than in fraternal twins, suggesting that genes ______________ (do/do not) play an important role.

45. Most developmentalists would say that the age at which a particular baby first displays a particular skill depends on the interaction between ______________ and ______________ factors.

Sensory and Perceptual Capacities (pp. 156–163)

46. The process by which the visual, auditory, and other sensory systems detect stimuli is called ______________; ______________ occurs when the brain tries to make sense out of a stimulus so that the individual becomes aware of it. At birth, both of these processes ______________ (are/are not) apparent.

Briefly describe the sensory abilities of the newborn.

47. An infant presented with an unfamiliar stimulus will respond with intensified sucking on a pacifier, or concentrated gazing. When the stimulus becomes so familiar that these responses no longer occur, ______________ is said to have occurred. If the infant reacts to a new stimulus, researchers conclude that the infant ______________ (can/cannot) perceive a difference between the stimuli. An alternative research strategy measures the infant's ______________ on a stimulus.

48. Newborns' visual focusing is best for objects between ______________ and ______________ inches away, giving them distance vision of about 20/______________. Distance vision improves rapidly, reaching 20/20 by ______________ of age. This improvement is due mostly to changes that have taken place in the newborn's ______________.

49. Increasing maturation of the visual cortex accounts for improvements in other visual abilities, such as ______________. The ability to use both eyes together to focus on one object, which is called ______________ ______________, develops at about ______________ of age. As a result of these changes, ______________ and ______________ perception improve dramatically.

50. Color vision ______________ (is/is not) present at birth.

Describe infant visual preferences.

51. Generally speaking, newborns' hearing is ______________ (more/less) sensitive than their vision. By ______________ of age, infants can perceive differences between very similar speech sounds.

52. Young infants ______________ (can/cannot) distinguish between speech sounds that are not used in their native language. This suggests that some features of speech perception may be ______________.

53. As infants' early language skills emerge, they ______________ (lose/gain) the ability to distinguish different ______________ sounds that are not heard in their culture.

54. About 1 in every ______________ infants is profoundly deaf.

55. A common cause of temporary hearing loss during infancy is a middle ear infection, or ______________ ______________.

When this condition becomes chronic, the ______________ ear fills with fluid. This condition may last for weeks or months, causing impairment in one or both ears.

56. (Research Report) Chronic otitis media may cause developmental lags in the ability to ______________, make ______________, and solve ______________ problems, and deflect ______________. Treatments include the use of ______________ drugs and placement of a ______________ to drain fluid from the inner ear.

57. Infants' hearing for low-frequency sounds is ______________ (more/less) acute than their hearing for high-frequency sounds. Infants are less capable of ______________ sounds than are older children.

58. At birth, infants can distinguish most of the basic tastes except ______________ tastes. Compared to their sense of taste, infants' sense of smell is ______________ (more/less) acute. By ______________ of age, taste and smell become quite sensitive.

59. The sense of touch ________________ (is/is not) very acute during the first year. By 6 months, infants can distinguish objects on the basis of their ________________, ________________, ________________, and ________________.

Nutrition (pp. 201–207)

60. More important than an infant's feeding schedule in fostering development is the overall ________________ and ________________ of the infant's nutritional intake.

State several advantages of breast milk over cow's milk for the developing infant.

61. The most serious nutritional problem of infancy is ________________-________________ ________________.

62. Severe protein-calorie deficiency in early infancy causes a disease called ________________. In toddlers, protein-calorie deficiency is more likely to cause a disease called ________________, which involves swelling or bloating of the face, legs, and abdomen.

63. The primary cause of malnutrition in developing countries is ________________ ________________.

Briefly explain why, in developing countries, bottle-fed babies have a higher risk of death and disease than do breast-fed babies.

64. In both developing and developed countries ________________, also called ________________-________________, is more prevalent than severe malnutrition. Worldwide, approximately ________________ percent of all children in the least developed countries are undernourished.

Identify several possible causes of infant undernutrition.

65. Children who were undernourished as infants show impaired learning, especially in ________________ and in ________________ skills.

Progress Test 1

Multiple-Choice Questions

Circle your answers to the following questions and check them with the answers on page 83. If your answer is incorrect, read the explanation for why it is incorrect and then consult the appropriate pages of the text (in parentheses following the correct answer).

1. The average North American newborn:
   a. weighs approximately 6 pounds.
   b. weighs approximately 7 pounds.
   c. is "overweight" because of the diet of the mother.
   d. weighs 10 percent less than what is desirable.

2. Compared to the first year, growth during the second year:
   a. proceeds at a slower rate.
   b. continues at about the same rate.
   c. includes more insulating fat.
   d. includes more bone and muscle.

3. The major motor skill most likely to be mastered by an infant before the age of 6 months is:
   a. rolling over.
   b. sitting without support.
   c. turning the head in search of a nipple.
   d. grabbing an object with thumb and forefinger.

4. Norms suggest that the earliest walkers in the world are infants from:
   a. Western Europe.
   b. the United States.
   c. Uganda.
   d. Denver.

5. The interaction between inherited and environmental factors is responsible for:
   a. variation in the age at which infants master specific motor skills.
   b. physical growth, but not the development of motor skills.
   c. the fact that babies in the United States walk earlier than do Ugandan babies.
   d. the fact that infants master motor skills more slowly today than they did fifty years ago.

6. The development of binocular vision at about 14 months results in:
   a. a dramatic improvement in depth and motion perception.
   b. the rapid development of distance vision.
   c. the refinement of the ability to discriminate colors.
   d. both a. and b.

7. Proportionally, the head of the infant is about __________ of total body length; the head of an adult is about __________ of total body length.
   a. one-fourth; one-third
   b. one-eighth; one-fourth
   c. one-fourth; one-eighth
   d. one-third; one-fourth

8. Research has shown that young animals prevented from using their senses in a normal way experience:
   a. no significant impairment.
   b. harmful overstimulation.
   c. deficits in behavior only.
   d. permanent impairment.

9. Compared with formula-fed infants, breast-fed infants tend to have:
   a. greater weight gain.
   b. fewer allergies and digestive upsets.
   c. less frequent feedings during the first few months.
   d. more social approval.

10. Marasmus and kwashiorkor are caused by:
    a. bloating.
    b. protein-calorie deficiency.
    c. living in a developing country.
    d. poor family food habits.

11. The infant's first motor skills are:
    a. fine motor skills.
    b. gross motor skills.
    c. reflexes.
    d. unpredictable.

12. Which of the following is *not* one of the basic physiological states of infancy?
    a. quiet sleep
    b. active sleep
    c. alert wakefulness
    d. relaxed wakefulness

13. Babies are referred to as toddlers when:
    a. their newborn reflexes have disappeared.
    b. they can walk well unassisted.
    c. they begin to creep or crawl.
    d. they speak their first word.

14. Which of the following is true of motor-skill development in healthy infants?
    a. It follows the same basic sequence the world over.
    b. It occurs at different rates from individual to individual.
    c. It follows norms that vary from one ethnic group to another.
    d. All of the above are true.

15. Most of the nerve cells a human brain will ever possess are present:
    a. at conception.
    b. about 1 month following conception.
    c. at birth.
    d. at age 5 or 6.

16. (Research Report) Toddlers with a history of frequent ear infections are much more likely to:
    a. lag behind in language development.
    b. play by themselves.
    c. be uninterested in watching other children play.
    d. all of the above.

Matching Items

Match each definition or description with its corresponding term.

Terms

_______ 1. neurons
_______ 2. dendrites
_______ 3. myelination
_______ 4. kwashiorkor
_______ 5. marasmus
_______ 6. habituation
_______ 7. gross motor skill
_______ 8. fine motor skill
_______ 9. reflex
_______ 10. sucking reflex
_______ 11. protein-calorie malnutrition
_______ 12. transient exuberance
_______ 13. developmental biodynamics
_______ 14. otitis media

Definitions or Descriptions

a. ear infection
b. protein deficiency during the first year in which growth stops and body tissues waste away
c. picking up an object
d. the most common serious nutrition problem of infancy
e. protein deficiency during toddlerhood
f. newborns suck anything that touches their lips
g. communication networks among nerve cells
h. declining physiological response to a familiar stimulus
i. running or climbing
j. the process in which axons are coated with an insulating sheath
k. an involuntary response
l. the phenomenal increase in neural connections over the first 2 years
m. nerve cells
n. maturation of the developing person's ability to move through, and with, the environment

Progress Test 2

Progress Test 2 should be completed during a final chapter review. Answer the following questions after you thoroughly understand the correct answers for the Chapter Review and Progress Test 1.

Multiple-Choice Questions

1. Dendrite is to axon as neural _______ is to neural _______.
   a. input; output
   b. output; input
   c. myelin; synapse
   d. synapse; myelin

2. A reflex is best defined as a(n):
   a. fine motor skill.
   b. motor ability mastered at a specific age.
   c. involuntary physical response to a given stimulus.
   d. gross motor skill.

3. Habituation describes the:
   a. increased physiological arousal of the newborn to unfamiliar or interesting stimuli.
   b. decreased physiological arousal of the newborn to stimuli that are familiar or no longer interesting.
   c. preterm infant's immature brain-wave patterns.
   d. universal sequence of motor-skill development in children.

4. Most babies can reach for, grasp, and hold onto an object by about the _______ month.
   a. second
   b. sixth
   c. ninth
   d. fourteenth

5. Activity level, rate of physical maturation, and how fat the infant is affect the age at which an infant walks and acquires other motor skills. They are examples of:
   a. norms.
   b. environmental factors.
   c. inherited factors.
   d. the interaction of environment and heredity.

6. During the first weeks of life, babies seem to focus reasonably well on:
   a. little in their environment.
   b. objects at a distance of 4 to 30 inches.
   c. objects at a distance of 1 to 3 inches.
   d. objects several feet away.

7. Which of the following provides evidence that some aspects of early speech perception are innate?
   a. Young infants are able to distinguish their mother's voice from others.
   b. Girls master the rules of grammar more readily than do boys.
   c. Young infants can distinguish between speech sounds that are not used in their native language.
   d. Newborns habituate rapidly to soothing sounds.

8. An EEG is best described as:
   a. a device that records electrical impulses from the nerve cells.
   b. a device that measures the physical growth of the skull and brain.
   c. a means of treating brain immaturity in preterm infants.
   d. a brain-wave pattern that is known as electrical silence.

9. An advantage of breast milk over formula is that it:
   a. is always sterile and at body temperature.
   b. contains traces of medications ingested by the mother.
   c. can be given without involving the father.
   d. contains more protein and vitamin D than does formula.

10. The primary cause of malnutrition in developing countries is:
    a. formula feeding.
    b. inadequate food supply.
    c. disease.
    d. early cessation of breast-feeding.

11. The cause of sudden infant death syndrome (SIDS) is:
    a. an inborn heart defect.
    b. a neurological disorder.
    c. inadequate infant care.
    d. a combination of factors.

12. Climbing is to using a crayon as ________ is to ________.
    a. fine motor skill; gross motor skill
    b. gross motor skill; fine motor skill
    c. reflex; fine motor skill
    d. reflex; gross motor skill

13. Some infant reflexes:
    a. are essential to life.
    b. disappear in the months after birth.
    c. provide the foundation for later motor skills.
    d. do all of the above.

14. When they are startled by a noise, newborns will fling their arms outward and then bring them together as if to hold on to something. This is an example of:
    a. a fine motor skill.
    b. a gross motor skill.
    c. the Babinski reflex.
    d. the Moro reflex.

15. (Research Report) A common cause of undernutrition in young children is:
    a. ignorance of the infant's nutritional needs.
    b. the absence of socioeconomic policies that reflect the importance of infant nutrition.
    c. problems in the family, such as maternal depression.
    d. all of the above.

16. Neurotransmitters are chemical messengers that diffuse across the:
    a. axon.
    b. myelin sheath.
    c. dendrite.
    d. synaptic gap.

True or False Items

Write *true* or *false* on the line in front of each statement.

________ 1. By age 2, boys are slightly taller than girls, but girls are slightly heavier.

________ 2. SIDS is the third leading cause of infant death in the United States.

________ 3. Reflexive hiccups, sneezes, and thrashing are signs that the infant's reflexes are not functioning properly.

________ 4. Infants of all ethnic backgrounds develop the same motor skills at approximately the same age.

________ 5. The typical 2-year-old is almost one-fifth its adult weight and one-half its adult height.

________ 6. Vision is better developed than hearing in most newborns.

_______ 7. Myelination and other processes of brain maturation are completed within the first few years of childhood.

_______ 8. Certain basic sensory experiences seem necessary to ensure full brain development in the human infant.

_______ 9. Severe malnutrition is not widespread among young children in the United States.

_______ 10. Ear infections are common during infancy and rarely a cause for concern.

Thinking Critically About Chapter 5

Answer these questions the day before an exam as a final check on your understanding of the chapter's terms and concepts.

1. Newborns cry, shiver, and tuck their legs close to their bodies. This set of reflexes helps them:
   a. ensure proper muscle tone.
   b. learn how to signal distress.
   c. maintain constant body temperature.
   d. communicate serious hunger pangs.

2. If a baby sucks harder on a nipple, evidences a change in heart rate, or stares longer at one image than at another when presented with a change of stimulus, the indication is that the baby:
   a. is annoyed by the change.
   b. is both hungry and angry.
   c. has become habituated to the new stimulus.
   d. perceives some differences between stimuli.

3. A classic experiment on hearing in infants (Eimas et al., 1971) showed that even 1-month-olds can detect:
   a. the father's voice more quickly than the mother's.
   b. sounds they won't be able to hear at age 2.
   c. differences between very similar sounds.
   d. the correct location of auditory stimuli about 80 percent of the time.

4. Mrs. Bartholomew opens the door to her infant's room to be sure everything is alright. She notices that her son's facial muscles are moving and his breathing is irregular and rapid. The infant is in which physiological state?
   a. quiet sleep
   b. active sleep
   c. alert wakefulness
   d. one somewhere between b. and c.

5. The brain development that permits seeing and hearing in human infants appears to be:
   a. totally dependent upon genetic programming, present at birth.
   b. totally dependent upon visual and auditory experiences in the first few months.
   c. "fine-tuned" by visual and auditory experiences in the first few months.
   d. independent of both genetic and environmental influences.

6. Disputing a classmate's contention that the high rate of SIDS among African-Americans implicates genetic causes in the syndrome, Renaldo notes that:
   a. the most recent statistics show that ethnic differences in SIDS rates among the major ethnic groups in the United States are decreasing.
   b. a higher proportion of low-birthweight infants and teenage mothers may explain this higher rate.
   c. African-American infants are almost always put to sleep on their stomachs.
   d. all of the above are true.

7. Michael has 20/400 vision and is able to discriminate subtle sound differences. Michael most likely:
   a. is a preterm infant.
   b. has brain damage in the visual processing areas of the cortex.
   c. is a newborn.
   d. is slow-to-mature.

8. A baby turns her head and starts to suck when her receiving blanket is brushed against her cheek. The baby is displaying the:
   a. sucking reflex.
   b. rooting reflex.
   c. Babinski reflex.
   d. Moro reflex.

9. (Research Report) Toddlers whose parents give them a bottle of milk before every nap and with every meal:
   a. may be at increased risk of undernutrition, because the milk reduces the child's appetite for other foods.
   b. are ensured of receiving a sufficient amount of iron in their diets.
   c. are more likely to develop lactose intolerance.
   d. are likely to be overweight throughout life.

10. Sensation is to perception as ______________ is to ______________.
   a. hearing; seeing
   b. detecting a stimulus; making sense of a stimulus
   c. making sense of a stimulus; detecting a stimulus
   d. tasting; smelling

11. Adults often speak to infants in a high-pitched voice. This is because they discover from experience that:
   a. low-pitched sounds are more frightening to infants.
   b. infants are more sensitive to high-pitched sounds.
   c. high-pitched sounds are more soothing to infants.
   d. all of the above are true.

12. Kittens who are blindfolded for the first several weeks of life:
   a. do not develop the visual pathways in their brains to allow normal vision.
   b. recover fully if visual stimulation is normal thereafter.
   c. develop only binocular vision.
   d. can see clearly, but lack sensitivity to color.

13. Your sister is worried that her 2-year-old son's first middle ear infection, which is being treated with antibiotics, is a sign of chronic otitis media. To help her reason about her son's condition, you wisely point out that:
   a. middle ear infections are common in infancy.
   b. most middle ear infections can be successfully treated with antibiotics and involve no permanent hearing damage.
   c. chronic otitis media is an inner ear disorder.
   d. all of the above are true.

14. Three-week-old Nathan should have the *least* difficulty focusing on the sight of:
   a. stuffed animals on a bookshelf across the room from his crib.
   b. his mother's face as she holds him in her arms.
   c. the checkerboard pattern in the wallpaper covering the ceiling of his room.
   d. the family dog as it dashes into the nursery.

15. (text and Changing Policy) Geneva has been undernourished throughout childhood. It is likely that she will be:
   a. smaller and shorter than her genetic potential would dictate.
   b. slow in intellectual development.
   c. less resistant to disease.
   d. all of the above.

16. Which of the following infants is likely to have the *lowest* risk of sudden infant death syndrome (SIDS)?
   a. a first-born, Asian female who sleeps on her back
   b. a later-born male of African descent
   c. a later-born female of European descent who sleeps on her stomach
   d. a first-born Asian male who sleeps on his back and was born during the winter

Key Terms

Writing Definitions

Using your own words, write a brief definition or explanation of each of the following terms on a separate piece of paper.

1. immunization
2. sudden infant death syndrome (SIDS)
3. neuron
4. axon
5. dendrites
6. synapses
7. cortex
8. transient exuberance
9. myelination
10. binocular vision
11. physiological states
12. electroencephalogram (EEG)
13. reflexes
14. developmental biodynamics
15. breathing reflex
16. sucking reflex
17. rooting reflex
18. gross motor skills
19. toddler
20. fine motor skills
21. pincer grasp

22. norms
23. sensation
24. perception
25. habituation
26. otitis media
27. protein-calorie malnutrition
28. marasmus
29. kwashiorkor
30. undernutrition
31. failure-to-thrive

Cross Check

After you have written the definitions of the key terms in this chapter, you should complete the crossword puzzle to ensure that you can reverse the process—recognize the term, given the definition.

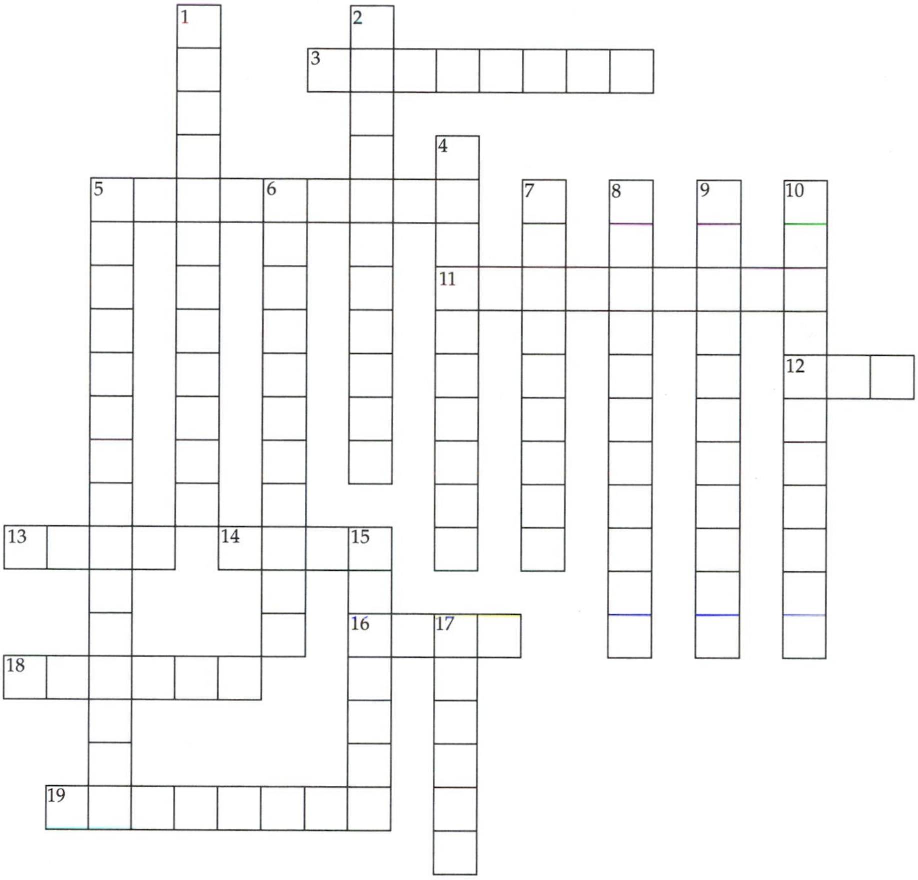

ACROSS

3. Disease caused by severe protein-calorie deficiency during the first year of life.
5. Physical abilities that require precise, small movements.
11. The process by which a sensory system detects a particular stimulus.
12. Device that records brain waves (abbrev.).
13. Nerve fiber extension that transmits an electrical impulse from one neuron to the dendrites of another neuron.
14. The third leading cause of infant death in the United States.
16. Average age for the acquisition of a particular behavior, developed for a specified group population.
18. The thin outer layer of the brain.
19. Nerve fiber extension that receives impulses from the axon of another neuron.

DOWN

1. The process that stimulates the immune system's ability to defend itself against a particular infectious disease.
2. Decline in responsiveness to a familiar stimulus.
4. Physical abilities that demand large body movements.
5. Undernutrition in a child who lives in an adequately nourished community.
6. The process in which axons are coated with an insulating sheath.
7. Vision involving the use of both eyes together to focus on an object.
8. Disease caused by protein-calorie deficiency during toddlerhood.
9. Infection of the middle ear.
10. Using the thumb and forefinger together to grasp an object.
15. The junction between the axon of a sending neuron and the dendrites of a receiving neuron.
17. Involuntary physical response to a specific stimulus.

ANSWERS

CHAPTER REVIEW

1. prenatal; size; proportion
2. 20 inches (51 centimeters); 7 pounds (3.2 kilograms)
3. lose
4. 22 pounds (10 kilograms); 30 inches (75 centimeters); one-fifth; half
5. one-fourth; one-fifth; one-eighth
6. one-fourth; one-half
7. 500; immunization
8. smallpox; polio; measles

Other reasons for the increased survival of young children include improved sanitation procedures that reduce the spread of disease and technological breakthroughs for high-risk infants.

9. month; congenital abnormalities such as heart defects and very low birthweight
10. sudden infant death syndrome; third

SIDS risk factors include a young, poverty-level mother who smokes; a male child, 1–3 months of age, born in winter, who sleeps on his stomach.

Potential culprits include a bacterium that is occasionally found in raw honey, cardiac instability, a brainstem defect, and an excessive intake of carbon dioxide.

11. backs
12. African; Asian; European; birthweight; socioeconomic status; lower

First, Chinese infants sleep on their backs. Second, Chinese parents tend to their babies periodically as they sleep. Third, most Chinese infants are breast-fed, which makes them sleep less soundly.

13. 25; 75; 20
14. neurons; dendrites; axons; dendrites; axon
15. synapses; axon; neurotransmitters; synaptic gap; dendrites; are; are not
16. cortex; perception; thinking
17. increases; five; transient exuberance; myelin; adolescence
18. frontal; self-control; self-regulation; sleep-wake; reflexes
19. is
20. blindfolded; binocular vision; neural pathways

Sensory restriction does not affect the vision of older animals. This demonstrates that the cat's genetic basis is present at birth, but early experiences are needed to make the genetic possibilities operative.

21. language; emotion
22. states

Quiet sleep: breathing is regular and relatively slow and muscles seem relaxed.

Active sleep: facial muscles move and breathing is less regular and more rapid.

Alert wakefulness: eyes are bright and breathing is relatively regular and rapid.

Active crying: the characteristics are obvious.

23. electroencephalogram (EEG)
24. does not; timing; one-third; 80; more; less
25. developmental biodynamics
26. reflex
27. breathing reflex; hiccups, sneezes, thrashing
28. body temperature
29. feeding; sucking; rooting
30. Babinski
31. stepping
32. swimming
33. Palmar grasping
34. Moro
35. gross motor; fine motor
36. 8; 10

On average, a child can walk while holding a hand at 9 months, can stand alone momentarily at 10 months, and can walk well unassisted at 12 months.

37. toddler
38. unfamiliar

Upright mobility literally gives the child a new viewpoint on the world. It also frees the child's hands, fostering the development of fine motor skills and perception.

39. 6 months

At first, infants use their whole hand, especially the palm and the fourth and fifth fingers to grasp. Then they use the middle fingers and the center of the palm, or the index finger and the side of the palm. Finally, they use thumb and forefinger together.

40. pincer grasp; 9; 14
41. sequence; age
42. norms; many
43. ethnic

Of primary importance in variations in the acquisition of motor skills are inherited factors, such as activity level, rate of physical maturation, and how fat the infant is. Particular patterns of infant care may also be influential.

44. is; do

45. inherited; environmental

46. sensation; perception; are

Although their sensory abilities are selective, newborns see, hear, smell, taste, and respond to pressure, motion, temperature, and pain.

47. habituation; can; fixation

48. 4; 30; 400; 1 year; brain

49. scanning; binocular vision; 14 weeks; depth; motion

50. is not

Infants prefer to look at novel images, complex patterns, stimuli with contrast and contour density, and visual events that represent incongruity or discrepancy from the usual.

51. more; 1 month

52. can; innate

53. lose; speech

54. 1,000

55. otitis media; inner

56. learn; friends; social; aggression; antibiotic; tube

57. less; locating

58. salty; more; 1 year

59. is; temperature; size; hardness; texture

60. quality; quantity

Breast milk is always sterile and at body temperature; it is more digestible and contains more iron, vitamin C, and vitamin A; it contains antibodies that provide the infant some protection against disease; it is more digestible than any formula; and it contains hormones that help regulate growth, encourage attachment, reduce pain, and regulate the brain, liver, intestines, and pancreas.

61. protein-calorie malnutrition

62. marasmus; kwashiorkor

63. early cessation of breast-feeding

For many people in the developing world, the hygienic conditions for the proper use of infant formula do not exist. The water and bottles are unclean, and the formula is often diluted to make it last longer.

64. undernutrition; failure-to-thrive; 56

Undernutrition is caused by the interaction of many factors, with insufficient food as the immediate cause, and problems in the family and/or society as underlying causes. For example, depressed mothers tend to feed their infants erratically, and some may be ignorant of the infant's nutritional needs.

65. concentration; language

PROGRESS TEST 1

Multiple-Choice Questions

1. b. is the answer. (p. 137)

2. a. is the answer. (p. 138)

3. a. is the answer. (p. 153)

b. The age norm for this skill is 7.8 months.

c. This is a reflex, rather than an acquired motor skill.

d. This skill is acquired between 9 and 14 months.

4. c. is the answer. (p. 154)

5. a. is the answer. (p. 154)

b. Inherited and environmental factors are important for both physical growth *and* the development of motor skills.

c. On average, Ugandan babies walk earlier than do babies in the United States.

d. In fact, just the opposite is true.

6. a. is the answer. (p. 158)

7. c. is the answer. (p. 138)

8. d. is the answer. (pp. 145–146)

a. & c. Research has shown that deprivation of normal sensory experiences prevents the development of normal neural pathways that transmit sensory information.

b. On the contrary, these studies demonstrate harmful sensory *restriction.*

9. b. is the answer. This is because breast milk is more digestible than cow's milk or formula. (p. 165)

a., c., & d. Breast- and bottle-fed babies do not differ in these attributes.

10. b. is the answer. (p. 166)

11. c. is the answer. (p. 148)

a. & b. These motor skills do not emerge until somewhat later; reflexes are present at birth.

d. On the contrary, reflexes are quite predictable.

12. d. is the answer. (p. 147)

13. b. is the answer. (p. 151)

14. d. is the answer. (p. 154)

15. c. is the answer. (p. 144)

16. b. is the answer. (p. 162)

Matching Items

1. m (p. 143)	**6.** h (p. 156)	**11.** d (p. 166)
2. g (p. 143)	**7.** i (p. 150)	**12.** l (p. 144)
3. j (p. 144)	**8.** c (p. 151)	**13.** n (p. 148)
4. e (p. 166)	**9.** k (p. 148)	**14.** a (p. 161)
5. b (p. 166)	**10.** f (p. 149)	

PROGRESS TEST 2

Multiple-Choice Questions

1. **a.** is the answer. (p. 143)
2. **c.** is the answer. (p. 148)

   a., b., & d. Each of these refers to voluntary responses that are acquired only after a certain amount of practice; reflexes are involuntary responses that are present at birth and require no practice.
3. **b.** is the answer. (p. 156)
4. **b.** is the answer. (p. 152)
5. **c.** is the answer. (p. 154)

   a. Norms are average ages at which certain motor skills are acquired.
6. **b.** is the answer. (p. 157)

   a. Although focusing ability seems to be limited to a certain range, babies do focus on many objects in this range.

   c. This is not within the range at which babies *can* focus.

   d. Babies have very poor distance vision.
7. **c.** is the answer. (p. 160)

   a. & c. These are examples of learned rather than innate behaviors.

   b. The text does not discuss the development of grammar in this chapter.
8. **a.** is the answer. (p. 147)
9. **a.** is the answer. (pp. 164–165)

   b. If anything, this is a potential *disadvantage* of breast milk over formula.

   c. So can formula.

   d. Breast milk contains more iron, vitamin C, and vitamin A than cow's milk; it does not contain more protein and vitamin D, however.
10. **d.** is the answer. (p. 166)
11. **d.** is the answer. (p. 141)
12. **b.** is the answer. (pp. 150, 151)

    c. & d. Reflexes are involuntary responses; climbing and using a crayon are both voluntary responses.
13. **d.** is the answer. (p. 150)
14. **d.** is the answer. (p. 143)

    a. & b. Fine and gross motor skills are voluntary responses; the response described here is clearly reflexive.

    c. The Babinski reflex is the response that infants make when their feet are stroked.
15. **d.** is the answer. (p. 168)
16. **d.** is the answer. (p. 144)

True or False Items

1. F Boys are both slightly heavier and taller than girls at 2 years. (p. 138)
2. T (p. 140)
3. F Hiccups, sneezes, and thrashing are common during the first few days, and they are entirely normal reflexes. (p. 149)
4. F Although all healthy infants develop the same motor skills in the same sequence, the age at which these skills are acquired can vary greatly from infant to infant. (p. 153)
5. T (p. 138)
6. F Vision is relatively poorly developed at birth, whereas hearing is well developed. (pp. 157–159)
7. F Myelination is not complete until adolescence. (p. 144)
8. T (p. 145)
9. T (p. 167)
10. F Although ear infections are common, they need prompt attention, since they can lead to hearing problems and social and cognitive difficulties. (p. 160)

THINKING CRITICALLY ABOUT CHAPTER 5

1. **c.** is the answer. (p. 149)
2. **d.** is the answer. (pp. 156–157)

   a. & b. These changes in behavior indicate that the newborn has perceived an unfamiliar stimulus, not that he or she is hungry, annoyed, or angry.

   c. Habituation refers to a *decrease* in physiological responsiveness to a familiar stimulus.
3. **c.** is the answer. (p. 160)

   a. & b. There is no evidence that infants can detect one parent's voice more easily than the other's, or that sounds perceived at 1 month can not be discriminated later.

   d. This experiment was not concerned with sound localization.
4. **b.** is the answer. (p. 147)

   a. This state is characterized by relatively slow and regular breathing and relaxed muscles.

   c. This state is characterized by bright eyes and regular and rapid breathing.

5. **c.** is the answer. The evidence for this comes from studies in which animals were prevented from using their senses in infancy; such animals became permanently handicapped. (p. 145)

   a. If this were true, research would show that restriction had no effect on sensory abilities.

   b. If this were true, sensory restriction would cause much more serious impairment than it does.

   d. Sensory restriction research demonstrates that both genetic and environmental factors are important in the development of sensory abilities.
6. **b.** is the answer. (pp. 141–142)
7. **c.** is the answer. (pp. 157, 159)
8. **b.** is the answer. (p. 149)

   a. This is the reflexive sucking of newborns in response to anything that touches their *lips*.

   c. This is the response that infants make when their feet are stroked.

   d. In this response to startling noises, newborns fling their arms outward and then bring them together on their chests as if to hold on to something.
9. **a.** is the answer. (p. 168)
10. **b.** is the answer. (p. 156)

    a. & d. Sensation and perception operate in all of these sensory modalities.
11. **b.** is the answer. (p. 161)

    a. & c. The text does not suggest that whether a sound is soothing or frightening is determined by its pitch.
12. **a.** is the answer. (p. 145)
13. **d.** is the answer. (p. 159)
14. **b.** is the answer. This is true because, at birth, focusing is best for objects between 4 and 30 inches away. (p. 157)

    a., c., & d. Newborns have very poor distance vision; each of these situations involves a distance greater than the optimal focus range.
15. **d.** is the answer. (pp. 206–207)
16. **a.** is the answer. (pp. 141–142)

KEY TERMS

Writing Definitions

1. **Immunization** is the process that stimulates the immune system's ability to defend itself against a particular infectious disease. (p. 138)
2. The third leading cause of infant death in the United States, **sudden infant death syndrome (SIDS)** is diagnosed when autopsy suggests that the infant simply stopped breathing during sleep, with other possible causes ruled out. (p. 140)
3. A **neuron**, or nerve cell, is the main component of the central nervous system. (p. 143)
4. An **axon** is the nerve fiber extension that sends impulses from one neuron to the dendrites of other neurons. (p. 143)
5. **Dendrites** are nerve fiber extensions that receive the impulses transmitted from other neurons via their axons. (p. 143)
6. A **synapse** is the point at which the axon of a sending neuron meets the dendrites of a receiving neuron. (p. 143)
7. The **cortex** is the thin outer layer of the brain that is involved in the voluntary, cognitive aspects of the mind. (p. 144)

   Memory aid: **Cortex** in latin means "bark." As bark covers a tree, the cortex in the "bark of the brain."
8. **Transient exuberance** is the dramatic increase in neural connections that occurs in an infant's brain over the first 2 years of life. (p. 144)
9. **Myelination** is the process in which axons are coated with myelin, a fatty substance that speeds neural communication. (p. 144)
10. **Binocular vision** is the ability to use both eyes together to focus on a single object. (p. 145)

    Memory aid: Bi- indicates "two"; *ocular* means something pertaining to the eye. **Binocular vision** is vision for "two eyes."
11. The **physiological states** of the infant refer to levels of an organism's mental and biological activity, including quiet sleep, active sleep, alert wakefulness, and active crying. (p. 147)
12. The **electroencephalogram (EEG)** is a device that records the electrical impulses or brain waves from neurons. (p. 147)
13. **Reflexes** are involuntary physical responses to specific stimuli. (p. 148)
14. **Developmental biodynamics** is the maturation of movement skills. (p. 148)
15. The **breathing reflex** is an involuntary physical response that ensures that the infant has an adequate supply of oxygen and discharges carbon dioxide. (p. 149)
16. The **sucking reflex** is the involuntary tendency of newborns to suck anything that touches their lips. This reflex fosters feeding. (p. 149)
17. The **rooting reflex**, which helps babies find a nipple, causes them to turn their heads and start

to suck when something brushes against their cheek. (p. 149)

18. **Gross motor skills** are physical abilities that demand large body movements, such as climbing, jumping, or running. (p. 150)
19. When babies can walk well without assistance (usually at about 12 months), they are given the name **toddler** because of the characteristic way they move their bodies from side to side. (p. 151)
20. **Fine motor skills** are physical abilities that require precise, small movements, such as picking up a coin. (p. 151)
21. The **pincer grasp** is when the thumb and forefinger are used together to hold an object. (p. 153)
22. **Norms** are age averages for the acquisition of a particular behavior, developed for a specific group population. (p. 154)
23. **Sensation** is the process by which a sensory system detects a particular stimulus. (p. 154)
24. **Perception** is the process by which the brain tries to make sense of a stimulus such that the individual becomes aware of it. (p. 156)
25. **Habituation** refers to the decline in physiological responsiveness that occurs when a stimulus becomes familiar. Habituation to stimuli is used by researchers to assess infants' ability to perceive by testing their ability to discriminate between very similar stimuli. (p. 156)
26. **Otitis media** is a middle ear infection that can impair hearing temporarily, which can slow language development and interfere with social development if allowed to continue too long. (p. 161)
27. **Protein-calorie malnutrition** results when a person does not consume enough nourishment to thrive. (p. 166)
28. **Marasmus** is a disease caused by severe protein-calorie deficiency during the first year of life. Growth stops, body tissues waste away, and the infant dies. (p. 166)
29. **Kwashiorkor** is a disease caused by protein-calorie deficiency during toddlerhood. The child's face, legs, and abdomen swell with water, sometimes making the child appear well fed. Other body parts are degraded, including the hair, which becomes thin, brittle, and colorless. (p. 166)
30. **Undernutrition** is a nutritional problem in which a child is noticeably underweight or short in stature compared to the norms. (p. 167)
31. **Failure-to-thrive** is undernutrition that involves a child who lives in an adequately nourished community but is not exhibiting normal childhood weight gain. (p. 167)

Cross-Check

ACROSS

3. marasmus
5. fine motor
11. sensation
12. EEG
13. axon
14. SIDS
16. norm
18. cortex
19. dendrite

DOWN

1. immunization
2. habituation
4. gross motor
5. failure to thrive
6. myelination
7. binocular
8. kwashiorkor
9. otitis media
10. pincer grasp
15. synapse
17. reflex

CHAPTER 6

The First 2 Years: Cognitive Development

Chapter Overview

Chapter 6 explores the ways in which the infant comes to learn about, think about, and adapt to his or her surroundings. It focuses on the various ways in which infant intelligence is revealed: through perception, cognition, memory, sensorimotor intelligence, and language development. The chapter begins with a description of infant perception and Eleanor and James Gibson's influential theory. Central to this theory is the idea that infants gain cognitive understanding of their world through the affordances of objects, that is, the activities they can do with them.

The second section discusses the key cognitive elements needed by the infant to structure the environment discovered through its newfound perceptual abilities. Using the habituation procedure, researchers have found that the speed with which infants recognize familiarity and seek something novel is related to later cognitive skill. It points out the importance of memory to cognitive development.

The third section describes Jean Piaget's theory of sensorimotor intelligence, which maintains that infants think exclusively with their senses and motor skills. Piaget's six stages of sensorimotor intelligence are examined.

Finally, the chapter turns to the most remarkable cognitive achievement of the first two years, the acquisition of language. Beginning with a description of the infant's first attempts at language, the chapter follows the sequence of events that leads to the child's ability to utter two-word sentences. The chapter concludes with an examination of language learning as teamwork involving babies and adults, who, in a sense, teach each other the unique human process of verbal communication.

NOTE: Answer guidelines for all Chapter 6 questions begin on page 98.

Guided Study

The text chapter should be studied one section at a time. Before you read, preview each section by skimming it, noting headings and boldface items. Then read the appropriate section objectives from the following outline. Keep these objectives in mind and, as you read the chapter section, search for the information that will enable you to meet each objective. Once you have finished a section, write out answers for its objectives.

Perception and Cognition (pp. 173–180)

1. Explain the Gibsons' contextual view of perception, and discuss the idea of affordances, giving examples of affordances perceived by infants.

2. Explain how the infant's understanding of perceptual constancy, along with the infant's focus on movement and change, enhance sensory and perceptual skills and thus overall cognitive growth.

3. Discuss the infant's ability to integrate perceptual information from different sensory systems, giving examples of intermodal and cross-modal perception.

Key Elements of Cognitive Growth (pp. 180–188)

4. Explain what habituation research has revealed about the infant's ability to categorize.

5. Explain what object permanence is, how it is tested in infancy, and what these tests reveal.

6. (text and Research Report) Discuss research findings on infant long-term memory and infants' understanding of causal relationships.

Active Intelligence: Piaget's Theory (pp. 188–194)

7. Identify and describe the first two of Piaget's stages of sensorimotor intelligence.

8. Identify and describe stages 3 and 4 of Piaget's theory of sensorimotor intelligence.

9. Identify and describe stages 5 and 6 of Piaget's theory of sensorimotor intelligence.

Language Development (pp. 195–204)

10. Describe language development during infancy, and identify its major hallmarks.

11. Contrast the theories of Skinner and Chomsky regarding early language development, and explain current views on language learning.

12. Explain the importance of baby talk, and identify its main features.

Chapter Review

When you have finished reading the chapter, work through the material that follows to review it. Complete the sentences and answer the questions. As you proceed, evaluate your performance for each section by consulting the answers on page 98. Do not continue with the next section until you understand each answer. If you need to, review or reread the appropriate section in the textbook before continuing.

Perception and Cognition (pp. 173–180)

1. The first major theorist to realize that infants are active learners was ________________ .
2. Much of the current research in perception and cognition has been inspired by the work of the Gibsons, who stress that perception is a(n) ________________ (active/passive/automatic) cognitive phenomenon.
3. According to the Gibsons, any object in the environment offers diverse opportunities for interaction; this property of objects is called an ________________ .
4. Which of these an individual perceives in an object depends on the individual's ________________ ________________ and ________________ ________________, on his or her ________________ ________________, and on his or her ________________ ________________ of what the object might be used for.
5. Infants perceive the affordance of ________________ long before their manual dexterity has matured.

List other affordances perceived by infants from a very early age.

6. A firm surface that appears to drop off is called a ________________ ________________ Although perception of this drop off was once linked to ________________ maturity, later research found that infants as young as ________________ are able to perceive the drop off, as evidenced by changes in their ________________ ________________ and their wide open eyes.
7. Central to the infant's ability to perceive affordances is gaining an understanding of the ________________ of objects. This begins to occur by the age of ________________, when infants are able to distinguish the ________________ of separate objects, even when objects are ________________ .
8. Infants also begin to develop an understanding of ________________ ________________, which is the awareness that the ________________ and ________________ of objects remain the same despite changes in their appearance due to changes in their location.
9. Perception that is primed to focus on movement and change is called ________________ ________________ .

Give several examples of how infants use movement cues in perceiving objects.

10. The ability to associate information from one sensory modality with information from another is called ________________ ________________ . This ability ________________ (is/is not) demonstrated by newborns.
11. The ability to use information from one sensory modality to imagine something in another is called ________________-________________ ________________ . The first evidence of this ability in very young infants involves the sense of ________________ .

Key Elements of Cognitive Growth (pp. 180–188)

12. From a very early age, infants coordinate and organize their perceptions into ____________. Researchers use the phenomenon of infant ____________ to study these abilities.

13. Infants younger than 6 months can categorize objects according to their ____________, ____________, ____________, ____________, ____________, and ____________. By the end of the first year, they can categorize ____________, ____________, and ____________.

14. A major cognitive accomplishment of infancy is the ability to understand that objects exist independently of ____________ ____________. This awareness is called ____________ ____________.

15. To test for this awareness, Piaget devised a procedure to observe whether an infant will ____________. Using this test, Piaget concluded that this awareness does not develop until about ____________ of age.

16. Using the habituation procedure, Renée Baillargeon has demonstrated that infants as young as ____________ months have an awareness of object permanence that is concealed by the traditional Piagetian hidden-object tests.

17. Researchers have generally considered infants' long-term memory to be quite ____________ (good/poor).

18. More recent studies demonstrate that babies have great difficulty storing new memories in their first ____________ (how long?). But they can show they remember when three conditions are met:

    (a) ____________
    (b) ____________
    (c) ____________

19. When these conditions are met, infants as young as ____________ months "remembered" events from one week earlier or two weeks earlier, if they experienced a ____________ ____________ prior to retesting.

20. The ability to remember and imitate behaviors that have been observed but never actually performed is called ____________ ____________. This ability becomes apparent toward the ____________.

21. By 18 months, toddlers are capable of remembering more complex sequences and can also ____________ their memories.

22. (Research Report) Most people cannot remember events from their early years, a phenomenon referred to as ____________ ____________. Memory of events, objects, or experiences that can be recognized but not necessarily ____________ is called ____________ ____________. Memory that a person can demonstrate on demand is called ____________ ____________. Recent research studies have demonstrated that early memories are usually ____________ and that ____________ memory improves with developing ____________ ability.

23. Another important cognitive accomplishment of infancy is the ability to recognize and associate ____________-____________-____________ relations. Research using the ____________ ____________ procedure reveals that infants as young as ____________ months have a rudimentary understanding of such relations.

Active Intelligence: Piaget's Theory (pp. 188–194)

24. A central concept in Piaget's theory of cognitive development is the notion of ____________ intelligence.

25. When infants begin to explore the environment through sensory and motor skills, they are displaying what Piaget called ____________ intelligence. In number, Piaget described ____________ stages of development of this type of intelligence.

26. Sensorimotor intelligence begins with newborns'

reflexes, such as ______________, ______________, ______________, and ______________. It lasts from birth to ______________ of age.

27. Stage 2 begins when newborns show signs of ______________ of their reflexes to the specifics of the environment. This is revealed in two ways: by ______________ of new information into previously developed mental categories, or ______________; and ______________ of previous mental categories to incorporate new information. During this stage, infants spend much time playing with their bodies. This provides them with information that is basic to an awareness of body ______________.

Describe the development of the sucking reflex during stages one and two.

28. During stage three, which occurs between ______________ and ______________ months of age, infants repeat a specific action that has just elicited a pleasing response.

Describe a typical stage-three behavior.

29. In stage four, which lasts from ______________ to ______________ months of age, infants can better ______________ events. At this stage babies also engage in purposeful actions, or ______________-______________ behavior.

30. During stage five, which lasts from ______________ to ______________ months, goal-directed activities become more expansive and creative.

Explain what Piaget meant when he described the stage-five infant as a "little scientist."

31. Stage six, which lasts from ______________ to ______________ months, is the stage of achieving new means by using ______________ ______________.

32. One sign that children have reached stage six is their ability to think more flexibly about ______________ and ______________ events and to enjoy a broader range of ______________ activities.

Language Development (pp. 195–204)

33. Children the world over ______________ (follow/do not follow) the same sequence of early language development. Long before using words, young infants communicate through ______________.

These early skills serve the primary role of ______________ ______________, which is to ______________, and be ______________ by, others. This ability gradually evolves into the ______________ ______________, which consists of sounds, words, and rules.

34. Newborns show a preference for hearing ______________ over other sounds.

35. By 4 months of age, most babies' verbal repertoire consists of ______________ ______________.

36. At ______________ months of age, babies begin to repeat certain syllables, a phenomenon referred to as ______________.

37. Deaf babies begin oral babbling ______________ (earlier/later) than hearing babies do. Deaf babies may also babble ______________, with this behavior emerging ______________ (earlier than/at the same time as/later than) hearing

infants begin oral babbling. The similar timing of babbling among hearing and deaf babies suggests that ______________ maturation, more than maturation of the ______________ ______________, underlies language development.

38. At every stage of development, children understand ______________ (more/less) than they express.

39. The average baby speaks a few words at about ______________ of age. At this time, vocabulary increases at a rate of ______________ words a month. When vocabulary reaches approximately 50 words, it suddenly begins to build rapidly, at a rate of ______________ or more words a month.

40. Toddlers who primarily learn naming words first are called ______________, whereas those who acquire mainly words that can be used in social interaction are called ______________. Language acquisition is also shaped by our ______________, as revealed by the fact that North American infants are more ______________ than Japanese infants.

41. One characteristic of infant speech is ______________, or overgeneralization, in which the infant applies a known word to a variety of objects and contexts. Initially, however, infants tend toward ______________ of word meanings. Another characteristic is the use of the ______________, in which a single word expresses a complete thought.

42. Vocabulary size ______________ (is/is not) the best measure of early language learning. The crux of early language is ______________.

43. Children begin to produce their first two-word sentences at about ______________ months.

44. Reinforcement and other conditioning processes account for language development, according to the learning theory of ______________.

45. The theorist who stressed the infant's innate language abilities is ______________, who maintained that all children are born with a LAD, or ______________ ______________ ______________.

Summarize the conclusions of recent research regarding the theories of Skinner and Chomsky.

46. Adults talk to infants using a special form of language called ______________ ______________, which is nicknamed ______________.

Briefly describe the type of speech adults use with infants.

47. Four ways that adults support infants in their acquisition of language are: (a) ______________ ______________; (b) ______________ ______________; (c) ______________ ______________; and (d) ______________ ______________.

Progress Test 1

Multiple-Choice Questions

Circle your answers to the following questions and check them with the answers on page 99. If your answer is incorrect, read the explanation for why it is incorrect and then consult the appropriate pages of the text (in parentheses following the correct answer).

1. In general terms, the Gibsons' concept of affordances emphasizes the idea that the individual perceives an object in terms of its:
   a. economic importance.
   b. physical qualities.
   c. function or use to the individual.
   d. role in the larger culture or environment.

2. According to Piaget, when a baby repeats an action that has just triggered a pleasing response from his or her caregiver, a stage ________ behavior has occurred.
   a. one
   b. two
   c. three
   d. six

3. Sensorimotor intelligence begins with a baby's first:
   a. attempt to crawl.
   b. reflex actions.
   c. auditory perception.
   d. adaptation of a reflex.

4. To study an infant's categorization ability, researchers show a baby different objects in a category until ____________ occurs. If the baby then ________ when an object from a different category is presented, it suggests that the child has discriminated between the different categories.
   a. intermodal perception; habituates
   b. cross-modal perception; dishabituates
   c. habituation; dishabituates
   d. dynamic perception; habituates

5. Piaget and the Gibsons would most likely agree that:
   a. perception is largely automatic.
   b. language development is biologically predisposed in children.
   c. learning and perception are active cognitive processes.
   d. it is unwise to "push" children too hard academically.

6. By the end of the first year, infants usually learn how to:
   a. accomplish simple goals.
   b. manipulate various symbols.
   c. solve complex problems.
   d. pretend.

7. When an infant begins to understand that objects exist even when they are out of sight, she or he has begun to understand the concept of object:
   a. displacement.
   b. importance.
   c. permanence.
   d. location.

8. Today, most cognitive psychologists view language acquisition as:
   a. primarily the result of imitation of adult speech.
   b. a behavior that is determined primarily by biological maturation.
   c. a behavior determined entirely by learning.
   d. determined by both biological maturation and learning.

9. Despite cultural differences, children all over the world attain very similar language skills:
   a. according to ethnically specific timetables.
   b. at about the same age in the same sequence.
   c. according to culturally specific timetables.
   d. according to timetables that vary from child to child.

10. The average baby speaks a few words at about:
    a. 6 months.
    b. 9 months.
    c. 12 months.
    d. 24 months.

11. A single word used by toddlers to express a complete thought is:
    a. a holophrase.
    b. baby talk.
    c. an overextension.
    d. an underextension.

12. Compared with children's *rate* of speech development, their *comprehension* of language develops:
    a. more slowly.
    b. at about the same pace.
    c. more rapidly.
    d. more rapidly in certain cultures than it does in other cultures.

13. A distinctive form of language, with a particular pitch, structure, etc., that adults use in talking to infants is called:
    a. a holophrase.
    b. the LAD.
    c. baby talk.
    d. conversation.

14. At 8 months, infants can categorize objects on the basis of
    a. angularity.
    b. shape.
    c. density.
    d. all of the above.

15. By what age can most infants properly interpret the cause-and-effect relations of the launching event experiment?
    a. 5 months
    b. 6 months
    c. 10 months
    d. 12 months

16. A toddler who taps on the computer's keyboard after observing her mother sending e-mail is demonstrating:
    a. assimilation.
    b. accommodation.
    c. deferred imitation.
    d. dynamic perception.

Matching Items

Match each definition or description with its corresponding term.

Terms

_____ 1. mental combinations
_____ 2. affordances
_____ 3. object permanence
_____ 4. intermodal perception
_____ 5. cross-modal perception
_____ 6. implicit memory
_____ 7. sensorimotor intelligence
_____ 8. babbling
_____ 9. holophrase
_____ 10. overextension
_____ 11. explicit memory
_____ 12. dynamic perception

Definitions or Descriptions

a. overgeneralization of a word to inappropriate objects, etc.
b. repetitive utterance of certain syllables
c. perception that focuses on movement and change
d. memory for events that can be recognized but not necessarily recalled
e. the realization that something that is out of sight continues to exist
f. trying out actions mentally
g. opportunities for interaction that an object offers
h. associating information from one sensory modality with information from another
i. a single word used to express a complete thought
j. using information from one sensory modality to imagine something in another
k. memory that is available for immediate recall
l. thinking through the senses and motor skills

Progress Test 2

Progress Test 2 should be completed during a final chapter review. Answer the following questions after you thoroughly understand the correct answers for the Chapter Review and Progress Test 1.

Multiple-Choice Questions

1. Stage five (12 to 18 months) of sensorimotor intelligence is best described as:
a. first acquired adaptations.
b. the period of the "little scientist."
c. procedures for making interesting sights last.
d. new means through symbolization.

2. Which of the following is *not* evidence of dynamic perception during infancy?
a. Babies prefer to look at things in motion.
b. Babies form simple expectations of the path that a moving object will follow.
c. Babies use movement cues to discern the boundaries of objects.
d. Babies quickly grasp that even though objects look different when seen from different viewpoints, they are the same objects.

3. Recent research suggests that the concept of object permanence:
a. fades after a few months.
b. is a skill some children never acquire.
c. may occur earlier and more gradually than Piaget recognized.
d. involves pretending as well as mental combinations.

4. According to the Gibsons, graspability is:
a. an opportunity perceived by a baby.
b. a quality that resides in toys and other objects.
c. an ability that emerges at about 6 months.
d. evidence of manual dexterity in the infant.

5. Both intermodal and cross-modal perception necessarily involve:
a. matching of sight and sound.
b. hand-eye coordination.
c. mental representation of a hidden object.
d. the ability to integrate perceptual information.

6. The best and most accurate measure of early language learning is the:
a. size of a child's vocabulary.
b. number of grammatical errors made by a child.
c. nature of the grammatical errors made by the child.
d. child's ability and willingness to communicate.

7. For Noam Chomsky, the "language acquisition device" refers to:
   a. the human predisposition to acquire language.
   b. the portion of the human brain that processes speech.
   c. the vocabulary of the language the child is exposed to.
   d. all of the above.

8. The first stage of sensorimotor intelligence lasts until:
   a. infants can anticipate events that will fulfill their needs.
   b. infants begin to adapt their reflexes to the environment.
   c. object permanence has been achieved.
   d. infants are capable of thinking about past and future events.

9. Experiments demonstrate that intermodal and cross-modal perceptual abilities begin to develop in infants:
   a. less than 6 months old.
   b. between 6 and 12 months old.
   c. between 12 and 18 months old.
   d. more than 18 months old.

10. Whether or not an infant perceives certain characteristics of objects, such as "suckability" or "graspability," seems to depend on:
    a. his or her prior experiences.
    b. his or her needs.
    c. his or her cognitive awareness.
    d. all of the above.

11. Piaget was *incorrect* in his belief that infants do not have:
    a. object permanence.
    b. intelligence.
    c. goal-directed behavior.
    d. all of the above.

12. The purposeful actions that begin to develop in sensorimotor stage four are called:
    a. reflexes.
    b. affordances.
    c. goal-directed behaviors.
    d. mental combinations.

13. What is the correct sequence of stages of language development?
    a. crying, babbling, cooing, first word
    b. crying, cooing, babbling, first word
    c. crying, babbling, first word, cooing
    d. crying, cooing, first word, babbling

14. Compared with hearing babies, deaf babies:
    a. are less likely to babble.
    b. are more likely to babble.
    c. begin to babble vocally at about the same age.
    d. begin to babble manually at about the same age as hearing babies begin to babble vocally.

15. According to Skinner, children acquire language:
    a. as a result of an inborn ability to use the basic structure of language.
    b. through reinforcement and conditioning.
    c. mostly because of biological maturation.
    d. in a fixed sequence of predictable stages.

16. Which of the following is most closely tied to language development?
    a. explicit memory
    b. cross-modal perception
    c. implicit memory
    d. intermodal perception

Matching Items

Match each definition or description with its corresponding term.

Terms

_______ 1. goal-directed behavior
_______ 2. perceptual constancy
_______ 3. infantile amnesia
_______ 4. baby talk
_______ 5. assimilation
_______ 6. little scientist
_______ 7. launching event
_______ 8. underextension
_______ 9. habituation study
_______ 10. accommodation
_______ 11. LAD

Definitions or Descriptions

a. the awareness that the size and shape of an object remains the same despite changes in its appearance
b. incorporating new information into an existing schema
c. research procedure for investigating cause-and-effect relations
d. the inability to access memories from the first years of life
e. a technique for studying categorization in infants
f. a word is used more narrowly than its true meaning allows
g. a hypothetical device that facilitates language development
h. also called "Motherese"
i. Piaget's term for the stage-five toddler
j. purposeful actions
k. modifying an existing schema to reflect new information

Thinking Critically About Chapter 6

Answer these questions the day before an exam as a final check on your understanding of the chapter's terms and concepts.

1. A 9-month-old repeatedly reaches for his sister's doll, even though he has been told "no" many times. This is an example of:
a. pretend play.
b. an overextension.
c. delayed imitation.
d. goal-directed behavior.

2. An infant who comes to expect the sound of music to emanate from a CD player is exhibiting:
a. cross-modal perception.
b. goal-directed behavior.
c. intermodal perception.
d. object permanence.

3. Experiments reveal that infants can "recognize" by sight an object that they have previously touched but have not seen. This is an example of:
a. delayed imitation.
b. two related affordances.
c. categorization.
d. cross-modal perception.

4. According to Skinner's theory, an infant who learns to delight his father by saying "da-da" is probably benefiting from:
a. social reinforcers, such as smiles and hugs.
b. modeling.
c. learning by imitation.
d. an innate ability to use language.

5. The child's tendency to call every animal "doggie" is an example of:
a. using a holophrase.
b. babbling.
c. motherese.
d. overextension.

6. About six months after speaking his or her first words, the typical child will:
a. have a vocabulary of between 250 and 350 words.
b. begin to speak in holophrases.
c. put words together to form rudimentary sentences.
d. do all of the above.

7. A 20-month-old girl who is able to try out various actions mentally without having to actually perform them is learning to solve simple problems by using:
   a. dynamic perception.
   b. object permanence.
   c. intermodal perception.
   d. mental combinations.

8. A baby who repeats an action he or she has seen trigger a reaction in someone else is demonstrating an ability that typically occurs in which stage of sensorimotor development?
   a. one
   b. two
   c. three
   d. four

9. (Research Report) One explanation for "infantile amnesia" is that:
   a. infants are incapable of forming long-term memories.
   b. infants and adults store memories differently.
   c. early memories are traumatic, and therefore repressed.
   d. infants' attentional processes are too immature to allow for adequate memory testing.

10. Sixteen-month-old Courtney reserves the word "cat" for her pet feline. Her failure to refer to other felines as cats is an example of:
    a. a holophrase.
    b. an overextension.
    c. babbling.
    d. an underextension.

11. A baby who realizes that a rubber duck that has fallen out of the tub must be somewhere on the floor has achieved:
    a. object permanence.
    b. intermodal perception.
    c. mental combinations.
    d. cross-modal perception.

12. As soon as her babysitter arrives, 21-month-old Christine holds on to her mother's legs and, in a questioning manner, says "bye-bye." Because Christine clearly is "asking" her mother not to leave, her utterance can be classified as:
    a. babbling.
    b. an overextension.
    c. a holophrase.
    d. subject-predicate order.

13. The 6-month-old infant's continual repetition of sound combinations such as "ba-ba-ba" is called:
    a. cooing.
    b. babbling.
    c. a holophrase.
    d. an overextension.

14. Which of the following is an example of a linguistic overextension that a 2-year-old might make?
    a. saying "bye-bye" to indicate that he or she wants to go out
    b. pointing to a cat and saying "doggie"
    c. repeating certain syllables, such as "ma-ma"
    d. reversing word order, such as "want it, paper"

15. Many researchers believe that the infant's ability to detect the similarities and differences between shapes and colors marks the beginning of:
    a. cross-modal perception.
    b. intermodal perception.
    c. category or concept formation.
    d. full object permanence.

16. Like most Japanese toddlers, Noriko has acquired a greater number of __________ words than her North American counterparts, who tend to be more __________ .
    a. referential; expressive
    b. expressive; referential
    c. labeling; expressive
    d. social; referential

Key Terms

Using your own words, write a brief definition or explanation of each of the following terms on a separate piece of paper.

1. affordance
2. graspability
3. visual cliff
4. object constancy
5. perceptual constancy
6. dynamic perception
7. intermodal perception
8. cross-modal perception
9. object permanence
10. reminder session
11. deferred imitation

12. implicit memory
13. explicit memory
14. launching event
15. sensorimotor intelligence
16. goal-directed behavior
17. little scientist
18. mental combinations
19. language function
20. language structure
21. babbling
22. underextension
23. overextension
24. holophrase
25. language acquisition device (LAD)
26. baby talk

ANSWERS

CHAPTER REVIEW

1. Piaget
2. active
3. affordance
4. past experiences; developmental level; present needs; cognitive awareness
5. graspability

From a very early age, infants understand which objects afford digestibility and suckability, which afford noisemaking, which afford movability, and so forth.

6. visual cliff; visual; 3 months; heart rate
7. constancy; 3 months; boundaries; in motion
8. perceptual constancy; size; shape
9. dynamic perception

Infants use movement cues to discern not only the boundaries of objects but also their rigidity, wholeness, shape, and size. They even form expectations of the path that a moving object will follow.

10. intermodal perception; is
11. cross-modal perception; touch
12. categories; habituation
13. angularity; shape; color; density; relative size; number (up to 3 objects); faces; animals; birds
14. one's perception of them; object permanence
15. search for a hidden object; 8 months
16. $4\,^1/_2$
17. poor
18. 6 months; (a) real-life situations are used; (b) motivation is high; c) special measures aid memory retrieval
19. 2 months; reminder session
20. deferred imitation; end of the first year
21. generalize
22. infantile amnesia; recalled; implicit memory; explicit memory; implicit; explicit; language
23. cause-and-effect; launching event; 6
24. active
25. sensorimotor; 6
26. sucking, grasping, looking, listening; 1 month
27. adaptation; assimilation; schemas; accommodation; integrity

Stage-one infants suck everything that touches their lips. At about 1 month, they start to adapt their sucking to specific objects. By 3 months, they have organized the world into objects to be sucked for nourishment, objects to be sucked for pleasure, and objects not to be sucked at all.

28. 4; 8

A stage-three infant may squeeze a duck, hear a quack, and squeeze the duck again.

29. 8; 12; anticipate; goal-directed
30. 12; 18

Having discovered some action or set of actions that is possible with a given object, stage-five "little scientists" seem to ask, "What else can I do with this?"

31. 18; 24; mental combinations
32. past; future; pretend
33. follow; cries, laughs, body movements, gestures, and facial expressions; language function; understand; understood; language structure
34. speech
35. squeals, growls, grunts, croons, and yells, as well as some speechlike sounds
36. 6 or 7; babbling;
37. later; manually; at the same time as; brain; vocal apparatus
38. more

39. 1 year; 10; 100
40. referential; expressive; culture; referential
41. overextension; underextension; holophrase
42. is not; communication
43. 21
44. B. F. Skinner
45. Noam Chomsky; language acquisition device

Recent research has suggested that both Skinner's and Chomsky's theories have some validity but that both miss the mark. Developmentalists today believe that language acquisition is an interactional process between the infant's genetic predisposition and the communication that occurs in the caregiver-child relationship.

46. baby talk; Motherese

Baby talk is higher in pitch; has a characteristically low-to-high intonation pattern; uses simpler and more concrete vocabulary and shorter sentence length; and employs more questions, commands, and repetitions, and fewer past tenses, pronouns, and complex sentences.

47. (a) holding prelinguistic "conversations with the infant; (b) engaging in baby talk; (c) persistently naming objects and events that capture the child's attention; (d) expanding the child's sounds and words into meaningful communications

PROGRESS TEST 1

Multiple-Choice Questions

1. **c.** is the answer. (p. 174)
2. **c.** is the answer. (p. 191)
3. **b.** is the answer. This was Piaget's most basic contribution to the study of infant cognition—that intelligence is revealed in behavior at every age. (p. 190)
4. **c.** is the answer. (p. 180)

   a. Intermodal perception involves associating information from one sensory modality with information from another.

   b. In cross-modal perception information from one sensory modality is used to imagine something in another modality.

   d. Dynamic perception is perception that focuses on movement.
5. **c.** is the answer. (pp. 174, 188)

   b. This is Chomsky's position.

   d. This issue was not discussed in the text.
6. **a.** is the answer. (p. 192)

   b. & c. These abilities are not acquired until children are much older.

   d. Pretending is associated with stage six (18 to 24 months).
7. **c.** is the answer. (p. 181)
8. **d.** is the answer. (pp. 199–200)
9. **b.** is the answer. (p. 194)

   a., c., & d. Children the world over, and in every Piagetian stage, follow the same sequence and approximately the same timetable for early language development.
10. **c.** is the answer. (p. 197)
11. **a.** is the answer. (p. 198)

    b. Baby talk is the speech adults use with infants.

    c. An overextension is a grammatical error in which a word is generalized to an inappropriate context.

    d. An underextension is the use of a word to refer to a narrower category of objects or events than the term signifies.
12. **c.** is the answer. At every age, children understand more speech than they can produce. (p. 196)
13. **c.** is the answer. (p. 200)

    a. A holophrase is a single word uttered by a toddler to express a complete thought.

    b. According to Noam Chomsky, the LAD, or language acquisition device, is an innate ability in humans to acquire language.

    d. These characteristic differences in pitch and structure are precisely what distinguish baby talk from regular conversation.
14. **d.** is the answer. (p. 181)
15. **c.** is the answer. (p. 187)
16. **c.** is the answer (p. 185)

    a. & b. In Piaget's theory, these refer to processes by which mental concepts incorporate new experiences (assimilation) or are modified in response to new experiences (accommodation).

    d. Dynamic perception is perception that is primed to focus on movement and change.

Matching Items

1. f (p. 193)	**5.** j (p. 179)	**9.** i (p. 198)
2. g (p. 174)	**6.** d (p. 187)	**10.** a (pp. 197–198)
3. e (p. 181)	**7.** l (p. 189)	**11.** k (p. 187)
4. h (p. 178)	**8.** b (p. 195)	**12.** c (p. 178)

PROGRESS TEST 2

Multiple-Choice Questions

1. **b.** is the answer. (p. 193)

   a. & c. These are stages two and three.

   d. This is not one of Piaget's stages of sensorimotor intelligence.

2. **d.** is the answer. This is an example of perceptual constancy. (pp. 177–178)

3. **c.** is the answer. (p. 183)

4. **a.** is the answer. (p. 174)

   b. Affordances are perceptual phenomena.

   c. & d. Infants perceive graspability at an earlier age and long before their manual dexterity enables them to actually grasp successfully.

5. **d.** is the answer. (pp. 177–178)

   a. Intermodal and cross-modal perception are not limited to vision and hearing.

   b. Intermodal and cross-modal perception are *perceptual* abilities and do not involve motor responses, as hand-eye coordination does.

   c. This ability is called object permanence.

6. **d.** is the answer. (p. 198)

7. **a.** is the answer. Chomsky believed this device is innate. (p. 200)

8. **b.** is the answer. (p. 190)

   a. & c. Both of these occur later than stage one.

   d. This is a hallmark of stage six.

9. **a.** is the answer. (pp. 178–179)

10. **d.** is the answer. (p. 173)

11. **a.** is the answer. (p. 183)

12. **c.** is the answer. (p. 192)

    a. Reflexes are involuntary (and therefore unintentional) responses.

    b. Affordances are perceived opportunities for interaction with objects.

    d. Mental combinations are actions that are carried out mentally, rather than behaviorally. Moreover, mental combinations do not develop until a later age, during sensorimotor stage six.

13. **b.** is the answer. (pp. 194–197)

14. **d.** is the answer. (p. 196)

    a. & b. Hearing and deaf babies do not differ in the overall likelihood that they will babble.

    c. Deaf babies begin to babble vocally several months later than hearing babies do.

15. **b.** is the answer. (p. 199)

    a., c., & d. These views on language acquisition describe the theory offered by Noam Chomsky.

16. **a.** is the answer. (p. 186)

    b. & d. These perceptual processes do not require language.

    c. Implicit memories often are triggered by nonlinguistic stimuli, such as sights or smells.

Matching Items

1. j (p. 192)	**5.** b (p. 190)	**9.** e (p. 180)
2. a (p. 177)	**6.** i (p. 193)	**10.** k (p. 190)
3. d (p. 186)	**7.** c (p. 187)	**11.** g (p. 200)
4. h (p. 200)	**8.** f (p. 197)	

THINKING CRITICALLY ABOUT CHAPTER 6

1. **d.** is the answer. The baby is clearly behaving purposefully, the hallmark of goal-directed behavior. (p. 192)

   a. There is nothing imaginary in the child's behavior.

   b. An overextension occurs when the infant overgeneralizes the use of a word to an inappropriate object or context.

   c. Delayed imitation is the ability to imitate actions seen in the past.

2. **c.** is the answer. Intermodal perception is the ability to associate information from one sensory modality with information from another. In the example, the infant is associating visual information (the sight of the CD player) with auditory information (the sound of a CD). (p. 178)

   a. Cross-modal perception is the ability to use information from one sensory modality to imagine something in another.

   b. Goal-directed behavior is purposeful action.

   d. Object permanence is the awareness that objects do not cease to exist when they are out of sight.

3. **d.** is the answer. (p. 179)

   a. Delayed imitation is the ability to imitate actions seen in the past.

   b. Affordances are perceived opportunities for interacting with objects.

   c. Categorization refers to cognitively classifying objects according to certain features.

4. **a.** is the answer. The father's expression of delight is clearly a reinforcer in that it has increased the likelihood of the infant's vocalization. (p. 199)

   b. & c. Modeling, or learning by imitation, would be implicated if the father attempted to increase the infant's vocalizations by repeatedly saying "da-da" himself, in the infant's presence.

   d. This is Chomsky's viewpoint; Skinner maintained that language is acquired through learning.

5. **d.** is the answer. The child is clearly overgeneralizing the word "dog" by applying it to other animals. (p. 197)

   a. The holophrase is a single word that is used to express a complete thought.

   b. Babbling is the repetitious uttering of certain syllables, such as "ma-ma," or "da-da."

   c. Motherese, or baby talk, is the characteristic manner in which adults change the structure and pitch of their speech when conversing with infants.

6. **c.** is the answer. (p. 198)

   a. At 18 months of age, most children have much smaller vocabularies.

   b. Speaking in holophrases is typical of younger infants.

7. **d.** is the answer. (p. 193)

   a. Dynamic perception is perception primed to focus on movement and change.

   b. Object permanence is the awareness that objects do not cease to exist when they are out of sight.

   c. Intermodal perception is the ability to associate information from one sensory modality with information from another.

8. **c.** is the answer. (p. 191)

9. **b.** is the answer. Infants can remember, but their recollections consist not of words but of sensations. (pp. 186–187)

10. **d.** is the answer. (p. 197)

11. **a.** is the answer. Before object permanence is attained, an object that disappears from sight ceases to exist for the infant. (p. 181)

    b. Intermodal perception is the ability to associate information from one sensory modality with information from another.

    c. Mental combinations are actions that are carried out mentally.

    d. Cross-modal perception is the ability to use information from one sensory modality to imagine something in another.

12. **c.** is the answer. (p. 198)

    a. Because Christine is expressing a complete thought, her speech is much more than babbling.

    b. An overextension is the application of a word the child knows to an inappropriate context, such as "doggie" to all animals the child sees.

    d. The ability to understand subject-predicate order emerges later, when children begin forming 2-word sentences.

13. **b.** is the answer. (p. 195)

    a. Cooing is the pleasant-sounding utterances of the infant at about 2 months.

    c. The holophrase occurs later and refers to the toddler's use of a single word to express a complete thought.

    d. An overextension, or overgeneralization, is the application of a word to an inappropriate context, such as "doed" for the past tense of "do."

14. **b.** is the answer. In this example, the 2-year-old has overgeneralized the concept "doggie" to all four-legged animals. (p. 197)

15. **c.** is the answer. (p. 180)

    a. & b. These perceptual abilities are based on the integration of perceptual information from different sensory systems.

    d. Object permanence, or the awareness that objects do not cease to exist simply because they are not in view, is not based on perceiving similarities among objects.

16. **b.** is the answer. (p. 197)

    c. & d. Referential language focuses on labeling; expressive language focuses on social interaction.

KEY TERMS

1. **Affordances** are perceived opportunities for interacting with objects in the environment. Infants perceive sucking, grasping, noisemaking, and many other affordances of objects at an early age. (p. 174)

2. **Graspability** is the perception of whether or not an object is of the proper size, shape, texture, and distance to afford grasping or grabbing. (p. 174)

3. A **visual cliff** is an apparent (but not actual) drop between one surface and another. (p. 175)

4. **Object constancy** is the concept that objects retain their identity, despite changes in their

appearance or movement caused by shifts in the observer, the object, or the context. (p. 177)

5. **Perceptual constancy** is the awareness that the size and shape of an object remain the same despite changes in the object's appearance due to changes in its location. (p. 177)

6. **Dynamic perception** is perception that is primed to focus on movement and change. (p. 178)

7. **Intermodal perception** is the ability to connect, simultaneously, information from one sensory modality with information from another. (p. 178)

8. **Cross-modal perception** is the ability to translate information from one sensory modality to another. (p. 179)

9. **Object permanence** is the understanding that objects continue to exist even when they cannot be seen, touched, or heard. (p. 181)

10. A **reminder session** involves the experiencing of some aspect of an event that triggers the entire memory of the event. (p. 184)

11. **Deferred imitation** is the ability to witness, remember, and later copy a behavior that has been witnessed. (p. 185)

12. **Implicit memory** is memory of experiences that can be recognized but not necessarily recalled. (p. 187)

13. **Explicit memory** is memory that can be recalled on demand and demonstrated verbally. (p. 187)

14. The **launching event** is a commonly used habituation technique for studying infants' awareness of cause-and-effect relationships. (p. 187)

15. Piaget's stages of **sensorimotor intelligence** (from birth to about 2 years old) are based on his theory that infants think exclusively with their senses and motor skills. (p. 189)

16. **Goal-directed behavior** refers to purposeful actions initiated by infants in anticipation of events that will fulfill their needs and wishes. (p. 192)

17. "**Little scientist**" is Piaget's term for the stage-five toddler who learns about the properties of objects in his or her world through active experimentation. (p. 193)

18. In Piaget's theory, **mental combinations** are sequences of actions that are carried out mentally. Mental combinations enable stage-six toddlers to begin to anticipate and solve problems without resorting to trial-and-error experiments. (p. 193)

19. **Language function** refers to the primary purpose of language—communication, allowing people to understand, and be understood by, others. (p. 194)

20. **Language structure** refers to the body of sounds, words, and rules of a particular language. (p. 194)

21. **Babbling**, which begins at 6 or 7 months, is characterized by the extended repetition of certain syllables (such as "ma-ma"). (p. 195)

22. An **underextension** of word meaning occurs when a baby applies a word more narrowly than its full meaning allows. (p. 197)

23. **Overextension** is a characteristic of infant speech in which the infant overgeneralizes a known word by applying it to a large variety of objects or contexts. (pp. 197–198)

    Memory aid: In this behavior, the infant *extends* a word or grammatical rule beyond, or *over* and above, its normal boundaries.

24. Another characteristic of infant speech is the use of the **holophrase**, in which a single word is used to convey a complete thought. (p. 198)

25. According to Chomsky, children possess an innate **language acquisition device (LAD)** that enables them to acquire language, including the basic aspects of grammar. (p. 198)

26. **Baby talk**, or motherese, is a form of speech used by adults when talking to infants. Its hallmark is exaggerated expressiveness; it employs more questions, commands, and repetitions and fewer past tenses, pronouns, and complex sentences; it uses simpler vocabulary and grammar; it has a higher pitch and more low-to-high fluctuations. (p. 200)

CHAPTER 7

The First 2 Years: Psychosocial Development

Chapter Overview

Chapter 7 describes the emotional and social life of the developing person during the first two years. It begins with a description of the infant's emerging emotions and how they reflect increasing cognitive abilities. Newborns are innately predisposed to sociability, and capable of expressing distress, sadness, contentment, and many other emotions, as well as responding to the emotions of other people.

The second section explores the social context in which emotions develop. By referencing their caregivers' signals, infants learn when and how to express their emotions. As self-awareness develops, many new emotions emerge, including embarrassment, shame, guilt, and pride.

The third section presents the theories of Freud and Erikson that help us understand how the infant's emotional and behavioral responses begin to take on the various patterns that form personality. Important research on the nature and origins of temperament, which informs virtually every characteristic of the individual's developing personality, is also considered.

In the final section, emotions and relationships are examined from a different perspective—that of parent–infant interaction. Videotaped studies of parents and infants, combined with laboratory studies of attachment, have greatly expanded our understanding of psychosocial development.

NOTE: Answer guidelines for all Chapter 7 questions begin on page 114.

Guided Study

The text chapter should be studied one section at a time. Before you read, preview each section by skimming it, noting headings and boldface items. Then read the appropriate section objectives from the following outline. Keep these objectives in mind and, as you read the chapter section, search for the information that will enable you to meet each objective. Once you have finished a section, write out answers for its objectives.

Early Emotions (pp. 207–210)

1. Describe the basic emotions expressed by infants during the first days and months.

2. Describe the main developments in the emotional life of the child between 6 months and 2 years.

Emotions as a Social Window (pp. 210–216)

3. Discuss the concept of social referencing, including its development and role in shaping later emotions.

4. (Changing Policy) Discuss contemporary views on the role of the father in infant psychosocial development.

5. Discuss the links between the infant's emerging self-awareness and its continuing emotional development.

The Origins of Personality (pp. 216–223)

6. Describe the evolution of learning theory with regard to personality development.

7. Describe Freud's psychosexual stages of infant development.

8. Describe Erikson's psychosocial stages of infant development.

9. Discuss the origins and development of temperament as an interaction of nature and nurture, and explain the significance of research on temperament for parents and caregivers.

Interaction Again (pp. 223–236)

10. Describe the synchrony of parent–infant interaction during the first year, and discuss its significance for the developing person.

11. Define attachment, explain how it is measured and how it is influenced by context, and discuss the long-term consequences of secure and insecure attachment.

12. (Research Report) Describe four categories of adult attachments and how each affects the child's attachment to the parent.

13. Discuss concerns regarding day care, and identify the factors that define high-quality day care.

Chapter Review

When you have finished reading the chapter, work through the material that follows to review it. Complete the sentences and answer the questions. As you proceed, evaluate your performance for each section by consulting the answers on page 114. Do not continue with the next section until you understand each answer. If you need to, review or reread the appropriate section in the textbook before continuing.

1. Developmentalists believe that infants ______________ (are/are not) innately predisposed to sociability.

Early Emotions (pp. 207–210)

2. The first emotion that can be reliably discerned in infants is ______________. Other early infant emotions include ______________, ______________, and ______________.

3. The infant's smile in response to a human face or voice, which is called a ______________, begins to appear at about ______________ of age. The development of smiling ______________ (is/is not) universal in infants. Infants begin to express anger when they are frustrated by about ______________ of age.

4. Infant emotions become more differentiated and distinct sometime between ______________ of age. At this age, individual differences in the ______________ and ______________ with which emotions occur are also apparent.

5. Stranger ______________ is first noticeable at about ______________ of age. All infants ______________ (do/do not) experience this fear. How a baby responds to a stranger depends on aspects of the infant, such as ______________, as well as on the situation and the stranger.

6. An infant's fear of being left by the mother or other caregiver, called ______________, peaks at about ______________ of age and then gradually subsides. Whether separation distresses an infant depends on such factors as ______________.

7. As infants become older, emotions such as frustration and anger ______________ (intensify/weaken) as cognition regarding ______________-______________ actions increases. At the same time, infants become ______________ (better/worse) at handling their emotions.

Emotions as a Social Window (pp. 210-216)

8. As early as ______________ of age, infants associate ______________ meanings with specific ______________ expressions and with different tones of voice. For example, infants look to trusted adults for emotional cues in uncertain situations; this is called ______________. This becomes increasingly important as the infant becomes more ______________.

9. Infants use their fathers for social reference ______________ (less than/about the same as/more than) their mothers. Fathers tend to be more ______________, and mothers more ______________.

Briefly contrast how mothers and fathers tend to play with their infants.

10. (Changing Policy) Traditional views of infant development focused ______________ (exclusively on mothers/on both mothers and fathers). Overall, researchers ______________ (have/have not) found evidence that women are biologically predisposed to be better parents than men are.

11. (Changing Policy) In contemporary marriages, with both parents working outside the home, most child caregiving is ______________

(shared equally by mothers and fathers/done by the mother). Even so, fathers spend more time ________________ with their children. Overall, fathering is more a result of ________________ ________________ and ________________ than mothering is.

12. At 12 months of age, infants look to caregivers for ________________ messages, rather than for ________________ attitudes of approval or disapproval. The social signals a young child receives might have an effect on future ________________ development as well as ________________ .

Briefly explain how the kinds of signals caregivers send to toddlers influence their overall emotionality.

13. The emerging sense of "me and mine" is part of what psychologists call ________________ . This makes possible many new self-conscious emotions, including ________________ , ________________ , ________________ , and ________________ .

14. In the first few months, infants ________________ (do/do not) have a sense of self and/or an awareness of their bodies as their own.

Briefly describe the nature and findings of the classic rouge-and-mirror experiment on self-awareness in infants.

15. Developing self-awareness also enhances the toddler's ________________ reactions and emotional responses such as ________________ . Furthermore, it allows the child to react to his or her misdeeds with ________________ at going against another's wishes.

The Origins of Personality (pp. 216–223)

16. An early prevailing view among psychologists was that the individual's personality was permanently molded by the actions of his or her ________________ . Two versions of this theory were the ________________ and ________________ theories.

17. According to early learning theory, personality is molded through the processes of ________________ and ________________ of the child's various behaviors. A strong proponent of this position was ________________ . Later theorists incorporated the role of ________________ learning, that is, infants' tendency to ________________ the personality traits of their parents.

18. According to Freud, the experiences of the first ________________ years of life and the child's relationship with his or her ________________ were decisive in personality formation.

19. In Freud's theory, development begins with the ________________ stage, so named because the ________________ is the infant's prime source of gratification and pleasure.

20. According to Freud, in the ________________ year the prime focus of gratification comes from stimulation and control of the bowels. Freud referred to this period as the ________________ stage. This stage represents a shift in the way the infant interacts with others, from the more ________________ , ________________ mode of orality to the more ________________ , ________________ mode of anality.

Describe Freud's ideas on the importance of early oral experiences to later personality development.

21. Research has shown that the parents' overall pattern of ______________________ is more important to the child's emotional development than the particulars of feeding and weaning or toilet training.

22. The theorist who believed that development occurs through a series of psychosocial crises is ______________. According to his theory, the crisis of infancy is one of ______________________, whereas the crisis of toddlerhood is one of ______________________. He maintained that experiences later in life ______________ (can alter/have little impact on) the effects of early experiences on personality development.

23. The traditional views of personality emphasize the importance of early ______________, particularly that provided by a child's ______________.

24. A person's inherent, relatively consistent, basic dispositions define his or her ______________. This overall makeup, which ______________ (is/is not) evident at birth, begins in the ______________ codes that guide the development of the brain and is affected by many prenatal experiences, including ______________ ______________________. However, as the person develops, the ______________ ______________ and the individual's ______________ increasingly influence the nature and expression of this trait.

25. List the nine temperamental characteristics measured in the NYLS study:

____

____

26. Most young infants can be described as one of three types: ______________, ______________ ______________, ______________ ______________, or ______________.

27. Although some researchers of adult personality see temperament types as ______________ patterns, temperament evolves over time, with shifts being particularly likely during the first ______________ years.

28. The "big five" dimensions of personality are ______________, ______________, ______________, ______________, and ______________.

29. Two aspects of temperament that are quite variable are ______________ and ______________.

Describe two ways in which the environment can influence a child's temperamental characteristics.

Interaction Again (pp. 223–236)

30. Although infants are social from birth, they are not necessarily socially ______________.

31. Infants under 3 months of age often become upset for reasons that have little to do with the ______________ they receive. At this age, ______________ (boys/girls) tend to be fussier than ______________ (boys/girls).

32. Babies begin to respond especially to their primary caregivers by ______________ months

of age. At this time, caregivers begin to initiate focused episodes of ______________-______________-______________ play.

33. The coordinated interaction of response between infant and caregiver is called ______________. Partly through this interaction, infants learn to ______________ and ______________ emotions.

Describe the social play behaviors of adults with infants.

34. Episodes of face-to-face play ______________ (are/are not) a universal feature of early interaction with infants.

35. Cultural variations in the ______________ and ______________ of social play, as well as the ______________ of the adults who initiate face-to-face episodes, are common.

36. (Children Up Close) The signs of dyssynchrony include ______________ ______________.The ease of synchrony is affected not only by the caregiver's personality but also by the infant's ______________ and ______________.

37. The emotional bond that develops between parents and infants is called ______________.

38. Approaching, following, and climbing onto the caregiver's lap are signs of ______________-______________ behaviors, while clinging and resisting being put down are signs of ______________-______________ behaviors.

39. An infant who derives comfort and confidence from the secure base provided by the caregiver is displaying ______________ ______________.

By contrast, ______________ ______________ is characterized by an infant's fear, anger, or seeming indifference to the caregiver.

40. The procedure developed by Ainsworth to measure attachment is called the ______________.

Approximately ______________-______________ (what proportion?) of American infants tested with this procedure demonstrate secure attachment.

Briefly describe three types of insecure attachment.

41. Among the features of caregiving that affect the quality of attachment are the following:

a. ______________

b. ______________

c. ______________

42. Attachment may also be affected by the broader family context, including the quality of the ______________'s involvement in child care, the ______________, ______________, and ______________. It is also affected by ______________ and by the infant's ______________.

43. Cross-cultural comparisons of the Strange Situation reveal that children from ______________ and ______________ show a higher rate of insecure-resistant attachment than do American infants, whereas infants from Germany show higher rates of ______________. Overall, such studies demonstrate that the majority of infants in the Strange Situation exhibit ______________ attachment.

44. Most infants ______________ (do/do not) show signs of attachment to other caregivers, such as fathers, siblings, and day-care workers.

45. By itself, a secure or insecure attachment in infancy ______________ (determines/does not determine) a child's later social relationships.

46. (Research Report) Mary Main has found that adults can be classified into one of four categories of attachment: ______________ adults, who value attachment relationships but can discuss them objectively; ______________ adults, who devalue attachment; ______________ adults, who dwell on past relationships; and ______________ adults, who have not yet reconciled their past experiences with the present.

47. (Research Report) Autonomous mothers tend to have infants who are ______________ attached, dismissing mothers tend to have ______________ babies, and preoccupied mothers tend to have ______________ infants.

State several possible reasons for the link between adult and infant attachment.

48. According to Jay Belsky, extended infant day care ______________ (is/is not) likely to result in negative developmental outcomes. Belsky admits, however—and other research has convincingly demonstrated—that when preschoolers experience early and extended amounts of high quality day care, they show more ______________ (positive/negative) outcomes than children without such experience.

49. Researchers have identified four factors that seem essential to high-quality day care:

(a) ______________

(b) ______________

(c) ______________

(d) ______________

50. A large-scale study of day care in the United States found that infants were likely to become insecurely attached only under three circumstances: (a) ______________; (b) ______________; and (c) ______________.

Progress Test 1

Multiple-Choice Questions

Circle your answers to the following questions and check them with the answers on page 116. If your answer is incorrect, read the explanation for why it is incorrect and then consult the appropriate pages of the text (in parentheses following the correct answer).

1. One of the first emotions that can be discerned in infancy is:

a. shame.
b. distress.
c. guilt.
d. pride.

2. The social smile begins to appear:

a. at about 6 weeks.
b. at about 8 months.
c. after stranger wariness has been overcome.
d. after the infant has achieved a sense of self.

3. An infant's fear of being left by the mother or other caregiver, called ______________, peaks at about ______________.

a. separation anxiety; 14 months
b. stranger wariness; 8 months
c. separation anxiety; 8 months
d. stranger wariness; 14 months

4. Social referencing refers to:

a. parenting skills that change over time.
b. changes in community values regarding, for example, the acceptability of using physical punishment with small children.
c. the support network for new parents provided by extended family members.
d. the infant response of looking to trusted adults for emotional cues in uncertain situations.

5. The "big five" personality dimensions are:
   a. emotional stability, openness, introversion, sociability, locus of control
   b. neuroticism, extroversion, openness, emotional stability, sensitivity
   c. agreeableness, conscientiousness, neuroticism, openness, extroversion
   d. neuroticism, gregariousness, extroversion, impulsiveness, sensitivity

6. Psychologists who favored the ______________ perspective believed that the personality of the child was virtually "created" through reinforcement and punishment.
   a. psychoanalytic
   b. learning
   c. psychosocial
   d. epigenetic

7. Freud's oral stage corresponds to Erikson's crisis of:
   a. orality versus anality.
   b. trust versus mistrust.
   c. autonomy versus shame and doubt.
   d. secure versus insecure attachment.

8. Erikson feels that the development of a sense of trust in early infancy depends on the quality of the:
   a. infant's food.
   b. child's genetic inheritance.
   c. maternal relationship.
   d. introduction of toilet training.

9. The increased tendency of toddlers to express frustration and anger is most closely linked to new developments in their cognitive abilities, especially those related to:
   a. goal-directed actions.
   b. social referencing.
   c. self-awareness.
   d. stranger wariness.

10. "Easy," "slow to warm up," and "difficult" are descriptions of different:
    a. forms of attachment.
    b. types of temperament.
    c. types of parenting.
    d. toddler responses to the Strange Situation.

11. Research studies of infant caregiving have found that all but which one of the following is true?
    a. When both parents work outside the home, child care tends to be shared equally by mothers and fathers.
    b. Fathers can provide the emotional and cognitive nurturing that children need.
    c. Divorced fathers spend less time caring for infants than married fathers do.
    d. Contemporary fathers are more actively engaged with their children than fathers were in 1970.

12. *Synchrony* is a term that describes:
    a. the carefully coordinated interaction between parent and infant.
    b. a mismatch of the temperaments of parent and infant.
    c. a research technique involving videotapes.
    d. the concurrent evolution of different species.

13. The emotional tie that develops between an infant and his or her primary caregiver is called:
    a. self-awareness.
    b. synchrony.
    c. affiliation.
    d. attachment.

14. An important effect of secure attachment is the promotion of:
    a. self-awareness.
    b. curiosity and self-directed behavior.
    c. dependency.
    d. all of the above.

15. The sight of almost any human face is most likely to produce a smile in a ____________-month-old.
    a. 3
    b. 6
    c. 9
    d. 12

True or False Items

Write *true* or *false* on the line in front of each statement.

_______ 1. Most developmentalists think that infants must learn to be sociable.

_______ 2. The major difference between a 6-month-old and a 12-month-old is that emotions become less intense.

_______ 3. A baby at 11 months is likely to display both stranger wariness and separation anxiety.

_______ 4. Emotional development is affected by cognitive development.

_______ 5. A securely attached toddler is most likely to stay close to his or her mother even in a familiar environment.

_______ 6. Current research shows that the majority of infants in day care are insecurely attached.

_______ 7. Women are biologically predisposed to be better parents than men are.

_______ 8. Temperament is genetically determined and is unaffected by environmental factors.

_______ 9. Self-awareness enables toddlers to be self-critical and to feel guilt.

_______ 10. Adult attachment classifications parallel those of infancy.

Progress Test 2

Progress Test 2 should be completed during a final chapter review. Answer the following questions after you thoroughly understand the correct answers for the Chapter Review and Progress Test 1.

Multiple-Choice Questions

1. Infants give their first real smiles, called _______, when they are about _______ of age.
   a. play smiles; 3 months
   b. play smiles; 6 weeks
   c. social smiles; 3 months
   d. social smiles; 6 weeks

2. Freud's anal stage corresponds to Erikson's crisis of:
   a. autonomy versus shame and doubt.
   b. trust versus mistrust.
   c. orality versus anality.
   d. identity versus role confusion.

3. Not until the sense of self begins to emerge do babies realize that they are seeing their own faces in the mirror. This realization usually occurs:
   a. shortly before 3 months.
   b. at about 6 months.
   c. between 15 and 24 months.
   d. after 24 months.

4. Infants who are placed in day care are most likely to become insecurely attached if they are in day care more than 20 hours a week, if the day care quality is poor, and if:
   a. their mothers are insensitive
   b. they come from broken homes.
   c. they have a difficult temperament.
   d. their own parents were insecurely attached.

5. Emotions such as shame, guilt, embarrassment, and pride emerge at the same time that:
   a. the social smile appears.
   b. aspects of the infant's temperament can first be discerned.
   c. self-awareness begins to emerge.
   d. parents initiate toilet training.

6. According to the research, the NYLS temperamental characteristics that are not particularly stable are quality of mood and:
   a. rhythmicity.
   b. activity level.
   c. self-awareness.
   d. sociability (or shyness).

7. In the second six months, stranger wariness is a:
   a. result of insecure attachment.
   b. result of social isolation.
   c. normal emotional response.
   d. setback in emotional development.

8. The caregiving environment can affect a child's temperament through:
   a. the child's temperamental pattern and the demands of the home environment.
   b. parental expectations.
   c. both a. and b.
   d. neither a. nor b.

9. Compared to children who are insecurely attached, those who are securely attached are:
   a. more independent.
   b. more curious.
   c. more sociable.
   d. characterized by all of the above.

10. The later consequences of secure attachment and insecure attachment for children are:
    a. balanced by the child's current rearing circumstances.
    b. irreversible, regardless of the child's current rearing circumstances.
    c. more significant in girls than in boys.
    d. more significant in boys than in girls.

11. Beginning at _______ of age, infants begin to associate emotional meaning with different facial expressions of emotion.
    a. 3 months
    b. 4 months
    c. 5 months
    d. 6 months

12. Compared with mothers, fathers are more likely to:
    a. engage in noisier, more boisterous play.
    b. encourage intellectual development in their children.
    c. encourage social development in their children.
    d. read to their toddlers.

13. Unlike Freud, Erikson believed that:
    a. problems arising in early infancy can last a lifetime.
    b. experiences later in life can alter the effects of early experiences.
    c. the first two years of life are fraught with potential conflict.
    d. all of the above are true.

14. Which of the following most accurately summarizes the relationship between early attachment and later social relationships?
    a. Attachment in infancy determines whether a child will grow to be sociable.
    b. Attachment relationships are sometimes, though rarely, altered as children grow older.
    c. There is, at best, only a weak correlation between early attachment and later social relationships.
    d. Early attachment biases, but does not inevitably determine, later social relationships.

15. In her research, Mary Main has discovered that:
    a. adult attachment classifications parallel those of infancy.
    b. autonomous mothers tend to have insecurely attached babies.
    c. preoccupied mothers tend to have avoidant babies.
    d. all of the above are true.

Matching Items

Match each theorist, term, or concept with its corresponding description or definition.

Theorists, Terms, or Concepts

_______ 1. temperament
_______ 2. Erikson
_______ 3. the Strange Situation
_______ 4. synchrony
_______ 5. trust versus mistrust
_______ 6. Freud
_______ 7. social referencing
_______ 8. autonomy versus shame and doubt
_______ 9. self-awareness
_______ 10. Ainsworth
_______ 11. proximity-seeking behaviors
_______ 12. contact-maintaining behaviors

Descriptions or Definitions

a. looking to caregivers for emotional cues
b. the crisis of infancy
c. the crisis of toddlerhood
d. approaching, following, and climbing
e. theorist who described psychosexual stages of development
f. researcher who devised a laboratory procedure for studying attachment
g. laboratory procedure for studying attachment
h. the relatively consistent, basic dispositions inherent in a person
i. clinging and resisting being put down
j. coordinated interaction between parent and infant
k. theorist who described psychosocial stages of development
l. a person's sense of being distinct from others

Thinking Critically About Chapter 7

Answer these questions the day before an exam as a final check on your understanding of the chapter's terms and concepts.

1. In laboratory tests of attachment, when the mother returns to the playroom after a short absence, a securely attached infant is most likely to:
   a. cry and protest the mother's return.
   b. climb into the mother's lap, then leave to resume play.
   c. climb into the mother's lap and stay there.
   d. continue playing without acknowledging the mother.

2. After a scary fall, 18-month-old Miguel looks to his mother to see if he should cry or laugh. Miguel's behavior is an example of:
   a. proximity-seeking behavior.
   b. contact-maintaining behavior.
   c. insecure attachment.
   d. the crisis of trust versus mistrust.

3. Which of the following is a clear sign of an infant's attachment to a particular person?
   a. The infant turns to that person when distressed.
   b. The infant protests when that person leaves a room.
   c. The infant may cry when strangers appear.
   d. All of the above are signs of infant attachment.

4. If you had to predict a newborn baby's personality "type" solely on the basis of probability, which classification would be the most likely?
   a. easy
   b. slow-to-warm-up
   c. difficult
   d. There is not enough information to make a prediction.

5. (Research Report) Kenny becomes very emotional when talking about his relationship with his parents; consequently, he is unable to discuss his early attachment experiences objectively. Kenny's attachment classification is probably:
   a. autonomous.
   b. dismissing.
   c. preoccupied.
   d. unresolved.

6. Which of the following mothers is most likely to have an avoidant son or daughter?
   a. Claudia, who is still coping with the loss of her parents
   b. Kaleen, who idealizes her parents, yet devalues the importance of her own relationships
   c. Pearl, who is able to discuss her own early attachment experiences quite objectively, despite their painful nature
   d. Carmen, who spends a lot of time thinking about her own relationship with her parents

7. One way in which infant psychosocial development has changed is that today:
   a. many infants have their first encounters with other infants at a younger age.
   b. parental influence is less important than it was in the past.
   c. social norms are nearly the same for the sexes.
   d. infants tend to have fewer social encounters than in the past.

8. (Changing Policy) Jack, who is about to become a father and primary caregiver, is worried that he will never have the natural caregiving skills that the child's mother has. Studies on father–infant relationships show that:
   a. infants nurtured by single fathers are more likely to be insecurely attached.
   b. fathers can provide the emotional and cognitive nurturing necessary for healthy infant development.
   c. women are biologically predisposed to be better parents than men are.
   d. social development is usually slightly delayed in children whose fathers are the primary caregiver.

9. Kalil's mother left him alone in the room for a few minutes. When she returned, Kalil seemed indifferent to her presence. According to Mary Ainsworth's research with children in the Strange Situation, Kalil is probably:
   a. a normal, independent infant.
   b. an abused child.
   c. insecurely attached.
   d. securely attached.

10. Connie and Lev, who are first-time parents, are concerned because their 1-month-old baby is difficult to care for and hard to soothe. They are worried that they are doing something wrong. You inform them that their child is probably that way because:
    a. they are reinforcing the child's tantrum behaviors.
    b. they are not meeting some biological need of the child's.
    c. of his or her inherited temperament.
    d. at 1 month of age all children are difficult to care for and hard to soothe.

11. Two-year-old Anita and her mother visit a day-care center. Seeing an interesting toy, Anita runs a few steps toward it, then stops and looks back to see if her mother is coming. Anita's behavior illustrates:
    a. the crisis of autonomy versus shame and doubt.
    b. synchrony.
    c. dyssynchrony.
    d. social referencing.

12. Felix has a biting, sarcastic manner. Freud would probably say that Felix is:
    a. anally expulsive.
    b. anally retentive.
    c. fixated in the oral stage.
    d. experiencing the crisis of trust versus mistrust.

13. A researcher at the child development center places a dot on an infant's nose and watches to see if the infant reacts to her image in a mirror by touching her nose. Evidently, the researcher is testing the child's:
    a. attachment.
    b. temperament.
    c. self-awareness.
    d. social referencing.

14. Four-month-old Carl and his 13-month-old sister Carla are left in the care of a babysitter. As their parents are leaving, it is to be expected that:
    a. Carl will become extremely upset, while Carla will calmly accept her parents' departure.
    b. Carla will become more upset over her parents' departure than will Carl.
    c. Carl and Carla will both become quite upset as their parents leave.
    d. Neither Carl nor Carla will become very upset as their parents leave.

15. You have been asked to give a presentation on "Mother–Infant Attachment" to a group of expectant mothers. Basing your presentation on the research of Mary Ainsworth, you conclude your talk by stating that mother–infant attachment depends mostly on:
    a. an infant's innate temperament.
    b. the amount of time mothers spend with their infants.
    c. sensitive and responsive caregiving in the early months.
    d. whether the mother herself was securely attached as an infant.

Key Terms

Using your own words, write a brief definition or explanation of each of the following terms on a separate piece of paper.

1. social smile
2. stranger wariness
3. separation anxiety
4. social referencing
5. self-awareness
6. personality
7. oral stage
8. anal stage
9. trust versus mistrust
10. autonomy versus shame and doubt
11. temperament
12. big five
13. goodness of fit
14. synchrony
15. attachment
16. proximity-seeking behaviors
17. contact-maintaining behaviors
18. secure attachment
19. insecure attachment
20. Strange Situation

ANSWERS

CHAPTER REVIEW

1. are
2. distress; sadness; interest; pleasure,

3. social smile; 6 weeks; is; 4 to 7 months
4. 6 and 9 months; intensity; speed
5. wariness; 6 months; do not; temperament and the security of the mother-infant relationship
6. separation anxiety; 14 months; the baby's prior experiences with separation and the manner in which the parent departs
7. intensify; goal-directed; better
8. 5 months; emotional; facial; social referencing; mobile
9. about the same as; encouraging; protective

Fathers' play is noisier, more boisterous, and idiosyncratic. Mothers' play is more physically restrained, and they tend to play conventional games.

10. exclusively on mothers; have not
11. done by the mother; playing; personal choice; culture
12. specific; overall; brain; cognition

If toddlers receive more signals of interest and encouragement than of fear and prohibition as they explore, they are likely to be friendlier and less aggressive. If an infant or toddler sees few signals of any kind, the child becomes relatively passive and emotionless.

13. self-awareness; embarrassment; guilt; shame; pride
14. do not

In the classic self-awareness experiment, babies look in a mirror after a dot of rouge is put on their nose. If the babies react to the mirror image by touching their nose, it is clear they know they are seeing their own face. Most babies demonstrate this self-awareness between 15 and 24 months of age.

15. self-critical; shame; guilt
16. parents; learning; psychoanalytic
17. reinforcement; punishment; John Watson; social; imitate
18. 4; mother
19. oral; mouth
20. second; anal; passive; dependent; active; controlling

Freud believed that the oral and anal stages are fraught with potential conflict that can have long-term consequences for the infant. If nursing is a hurried or tense event, for example, the child may become fixated at the oral stage, excessively eating, drinking, smoking, or talking in quest of oral satisfaction.

21. warmth and sensitivity or coldness and domination
22. Erikson; trust versus mistrust; autonomy versus shame and doubt; can alter
23. nurture; mother
24. temperament; is; genetic; the nutrition and health of the mother; social context; experiences
25. activity level; rhythmicity; approach-withdrawal; adaptability; intensity of reaction; threshold of responsiveness; quality of mood; distractibility; attention span
26. easy; slow to warm up; difficult
27. lifelong; 2
28. extroversion; agreeableness; conscientiousness; neuroticism; openness
29. rhythmicity; quality of mood

One way is through the "goodness of fit" between the child's temperamental patterns and the demands of the home environment. Parents' expectations also can influence temperament.

30. competent
31. care; boys; girls
32. 2 to 3; face-to-face
33. synchrony; express; read

Adults tend to open their eyes and mouths wide in exaggerated expressions, make rapid clicking noises or repeated one-syllable sounds, raise and lower the pitch of their voice, change the pace of their movements, and imitate the infant's actions, for example.

34. are
35. frequency; duration; goals
36. averted eyes, stiffening or abrupt shifting of the body, and/or an unhappy noise; personality; predispositions
37. attachment
38. proximity-seeking; contact-maintaining
39. secure attachment; insecure attachment
40. Strange Situation; two-thirds

Some infants are avoidant: They engage in little interaction with their mother before and after her departure. Others are anxious and resistant: They cling nervously to their mother, are unwilling to explore, cry loudly when she leaves, and refuse to be comforted when she returns. Others are disoriented: They show an inconsistent mixture of behavior toward the mother.

41. a. general sensitivity to the infant's needs
    b. responsiveness to the infant's specific signals

c. talking and playing with the infant in ways that actively encourage growth and development

42. father; marital relationship; overall social context; changes in family circumstances; temperament

43. Israel; Japan; avoidance; secure

44. do

45. does not determine

46. autonomous; dismissing; preoccupied; unresolved

47. securely; avoidant; resistant

Parents who value attachment may be more sensitive to their offspring and inspire secure attachment as a result; or innate temperament may predispose a certain attachment pattern across most relationships; or the nature of parents' attachment with their children may influence their memories of, and attitudes about, other attachments.

48. is; positive

49. (a) adequate attention to each child; (b) encouragement of sensorimotor exploration and language development; (c) attention to health and safety; (d) well-trained and professional caregivers.

50. (a) if their mothers were insensitive; (b) if the day-care quality was poor, (c) if they were in day care more than 20 hours per week

PROGRESS TEST 1

Multiple-Choice Questions

1. **b.** is the answer. (p. 207)

   a., c., & d. These emotions emerge later in infancy, at about the same time as self-awareness emerges.

2. **a.** is the answer. (p. 208)

3. **a.** is the answer. (p. 209)

   b. & d. This fear, which is also called fear of strangers, peaks by 10 to 14 months.

4. **d.** is the answer. (p. 210)

5. **c.** is the answer. (p. 222)

6. **b.** is the answer. (p. 217)

   a. Reinforcement and punishment have no place in the psychoanalytic perspective.

   c. This is Erikson's theory, which sees development as occurring through a series of basic crises.

   d. This perspective analyzes how genes and environment contribute to development.

7. **b.** is the answer. (pp. 217–218)

   a. Orality and anality refer to personality traits that result from fixation in the oral and anal stages, respectively.

   c. According to Erikson, this is the crisis of toddlerhood, which corresponds to Freud's anal stage.

   d. This is not a developmental crisis in Erikson's theory.

8. **c.** is the answer. (p. 219)

9. **a.** is the answer. Anger increases with age because toddlers are able to anticipate events and realize that other people's actions sometimes block their own efforts. (p. 210)

10. **b.** is the answer. (p. 221)

    a. "Secure" and "insecure" are different forms of attachment.

    c. The chapter does not describe different types of parenting.

    d. The Strange Situation is a test of attachment, rather than of temperament.

11. **a.** is the answer. (pp. 211–213)

12. **a.** is the answer. (p. 224)

13. **d.** is the answer. (p. 226)

    a. Self-awareness refers to the infant's developing sense of "me and mine."

    b. Synchrony describes the coordinated interaction between infant and caregiver.

    c. Affiliation describes the tendency of people at any age to seek the companionship of others.

14. **b.** is the answer. (p. 227)

    a. The text does not link self-awareness to secure attachment.

    c. On the contrary, secure attachment promotes *independence* in infants and children.

15. **a.** is the answer. (p. 208)

    b., c., & d. As infants become older, they smile more selectively.

True or False Items

1. F Most developmentalists believe that infants are born with a tendency toward sociability as a means of survival. (p. 207)

2. F Emotions become more intense and are manifested more quickly and more persistently. (p. 210)

3. T (p. 209)

4. T (pp. 210–211)

5. F A securely attached toddler is most likely to explore the environment, the mother's presence being enough to give him or her the courage to do so. (pp. 228–229)
6. F Jay Belsky and other researchers believe that high-quality day care is not likely to harm the child. In fact, it is thought to be beneficial to the development of cognitive and social skills. (p. 234)
7. F (p. 211)
8. F Temperament is a product of both nature and nurture. (pp. 219–220)
9. T (p. 214)
10. T (pp. 232–233)

PROGRESS TEST 2

Multiple-Choice Questions

1. **d.** is the answer. (p. 208)
2. **a.** is the answer. (p. 218)
3. **c.** is the answer. (p. 215)
4. **a.** is the answer. (p. 234)
5. **c.** is the answer. (pp. 214–215)

   a. & b. The social smile, as well as temperamental characteristics, emerge well before the first signs of self-awareness.

   d. Contemporary developmentalists link these emotions to self-consciousness, rather than any specific environmental event such as toilet training.
6. **a.** is the answer. (p. 221)

   b. & d. Activity level and sociability are much less variable than rhythmicity and quality of mood.

   c. Self-awareness is not a temperamental characteristic.
7. **c.** is the answer. (p. 209)
8. **c.** is the answer. (pp. 221–222)
9. **d.** is the answer. (p. 231)
10. **a.** is the answer. (p. 231)

    c. & d. The text does not suggest that the consequences of secure and insecure attachment differ in boys and girls.
11. **c.** is the answer. (p. 208)
12. **a.** is the answer. (pp. 212–213)
13. **b.** is the answer. (p. 219)

    a. & c. Freud would have agreed with both of these statements.
14. **d.** is the answer. (p. 231)
15. **a.** is the answer. (p. 232)

    b. Autonomous mothers tend to have securely attached infants.

    c. Preoccupied mothers tend to have resistant infants.

Matching Items

1. h (p. 219)	5. b (p. 218)	9. l (p. 214)
2. k (p. 218)	6. e (p. 217)	10. f (p. 228)
3. g (p. 228)	7. a (p. 210)	11. d (p. 226)
4. j (p. 224)	8. c (p 218)	12. i (p. 226)

THINKING CRITICALLY ABOUT CHAPTER 7

1. **b.** is the answer. (p. 229)

   a., c., & d. These responses are more typical of insecurely attached infants.
2. **b.** is the answer. (p. 210)
3. **d.** is the answer. (p. 228)
4. **a.** is the answer. About 40 percent of young infants can be described as "easy." (p. 221)

   b. About 15 percent of infants are described as "slow to warm up."

   c. About 10 percent of infants are described as "difficult."
5. **c.** is the answer. (p. 232)

   a. Autonomous adults are able to talk objectively about their own early attachments.

   b. Dismissing adults devalue the importance of attachment relationships.

   d. Unresolved adults have not yet reconciled their own early attachments.
6. **b.** is the answer. (pp. 232–233)

   a. Claudia would be classified as "unresolved."

   c. Autonomous adults, such as Pearl, tend to have securely attached infants.

   d. Preoccupied adults, such as Carmen, tend to have resistant offspring.
7. **a.** is the answer. (p. 234)
8. **b.** is the answer. (pp. 212–213)
9. **c.** is the answer. (p. 228)

   a. & d. When their mothers return following an absence, securely attached infants usually re-establish social contact (with a smile or by climbing into their laps) and then resume playing.

   b. There is no evidence in this example that Kalil is an abused child.
10. **c.** is the answer. (p. 219)

    a. & b. There is no evidence in the question that the parents are reinforcing tantrum behavior or failing to meet some biological need of the child's.

d. On the contrary, about 40 percent of infants are "easy" in temperamental style.

11. d. is the answer. (p. 210)

a. According to Erikson, this is the crisis of toddlerhood.

b. This describes a moment of coordinated and mutually responsive interaction between a parent and an infant.

c. Dyssynchrony occurs when the coordinated pace and timing of a synchronous interaction are temporarily lost.

12. c. is the answer. (p. 217)

a. & b. In Freud's theory, a person who is fixated in the anal stage exhibits messiness and disorganization or compulsive neatness.

d. Erikson, rather than Freud, proposed crises of development.

13. c. is the answer. (p. 215)

14. b. is the answer. The fear of being left by a caregiver (separation anxiety) emerges at about 8 or 9 months, and peaks at about 14 months. For this reason, 4-month-old Carl can be expected to become less upset than his older sister. (p. 209)

15. c. is the answer. (p. 231)

KEY TERMS

1. The **social smile**—a smile of pleasure in response to a human face or voice—appears at about 6 weeks. (p. 208)
2. A common early fear, **stranger wariness** (also called fear of strangers) is first noticeable at about 6 months. (p. 209)
3. **Separation anxiety**, which is the infant fear of being left by the mother or other caregiver, emerges at about 8 or 9 months, peaks at about 14 months, and then gradually subsides. (p. 209)
4. When infants engage in **social referencing**, they are looking to trusted adults for emotional cues on how to interpret uncertain situations. (p. 210)
5. **Self-awareness** refers to a person's sense of himself or herself as being distinct from other people that makes possible many new self-conscious emotions, including shame, guilt, embarrassment, and pride. (p. 214)
6. **Personality** refers to the emotions, behaviors, and attitudes that make an individual unique. (p. 216)
7. In Freud's first stage of psychosexual development, the **oral stage**, the mouth is the most important source of gratification for the infant. (p. 217)
8. According to Freud, during the second year infants are in the **anal stage** of psychosexual development and derive sensual pleasure from the stimulation of the bowels and psychological pleasure from their control. (p. 217)
9. In Erikson's theory, the crisis of infancy is one of **trust versus mistrust**, in which the infant learns whether the world is a secure place in which basic needs will be met. (p. 218)
10. In Erikson's theory, the crisis of toddlerhood is one of **autonomy versus shame and doubt**, in which toddlers strive to rule their own actions and bodies. (p. 218)
11. **Temperament** refers to the set of innate tendencies, or dispositions, that underlie and affect each person's interactions with people, situations, and events. (p. 219)
12. The **"big five"** are the five major clusters of personality found in adults, including extroversion, agreeableness, conscientiousness, neuroticism, and openness. (p. 221)
13. **Goodness of fit** is the match between the child's temperamental pattern and the demands of the environment. (p. 222)
14. **Synchrony** refers to the coordinated interaction between caregiver and infant that helps infants learn to express and read emotions. (p. 224)
15. **Attachment** is the enduring emotional tie that a person or animal forms with another. (p. 211)
16. Following, approaching, and other **proximity-seeking behaviors** are intended to place an individual close to another person to whom he or she is attached. (p. 226)
17. Clinging, resisting being put down, and other **contact-maintaining behaviors** are intended to keep a person near another person to whom he or she is attached. (p. 226)
18. A **secure attachment** is one in which the infant derives comfort and confidence from the "secure base" provided by a caregiver. (p. 228)
19. **Insecure attachment** is characterized by the infant's fear, anger, or seeming indifference toward the caregiver. (p. 228)
20. The **Strange Situation** is a laboratory procedure developed by Ainsworth for assessing attachment. Infants are observed in a playroom, in several successive episodes, while the caregiver (usually the mother) and a stranger move in and out of the room. (p. 228)

CHAPTER 8

The Play Years: Biosocial Development

Chapter Overview

Chapter 8 introduces the developing person between the ages of 2 and 6. This period is called the play years, emphasizing the central importance of play to the biosocial, cognitive, and psychosocial development of preschoolers.

The chapter begins by outlining the changes in size and shape that occur from ages 2 through 6. This is followed by a look at brain growth and development and its role in the development of physical and cognitive abilities. The Changing Policy box addresses the important issues of injury control and accidents, the major cause of childhood death in all but the most disease-ridden or war-torn countries. A description of the acquisition of gross and fine motor skills follows, noting that mastery of such skills develops steadily during the play years along with intellectual growth. The chapter concludes with an in-depth exploration of child maltreatment, including its prevalence, contributing factors, consequences for future development, treatment, and prevention.

NOTE: Answer guidelines for all Chapter 8 questions begin on page 129.

Guided Study

The text chapter should be studied one section at a time. Before you read, preview each section by skimming it, noting headings and boldface items. Then read the appropriate section objectives from the following outline. Keep these objectives in mind and, as you read the chapter section, search for the information that will enable you to meet each objective. Once you have finished a section, write out answers for its objectives.

Size and Shape (pp. 243–246)

1. Describe normal physical growth during the play years, and account for variations in height and weight.

2. Describe changes in eating habits during the preschool years.

Brain Growth and Development (pp. 246–248)

3. Discuss brain growth and development and its effect on development during the play years.

4. Identify several factors that contribute to variation in the risk of accidental injury among children.

5. Explain how the maturation of the visual pathways and cerebral hemispheres allows for formal education to begin at about age 6.

Mastering Motor Skills (pp. 249–253)

6. Distinguish between gross and fine motor skills, and discuss the development of each during the play years.

7. (Changing Policy) Explain what is meant by "injury control," and describe some measures that have significantly reduced accidental death rates for children.

8. Discuss the significance of drawing during the play years.

Child Maltreatment (pp. 254–267)

9. Identify the various categories of child maltreatment, and discuss several factors that contribute to its occurrence.

10. Discuss the consequences of child maltreatment.

11. Describe current efforts to treat child maltreatment, and differentiate four categories of families involved in maltreatment.

12. Discuss foster care, kinship care, and adoption as intervention options in cases of child maltreatment.

13. Compare and contrast three approaches to the prevention of child maltreatment.

Chapter Review

When you have finished reading the chapter, work through the material that follows to review it. Complete the sentences and answer the questions. As you proceed, evaluate your performance for each section by consulting the answers on page 129. Do not continue with the next section until you understand each answer. If you need to, review or reread the appropriate section in the textbook before continuing.

Size and Shape (pp. 243–246)

1. During the preschool years, from age ______________ to ______________, children add almost ______________ in height and gain about ______________ in weight per year. By age 6, the average child in a developed nation weighs about ______________ and measures ______________ in height.
2. The range of normal physical development is quite ______________ (narrow/broad).
3. Of the many factors that influence height and weight, the most influential are the child's ______________ ______________, ______________ ______________, and ______________.
4. The dramatic differences between physical development in developed and developing countries are largely due to differences in the average child's ______________.

Compare the size and shape of boys and girls during childhood.

5. In multiethnic countries, children of ______________ descent tend to be tallest, followed by ______________, then ______________, and then ______________. The impact of ______________ patterns on physical development can be seen in families in South Asia and the Indian subcontinent, where ______________ (which gender?) are more highly valued and consequently better fed than the other sex when food is scarce.
6. During the preschool years, annual height and weight gain is much ______________ (greater/less) than during infancy. This means that children need ______________ (fewer/more) calories per pound during this period.
7. The most prevalent nutritional problem in developed countries during the preschool years is ______________ ______________ ______________, the chief symptom of which is ______________ ______________. This problem stems from a diet deficient in ______________ ______________. This problem is ______________ (more/less) common among low-income families than among others.
8. An additional problem for American children is that they, like most American adults, consume too much ______________ and too much ______________.

Brain Growth and Development (pp. 246–248)

9. By age 5, the brain has attained about ______________ percent of its adult weight; in contrast, total body weight is about ______________ percent of that of the average adult.
10. Part of the brain's increase in size during childhood is due to the continued proliferation of ______________ pathways and the ongoing process of ______________. In addition, there is notable expansion of brain areas

dedicated to ______________ and ______________, the ______________, and ______________ processes. This helps children to develop ______________ reactions to stimuli and to be able to control their reactions.

11. The band of nerve fibers that connects the right and left sides of the brain, called the ______________ ______________, which becomes thicker due to ______________ growth and ______________. This helps children better coordinate functions that involve ______________.

12. In all but the most disease-ridden or war-torn countries of the world, the leading cause of childhood death is ______________.

13. The accident risk for a particular child depends on several factors, including ______________ ______________.

14. Injuries and accidental deaths are ______________ (more/less) frequent among boys than girls.

15. The clearest risk factor in accident rates is ______________, with ______________ (high/low)-status children being three times more likely than other children to die an accidental death.

16. (Changing Policy) Instead of "accident prevention," many experts speak of ______________ ______________, an approach based on the belief that most accidents ______________ (are/are not) preventable.

17. (Changing Policy) Safety laws that include penalties for noncompliance seem to be even ______________ (less/more) effective than educational measures in reducing injury rates.

18. (Changing Policy) The accidental death rate for American children between the ages of 1 and 5 has ______________ (increased/decreased) between 1980 and 1986.

19. Throughout the preschool years, the visual pathways of the brain that are associated with control of ______________ and ______________ undergo considerable growth. This, along with improved ______________ between the left and right sides of the brain, enhances children's ______________-______________ coordination.

20. Brain growth during childhood ______________ (is/is not) necessarily linear, sometimes occurring in ______________ and ______________.

21. Development of the corpus callosum and development of the frontal lobes of the brain at around age 5 facilitates formal schooling, because children are now able to begin forming links between ______________ and ______________ ______________.

Mastering Motor Skills (pp. 249–253)

22. Large body movements such as running, climbing, jumping, and throwing are called ______________ ______________ ______________. These skills, which improve dramatically during the preschool years, require guided ______________, as well as a certain level of ______________ ______________. Most children learn these skills ______________ (by themselves/from parents).

23. Skills that involve small body movements, such as pouring liquids and cutting food, are called ______________ ______________ ______________. Preschoolers have greater difficulty with these skills primarily because they have not developed the ______________ control, patience, or ______________ needed—in part because the ______________ of the central nervous system is not complete.

24. Many developmentalists believe that ______________ is a form of play that enhances the child's sense of accomplish-

ment. This form of play also provides a testing ground for another important skill, ______________. Mastery of this skill is related to overall ______________ growth.

Child Maltreatment (pp. 254–267)

25. Until a few decades ago, the concept of child maltreatment was mostly limited to obvious ______________ assault, which was thought to be the outburst of a mentally disturbed person. Today, it is known that most perpetrators of maltreatment ______________ (are/are not) mentally ill.

26. Intentional harm to, or avoidable endangerment of, someone under age 18 defines child ______________. Actions that are deliberately harmful to a child's well-being are classified as ______________. A failure to act appropriately to meet a child's basic needs is classified as ______________.

27. Ideas about what constitutes child maltreatment vary with ______________ and ______________ norms. Each culture develops a particular ______________ that creates a climate that is more or less conducive to maltreatment than others.

28. An important factor in understanding child maltreatment in context is ______________ ______________.

29. Two aspects of the overall context that seem universally conducive to maltreatment are ______________ and ______________ ______________.

30. The daily routines of maltreating families typically are either very rigid in their ______________ and ______________ ______________ such that no one can measure up, or they are so ______________ and ______________ that no one can be certain of what is expected.

31. Maltreatment is more likely if the family is ______________ and distrusting of others. Also, maltreatment may result when there is ______________ or ______________ among other family members.

32. According to case workers, the most frequent major problem interfering with effective child care is ______________. The second most common problem is ______________ ______________.

Describe some of the deficits of children who have been maltreated.

33. The phenomenon of maltreated children growing up to become abusive or neglectful parents themselves is called ______________ ______________. A widely held misconception is that this phenomenon ______________ (is/is not) avoidable.

34. Approximately ______________ percent of abused children actually become abusive parents.

35. New laws requiring teachers, social workers, and other professionals to report possible maltreatment ______________ (have/have not) resulted in increased reporting. Out of their concern that reporting does not create enough protection for a maltreated child, some experts advocate a policy of ______________ ______________. This policy separates high-risk cases that may require complete investigation and ______________ of the child from low-risk cases that may require some sort of ______________ measure.

36. Maltreating families who are experiencing unusual problems, such as divorce or the loss of a job, are classified as ______________ ______________ ______________.

It is relatively ________________ (easy/difficult) to help these families overcome their dysfunctional ways.

37. Maltreating families that have many problems, caused by their immediate situation, past history, and temperament, that seriously impair their parenting abilities, are classified as ________________. Treatment of these families is ________________ (more/less) difficult.

38. Maltreating families who will probably never be able to function adequately and independently of the help of social workers, therapists, and others until the children are grown are classified as ________________.

39. Maltreating families that are so impaired by deep emotional problems or serious cognitive deficiencies that they may never be able to meet the needs of their children are classified as ________________. For children born into these families, long-term ________________ ________________ is the best solution.

40. A reason that foster care has been stereotyped as inadequate care is that, compared with children overall, foster children tend to do less well in ________________, have fewer ________________, and are more likely to become ________________.

41. In another type of foster care, called ________________ ________________, a relative of the maltreated child becomes the approved caregiver. A final option is ________________, which is ideal when families are ________________ and children are ________________.

42. Public policy measures and other efforts designed to prevent maltreatment from ever occurring are called ________________ ________________. An approach that focuses on spotting and treating the first symptoms of maltreatment is called ________________ ________________. A specific example of this approach occurs in countries such as England and New Zealand, where ________________ ________________ of families with young infants is routinely practiced. Last ditch measures such as removing a child from an abusive home, jailing the perpetrator, and so forth constitute ________________ ________________.

Progress Test 1

Multiple-Choice Questions

Circle your answers to the following questions and check them with the answers on page 130. If your answer is incorrect, read the explanation for why it is incorrect and then consult the appropriate pages of the text (in parentheses following the correct answer).

1. During the preschool years, the most common nutritional problem in developed countries is:

a. serious malnutrition.
b. excessive intake of sweets.
c. iron deficiency anemia.
d. excessive caloric intake.

2. The brain center for speech is usually located in the:

a. right brain.
b. left brain.
c. corpus callosum.
d. space just below the right ear.

3. Gender differences in childhood size and shape:

a. are consistent throughout the world.
b. vary from one culture to another.
c. are more pronounced in Western cultures.
d. are more pronounced today than in the past.

4. (Changing Policy) Which of the following is *not* true regarding injury control?

a. Broad-based television announcements do not have a direct impact on children's risk taking.
b. Unless parents become involved, classroom safety education has little effect on children's actual behavior.
c. Safety laws that include penalties are more effective than educational measures.
d. Accidental deaths of 1- to 5-year-olds have held steady in the United States over the past two decades.

5. Like most Americans, children tend to have too much ________________ in their diet.

a. iron
b. fat
c. sugar
d. b. and c.

6. Skills that involve large body movements, such as running and jumping, are called:
   a. activity-level skills.
   b. fine motor skills.
   c. gross motor skills.
   d. left-brain skills.

7. The brain's ongoing myelination during childhood helps children:
   a. control their actions more precisely.
   b. react more quickly to stimuli.
   c. focus more easily on printed letters.
   d. do all of the above.

8. The leading cause of death in childhood is:
   a. accidents.
   b. untreated diabetes.
   c. malnutrition.
   d. iron deficiency anemia.

9. At age 6, the proportions of a child's body:
   a. still retain the "top-heavy" look of infancy.
   b. are more adultlike in girls than in boys.
   c. are not very different from those of an adult.
   d. are influenced more by heredity than by health care or nutrition.

10. Which of the following factors is *most* responsible for differences in height and weight between children in developed and developing countries?
    a. the child's genetic background
    b. health care
    c. nutrition
    d. age of weaning

11. In which of the following age periods is serious malnutrition *least* likely to occur?
    a. infancy
    b. early childhood
    c. adolescence
    d. Serious malnutrition is equally likely in each of these age groups.

12. The relationship between accident rate and SES can be described as:
    a. a positive correlation.
    b. a negative correlation.
    c. curvilinear.
    d. no correlation.

13. Which of the following is true of the corpus callosum?
    a. It enables short-term memory.
    b. It connects the two halves of the brain.
    c. It must be fully myelinated before gross motor skills can be acquired.
    d. All of the above are correct.

14. Eye-hand coordination improves during the play years, in part because:
    a. the brain areas associated with this ability become more fully myelinated.
    b. the corpus callosum begins to function.
    c. fine motor skills have matured by age 2.
    d. gross motor skills have matured by age 2.

15. Adoption is most likely to be successful as an intervention for maltreatment when:
    a. children are young and biological families are inadequate.
    b. efforts at tertiary prevention have already failed.
    c. children have endured years of maltreatment in their biological family.
    d. foster care and kinship care have failed.

True or False Items

Write *true* or *false* on the line in front of each statement.

_______ 1. Growth between ages 2 and 6 is more rapid than at any other period in the lifespan.

_______ 2. During childhood, the legs develop faster than any other part of the body.

_______ 3. For most people, the brain center for speech is located in the left hemisphere .

_______ 4. The health care, genetic background, and nutrition of the preschool child are major influences on growth.

_______ 5. Brain growth during childhood proceeds in spurts and plateaus.

_______ 6. Fine motor skills are usually easier for preschoolers to master than are gross motor skills.

_______ 7. Most serious childhood injuries truly are "accidents."

_______ 8. Children often fare as well in kinship care as they do in conventional foster care.

_______ 9. Concern for and protection of the well-being of children varies markedly from culture to culture.

_______ 10. Most child maltreatment does not involve serious physical abuse.

Progress Test 2

Progress Test 2 should be completed during a final chapter review. Answer the following questions after you thoroughly understand the correct answers for the Chapter Review and Progress Test 1.

Multiple-Choice Questions

1. Each year from ages 2 to 6, the average child gains and grows, respectively:
   a. 2 pounds and 1 inch.
   b. 3 pounds and 2 inches.
   c. 4 1/2 pounds and 3 inches.
   d. 6 pounds and 6 inches.

2. The center for perceiving various types of visual configurations is usually located in the brain's:
   a. right hemisphere.
   b. left hemisphere.
   c. right or left hemisphere.
   d. corpus callosum.

3. Which of the following best describes brain growth during childhood?
   a. It proceeds at a slow, steady, linear rate.
   b. The left hemisphere develops more rapidly than the right.
   c. The right hemisphere develops more rapidly than the left.
   d. It involves a nonlinear series of spurts and plateaus.

4. The text notes that art provides an important opportunity for the child to develop the skill of:
   a. realistic representation of objects.
   b. reading.
   c. perspective.
   d. self-correction.

5. Which of the following is an example of secondary prevention of child maltreatment?
   a. removing a child from an abusive home
   b. jailing a maltreating parent
   c. home visitation of families with infants by health professionals
   d. public-policy measures aimed at creating stable neighborhoods

6. When parents or caregivers do not provide adequate food, shelter, attention, or supervision, it is referred to as:
   a. abuse.
   b. neglect.
   c. endangering.
   d. maltreatment.

7. Which of the following is true of a developed nation in which many ethnic groups live together?
   a. Ethnic variations in height and weight disappear.
   b. Ethnic variations in stature persist, but are substantially smaller.
   c. Children of African descent tend to be tallest, followed by Europeans, Asians, and Latinos.
   d. Cultural patterns exert a stronger-than-normal impact on growth patterns.

8. Most families involved in maltreatment of children are classified as ________________, which means that while they have the potential to provide adequate care, they have many problems that seriously impair their parenting abilities.
   a. vulnerable to crisis.
   b. restorable.
   c. supportable.
   d. inadequate.

9. Which of the following is an example of a fine motor skill?
   a. kicking a ball
   b. running
   c. drawing with a pencil
   d. jumping

10. During the play years, boys generally are:
    a. taller and heavier than girls.
    b. shorter and heavier than girls.
    c. taller and lighter than girls.
    d. about the same weight and height as girls.

11. A contributing factor in one of every four cases of child maltreatment is:
    a. mental illness.
    b. drug dependency.
    c. a large child-adult ratio in the family.
    d. a preterm child.

12. Most gross motor skills can be learned by healthy children by about age:
    a. 2.
    b. 3.
    c. 5.
    d. 7.

13. Two of the most important factors that affect height during the play years are:
    a. socioeconomic status and health care.
    b. gender and health care.
    c. heredity and nutrition.
    d. heredity and activity level.

14. (Public Policy) Over the past two decades, the accidental death rate for American children between the ages of 1 and 5 has:
   a. decreased, largely as a result of new city, state, and federal safety laws.
   b. decreased, largely because parents are more knowledgeable about safety practices.
   c. increased.
   d. remained unchanged.

15. During the play years, because growth is slow, children's appetites seem ________ they were in the first two years of life.
   a. larger than
   b. smaller than
   c. about the same as
   d. erratic, sometimes smaller and sometimes larger than

Matching Items

Match each term or concept with its corresponding description or definition.

Terms or Concepts

________ 1. corpus callosum
________ 2. gross motor skills
________ 3. fine motor skills
________ 4. restorable
________ 5. vulnerable to crisis
________ 6. injury control
________ 7. supportable
________ 8. inadequate
________ 9. abuse
________ 10. neglect
________ 11. primary prevention
________ 12. secondary prevention
________ 13. tertiary prevention

Descriptions or Definitions

a. maltreating family for which foster care of children is the best solution
b. maltreating family that needs temporary help to resolve unusual problems
c. maltreating family that requires a variety of helping services until the children are grown
d. maltreating family that seems to have the potential to provide adequate care, but has serious problems that impair its parenting abilities
e. procedures to prevent child maltreatment from ever occurring
f. running and jumping
g. actions that are deliberately harmful to a child's well-being
h. procedures for spotting and treating the early warning signs of child maltreatment
i. painting a picture or tying shoelaces
j. failure to appropriately meet a child's basic needs
k. an approach emphasizing "accident" prevention
l. procedures to halt maltreatment that has already occurred
m. band of nerve fibers connecting the right and left hemispheres of the brain

Thinking Critically About Chapter 8

Answer these questions the day before an exam as a final check on your understanding of the chapter's terms and concepts.

1. An editorial in the local paper claims that there is no reason children younger than 6 cannot be taught basic literacy skills. You write to the editor, noting that:
   a. she has an accurate grasp of developmental processes.
   b. before age 6, brain myelination and development are too immature to enable children to form links between spoken and written language.
   c. although the right hemisphere is relatively mature at age 6, the left is not.
   d. although this may be true for girls, boys (who are slower to mature neurologically) would struggle.

2. Four-year-old Deon is tired all the time. On questioning Deon's mother, the pediatrician learns that Deon's diet is deficient in quality meats, whole grains, eggs, and dark green vegetables. The doctor believes that Deon may be suffering from:
   a. malnutrition.
   b. protein anemia.
   c. iron deficiency anemia.
   d. an inherited fatigue disorder.

3. Following an automobile accident, Amira developed severe problems with her speech. Her doctor believes that the accident injured the ______________ of her brain.
   a. left side
   b. right side
   c. communication pathways
   d. corpus callosum

4. Two-year-old Ali is quite clumsy, falls down frequently, and often bumps into stationary objects. Ali most likely:
   a. has a neuromuscular disorder.
   b. has an underdeveloped right hemisphere of the brain.
   c. is suffering from iron deficiency anemia.
   d. is a normal 2-year-old whose gross motor skills will improve dramatically during the preschool years.

5. Climbing a fence is an example of a:
   a. fine motor skill.
   b. gross motor skill.
   c. circular reaction.
   d. launching event.

6. (Changing Policy) To prevent accidental death in childhood, some experts urge forethought and planning for safety and measures to limit the damage of such accidents as do occur. This approach is called:
   a. protective analysis.
   b. safety education.
   c. injury control.
   d. childproofing.

7. Recent research reveals that some children are poor readers because they have trouble connecting visual symbols, phonetic sounds, and verbal meanings. This occurs because:
   a. their sugary diets make concentration more difficult.
   b. the brain areas involved in reading have not become localized in the left hemisphere.
   c. they use one side of the brain considerably more than the other.
   d. their underdeveloped corpus callosums limit communication between the two brain hemispheres.

8. Which of the following activities would probably be the most difficult for a 5-year-old child?
   a. climbing a ladder
   b. catching a ball
   c. throwing a ball
   d. pouring juice from a pitcher without spilling it

9. Tanya's family is under a lot of stress. Her mother was laid off from her job, her grandfather recently died, and her parents are contemplating divorce. If Tanya were being maltreated, how would her family be classified?
   a. vulnerable-to-crisis
   b. inadequate
   c. supportable
   d. There is not enough information.

10. Most child maltreatment:
    a. does not involve serious physical abuse.
    b. involves a rare outburst from the perpetrator.
    c. involves a mentally ill perpetrator.
    d. can be predicted from the victim's personality characteristics.

11. A mayoral candidate is calling for sweeping policy changes to help ensure the well-being of children by promoting home ownership, high-quality community centers, and more stable neighborhoods. If these measures are effective in reducing child maltreatment, they would be classified as:
    a. primary prevention.
    b. secondary prevention.
    c. tertiary prevention.
    d. differential response.

12. A factor that would figure very little into the development of fine motor skills, such as drawing and writing, is:
    a. strength.
    b. muscular control.
    c. judgment.
    d. short, fat fingers.

13. Parents who were abused as children:
    a. almost always abuse their children.
    b. are more likely to neglect, but not necessarily abuse, their children.
    c. are no more likely than anyone else to mistreat their children .
    d. do none of the above.

14. Which aspect of brain development during the play years contributes *most* to enhancing communication among the brain's various specialized areas?
    a. increasing brain weight
    b. proliferation of dendrite networks
    c. myelination
    d. increasing specialization of brain areas

15. Three-year-old Kyle's parents are concerned because Kyle, who generally seems healthy, doesn't seem to have the hefty appetite or rate of growth he had as an infant. Should they be worried?
    a. Yes, because both appetite and growth rate normally increase throughout the preschool years.
    b. Yes, because appetite (but not necessarily growth rate) normally increases during the preschool years.
    c. No, because growth rate (and hence caloric need) is less during the preschool years than during infancy.
    d. There is not enough information to determine whether Kyle is developing normally.

Key Terms

Using your own words, write a brief definition or explanation of each of the following terms on a separate piece of paper.

1. corpus callosum
2. injury control
3. child maltreatment
4. abuse
5. neglect
6. intergenerational transmission
7. differential response
8. vulnerable-to-crisis families
9. restorable families
10. supportable families
11. inadequate families
12. foster care
13. kinship care
14. primary prevention
15. secondary prevention
16. tertiary prevention

ANSWERS

CHAPTER REVIEW

1. 2; 6; 3 inches (7 centimeters); 4 1/2 pounds (2 kilograms); 46 pounds (21 kilograms); 46 inches (117 centimeters)
2. broad
3. genetic background; health care; nutrition
4. nutrition

Generally, boys are more muscular, have less body fat, and are slightly taller and heavier than girls throughout childhood.

5. African; Europeans; Asians; Latinos; cultural; boys
6. less; fewer
7. iron deficiency anemia; chronic fatigue; quality meats, whole grains, eggs, and dark green vegetables; more
8. sugar; fat
9. 90; 30
10. communication; myelination; control; coordination; emotions; thinking; quicker
11. corpus callosum; dendrite; myelination; both sides of the brain and body
12. accidents
13. the child's sex, socioeconomic status, and community setting
14. more
15. socioeconomic status (SES); low
16. injury control; are
17. more
18. decreased
19. eye movements; focusing; communication; eye-hand
20. is not; spurts; plateaus
21. spoken; written language

22. gross motor skills; practice; brain maturation; by themselves
23. fine motor skills; muscular; judgment; myelination
24. drawing; self-correction; intellectual
25. physical; are not
26. maltreatment; abuse; neglect
27. historical; cultural; ecosystem
28. community standards
29. poverty; social isolation
30. schedules; role demands; chaotic; disorganized
31. isolated; abuse; neglect
32. substance abuse; lack of parental capacity and skill

Compared to well-cared-for children, chronically abused and neglected children are slower to talk, underweight, less able to concentrate, and behind in school. They also tend to regard others as hostile and exploitative, and so are less friendly, more aggressive, and more isolated than other children. As adolescents and adults, they often engage in self-destructive and/or other destructive behaviors.

33. intergenerational transmission; is not
34. 30–40
35. have; differential response; removal; supportive
36. vulnerable to crisis; easy
37. restorable; more
38. supportable
39. inadequate; foster care
40. school; friends; criminals
41. kinship care; adoption; inadequate; young
42. primary prevention; secondary prevention; home visitation; tertiary prevention

PROGRESS TEST 1

Multiple-Choice Questions

1. **c.** is the answer. (p. 245)

   a. Serious malnutrition is much more likely to occur in infancy or in adolescence than in early childhood.

   b. Although an important health problem, eating too much candy or other sweets is not as serious as iron deficiency anemia.

   d. Since growth is slower during the preschool years, children need fewer calories per pound during this period.

2. **b.** is the answer. (p. 247)

   a. & d. The right brain is the location of areas associated with recognition of visual configurations.

   c. The corpus callosum helps integrate the functioning of the two halves of the brain; it does not contain areas specialized for particular skills.

3. **b.** is the answer. (p. 244)
4. **d.** is the answer. Accident rates have *decreased* during this time period. (p. 247)
5. **d.** is the answer. (p. 245)
6. **c.** is the answer. (p. 249)
7. **d.** is the answer. (pp. 246–247)
8. **a.** is the answer. (p. 247)
9. **c.** is the answer. (p. 243)

   b. The proportions are more adultlike in both girls and boys.

   d. Nutrition is a bigger factor in growth at this age than either heredity or health care.

10. **c.** is the answer. (p. 245)
11. **b.** is the answer. (p. 245)
12. **b.** is the answer. Children with *lower* SES have *higher* accident rates. (p. 248)
13. **b.** is the answer. (p. 246)

    a. The corpus callosum is not directly involved in memory.

    c. Myelination of the central nervous system is important to the mastery of *fine* motor skills.

14. **a.** is the answer. (p. 247)

    b. The corpus callosum begins to function long before the play years.

    c. & d. Neither fine nor gross motor skills have fully matured by age 2.

15. **a.** is the answer. (p. 264)

    b. Removing a child from an abusive home is itself a form of tertiary prevention.

    c. Such children tend to fare better in group homes.

    d. Although adoption is the final option, children who have been unable to thrive in foster care or kinship care will probably not thrive in an adoptive home either.

True or False Items

1. F Growth actually slows down during the play years. (p. 243)
2. F During childhood, the brain develops faster than any other part of the body. (p. 246)

3. T (p. 248)
4. T (p. 244)
5. T (p. 248)
6. F Fine motor skills are more difficult for preschoolers to master than are gross motor skills. (p. 252)
7. F Most serious accidents involve someone's lack of forethought. (pp. 250–251)
8. T (p. 263)
9. T (p. 255)
10. T (p. 254)

PROGRESS TEST 2

Multiple-Choice Questions

1. **c.** is the answer. (p. 243)
2. **a.** is the answer. (p. 247)

   b. & c. The left hemisphere of the brain contains areas associated with language development.

   d. The corpus callosum does not contain areas for specific behaviors.
3. **d.** is the answer. (p. 248)

   b. & c. The left and right hemispheres develop at similar rates.
4. **d.** is the answer. (p. 253)
5. **c.** is the answer. (p. 266)

   a. & b. These are examples of tertiary prevention.

   d. This is an example of primary prevention.
6. **b.** is the answer. (p. 255)

   a. Abuse is deliberate, harsh injury to the body.

   c. Endangerment was not discussed.

   d. Maltreatment is too broad a term.
7. **c.** is the answer. (p. 244)
8. **b.** is the answer. (p. 262)

   a. Families that are vulnerable to crisis are experiencing unusual problems, such as divorce or loss of a job, and need temporary help to resolve these problems.

   c. Supportable families will probably never be able to function adequately and independently until the children are grown.

   d. Inadequate families are so impaired by problems that long-term foster care of the children is usually the best solution.
9. **c.** is the answer. (p. 252)

   a., b., & d. These are gross motor skills.
10. **a.** is the answer. (p. 244)
11. **b.** is the answer. (p. 254)
12. **c.** is the answer. (p. 249)
13. **c.** is the answer. (p. 244)
14. **a.** is the answer. (pp. 250–251)

    b. Although safety education is important, the decrease in accident rate is largely the result of new safety laws.
15. **b.** is the answer. (p. 244)

Matching Items

1. m (p. 246)	**6.** k (p. 250)	**11.** e (p. 265)
2. f (p. 249)	**7.** c (p. 262)	**12.** h (p. 266)
3. i (p. 252)	**8.** a (p. 262)	**13.** l (p. 267)
4. d (p. 262)	**9.** g (p. 255)	
5. b (p. 263)	**10.** j (p. 255)	

THINKING CRITICALLY ABOUT CHAPTER 8

1. **b.** is the answer. (p. 248)
2. **c.** is the answer. Chronic fatigue is the major symptom of iron deficiency anemia, which is caused by a diet deficient in quality meats, whole grains, eggs, and dark green vegetables and is the most prevalent nutritional deficiency in developed countries. (p. 245)
3. **a.** is the answer. In most people, the left hemisphere of the brain contains centers for language, including speech. (p. 248)
4. **d.** is the answer. (p. 249)
5. **b.** is the answer. (p. 249)

   a. Fine motor skills involve small body movements, such as the hand movements used in painting.

   c. & d. These events were not discussed in this chapter.
6. **c.** is the answer. (p. 250)
7. **c.** is the answer. Analysis of the brain's electrical activity reveals that areas in both halves of the brain are involved in reading. (p. 248)
8. **d.** is the answer. (p. 252)

   a., b., & c. Preschoolers find these gross motor skills easier to perform than fine motor skills such as that described in d.
9. **a.** is the answer. The family's problems are unusual and, hopefully, temporary. (p. 261)

   b. & c. There is no evidence that Tanya's family is so severely impaired as to never be able to meet Tanya's needs, with or without assistance.

10. **a.** is the answer. (p. 254)
11. **a.** is the answer. (pp. 263-264)

    b. Had the candidate called for measures to spot the early warning signs of maltreatment, this answer would be true.

    c. Had the candidate called for jailing those who maltreat children or providing greater counseling and health care for victims, this answer would be true.

    d. Differential response is not an approach to prevention of maltreatment; rather, it refers to separate reporting procedures for high- and low-risk families.
12. **a.** is the answer. Strength is a more important factor in the development of gross motor skills. (p. 252)
13. **d.** is the answer. Approximately 30 percent of adults who were abused as children themselves become abusive parents. (p. 259)
14. **b.** is the answer. (p. 246)
15. **c.** is the answer. (p. 243)

KEY TERMS

1. The **corpus callosum** is a band of nerve fibers that connects the right and left sides of the brain. (p. 246)
2. **Injury control** is the practice of limiting the extent of injuries by planning ahead, controlling the circumstances, preventing certain dangerous activities, and adding safety features to others. (p. 250)
3. **Child maltreatment** is intentional harm to, or avoidable endangerment of, anyone under age 18. (p. 255)
4. **Abuse** refers to deliberate actions that are harmful to a child's well-being. (p. 255)
5. **Neglect** refers to failure to appropriately meet a child's basic needs. (p. 255)
6. **Intergenerational transmission** is the assumption that mistreated children grow up to become abusive or neglectful parents themselves. (p. 259)
7. **Differential response** refers to separating child maltreatment reports into two categories: high-risk cases that require immediate investigation and possible removal of the child, and low-risk cases that require supportive measures to encourage better parental care. (p. 260)
8. **Vulnerable-to-crisis families** are families involved in maltreatment in which parents are experiencing unusual problems (such as divorce or death) and need only temporary help to resolve them. (pp. 261–262)
9. **Restorable families** are families involved in maltreatment that have the potential to provide adequate care for children but, because of past and present problems, are not doing so. (p. 262)
10. **Supportable families** are families involved in maltreatment that are able to meet their children's basic needs and avoid maltreatment only with extensive, ongoing support. (p. 262)
11. **Inadequate families** are families involved in maltreatment that have so many emotional and/or cognitive problems that caregivers can never adequately meet their children's basic needs. (p. 262)
12. **Foster care** is a legally sanctioned, publicly supported arrangement in which children are removed from their biological parents and temporarily given to another adult to nurture. (p. 263)
13. **Kinship care** is a form of foster care in which a relative of a maltreated child becomes the child's legal caregiver. (p. 263)
14. **Primary prevention** refers to public policy measures designed to prevent child maltreatment (or other harm) from ever occurring. (p. 265)
15. **Secondary prevention** involves home visitation and other efforts to spot and treat the early warning signs of maltreatment before problems become severe. (p. 266)
16. **Tertiary prevention** involves efforts to stop child maltreatment after it occurs and to treat the victim. Removing a child from an abusive home, jailing the perpetrator, and providing health care to the victim are examples of tertiary prevention. (p. 267)

CHAPTER 9

The Play Years: Cognitive Development

Chapter Overview

In countless everyday instances, as well as in the findings of numerous research studies, young children reveal themselves to be remarkably thoughtful, insightful, and perceptive thinkers whose grasp of the causes of everyday events, memory of the past, and mastery of language is sometimes astonishing. Chapter 9 begins by comparing Piaget's and Vygotsky's views of cognitive development at this age. According to Piaget, young children's thought is prelogical: between the ages of 2 and 6, they are unable to perform many logical operations and are limited by irreversible, centered, and static thinking. Lev Vygotsky, a contemporary of Piaget's saw learning as a social activity more than as a matter of individual discovery. Vygotsky focused on the child's "zone of proximal development" and the relationship between language and thought.

The chapter next focuses on what preschoolers can do, including their competence in understanding number concepts, solving problems, storing and retrieving memories, and theorizing about the world. This leads into a description of language development during the play years. Although young children demonstrate rapid improvement in vocabulary and grammar, they have difficulty with abstractions, metaphorical speech, and certain rules of grammar. The chapter concludes with a discussion of preschool education, including a description of "quality" preschool programs and an evaluation of their lifelong impact on children.

NOTE: Answer guidelines for all Chapter 9 questions begin on page 144.

Guided Study

The text chapter should be studied one section at a time. Before you read, preview each section by skimming it, noting headings and boldface items. Then read the appropriate section objectives from the following outline. Keep these objectives in mind and, as you read the chapter section, search for the information that will enable you to meet each objective. Once you have finished a section, write out answers for its objectives.

How Young Children Think (pp. 271–280)

1. Describe and discuss the major characteristics of preoperational thought, according to Piaget.

2. Contrast Vygotsky's views on cognitive development with those of Piaget, focusing on the concept of guided participation.

3. Explain the significance of the zone of proximal development and scaffolding in promoting cognitive growth.

4. Describe Vygotsky's view of the role of language in cognitive growth.

5. Discuss more recent research on conservation, and explain why findings have led to qualification or revision of Piaget's description of cognition during the play years.

What Preschoolers Can Do (pp. 280–290)

6. Discuss preschoolers' understanding of number concepts.

7. Discuss young children's memory abilities and limitations, noting the role of meaning in their ability to recall events.

8. (Changing Policy) Discuss the reliability of children's eyewitness testimony.

9. (text and Research Report) Explain the typical young child's theory of mind, noting how it is affected by cultural context, and relate it to the child's developing ability to understand pretense.

Language Learning (pp. 290–295)

10. Outline the sequence by which vocabulary and grammar develop during the play years, and discuss limitations in the young child's language abilities.

11. Explain the role of fast mapping in children's acquisition of language.

Preschool Education (pp. 295–299)

12. Identify the characteristics of a high-quality preschool program, and discuss the long-term benefits of preschool education for the child and his or her family.

Chapter Review

When you have finished reading the chapter, work through the material that follows to review it. Complete the sentences and answer the questions. As you proceed, evaluate your performance for each section by consulting the answers on page 144. Do not continue with the next section until you understand each answer. If you need to, review or reread the appropriate section in the textbook before continuing.

How Young Children Think (pp. 271–280)

1. For many years, researchers maintained that young children's thinking abilities were sorely limited by their ______________ .

2. According to Piaget, the most striking difference between cognition during infancy and the preschool years is ______________ ______________ . He referred to cognitive development the ages of 2 and 6 as ______________ thought.

3. Young children's tendency to think about one aspect of a situation at a time is called ______________ . One particular form of this characteristic is children's tendency to contemplate the world exclusively from their personal perspective, which is referred to as ______________ . They also tend to focus on ______________ to the exclusion of other attributes of objects and people.

4. Preschoolers' understanding of the world tends to be ______________ (static/dynamic), which means that they tend to think of their world as ______________ . A closely related characteristic is ______________ —the inability to recognize that reversing a process will restore the original conditions from which the process began.

5. The idea that amount is unaffected by changes in shape or configuration is called ______________ . In the case of ______________ ______________ ______________ , preschoolers who are shown pairs of checkers in two even rows and who then observe one row being spaced out will say that the spaced-out row has more checkers.

6. The idea that children are "apprentices in thinking" emphasizes that children's intellectual growth is stimulated by their ______________ in ______________ experiences of their environment. The critical element in this process is that the mentor and the child ______________ to accomplish a task.

7. Much of the research and perspective on the young child's emerging cognition is inspired by the Russian psychologist ______________ .

8. Unlike Piaget, this psychologist believed that cognitive growth is a ______________ more than a matter of individual discovery.

9. Vygotsky suggested that for each developing individual there is a ______________ ______________ , a range of skills that the person can exercise with assistance but is not yet able to perform independently.

10. How and when new skills are developed depends, in part, on the willingness of tutors to ______________ the child's participation in learning encounters.

Identify several steps that contribute to effective scaffolding.

11. Vygotsky believed that language is essential to the advancement of thinking in two crucial ways. The first is through the internal dialogue in which a person talks to himself or herself, called ______________. In preschoolers, this dialogue is likely to be ______________ (expressed silently/uttered aloud).

12. According to Vygotsky, another way language advances thinking is as the ______________ of social interaction.

13. Piaget believed that it is ______________ (possible/impossible) for preoperational children to grasp logical reasoning processes. It is now clear that with more ______________ test conditions and special training, preschoolers can succeed at some tests of ______________.

14. Vygotsky would explain preschoolers' difficulty mastering conservation as the result of an inadequate ______________ for this logical principle. One piece of evidence that this is true is that throughout the world, children become more adept at those cognitive skills that are most valued by their ______________.

What Preschoolers Can Do (pp. 280–290)

15. Although preschoolers generally cannot count well, they often possess sophisticated number concepts, such as the ______________-______________ principle, the ______________-______________-______________ principle, and the ______________ principle.

16. The preschooler's developing understanding of number is influenced by ______________ development and the emerging ability to use ______________ to conceptualize number, as well as the flowering of the child's innate ______________. The overall importance the child's ______________ places on number competence also plays an important role.

17. The structure of the ______________ in a particular culture may promote preschool number competence. One hypothesis for the superiority of ______________ children over ______________ and ______________ children in math is that languages such as ______________, ______________, and ______________ are more logical in their labeling of numbers.

18. A final factor in promoting number competence is the ______________ and ______________ provided by parents, other adults, and older children.

19. Preschoolers are notorious for having a poor ______________. This shortcoming is due to the fact that they have not yet acquired skills for deliberate ______________ and efficient ______________ of information.

20. One way in which preschoolers are quite capable of storing in mind a representation of past events is by retaining ______________ of familiar, recurrent past experiences. These devices reflect an awareness of the correct ______________ and causal ______________ of remembered events.

21. Another reason young children sometimes appear deficient in their memory ability is that they often do not ______________.

22. A study compared preschoolers' memory of Disney World in response to a series of focused questions. The results showed that age ______________ (did/did not) significantly affect the amount of information the children remembered.

23. The "Disney World" study strongly suggests that even very young preschoolers can recall a great deal of information when they are given appropriate ______________ and when the material is ______________ to them.

24. (Changing Policy) Until quite recently, young children in most countries ______________ (were/were not) prohibited from providing courtroom testimony.

25. (Changing Policy) Recent research has found that, particularly for young children, the ________________ context in which children considered to be eyewitnesses are questioned is an important factor in the accuracy of their memory. Specifically, the ________________ of the child to the questioner, the ________________ of the questioner, and the ________________ of the interview have a substantial influence on his or her testimony.

26. (Changing Policy) Research demonstrates that the great majority of children when questioned as eyewitnesses ________________ (resist/fail to resist) suggestive questioning.

27. As a result of their experiences with others, young children acquire a ________________ ________________ ________________ that reflects their developing concepts about human mental processes.

28. Developmentalists have discovered that young children generally ________________ (are/are not) aware of divergent psychological perspectives.

Describe the young child's theory of mind by age 3 or 4.

29. The growth of children's theory of mind has broader implications for ________________ understanding. For example, children become far more capable of ________________ and ________________ the thoughts, emotions, and intentions of others.

30. Research studies reveal that theory-of-mind development depends as much on general ________________ ability as it does on ________________ ________________. A third helpful factor is having at least one ________________. Finally, ________________ may be a factor.

31. (Research Report) An important advance in preschoolers' theory of mind occurs when they realize that mental states may not accurately reflect ________________. This occurs between ages ________________, when the brain undergoes a growth spurt.

Language Learning (pp. 290–295)

32. During the preschool years a dramatic increase in language occurs, with ________________ increasing exponentially.

33. Through the process called ________________ preschoolers often learn words after only one or two hearings.

34. The learning of new words ________________ (does/does not) follow a predictable sequence according to parts of speech.

35. In building vocabulary, preschoolers generally learn ________________ more readily than ________________, which are learned more readily than ________________ ________________.

36. Abstract nouns, metaphors, and analogies are ________________ (more/no more) difficult for preschoolers to understand.

37. Because preschool children tend to think in absolute terms, they have difficulty with words that express ________________, as well as words expressing relativities of ________________ and ________________.

38. The structures, techniques, and rules that a language uses to communicate meaning define its ________________. By age ________________, children typically demonstrate extensive understanding of this aspect of language.

39. Humans possess an innate ________________ that facilitates their mastery of grammar.

40. Children's understanding of grammar is also facilitated by ______________________ and by ______________________.

41. Preschoolers' tendency to apply rules of grammar when they should not is called ______________________.

Give several examples of this tendency.

42. During the preschool years, children are able to comprehend ______________ (more/less) complex grammar and vocabulary than they can produce.

Preschool Education (pp. 295–299)

List several characteristics of a high-quality preschool program.

43. Japanese culture places great emphasis on ______________ ______________ and ______________. Reflecting this emphasis, Japanese preschools provide training in the behavior and attitudes appropriate for ______________ ______________. In contrast, preschools in the United States are often designed to foster ______________ ______________ and ______________ ______________.

44. In 1965, ______________ ______________ was inaugurated to give low-income children some form of compensatory education during the preschool years. Longitudinal research found that, as they made their way through elementary school, graduates of this program scored ______________ (higher/no higher) on achievement tests and had more positive school report cards than their non-Headstart counterparts. This type of hidden outcome that later becomes apparent is called a ______________ ______________.

45. The better the ______________ ______________ the less pronounced the influence of a preschool is likely to be.

Progress Test 1

Multiple-Choice Questions

Circle your answers to the following questions and check them with the answers on page 145. If your answer is incorrect, read the explanation for why it is incorrect and then consult the appropriate pages of the text (in parentheses following the correct answer).

1. Piaget believed that children are in the preoperational stage from ages:
   a. 6 months to 1 year.
   b. 1 to 3 years.
   c. 2 to 6 years.
   d. 5 to 11 years.

2. Compared with children in other developed countries, ______________ children in the United States attend preschool.
   a. fewer
   b. about the same number of
   c. a slightly higher percentage of
   d. a significantly higher percentage of

3. (Changing Policy) When questioned as eyewitnesses to an event, most young children:
   a. are unable to resist suggestive questioning.
   b. are able to resist suggestive questioning.
   c. provide very inaccurate answers.
   d. have reliable short-term memories, but very unreliable long-term memories.

4. The results of experiments on preschoolers' understanding of number concepts demonstrate that:
   a. supportive guidance provided by adults can stimulate the growth of number understanding in preschoolers.
   b. preschoolers have little or no number understanding.
   c. early developmentalists overestimated preschoolers' understanding of number.
   d. preschoolers are able to master the cardinal principle but not the one-to-one principle.

5. Preschoolers' poor performance on memory tests is primarily due to:
   a. their tendency to rely too extensively on scripts.
   b. their lack of efficient storage and retrieval skills.
   c. the incomplete myelination of cortical neurons.
   d. their short attention span.

6. The vocabulary of preschool children consists primarily of:
   a. metaphors.
   b. self-created words.
   c. abstract nouns.
   d. verbs and concrete nouns.

7. Preschoolers sometimes apply the rules of grammar even when they shouldn't. This tendency is called:
   a. overregularization.
   b. literal language.
   c. practical usage.
   d. single-mindedness.

8. The Russian psychologist Vygotsky emphasized that:
   a. language helps children form ideas.
   b. children form concepts first, then find words to express them.
   c. language and other cognitive developments are unrelated at this stage.
   d. preschoolers learn language only for egocentric purposes.

9. Private speech can be described as:
   a. a way of formulating ideas to oneself.
   b. fantasy.
   c. an early learning difficulty.
   d. the beginnings of deception.

10. The child who has not yet grasped the principle of conservation is likely to:
    a. insist that a tall, narrow glass contains more liquid than a short, wide glass, even though both glasses actually contain the same amount.
    b. be incapable of egocentric thought.
    c. be unable to reverse an event.
    d. do all of the above.

11. In later life, Headstart graduates showed:
    a. better report cards, but more behavioral problems.
    b. significantly higher IQ scores.
    c. higher scores on achievement tests.
    d. alienation from their original neighborhoods and families.

12. The best preschool programs are generally those that provide the greatest amount of:
    a. behavioral control.
    b. adult-child conversation.
    c. instruction in conservation and other logical principles.
    d. demonstration of toys by professionals.

13. Compared with their rate of speech development, children's understanding of language develops:
    a. more slowly.
    b. at about the same pace.
    c. more rapidly.
    d. more rapidly in some cultures than in others.

14. Relatively recent experiments have demonstrated that preschoolers *can* succeed at tests of conservation when:
    a. they are allowed to work cooperatively with other children.
    b. the test is presented as a competition.
    c. the children are informed that they are being observed by their parents.
    d. the test is presented in a simple, gamelike way.

15. Through the process called fast mapping, children:
    a. immediately assimilate new words by connecting them through their assumed meaning to categories of words they have already mastered.
    b. acquire the concept of conservation at an earlier age than Piaget believed.
    c. are able to move beyond egocentric thinking.
    d. become skilled in the practical use of language.

True or False Items

Write *true* or *false* on the line in front of each statement.

_______ 1. Piaget's description of cognitive development in early childhood has been universally rejected by contemporary developmentalists.

_______ 2. In conservation problems, many preschoolers are unable to understand the transformation because they focus exclusively on appearances.

_______ 3. Preschoolers who use private speech have slower cognitive growth than those who do not.

_______ 4. Whether or not a preschooler demonstrates conservation in an experiment depends in part on the conditions of the experiment.

_____ 5. One reason Japanese children are superior to American children in math may be that the Japanese language is more logical in its labeling of numbers.

_____ 6. Piaget believed that preschoolers' acquisition of language makes possible their cognitive development.

_____ 7. With the beginning of preoperational thought, most preschoolers can understand abstract words.

_____ 8. A preschooler who says "You comed up and hurted me" is demonstrating a lack of understanding of English grammar.

_____ 9. Successful preschool programs generally have a low teacher-to-child ratio.

_____ 10. Vygotsky believed that cognitive growth is largely a social activity.

Progress Test 2

Progress Test 2 should be completed during a final chapter review. Answer the following questions after you thoroughly understand the correct answers for the Chapter Review and Progress Test 1.

Multiple-Choice Questions

1. (Changing Policy) When children are required to give eyewitness testimony:
   a. they should be interviewed by a neutral professional.
   b. they should be interviewed by a family member.
   c. the atmosphere of the interview should be fairly intense, to impress upon them the importance of their answers.
   d. both b. and c. should be done.

2. In one study, 3- and 4-year-old children were interviewed after visiting Disney World. The results demonstrated that:
   a. age did not significantly affect the amount of information children remembered.
   b. the children provided much more information in response to open-ended questions than they did to directive questions.
   c. older children recalled less information spontaneously than did younger children.
   d. all of the above were true.

3. A preschooler who focuses his or her attention on only one feature of a situation is demonstrating a characteristic of preoperational thought called:
   a. centration.
   b. overregularization.
   c. reversibility.
   d. egocentrism.

4. One characteristic of preoperational thought is:
   a. the ability to categorize objects.
   b. the ability to count in multiples of 5.
   c. the inability to perform logical operations.
   d. difficulty adjusting to changes in routine.

5. The zone of proximal development represents the:
   a. skills or knowledge that are within the potential of the learner but are not yet mastered.
   b. influence of a child's peers on cognitive development.
   c. explosive period of language development during the play years.
   d. normal variations in children's language proficiency.

6. According to Vygotsky, language advances thinking through private speech, and by:
   a. helping children to privately review what they know.
   b. helping children explain events to themselves.
   c. serving as a mediator of the social interaction that is a vital part of learning.
   d. facilitating the process of fast mapping.

7. Irreversibility refers to the:
   a. inability to understand that other people view the world from a different perspective than one's own.
   b. inability to think about more than one idea at a time.
   c. failure to understand that changing the arrangement of a group of objects doesn't change their number.
   d. failure to understand that undoing a process will restore the original conditions.

8. According to Piaget:
   a. it is impossible for preoperational children to grasp the concept of conservation, no matter how carefully it is explained.
   b. preschoolers fail to solve conservation problems because they center their attention on the transformation that has occurred and ignore the changed appearances of the objects.
   c. with special training, even preoperational children are able to grasp some aspects of conservation.
   d. preschoolers fail to solve conservation problems because they have no theory of mind.

9. In order to scaffold a child's cognitive skills, parents:
   a. simplify tasks.
   b. interpret the activity.
   c. solve problems, anticipating mistakes.
   d. do all of the above.

10. Which theorist would be most likely to agree with the statement, "Learning is a social activity more than it is a matter of individual discovery"?
   a. Piaget
   b. Vygotsky
   c. both a. and b.
   d. neither a. nor b.

11. Children first demonstrate some understanding of grammar:
   a. as soon as the first words are produced.
   b. once they begin to use language for practical purposes.
   c. through the process called fast mapping.
   d. in their earliest two-word sentences.

12. Preschoolers sometimes seem forgetful because they:
   a. are unable to benefit from using mental scripts.
   b. often do not attend to event features that are pertinent to older people.
   c. are egocentric in their thinking.
   d. have all of the above limitations.

13. During the preschool years, the learning of new words tends to follow this sequence:
   a. verbs, followed by nouns, then adjectives, adverbs, and interrogatives.
   b. nouns, followed by verbs, then adjectives, adverbs, and interrogatives.
   c. adjectives, followed by verbs, then nouns, adverbs, and interrogatives.
   d. interrogatives, followed by nouns, then verbs, adjectives, and adverbs.

14. Overregularization indicates that a child:
   a. is clearly applying rules of grammar.
   b. persists in egocentric thinking.
   c. has not yet mastered the principle of conservation.
   d. does not yet have a theory of mind.

15. Regarding the value of preschool education, most developmentalists believe that:
   a. most disadvantaged children will not benefit from an early preschool education.
   b. most disadvantaged children will benefit from an early preschool education.
   c. because of sleeper effects, the early benefits of preschool education are likely to disappear by grade 3.
   d. the relatively small benefits of antipoverty measures such as Headstart do not justify their huge costs.

Matching Items

Match each term or concept with its corresponding description or definition.

Terms or Concepts

_____ 1. script
_____ 2. scaffold
_____ 3. theory of mind
_____ 4. zone of proximal development
_____ 5. overregularization
_____ 6. fast mapping
_____ 7. irreversibility
_____ 8. centration
_____ 9. conservation
_____ 10. private speech
_____ 11. guided participation

Descriptions or Definitions

a. the idea that amount is unaffected by changes in shape or placement
b. memory-facilitating outline of past experiences
c. the cognitive distance between a child's actual and potential levels of development
d. the tendency to think about one aspect of a situation at a time
e. the process whereby the child learns through social interaction with a "tutor"
f. our understanding of mental processes in ourselves and others
g. the process by which words are learned after only one hearing
h. an inappropriate application of rules of grammar
i. the internal use of language to form ideas
j. the inability to understand that original conditions are restored by the undoing of some process
k. to structure a child's participation in learning encounters

Thinking Critically About Chapter 9

Answer these questions the day before an exam as a final check on your understanding of the chapter's terms and concepts.

1. An experimenter first shows a child two rows of checkers that each have the same number of checkers. Then, with the child watching, the experimenter elongates one row and asks the child if each of the two rows still has an equal number of checkers. This experiment tests the child's understanding of:
   a. reversibility.
   b. conservation of matter.
   c. conservation of number.
   d. centration.

2. A preschooler believes that a "party" is the one and only attribute of a birthday. She says that Daddy doesn't have a birthday because he never has a party. This thinking demonstrates the tendency Piaget called:
   a. egocentrism.
   b. centration.
   c. conservation of events.
   d. mental representation.

3. A child who understands that 3 + 4 = 7 means that 7 – 4 = 3 has had to master the concept of:
   a. reversibility.
   b. number.
   c. conservation.
   d. egocentrism.

4. A 4-year-old tells the teacher that a clown should not be allowed to visit the class because "Pat is 'fraid of clowns." The 4-year-old thus shows that he can anticipate how another will feel. This is evidence of the beginnings of:
   a. egocentrism.
   b. deception.
   c. a theory of mind.
   d. conservation.

5. A Chinese visitor to an American preschool would probably be struck by its emphasis on fostering ____________ in children.
   a. conformity
   b. concern for others
   c. cooperation
   d. self-reliance

6. A nursery school teacher is given the job of selecting holiday entertainment for a group of preschool children. If the teacher agrees with the ideas of Vygotsky, she is most likely to select:
   a. a simple TV show that every child can understand.
   b. a hands-on experience that requires little adult supervision.
   c. brief, action-oriented play activities that the children and teachers will perform together.
   d. holiday puzzles for children to work on individually.

7. When asked to describe her friend's birthday party, 3-year-old Hilary gives a general description of events that form a composite of all the parties she has attended. Hilary evidently:
   a. is very egocentric in her thinking.
   b. is retrieving from a "birthday party script."
   c. failed to store memories that are specific to this party.
   d. has acquired a sophisticated theory of mind.

8. That a child produces sentences that follow such rules of word order as "the initiator of an action precedes the verb, the receiver of an action follows it" demonstrates a knowledge of:
   a. grammar.
   b. semantics.
   c. pragmatics.
   d. phrase structure.

9. The 2-year-old child who says, "We goed to the store," is making a grammatical:
   a. centration.
   b. overregularization.
   c. extension.
   d. script.

10. An experimenter who makes two balls of clay of equal amount, then rolls one into a long, skinny rope and asks the child if the amounts are still the same, is testing the child's understanding of:
    a. conservation.
    b. reversibility.
    c. perspective-taking.
    d. centration.

11. Dr. Jones, who believes that children's language growth greatly contributes to their cognitive growth, evidently is a proponent of the ideas of:
    a. Piaget.
    b. Chomsky.
    c. Flavell.
    d. Vygotsky.

12. Jack constantly "talks down" to his 3-year-old son's speech level. Jack's speech is:
    a. appropriate because 3-year-olds have barely begun to comprehend grammatical rules.
    b. commendable, given the importance of scaffolding in promoting cognitive growth.
    c. unnecessary because preschoolers are able to comprehend more complex grammar and vocabulary than they can produce.
    d. clearly within his son's zone of proximal development.

13. In describing the limited logical reasoning of preschoolers, a *contemporary* developmentalist is *least* likely to emphasize:
    a. irreversibility.
    b. centration.
    c. egocentrism.
    d. its static nature.

14. A preschooler fails to put together a difficult puzzle on her own, so her mother encourages her to try again, this time guiding her by asking questions such as, "For this space do we need a big piece or a little piece?" With Mom's help, the child successfully completes the puzzle. Lev Vygotsky would attribute the child's success to:
    a. additional practice with the puzzle pieces.
    b. imitation of her mother's behavior.
    c. the social interaction with her mother that restructured the task to make its solution more attainable.
    d. modeling and reinforcement.

15. Mark is answering an essay question that asks him to "discuss the positions of major developmental theorists regarding the relationship between language and cognitive development." To help organize his answer, Mark jots down a reminder that ________ contended that language is essential to the advancement of thinking, as private speech, and as a ________ of social interactions.
    a. Piaget; mediator
    b. Vygotsky; mediator
    c. Piaget; theory
    d. Vygotsky; theory

Key Terms

Writing Definitions

Using your own words, write a brief definition or explanation of each of the following terms on a separate piece of paper.

1. symbolic thought
2. preoperational thought
3. centration
4. egocentrism
5. irreversibility
6. conservation
7. guided participation
8. zone of proximal development
9. scaffold
10. private speech
11. social mediation
12. scripts
13. theory of mind
14. fast mapping
15. overregularization
16. Project Headstart
17. sleeper effect

Cross Check

After you have written the definitions of the key terms in this chapter, you should complete the crossword puzzle to ensure that you can reverse the process—recognize the term, given the definition.

ACROSS

2. The structure, techniques, and rules of a language.
6. Theorist who described the young child's thinking as lacking in logical reasoning ability.
11. Process by which children quickly learn new words.
12. The tendency of preschoolers to see things exclusively from their own perspective.
13. Mental outlines of familiar experiences.
14. Thinking that uses words or gestures to represent other objects or experiences.
15. Theorist who viewed cognitive development as a social interaction.

DOWN

1. What preschool learners are, according to Vygotsky.
2. The process by which parents and teachers assist preschoolers with challenging tasks and support the child's interest and motivation.
3. Piaget's term for the young child's thinking.
4. The tendency of young children to focus on only a single aspect of a situation.
5. The internal dialogue a person has with himself or herself.
7. The use of speech as a tool to bridge the zone of proximal development between a child and a tutor.
8. The understanding that the amount or quantity of a substance or object is unaffected by changes in its shape or configuration.
9. The counting principle that the last number in a count represents the total.
10. The inability to recognize that reversing a transformation brings about the same conditions that existed prior to the transformation.

ANSWERS

CHAPTER REVIEW

1. self-absorption
2. symbolic thought; preoperational
3. centration; egocentrism; appearances
4. static; unchanging; irreversibility
5. conservation; conservation of number
6. guided participation; social; interact
7. Lev Vygotsky
8. social activity
9. zone of proximal development
10. scaffold

Parents who scaffold effectively arouse and maintain the child's interest; simplify tasks; break the task down into steps within the child's ability; interpret the activity; solve problems, anticipating mistakes; and teach enthusiasm.

11. private speech; uttered aloud
12. mediator
13. impossible; gamelike; conservation
14. scaffold; culture
15. stable-order; one-to-one; cardinal
16. brain; language; curiosity; culture
17. language; East Asian; European; American; Japanese; Korean; Chinese
18. structure; support
19. memory; storage; retrieval

20. scripts; sequence; flow
21. attend to the features of an event that an older person would consider pertinent
22. did not
23. cues (or prompts); meaningful
24. were
25. social; relationship; age; atmosphere
26. resist
27. theory of mind
28. are

By age 3 or 4, young children distinguish between mental phenomena and the physical events to which they refer; they appreciate how mental states arise from experiences in the world; they understand that mental phenomena are subjective; they recognize that people have differing opinions and preferences; they realize that beliefs and desires can form the basis for human action; and they realize that emotion arises not only from physical events but also from one's goals, expectations, and other mental phenomena.

29. social; anticipating; influencing
30. language; brain maturation; brother or sister; culture
31. reality; 4 and 5
32. vocabulary
33. fast mapping
34. does
35. nouns; verbs; adjectives, adverbs, conjunctions, and interrogatives
36. more
37. comparisons; time; place
38. grammar; 3
39. mental program
40. hearing conversations at home that model good grammar; receiving helpful feedback about their language use
41. overregularization

Many preschoolers overapply the rule of adding "s" to form the plural, as well as the rule of adding "ed" to form the past tense. Thus, preschoolers are likely to say "foots" and "snows," and that someone "broked" a toy.

42. more

High-quality preschools are characterized by (a) a low teacher-child ratio, (b) a staff with training and credentials in early-childhood education, (c) a curriculum geared toward cognitive development, and (d) an organization of space that facilitates creative and constructive play.

43. social consensus; conformity; group activity; self-confidence; self-reliance
44. Project Headstart; higher; sleeper effect
45. home environment

PROGRESS TEST 1

Multiple-Choice Questions

1. **c.** is the answer. (p. 272)
2. **a.** is the answer. Unlike the U.S. government, the governments of many other developed countries sponsor preschool education. (p. 296)
3. **b.** is the answer. (pp. 284–285)

   c. & d. Research demonstrates that even young children often have very accurate *long*-term recall.
4. **a.** is the answer. (p. 280)

   b. & c. Experiments have demonstrated that preschoolers have *greater* number awareness than was once believed.

   d. Preschoolers are able to recognize *both* of these principles.
5. **b.** is the answer. (p. 282)

   a. Scripts tend to *improve* preschoolers' memory.

   c. & d. Although true, neither of these is the *primary* reason for preschoolers' poor memory.
6. **d.** is the answer. (p. 291)

   a. & c. Preschoolers generally have great difficulty understanding, and therefore using, metaphors and abstract nouns.

   b. Other than the grammatical errors of overregularization, the text does not indicate that preschoolers use a significant number of self-created words.
7. **a.** is the answer. (p. 294)

   b. & d. These terms are not identified in the text and do not apply to the use of grammar.

   c. Practical usage, which also is not discussed in the text, refers to communication between one person and another in terms of the overall context in which language is used.
8. **a.** is the answer. (p. 277)

   b. This expresses the views of Piaget.

   c. Because he believed that language facilitates thinking, Vygotsky obviously felt that language and other cognitive developments are intimately related.

d. Vygotsky did not hold this view.

9. **a.** is the answer. (p. 277)

10. **a.** is the answer. (p. 273)

b., c., & d. Failure to conserve is the result of thinking that is centered on appearances. Egocentrism and irreversibility are also examples of centered thinking.

11. **c.** is the answer. (p. 299)

b. This is not discussed in the text. However, although there was a slight early IQ advantage in Headstart graduates, the difference disappeared by grade 3.

a. & d. There was no indication of greater behavioral problems or alienation in Headstart graduates.

12. **b.** is the answer. (p. 296)

13. **c.** is the answer. (p. 295)

14. **d.** is the answer. (p. 278)

15. **a.** is the answer. (p. 291)

True or False Items

1. F More recent research has found that children may understand conservation earlier than Piaget thought, given a more gamelike presentation. His theory has not been rejected overall, however. (p. 278)
2. T (p. 274)
3. F In fact, just the opposite is true. Children who have learning difficulties tend to be slower to develop private speech. (p. 277)
4. T (p. 278)
5. T (p. 281)
6. F Piaget believed that language ability builds on the sensorimotor and conceptual accomplishments of infancy and toddlerhood. (p. 272)
7. F Preschoolers have difficulty understanding abstract words; their vocabulary consists mainly of concrete nouns and verbs. (p. 291)
8. F In adding "ed" to form a past tense, the child has indicated an understanding of the grammatical rule for making past tenses in English, even though the construction in these two cases is incorrect. (p. 295)
9. T (p. 296)
10. T (p. 274)

PROGRESS TEST 2

Multiple-Choice Questions

1. **a.** is the answer. (p. 285)

2. **a.** is the answer. (p. 286)

b. The children provided more information in response to *directive* questions.

c. Older children recalled *more* information spontaneously than did younger children.

3. **a.** is the answer. (p. 272)

b. Overregularization is the child's tendency to apply grammatical rules even when he or she shouldn't.

c. Reversibility is the concept that reversing an operation, such as addition, will restore the original conditions.

d. This term is used to refer to the young child's belief that people think as he or she does.

4. **c.** is the answer. This is why the stage is called *pre*operational. (p. 272)

5. **a.** is the answer. (p. 276)

6. **c.** is the answer. (p. 277)

a. & b. These are both advantages of private speech.

d. Fast mapping is the process by which new words are acquired, often after only one hearing.

7. **d.** is the answer. (p. 273)

a. This describes egocentrism.

b. This is the opposite of centration.

c. This defines conservation of number.

8. **a.** is the answer. (p. 274)

b. According to Piaget, preschoolers fail to solve conservation problems because they focus on the *appearance* of objects and ignore the transformation that has occurred.

d. Piaget did not relate conservation to a theory of mind.

9. **d.** is the answer. (p. 276)

10. **b.** is the answer. (pp. 274–275)

a. Piaget believed that learning is a matter of individual discovery.

11. **d.** is the answer. Preschoolers almost always put subject before verb in their two-word sentences. (p. 293)

12. **b.** is the answer. (p. 283)

a. Preschoolers *do* tend to use mental scripts.

c. Although this type of thinking is somewhat characteristic of preschoolers, it has no impact on memory per se.

13. **b.** is the answer. (p. 291)

14. **a.** is the answer. (p. 295)

b. c, & d. Overregularization is a *linguistic* phenomenon rather than a characteristic type of thinking (b. and d.), or a logical principle (c.).

15. **b.** is the answer. (p. 299)

Matching Items

1. b (p. 283)
2. k (p. 276)
3. f (p. 287)
4. c (p. 276)
5. h (p. 294)
6. g (p. 291)
7. j (p. 273)
8. d (p. 273)
9. a (p. 273)
10. i (p. 277)
11. e (p. 275)

THINKING CRITICALLY ABOUT CHAPTER 9

1. **c.** is the answer. (pp. 273–274)

   a. A test of reversibility would ask a child to perform an operation, such as adding 4 to 3, and then reverse the process (subtract 3 from 7) to determine whether the child understood that the original condition (the number 4) was restored.

   b. A test of conservation of matter would transform the appearance of an object, such as a ball of clay, to determine whether the child understood that the object remained the same.

   d. A test of centration would involve the child's ability to see various aspects of a situation.

2. **b.** is the answer. (p. 272)

   a. Egocentrism is thinking that is self-centered.

   c. This is not a concept in Piaget's theory.

   d. Mental representation is an example of symbolic thought.

3. **a.** is the answer. (p. 273)

4. **c.** is the answer. (p. 287)

   a. Egocentrism is self-centered thinking.

   b. Although deception provides evidence of a theory of mind, the child in this example is not deceiving anyone.

   d. Conservation is the understanding that the amount of a substance is unchanged by changes in its shape or placement.

5. **d.** is the answer. (p. 297)

   a., b., & c. Chinese preschools place *more* emphasis on these attitudes and behaviors than do American preschools.

6. **c.** is the answer. In Vygotsky's view, learning is a social activity more than a matter of individual discovery. Thus, social interaction that provides motivation and focuses attention facilitates learning. (p. 274)

   a., b., & d. These situations either provide no opportunity for social interaction (b. & d.) or do not challenge the children (a.).

7. **b.** is the answer. (p. 283)

   a. Egocentrism is thinking that is self-focused.

   c. Preschoolers do form memories of specific events; their retrieval, however, is often a composite of similar experiences.

   d. This refers to preschoolers' emerging social understanding of others' perspectives.

8. **a.** is the answer. (p. 293)

   b. & d. The text does not discuss these aspects of language.

   c. Pragmatics, which is not mentioned in the text, refers to the practical use of language in varying social contexts.

9. **b.** is the answer. (p. 294)

10. **a.** is the answer. (pp. 273–274)

11. **d.** is the answer. (p. 277)

    a. Piaget believed that cognitive growth precedes language development.

    b. & c. Chomsky focused on the *acquisition* of language, and Flavell emphasizes cognition.

12. **c.** is the answer. (p. 295)

13. **d.** is the answer. (pp. 272–273)

14. **c.** is the answer. (p. 276)

15. **b.** is the answer. (p. 277)

KEY TERMS

Writing Definitions

1. **Symbolic thought** is thinking that involves the use of words, gestures, pictures, or actions to represent other objects, behaviors, or experiences. (p. 272)

2. According to Piaget, thinking between ages 2 and 6 is characterized by **preoperational thought**, meaning that children cannot yet perform logical operations; that is, they cannot use logical principles. (p. 272)

   Memory aid: Operations are mental transformations involving the manipulation of ideas and symbols. *Pre*operational children, who lack the ability to perform transformations, are "before" this developmental milestone.

3. **Centration** is the tendency of young children to focus only on a single aspect of a situation or object. (p. 272)

4. **Egocentrism** refers to the tendency of young children to view the world exclusively from their own perspective. (p. 272)

5. **Irreversibility** is the inability to recognize that reversing a transformation brings about the same

conditions that existed prior to the transformation. (p. 273)

6. **Conservation** is the understanding that the amount or quantity of a substance or object is unaffected by changes in its shape or configuration. (p. 273)
7. According to Vygotsky, intellectual growth in young children is stimulated and directed by their **guided participation** in learning experiences. As guides, parents, teachers, and older children offer assistance with challenging tasks, model problem-solving approaches, provide explicit instructions as needed, and support the child's interest and motivation. (p. 275)
8. According to Vygotsky, for each individual there is a **zone of proximal development**, which represents the skills that are within the potential of the learner but cannot be performed independently. (p. 276)
9. Tutors who **scaffold** structure children's learning experiences by simplifying tasks, maintaining children's interest, and solving problems, anticipating mistakes, among other things. (p. 276)
10. **Private speech** is the internal dialogue in which a person talks to himself or herself. Preschoolers' private speech, which often is uttered aloud, helps them think, review what they know, and decide what to do. (p. 277)
11. In Vygotsky's theory, **social mediation** refers to the use of speech as a tool to bridge the gap in understanding or knowledge between a child and a tutor. (p. 277)
12. **Scripts** are mental outlines of familiar, recurrent past experiences used to facilitate the storage and retrieval of memories. (p. 283)
13. A **theory of mind** is an understanding of mental processes, that is, of one's own or another's emotions, perceptions, intentions, and thoughts. (p. 287)
14. **Fast mapping** is the process by which children rapidly learn new words by quickly connecting them to words and categories that are already understood. (p. 291)
15. **Overregularization** occurs when children apply rules of grammar when they should not. It is seen in English, for example, when children add "s" to form the plural even in irregular cases that form the plural in a different way. (p. 294)
16. **Project Headstart** is a preschool program that was initiated in 1965 in response to a perceived need to improve the educational future of low-income children. (p. 297)
17. A **sleeper effect** is an outcome of a program (such as Headstart) that is hidden for a while but later becomes apparent. (p. 299)

Cross Check

ACROSS

2. grammar
6. Piaget
11. fast mapping
12. egocentrism
13. scripts
14. symbolic
15. Vygotsky

DOWN

1. apprentices
2. guided participation
3. preoperational
4. centration
5. private speech
7. social mediation
8. conservation
9. cardinal

CHAPTER 10

The Play Years: Psychosocial Development

Chapter Overview

Chapter 10 explores the ways in which young children begin to relate to others in an ever-widening social environment. The chapter begins where social understanding begins, with the emergence of the sense of self. With their increasing social awareness, children become more concerned with how others evaluate them and better able to regulate their emotions.

The next section explores the origins of helpful, prosocial behaviors in young children, as well as aggression, and other hurtful antisocial behaviors. These social skills reflect many influences, including early attachments, learning from playmates through various types of play, as well as from television.

The third section describes the increasing complexity of children's interactions with others, paying special attention to the parent-child relationship in terms of different styles of parenting and how factors such as the cultural, ethnic, and community context influence the effectiveness of parenting.

The chapter concludes with a description of children's emerging awareness of male-female differences and gender identity. Five major theories of gender-role development are considered.

NOTE: Answer guidelines for all Chapter 10 questions begin on page 159.

Guided Study

The text chapter should be studied one section at a time. Before you read, preview each section by skimming it, noting headings and boldface items. Then read the appropriate section objectives from the following outline. Keep these objectives in mind and, as you read the chapter section, search for the information that will enable you to meet each objective. Once you have finished a section, write out answers for its objectives.

The Self and the Social World (pp. 303–310)

1. Discuss the relationship between the child's developing sense of self and social awareness.

2. Discuss the importance of positive self-evaluation during this period, noting the role of mastery play in gaining self-esteem.

3. Discuss emotional development during early childhood, focusing on emotional regulation.

Antisocial and Prosocial Behavior (pp. 310–315)

4. Discuss the nature and significance of rough-and-tumble and sociodramatic play during the play years.

5. (text and Children Up Close) Discuss how playing with peers and watching television contributes to the development of aggression and other antisocial behaviors.

Parenting Patterns (pp. 315–326)

6. Compare and contrast three classic patterns of parenting and their effect on children.

7. Discuss the pros and cons of punishment, and describe the most effective method for disciplining a child.

8. Discuss how parenting style is determined by economic well-being, family pattern and size, ethnicity, and culture.

9. (Changing Policy) Discuss the impact of being an only child on cognitive and social development.

Boy or Girl: So What? (pp. 326–335)

10. Describe the developmental progression of gender awareness in young children.

11. Summarize five theories of gender-role development during the play years, noting important contributions of each.

Chapter Review

When you have finished reading the chapter, work through the material that follows to review it. Complete the sentences and answer the questions. As you proceed, evaluate your performance for each section by consulting the answers on page 159. Do not continue with the next section until you understand each answer. If you need to, review or reread the appropriate section in the textbook before continuing.

1. Psychosocial advances during the play years are partly the result of cognitive growth in the child's ________________ ________________ ________________.

The Self and the Social World (pp. 303–310)

2. The play years are filled with examples of the child's emerging ________________.
3. The growth of preschoolers' self-awareness is especially apparent in their ________________ with others.
4. As their theory of mind expands, preschoolers become less ________________ and more ________________. They also become less ________________ and ________________, although some develop irrational fears, or ________________.

5. Psychologists emphasize the importance of children's developing a positive ____________. Preschoolers typically form impressions of themselves that are quite ____________. One manifestation of this tendency is that preschoolers regularly ____________ (overestimate/underestimate) their own abilities. Most preschoolers think of themselves as competent ____________ (in all/only in certain) areas.

6. Most developmentalists believe that ____________ is the work of early childhood. An important part of preschoolers' lives is ____________ ____________—practicing a skill until one is proficient at it. This type of play involves not only physical skills but also ____________ and ____________ abilities.

7. At this point, according to Erikson, children are in the stage of ____________.

8. As they grow, preschoolers become ____________ (more/less) concerned with how others evaluate their behavior.

9. Preschoolers' self-evaluation and initiative stem from their growing ____________ ____________.

10. The most significant emotional development during early childhood is ____________ ____________, which is the growing ability to direct or modify one's feelings in response to expectations from ____________. This ability develops partly as the result of ____________ maturation and partly as a result of ____________. According to Daniel Goleman, this ability is crucial to ____________ ____________.

11. How children regulate their emotions reflects the results of past ____________. For example, children who respond unsympathetically to another child's distress may have ____________ ____________.

12. Another example of emotional regulation is appropriate expression of ____________.

Antisocial and Prosocial Behavior (pp. 310–315)

13. Sharing, cooperating, and sympathizing are examples of ____________ ____________. Conversely, actions that are destructive or deliberately hurtful are called ____________ ____________.

14. According to Mildred Parten, young children progress from ____________ play, in which they play alone, to ____________ play, in which they watch others play, to ____________ play, in which children play alongside others without interacting, to ____________ play, in which there is some interaction with playmates, to ____________ play, in which children fully interact while playing together. With the advent of ____________, the progression of ____________ play is more rapid and variable today.

15. The type of physical play that mimics aggression is called ____________-____________-____________ play. A distinctive feature of this form of play, which ____________ (occurs only in some cultures/is universal), is the positive facial expression that characterizes the ____________ ____________.

Gender differences ____________ (are/are not) evident in rough-and-tumble play.

16. In ____________ play, children act out various roles and themes in stories of their own creation. The increase in this form of play is related to the development of the child's ____________ ____________ ____________ and emotional regulation, as well as the development of ____________.

17. A typical preschool child In the United States watches more than ____________ hours of television per day. The most troubling criticism of television is that it encourages ____________ ____________ in young children, in part by ____________ children to violence in real life.

State several other criticisms of television from a developmental perspective.

18. The roots of aggression are inadequate ______________ and ______________ ______________ during the early preschool years.

19. Developmentalists distinguish three types of physical aggression: ______________, used to obtain or retain a toy or other object; ______________, used in angry retaliation against an intentional or accidental act committed by a peer; and ______________, used in an unprovoked attack on a peer.

20. Social aggression that involves insults or social rejection is called ______________ ______________. This type of aggression is more common among ______________ than those of the other gender, and ______________ (younger/older) children.

Parenting Patterns (pp. 315–326)

21. A significant influence on early psychosocial growth is the style of ______________ that characterizes a child's family life.

22. There ______________ (is/is not) a single best style of parenting that will guarantee a child's successful upbringing. The seminal research on parenting styles, which was conducted by ______________, found that parents varied in their ______________ toward offspring, in their strategies for ______________, in how well they ______________, and in their expectations for ______________.

23. Parents who adopt the ______________ style demand unquestioning obedience from their children. In this style of parenting, nurturance tends to be ______________ (low/high), maturity demands are ______________ (low/high), and parent-child communication tends to be ______________ (low/high).

24. Parents who adopt the ______________ style make few demands on their children and are lax in discipline. Such parents ______________ (are/are not very) nurturant, communicate ______________ (well/poorly), and make ______________ (few/extensive) maturity demands.

25. Parents who adopt the ______________ style democratically set limits and enforce rules. Such parents make ______________ (high/low) maturity demands, communicate ______________ (well/poorly), and ______________ (are/are not) nurturant.

26. Follow-up studies indicate that children raised by ______________ parents are likely to be obedient but unhappy; those raised by ______________ parents are likely to lack self-control; and those raised by ______________ parents are more likely to be successful, happy with themselves, and generous with others. These advantages ______________ (grow stronger/weaken) over time.

27. Parents who take somewhat old-fashioned male and female roles are labeled ______________ parents. This style of parenting ______________ (does/does not) tend to lead to good outcomes.

28. To be effective, punishment should be more ______________ than ______________.

29. (Research Report) A 1994 study investigated the relationship between spanking and aggressive behavior in the child. Observers scored kindergartners for instances of aggressive behavior. Compared with children who were not spanked, those children who were spanked were more likely to engage in ______________ aggression.

30. Japanese mothers tend to use ______________ as disciplinary techniques more often than do North American mothers, who are more likely to encourage ______________ expressions of all sorts in their children. Throughout the world, most parents ______________ (believe/do not believe) that spanking is acceptable at times. Although spanking ______________ (is/is not) effective, it may teach children to be more ______________.

Identify several influences that contribute to shaping parenting style.

31. Many parents use ______________ ______________ to adapt their parenting style to the age, birth order, and sex of a particular child. Although this makes logical sense, one disadvantage is that ______________ ______________.

32. The impact of a particular parenting style may also depend on the child's ______________. For example, one study found that ______________ parenting was associated with the best outcomes among European-American youths, whereas ______________ parenting was associated with the best outcomes among African-American youths.

33. In most ways, only children fare ______________ (as well as or better/worse) than children with siblings. Only children are particularly likely to benefit ______________, becoming more ______________ and more ______________. A potential problem for only children is in their development of ______________ skills.

Boy or Girl: So What? (pp. 326–335)

34. Social scientists distinguish between biological, or ______________ ______________ between males and females, and cultural, or ______________ ______________ in the ______________ and behaviors of the two sexes.

35. True sex differences are ______________ (more/less) apparent in childhood than in adulthood.

36. By age ______________, children can consistently apply gender labels and have a rudimentary understanding of the permanence of their own gender. By age ______________, most children express stereotypic ideas of each sex. Such stereotyping ______________ (does/does not) occur in children whose parents provide nontraditional gender role models.

37. Freud called the period from age 3 to 7 the ______________ ______________. According to his view, boys in this stage develop sexual feelings about their ______________ and become jealous of their ______________. Freud called this phenomenon the ______________ ______________.

38. In Freud's theory, preschool boys resolve their guilty feelings defensively through ______________ with their father. Boys also develop, again in self-defense, a powerful conscience called the ______________.

39. According to Freud, during the phallic stage little girls may experience the ______________ ______________, in which they want to get rid of their mother and become intimate with their father. Alternatively, they may become jealous of boys because they have a penis; this emotion Freud called ______________ ______________.

40. According to learning theory, preschool children develop gender-role ideas by being ______________ for behaviors deemed appropriate for their sex and ______________ for behaviors deemed inappropriate.

41. Social learning theorists maintain that children learn gender-appropriate behavior by ______________________.

42. Cognitive theorists focus on children's ______________ of male-female differences. According to ______________-______________ theory, children develop a simple ______________ of gender roles, and then apply it universally.

43. According to the ______________ theory, gender education varies by region, socioeconomic status, and historical period. Gender distinctions are emphasized in many ______________ cultures. This theory points out that children can maintain a balance of male and female characteristics, or ______________, only if their culture promotes that idea.

44. According to ______________ ______________ theory, gender attitudes and roles are the result of interaction between ______________ and ______________ ______________.

45. One idea that has recently found greater acceptance is the idea that some gender differences are ______________ rather than ______________ based.

46. In some respects, the two sexes are different because there are subtle differences in ______________ development.

Describe several of these differences.

47. These differences probably ______________ (are/are not) the result of any single gene. More likely, they result from the differing ______________ ______________ that influence brain development. One piece of evidence that this is true comes from girls who have the disorder ______________ ______________ ______________, that causes their hormone balance to be more like a boy's than a girl's. Such girls tend to prefer ______________.

Progress Test 1

Multiple-Choice Questions

Circle your answers to the following questions and check them with the answers on page 160. If your answer is incorrect, read the explanation for why it is incorrect and then consult the appropriate pages of the text (in parentheses following the correct answer).

1. Preschool children have a clear (but not necessarily accurate) concept of self. Typically, the preschooler believes that she or he:
   a. owns all objects in sight.
   b. is great at almost everything.
   c. is much less competent than peers and older children.
   d. is more powerful than her or his parents.

2. According to Freud, the third stage of psychosexual development, during which the penis is the focus of psychological concern and pleasure, is the:
   a. oral stage.
   b. anal stage.
   c. phallic stage.
   d. latency period.

3. Because it helps children rehearse social roles, work out fears and fantasies, and learn cooperation, an important form of social play is:
   a. sociodramatic play.
   b. mastery play.
   c. rough-and-tumble play.
   d. sensorimotor play.

4. The three *basic* patterns of parenting described by Diana Baumrind are:
   a. hostile, loving, and harsh.
   b. authoritarian, permissive, and authoritative.
   c. positive, negative, and punishing.
   d. indulgent, neglecting, and traditional.

5. Authoritative parents are receptive and loving, but they also normally:
   a. set limits and enforce rules.
   b. have difficulty communicating.
   c. withhold praise and affection.
   d. encourage aggressive behavior.

6. Children who watch a lot of violent television:
   a. are more likely to be aggressive.
   b. become desensitized to violence.
   c. are less likely to attempt to mediate a quarrel between other children.
   d. have all of the above characteristics.

7. Four-year-old Lauren draws the same picture over and over, each time becoming a little more proficient at this difficult motor skill. A developmentalist would say Lauren is engaging in:
   a. associative play.
   b. parallel play.
   c. mastery play.
   d. sociodramatic play.

8. During the play years, a child's self-concept is defined largely by his or her:
   a. expanding range of skills and competencies.
   b. physical appearance.
   c. gender.
   d. relationship with family members.

9. Learning theorists emphasize the importance of ____________ in the development of the preschool child.
   a. identification
   b. praise and blame
   c. initiative
   d. a theory of mind

10. Children apply gender labels, and have definite ideas about how boys and girls behave, as early as age:
    a. 3.
    b. 4.
    c. 5.
    d. 7.

11. In chaotic and dangerous environments, ____________ parenting may be most beneficial to children.
    a. authoritative
    b. authoritarian
    c. traditional
    d. permissive

12. Six-year-old Leonardo has superior verbal ability rivaling that of most girls his age. Dr. Laurent believes this is due to the fact that although his sex is predisposed to slower language development, Leonardo's upbringing in a linguistically rich home enhanced his biological capabilities. Dr. Laurent is evidently a proponent of:
    a. cognitive theory.
    b. gender-schema theory.
    c. sociocultural theory.
    d. epigenetic systems theory.

13. Compared with children with siblings, only children are likely to:
    a. be less verbal.
    b. fare as well or better in most ways.
    c. have greater competence in social skills.
    d. be less creative.

14. Which of the following was not identified as a reason for variations in parenting styles?
    a. the parent's ethnic and cultural background
    b. the family's economic well-being
    c. the parent's personality
    d. the parents' ages

15. When her friend hurts her feelings, Maya shouts that she is a "mean old stinker!" Maya's behavior is an example of:
    a. instrumental aggression.
    b. reactive aggression.
    c. bullying aggression.
    d. relational aggression.

True or False Items

Write *true* or *false* on the line in front of each statement.

________ 1. According to Baumrind, only authoritarian parents make maturity demands on their children.

________ 2. Children of authoritative parents tend to be successful, happy with themselves, and generous with others.

________ 3. True sex differences are more apparent in childhood than in adulthood.

________ 4. (Research Report) Spanking is associated with higher rates of aggression toward peers.

________ 5. Many gender differences are genetically based.

________ 6. Children from feminist or nontraditional homes seldom have stereotypic ideas about feminine and masculine roles.

________ 7. Developmentalists do not agree about how children acquire gender roles.

________ 8. By age 3, most children have definite ideas about what constitutes typical masculine and feminine behavior.

________ 9. Identification was defined by Freud as a defense mechanism in which people identify with others who may be stronger and more powerful than they.

________ 10. Sociodramatic play is free-wheeling, creative, and fluid.

Progress Test 2

Progress Test 2 should be completed during a final chapter review. Answer the following questions after you thoroughly understand the correct answers for the Chapter Review and Progress Test 1.

Multiple-Choice Questions

1. Children of permissive parents are *most* likely to lack:
   a. social skills.
   b. self-control.
   c. initiative and guilt.
   d. care and concern.

2. Children learn reciprocity, nurturance, and cooperation most readily from their interaction with:
   a. their mothers.
   b. their fathers.
   c. friends.
   d. others of the same sex.

3. The initial advantages of parenting style:
   a. do not persist past middle childhood.
   b. remain apparent through adolescence.
   c. are likely to be even stronger over time.
   d. have an unpredictable impact later in children's lives.

4. Which theory maintains that children's ideas about gender are based on simple scripts developed from their experience?
   a. psychoanalytic theory
   b. epigenetic systems theory
   c. sociocultural theory
   d. gender-schema theory

5. Which of the following best summarizes the current view of developmentalists regarding gender differences?
   a. Some gender differences are biological in origin.
   b. Most gender differences are biological in origin.
   c. Nearly all gender differences are cultural in origin.
   d. There is no consensus among developmentalists regarding the origin of gender differences.

6. According to Freud, a young boy's jealousy of his father's relationship with his mother, and the guilt feelings that result, are part of the:
   a. Electra complex.
   b. Oedipus complex.
   c. phallic complex.
   d. penis envy complex.

7. The style of parenting in which the parents make few demands on children, the discipline is lax, and the parents are nurturant and accepting is:
   a. authoritarian.
   b. authoritative.
   c. permissive.
   d. rejecting-neglecting.

8. Cooperating with a playmate is to ______________ as insulting a playmate is to ______________.
   a. antisocial behavior; prosocial behavior
   b. prosocial behavior; antisocial behavior
   c. emotional regulation; antisocial behavior
   d. prosocial behavior; emotional regulation

9. Which of the following children would probably be said to have a phobia?
   a. Nicky, who has an exaggerated and irrational fear of furry animals
   b. Nairobi, who is frightened by loud thunder
   c. Noriko, who doesn't like getting shots
   d. All of the above have phobias.

10. Which of the following theories advocates the development of gender identification as a means of avoiding guilt over feelings for the opposite-sex parent?
    a. learning
    b. sociocultural
    c. psychoanalytic
    d. social learning

11. Compared to children with siblings, only children are more likely to be:
    a. overly dependent upon their parents.
    b. very spoiled.
    c. both a. and b.
    d. neither a. nor b.

12. The preschooler's readiness to learn new tasks and play activities reflects his or her:
    a. emerging competency and self-awareness.
    b. theory of mind.
    c. relationship with parents.
    d. growing identification with others.

13. Emotional regulation is in part related to maturation of a specific part of the brain in the:
    a. frontal cortex.
    b. parietal cortex.
    c. temporal lobe.
    d. occipital lobe.

14. In which style of parenting is the parents' word law and misbehavior strictly punished?

a. permissive
b. authoritative
c. authoritarian
d. traditional

15. Erikson noted that preschoolers eagerly begin many new activities but are vulnerable to criticism and feelings of failure; they experience the crisis of:

a. identity versus role confusion.
b. initiative versus guilt.
c. basic trust versus mistrust.
d. efficacy versus helplessness.

Matching Items

Match each term or concept with its corresponding description or definition.

Terms or Concepts

_______ **1.** rough-and-tumble play
_______ **2.** androgyny
_______ **3.** sociodramatic play
_______ **4.** prosocial behavior
_______ **5.** antisocial behavior
_______ **6.** Electra complex
_______ **7.** Oedipus complex
_______ **8.** authoritative
_______ **9.** authoritarian
_______ **10.** identification
_______ **11.** instrumental aggression

Descriptions or Definitions

a. aggressive behavior whose purpose is to obtain an object desired by another
b. Freudian theory that every daughter secretly wishes to replace her mother
c. parenting style associated with high maturity demands and low parent-child communication
d. an action performed for the benefit of another person without the expectation of reward
e. Freudian theory that every son secretly wishes to replace his father
f. parenting style associated with high maturity demands and high parent-child communication
g. two children wrestle without serious hostility
h. an action that is intended to harm someone else
i. two children act out roles in a story of their own creation
j. a defense mechanism through which children cope with their feelings of guilt during the phallic stage
k. a balance of traditional male and female characteristics in an individual

Thinking Critically About Chapter 10

Answer these questions the day before an exam as a final check on your understanding of the chapter's terms and concepts.

1. Bonita eventually copes with the fear and anger she feels over her hatred of her mother and love of her father by:
   a. identifying with her mother.
   b. copying her brother's behavior.
   c. adopting her father's moral code.
   d. competing with her brother for her father's attention.

2. A little girl who says she wants her mother to go on vacation so that she can marry her father is voicing a fantasy consistent with the ________________ described by Freud.
   a. Oedipus complex
   b. Electra complex
   c. theory of mind
   d. crisis of initiative versus guilt

3. According to Erikson, before the preschool years children are incapable of feeling guilt because:
   a. guilt depends on a sense of self, which is not sufficiently established in preschoolers.
   b. they do not yet understand that they are male or female for life.
   c. this emotion is unlikely to have been reinforced at such an early age.
   d. guilt is associated with the resolution of the Oedipus complex, which occurs later in life.

4. Parents who are strict and aloof are *most* likely to make their children:
   a. cooperative and trusting.
   b. obedient but unhappy.
   c. violent.
   d. withdrawn and anxious.

5. When 4-year-old Seema grabs for Vincenzo's beanie baby, Vincenzo slaps her hand away, displaying an example of:
   a. bullying aggression.
   b. reactive aggression.
   c. instrumental aggression.
   d. relational aggression.

6. The belief that almost all sexual patterns are learned rather than inborn would find its strongest adherents among __________ theorists.
   a. cognitive
   b. learning
   c. psychoanalytic
   d. epigenetic systems

7. In explaining the origins of gender distinctions, Dr. Christie notes that every society teaches its children its values and attitudes regarding preferred behavior for men and women. Dr. Christie is evidently a proponent of:
   a. gender-schema theory.
   b. sociocultural theory.
   c. epigenetic systems theory.
   d. psychoanalytic theory.

8. Five-year-old Rodney has a better-developed sense of self and is more confident than Darnell. According to the text, it is likely that Rodney will also be more skilled at:
   a. tasks involving verbal reasoning.
   b. social interaction.
   c. deception.
   d. all of the above.

9. Your sister and brother-in-law are thinking of having a second child because they are worried that only children miss out on the benefits of social play. You tell them that:
   a. parents can compensate for this by making sure the child has regular contact with other children.
   b. only children are likely to possess *superior* social skills because of the greater attention they receive from their parents.
   c. the style of parenting, rather than the presence of siblings, is the most important factor in social and intellectual development.
   d. unfortunately, this is true and nothing can replace the opportunities for acquiring social skills that siblings provide.

10. Concerning children's concept of gender, which of the following statements is true?
   a. Before the age of 3 or so, children think that boys and girls can change gender as they get older.
   b. Children as young as 2 years have a clear understanding of the physical differences between girls and boys and can consistently apply gender labels.
   c. Not until age 5 or 6 do children show a clear preference for gender-typed toys.
   d. All of the above are true.

11. Which of the following is *not* one of the features of parenting used by Baumrind to differentiate authoritarian, permissive, and authoritative parents?
    a. maturity demands for the child's conduct
    b. efforts to control the child's actions
    c. nurturance
    d. adherence to stereotypic gender roles

12. Jan recalls her mother as being nurturant and permissive, and her father was much more authoritarian. It is likely that Jan's parents would be classified as ______________ by Diana Baumrind.
    a. democratic-indulgent
    b. traditional
    c. androgynous
    d. authoritative

13. Which of the following is *not* a gender difference cited in the text?
    a. Right hemisphere activity is more pronounced in females.
    b. The corpus callosum is thicker in females.
    c. Brain maturation is faster in females.
    d. Right hemisphere dendrite formation is more pronounced in males.

14. (Research Report) Which of the following is true regarding the effects of spanking?
    a. Spanking seems to reduce reactive aggression.
    b. When administered appropriately, spanking promotes psychosocial development.
    c. Spanking is associated with increased aggression toward peers.
    d. None of the above is true.

15. Aldo and Jack are wrestling and hitting each other. Although this rough-and-tumble play mimics negative, aggressive behavior, it serves a useful purpose, which is to:
    a. rehearse social roles.
    b. develop interactive skills.
    c. improve fine motor skills.
    d. do both b. and c.

Key Terms

Using your own words, write a brief definition or explanation of each of the following terms on a separate piece of paper.

1. phobia
2. mastery play
3. initiative versus guilt
4. emotional regulation
5. prosocial behavior
6. antisocial behavior
7. rough-and-tumble play
8. play face
9. sociodramatic play
10. instrumental aggression
11. reactive aggression
12. bullying aggression
13. relational aggression
14. authoritarian parenting
15. permissive parenting
16. authoritative parenting
17. differential treatment
18. sex differences
19. gender differences
20. phallic stage
21. Oedipus complex
22. identification
23. superego
24. Electra complex
25. gender-schema theory
26. androgyny

ANSWERS

CHAPTER REVIEW

1. theory of mind
2. self-concept
3. negotiations
4. stubborn (or demanding); compromising; ritualistic; superstitious; phobias
5. self-concept; optimistic; overestimate; in all
6. play; mastery play; language; intellectual
7. initiative versus guilt
8. more
9. social awareness
10. emotional regulation; society; neurological; learning; emotional intelligence
11. caregiving; insecure attachments
12. friendliness
13. prosocial behavior; antisocial behavior
14. solitary; onlooker; parallel; associative; cooperative; preschool; social
15. rough-and-tumble; is universal; play face; are
16. sociodramatic; theory of mind; self-understanding
17. 3; antisocial behavior; desensitizing

Television takes away from active, interactive, and imaginative play; exposes children to faulty nutritional messages and sexist, racist, and ageist stereotypes.

18. self-concept; emotional regulation
19. instrumental; reactive; bullying
20. relational aggression; girls; older
21. parenting
22. is not; Baumrind; nurturance; discipline; communicate; maturity
23. authoritarian; low; high; low
24. permissive; are; well; few
25. authoritative; high; well; are
26. authoritarian; permissive; authoritative; grow stronger
27. traditional; does
28. proactive; punitive
29. reactive
30. reasoning; emotional; believe; is; aggressive

Parenting style derives, in part, from the parents' child-rearing goals and from beliefs about the nature of children, the proper role of parents, and the best way to raise children. The parents' personality, economic well-being, and memory of their own upbringing are also important influences.

31. differential treatment; siblings who notice they are being treated differently may resent it
32. ethnicity; authoritative; authoritarian
33. as well as or better; intellectually; verbal; creative; social
34. sex differences; gender differences; roles
35. less
36. 2; 6; does
37. phallic stage; mother; father; Oedipus complex
38. identification; superego
39. Electra complex; penis envy
40. reinforced; punished
41. observing and interacting with other people
42. understanding; gender-schema; script
43. sociocultural; traditional; androgyny
44. epigenetic systems; genes; early experience
45. biologically; culturally
46. brain

In females, the corpus callosum is thicker, and overall brain maturation occurs more quickly. In males, right-hemisphere activity and dendrite formation tend to be more pronounced.

47. are not; sex hormones; congenital adrenal hyperplasia; boys' toys and play activities

PROGRESS TEST 1

Multiple-Choice Questions

1. **b.** is the answer. (p. 306)

2. **c.** is the answer. (p. 328)

a. & b. In Freud's theory, the oral and anal stages are associated with infant and early childhood development, respectively.

d. In Freud's theory, the latency period is associated with development during the school years.

3. **a.** is the answer. (p. 312)

b. Mastery play is play that helps children develop new physical and intellectual skills.

c. Rough-and-tumble play is physical play that mimics aggression.

d. Sensorimotor play captures the pleasures of using the senses and motor skills.

4. **b.** is the answer. (pp. 318–319)

d. Traditional is a variation of the basic styles uncovered by later research. Indulgent and neglecting are not discussed in the text.

5. **a.** is the answer. (p. 319)

b. & c. Authoritative parents communicate very well and are quite affectionate.

d. This is not typical of authoritative parents.

6. **d.** is the answer. (pp. 313–314)

7. **c.** is the answer. (p. 306)

a. & b. In these forms of play, a child interacts, to varying degrees, with other playmates.

d. This is pretend play, in which children act out various roles.

8. **a.** is the answer. (p. 304)

9. **b.** is the answer. (p. 329)

a. This is the focus of Freud's phallic stage.

c. This is the focus of Erikson's psychosocial theory.

d. This is the focus of cognitive theorists.

10. **a.** is the answer. (p. 326)

11. **b.** is the answer. (p. 324)

12. **d.** is the answer. In accounting for Leonardo's verbal ability, Dr. Laurent alludes to both genetic and environmental factors, a dead-giveaway for epigenetic systems theory. (pp. 333–334)

a., b., & c. These theories do not address biological or genetic influences on development.

13. **b.** is the answer. (p. 325)

a. & d. Only children often benefit intellectually, becoming more verbal and more creative.

c. Because only children may miss out on the benefits of social play, they may be weaker in their social skills.

14. **d.** is the answer. (pp. 320–324)
15. **d.** is the answer. (p. 315)

a., b., & c. Each of these is an example of *physical* rather than verbal aggression.

True or False Items

1. F All parents make some maturity demands on their children; maturity demands are high in both the authoritarian and authoritative parenting styles. (pp. 318–319)
2. T (p. 319)
3. F Just the opposite is true. (p. 326)
4. T (p. 322)
5. T (p. 333)
6. F Children raised in feminist or nontraditional homes often surprise their parents by expressing stereotypic ideas about feminine and masculine roles. (p. 333)
7. T (pp. 328–334)
8. T (p. 326)
9. T (p. 329)
10. F Although sociodramatic play appears creative and fluid, it actually involves complex rules and structures. (p. 313)

PROGRESS TEST 2

Multiple-Choice Questions

1. **b.** is the answer. (p. 319)
2. **c.** is the answer. (p. 316)

a. & b. Siblings often provide better instruction than adults because they are likely to guide, challenge, and encourage a child's social interactions more frequently and intimately.

d. The text does not indicate that same-sex friends are more important in learning these than friends of the other sex.

3. **c.** is the answer. (p. 319)
4. **d.** is the answer. (pp. 331–332)
5. **a.** is the answer. Recent research has found that the sexes are different in part because of subtle differences in brain development. (p. 333)
6. **b.** is the answer. (p. 328)

a. & d. These are Freud's versions of phallic-stage development in little girls.

c. There is no such thing as the "phallic complex."

7. **c.** is the answer. (p. 318)

a. & b. Both authoritarian and authoritative parents make high demands on their children.

d. Rejecting-neglecting parents are quite cold and unengaged.

8. **b.** is the answer. (pp. 310–311)
9. **a.** is the answer. Exaggeration and irrationality are two hallmarks of phobias. (p. 305)

b. & c. Neither of these fears seems exaggerated or irrational.

10. **c.** is the answer. (p. 328)

a. & d. Learning and social learning theories emphasize that children learn about gender by rewards and punishments and by observing others.

b. Sociocultural theory focuses on the impact of the environment on gender identification.

11. **d.** is the answer. (p. 325)
12. **a.** is the answer. (pp. 304–305)

b. This viewpoint is associated only with cognitive theory.

c. Although parent-child relationships are important to social development, they do not determine readiness.

d. Identification is a Freudian defense mechanism.

13. **a.** is the answer. (p. 309)
14. **c.** is the answer. (p. 318)
15. **b.** is the answer. (p. 307)

a. & c. According to Erikson, these are the crises of adolescence and infancy, respectively.

d. This is not a crisis described by Erikson.

Matching Items

1. g (p. 311)	**5.** h (p. 310)	**9.** c (p. 318)
2. k (p. 333)	**6.** b (p. 329)	**10.** j (p. 329)
3. i (p. 312)	**7.** e (p. 328)	**11.** a (p. 315)
4. d (p. 310)	**8.** f (p. 319)	

THINKING CRITICALLY ABOUT CHAPTER 10

1. **a.** is the answer. (p. 329)
2. **b.** is the answer. (p. 329)

a. According to Freud, the Oedipus complex refers to the male's sexual feelings toward his mother and resentment toward his father.

c. & d. These are concepts introduced by cognitive theorists and Erik Erikson, respectively.

3. **a.** is the answer. (p. 306)

   b. Erikson did not equate gender constancy with the emergence of guilt.

   c. & d. These reflect the viewpoints of learning theory and Freud, respectively.

4. **b.** is the answer. (p. 319)
5. **c.** is the answer. The purpose of Vincenzo's action is clearly to retain the beanie baby, rather than to retaliate **(b)**, or bully Seema **(a)**. (p. 315)

   d. Relational aggression takes the form of a verbal insult.

6. **b.** is the answer. (p. 329)
7. **b.** is the answer. (p. 332–333)
8. **b.** is the answer. (p. 306)

   a. & c. The chapter does not link self-understanding with verbal reasoning or deception.

9. **a.** is the answer. (p. 325)
10. **a.** is the answer. (p. 326)

    b. Not until about age 3 can children consistently apply gender labels.

    c. By age 2, children prefer gender-typed toys.

11. **d.** is the answer. (pp. 318–319)
12. **b.** is the answer. (p. 319)

    a. Democratic-indulgent parents, although not mentioned in the text, would make fewer demands on their children than her father would.

    c. Androgynous parents, although not specifically mentioned in the text, would be more flexible in their gender roles than Jan's parents evidently were.

    d. Authoritative parents are more democratic than Jan's father evidently was.

13. **a.** is the answer. Right hemisphere activity is more pronounced in males. (pp. 333)
14. **c.** is the answer. (pp. 322–323)
15. **b.** is the answer. (p. 312)

KEY TERMS

1. A **phobia** is an exaggerated and irrational fear of an object or experience. (p. 305)
2. **Mastery play** is any form of play in which a skill is practiced until one is proficient at it. (p. 306)
3. According to Erikson, the crisis of the preschool years is **initiative versus guilt**. In this crisis, young children eagerly take on new tasks and play activities and feel guilty when their efforts result in failure or criticism. (p. 307)
4. **Emotional regulation** is the ability to manage and modify one's feelings, particular feelings of fear, frustration, and anger. (p. 308).
5. **Prosocial behavior** is an action, such as cooperating or sharing, that is performed to benefit another person without the expectation of reward. (p. 310)
6. **Antisocial behavior** is an action, such as hitting or insulting, that is intended to hurt another person. (p. 310).
7. **Rough-and-tumble play** is physical play that often mimics aggression, but involves no intent to harm. (p. 311)
8. A distinguishing feature of rough-and-tumble play is the **play face**—a smiling or relaxed expression that indicates that a child does not intend to be aggressive. (p. 312)
9. In **sociodramatic play**, children act out roles and themes in stories of their own creation, allowing them to examine personal concerns in a non-threatening manner. (p. 312)
10. **Instrumental aggression** is an action whose purpose is to obtain or retain an object desired by another. (p. 315).
11. **Reactive aggression** is aggressive behavior that is an angry retaliation for some intentional or incidental act by another person. (p. 315)

    Memory aid: Instrumental aggression is behavior that is *instrumental* in allowing a child to retain a favorite toy. **Reactive aggression** is a *reaction* to another child's behavior.

12. An unprovoked attack on another child is an example of **bullying aggression**. (p. 315)
13. Aggressive behavior that takes the form of verbal insults or social rejection is called **relational aggression**. (p. 315)
14. **Authoritarian parenting** is a style of child rearing in which the parents show little affection or nurturance for their children; maturity demands are high and parent-child communication is low. (p. 318)

    Memory aid: Someone who is an *authoritarian* demands unquestioning obedience and acts in a dictatorial way.

15. **Permissive parenting** is a style of parenting in which the parents make few demands on their children, yet are nurturant and accepting, and communicate well with their children. (p. 318)
16. **Authoritative parenting** is a style of parenting in which the parents set limits and enforce rules but do so more democratically than do authoritarian parents. (p. 318)

    Memory aid: *Authoritative parents* act as *authorities*

do on a subject—by discussing and explaining why certain family rules are in place.

17. In parenting, **differential treatment** is the practice of tailoring parental style to a particular child based on his or her age, birth order, and sex. (p. 321)

18. **Sex differences** are biological differences between females and males. (p. 326)

19. **Gender differences** are cultural differences in the roles and behavior of males and females. (p. 326).

20. In psychoanalytic theory, the **phallic stage** is the third stage of psychosexual development, in which the penis becomes the focus of psychological concerns and physiological pleasure. (p. 328)

21. According to Freud, boys in the phallic stage of psychosexual development develop a collection of feelings, known as the **Oedipus complex**, that center on sexual attraction to the mother and resentment of the father. (p. 281)

22. In Freud's theory, **identification** is the defense mechanism through which a person takes on the role and attitudes of a person more powerful than himself or herself. (p. 281)

23. In psychoanalytic theory, the **superego** is the self-critical and judgmental part of personality that internalizes the moral standards set by parents and society. (p. 329)

24. According to Freud, girls in the phallic stage may develop a collection of feelings, known as the **Electra complex**, that center on sexual attraction to the father and resentment of the mother. (p. 329)

25. A cognitive theory of development, **gender-schema** theory holds that children's ideas about gender are based on simple scripts about males and females that are developed from experience. (p. 331)

26. **Androgyny** is a balance of traditionally female and male gender characteristics in a person. (p. 333)

CHAPTER 11

The School Years: Biosocial Development

Chapter Overview

This chapter introduces middle childhood, the years from 7 to 11. Changes in physical size and shape are described, and the problem of obesity is addressed. The discussion then turns to the continuing development of motor skills during the school years. A final section examines the experiences of children with special needs, such as autistic children, children with learning disabilities, and those diagnosed as having attention-deficit hyperactivity disorder. The causes of and treatments for these problems are discussed, with emphasis placed on insights arising from the new developmental psychopathology perspective. This perspective makes it clear that the manifestations of any special childhood problem will change as the child grows older and that treatment must often focus on all three domains of development.

NOTE: Answer guidelines for all Chapter 11 questions begin on page 174.

Guided Study

The text chapter should be studied one section at a time. Before you read, preview each section by skimming it, noting headings and boldface items. Then read the appropriate section objectives from the following outline. Keep these objectives in mind and, as you read the chapter section, search for the information that will enable you to meet each objective. Once you have finished a section, write out answers for its objectives.

Size and Shape (pp. 341–347)

1. Describe normal physical growth and development during middle childhood, and account for the usual variations among children.

2. Discuss the problems—both physical and psychological—of obese children in middle childhood.

3. (Research Report) Identify the major causes of obesity, and outline the best approaches to treating obesity.

4. Discuss several other common physical problems of the school years, focusing on their causes, treatment, and impact on development in the other domains.

Motor Skills (pp. 348–350)

5. Describe motor-skill development during the school years, focusing on variations due to gender, culture, and genetics.

Children with Special Needs (pp. 350–362)

6. Explain the new developmental psychopathology perspective, and discuss its value in treating children with special needs.

7. Identify the symptoms of autism, discuss its possible causes, and describe its most effective treatment.

8. Discuss the characteristics and possible causes of learning disabilities.

9. Describe the symptoms and possible causes of attention-deficit hyperactivity disorder and attention-deficit hyperactivity disorder with aggression.

10. Discuss the types of treatment available for children with attention-deficit hyperactivity disorder.

11. (Children Up Close) Describe techniques that have been tried in efforts to educate children with special needs.

Chapter Review

When you have finished reading the chapter, work through the material that follows to review it. Complete the sentences and answer the questions. As you proceed, evaluate your performance for each section by consulting the answers on page 174. Do not continue with the next section until you understand each answer. If you need to, review or reread the appropriate section in the textbook before continuing.

1. Compared with biosocial development during other periods of the lifespan, biosocial development during middle childhood is ________ (relatively smooth/often fraught with problems). For example, disease and death during these years are ________ (more common/rarer) than during any other period. For another, sex differences in physical development and ability are ________ (very great/minimal).

Size and Shape (pp. 341–348)

2. Children grow ________ (faster/more slowly) during middle childhood than they did earlier or than they will in adolescence. The typical child gains about ________ pounds and ________ inches per year.

Describe several other features of physical development during the school years.

3. In some undeveloped countries, most of the variation in children's height and weight is caused by differences in ________. In developed countries, most children grow as tall as their ________ allow. These factors affect not only size but also rate of ________.

4. Among Americans, those of African descent tend to mature more ________ (quickly/slowly) than those of European descent, who tend to mature more ________ (quickly/slowly) than those of Asian descent.

5. The precise point at which a child is considered obese depends on ________ ________, on the proportion of ________ to ________, and on ________ ________. At least ________ percent of American children are 20 pounds or more above the average weight for their age.

6. One measure of obesity is the ________ ________ ________, which is the child's weight in ________ divided by the square of the ________ in meters. At age 8, obesity begins at a value of ________ on this index.

7. Experts estimate that between ________ and ________ percent of American children are obese.

8. Two physical problems associated with childhood obesity are ________ and ________ problems.

(Research Report) Identify several inherited characteristics that might contribute to obesity.

9. (Research Report) Inactive people burn ________ (more/fewer) calories and are ________ (no more/more) likely to be obese than active people.

10. (Research Report) Excessive television-watching by children ________ (is/is not) directly correlated with obesity. When children watch TV their metabolism ________ (slows down/speeds up).

(Research Report) Identify three factors that make television-watching fattening.

11. (Research Report) American children whose parents were immigrants from developing countries are __________ (more/less) likely to be overweight. This demonstrates the importance of another factor in obesity: __________ __________.

12. (Research Report) The onset of childhood obesity __________ (is/is not) commonly associated with a traumatic experience.

13. (Research Report) Fasting and/or repeated dieting __________ (lowers/raises) the rate of metabolism. For this reason, after a certain amount of weight loss, additional pounds become __________ (more/less) difficult to lose.

14. (Research Report) Strenuous dieting during childhood __________ (is/is not) potentially dangerous.

15. (Research Report) The best way to get children to lose weight is to increase their __________ __________. Developmentalists agree that treating obesity early in life __________ (is/is not) very important in ensuring the child's overall health later in life.

16. During the school years, the sense of __________ is sharper than at any other period of life. Minor problems in this sense, such as __________ __________, may become handicapping when __________ begins.

17. Another common problem that may affect school performance is disturbances of __________. This condition is more closely related to __________ __________ than to any emotional or neurological problem. In contrast, children with __________ __________ sleep too soundly and wet their beds at least __________ a month. Bed-wetting that returns after a year of being absent is called __________ __________. This condition may be a sign of __________ troubles at school or at home.

18. A chronic inflammatory disorder of the airways is called __________. This health problem is becoming increasingly prevalent in __________ nations, but usually disappears by __________ __________. Crucial in the epidemiology of this disorder are __________ factors.

State three pieces of evidence that environmental factors are implicated in asthma.

19. Among the aspects of modern life that contribute to asthma are __________ __________ __________.

Motor Skills (pp. 348–350)

20. Children become more skilled at controlling their bodies during the school years, in part because they __________.

21. The length of time it takes a person to respond to a particular stimulus is called __________ __________. A key factor in this motor skill is __________ __________.

22. Other important abilities that continue to develop during the school years are __________-__________ __________, balance, and judgment of __________.

23. Because during the school years boys have greater __________-__________ strength than girls, they tend to have an advantage in sports such as __________, whereas girls have an advantage in sports such as __________.

24. For most physical activities during middle childhood, biological sex differences are __________, with expertise depending on three elements: __________,

_______________, and _______________.
The development of specific motor skills also depends on _______________ and _______________ _______________.

25. Many of the sports that adults value _______________ (are/are not) well suited for children.

26. Due to _______________ differences, some children are simply more gifted in developing specific motor skills.

Children with Special Needs (pp. 350–362)

27. Among the psychological disorders that impair the development of children with special needs are _______________ _______________.

28. The field of study that is concerned with childhood psychological disorders is _______________ _______________.

29. This perspective has made diagnosticians much more aware of the _______________ _______________ of childhood problems. This awareness is reflected in the official diagnostic guide of the American Psychiatric Association, which is the _______________ _______________.

30. One of the most severe disturbances of early childhood is _______________, a term that Leo Kanner first used to describe children who are _______________. Today, this definition _______________ (is/is not) considered too narrow.

31. Children who have autistic symptoms that are less severe than those in the classic syndrome are sometimes diagnosed with _______________ _______________.

32. Autism is more common in _______________ (boys/girls).

33. In early childhood autism, severe deficiencies appear in three areas: _______________ _______________, _______________ _______________, and _______________ _______________. The first two deficiencies are usually apparent during _______________.

34. Some autistic children engage in a type of speech called _______________, in which they repeat, word for word, things they have heard.

35. The unusual play patterns of autistic children are characterized by repetitive _______________ and an absence of spontaneous _______________ play.

36. The most devastating problem of autistic children often proves to be the lack of _______________ _______________.
Autistic children appear to lack a _______________ _______________ _______________.

37. Unaffected by others' opinions, autistic children also lack _______________ _______________.

38. Autism probably results from a _______________ vulnerability in combination with some sort of _______________ during _______________ development or soon after _______________.

39. The most crucial period for intervention in the treatment of autism are the years between ages _______________ and _______________.
This is because _______________ skills develop most rapidly during these years.

40. The most successful treatment method for autism seems to be _______________ _______________ therapy to shape particular _______________.

41. Some children have difficulty in school due to an overall slowness in development; that is, they suffer _______________ _______________.
If that difficulty _______________ (is/is not) attributable to an overall intellectual slowness, a physical handicap, a severely stressful situation, or a lack of basic education, the child is said to have a _______________ _______________.

42. A disability in reading is called ______________; in math, it is called ______________. Other specific academic subjects that may show a learning disability are ______________ and ______________.

43. In many cases, it seems as if some particular part of the learning-disabled child's ______________ is not functioning properly. In the case of dyslexia, the disability may originate in ______________ areas of the brain.

44. A disability that manifests itself in a difficulty in concentrating for more than a few moments and a need to be active, often accompanied by excitability and impulsivity, is called ______________-______________ ______________ ______________.
The crucial problem in these conditions seems to be a neurological difficulty in paying ______________.

45. Researchers have identified several factors that may contribute to ADHD. These include ______________ ______________, prenatal damage from ______________, and postnatal damage, such as from ______________ ______________.

46. Many children with this disorder are prone to ______________, a fact that has led some researchers to propose a subtype of the disorder called ______________ ______________.
Such children also are at risk for developing ______________ and ______________ disorders.

47. Children with ADD with neither hyperactivity nor aggression appear to be prone to ______________ and ______________.

48. Developmental and contextual variations in ADHD help explain ______________ differences in the frequency of this disorder. For example, children in ______________ are less likely to be diagnosed as having ADHD than U.S. children, but they are more likely to be diagnosed with ______________ ______________.

49. Children with ADHD ______________ (do/do not) tend to have continuing problems as adults.

50. In childhood, the most effective forms of treatment for ADHD are ______________, ______________ therapy, and changes in the ______________.

51. Certain drugs that stimulate adults, such as ______________ and ______________, have a reverse effect on hyperactive children.

52. Teacher behavior that is too ______________ or too ______________ tends to exacerbate ADHD.

53. (Children Up Close) The training approach in which learning-disabled children are not separated into special classes is called ______________. More recently, some schools have developed a ______________ ______________, in which such children spend part of each day with a teaching specialist. In the most recent approach, called ______________, learning-disabled children receive targeted help within the setting of a regular classroom.

Progress Test 1

Multiple-Choice Questions

Circle your answers to the following questions and check them with the answers on page 175. If your answer is incorrect, read the explanation for why it is incorrect and then consult the appropriate pages of the text (in parentheses following the correct answer).

1. As children move into middle childhood:
- **a.** the rate of accidental death increases.
- **b.** sexual urges intensify.
- **c.** the rate of weight gain increases.
- **d.** biological growth slows and steadies.

2. During middle childhood:
   a. girls are usually stronger than boys.
   b. boys have greater physical flexibility than girls.
   c. boys have greater upper-arm strength than girls.
   d. the development of motor skills slows drastically.

3. To help obese children, nutritionists usually recommend:
   a. strenuous dieting to counteract early overfeeding.
   b. the use of amphetamines and other drugs.
   c. more exercise, stabilization of weight, and time to "grow out" of the fat.
   d. no specific actions.

4. A factor that is *not* primary in the development of motor skills during middle childhood is:
   a. practice.
   b. gender.
   c. brain maturation.
   d. age.

5. Dyslexia is a learning disability that affects the ability to:
   a. do math.
   b. read.
   c. write.
   d. speak.

6. In relation to weight in later life, childhood obesity is:
   a. not an accurate predictor of adolescent or adult weight.
   b. predictive of adolescent but not adult weight.
   c. predictive of adult but not adolescent weight.
   d. predictive of both adolescent and adult weight.

7. The developmental psychopathology perspective is characterized by its:
   a. contextual approach.
   b. emphasis on individual therapy.
   c. emphasis on the cognitive domain of development.
   d. concern with all of the above.

8. The time—usually measured in fractions of a second—it takes for a person to respond to a particular stimulus is called:
   a. the interstimulus interval.
   b. reaction time.
   c. the stimulus-response interval.
   d. response latency.

9. Researchers have suggested that excessive television-watching is a possible cause of childhood obesity because:
   a. TV bombards children with persuasive junk food commercials.
   b. children often snack while watching TV.
   c. body metabolism slows while watching TV.
   d. of all the above reasons.

10. The underlying problem in attention-deficit hyperactivity disorder appears to be:
    a. low overall intelligence.
    b. a neurological difficulty in paying attention.
    c. a learning disability in a specific academic skill.
    d. the existence of a conduct disorder.

11. Teacher behavior that seem to aggravate or increase problems in children with attention-deficit hyperactivity disorder tends to be:
    a. too rigid.
    b. too permissive.
    c. too rigid or permissive.
    d. none of the above.

12. In developed countries, most of the variation in children's size and shape can be attributed to:
    a. the amount of daily exercise.
    b. nutrition.
    c. genes.
    d. the interaction of the above factors.

13. Autistic children generally have severe deficiencies in all but which of the following?
    a. social skills
    b. imaginative play
    c. echolalia
    d. communication ability

14. The most likely cause of autism is:
    a. abnormal genes.
    b. prenatal exposure to teratogens.
    c. maternal stress.
    d. genetic vulnerability in combination with prenatal or early postnatal damage.

15. Psychoactive drugs are most effective in treating attention-deficit hyperactivity disorder when they are administered:
    a. before the diagnosis becomes certain.
    b. for several years after the basic problem has abated.
    c. as part of the labeling process.
    d. with psychological support or therapy.

True or False Items

Write *true* or *false* on the line in front of each statement.

_______ 1. Physical variations in North American children are usually caused by diet rather than heredity.

_______ 2. Childhood obesity usually does not correlate with adult obesity.

_______ 3. Research shows a direct correlation between television-watching and obesity.

_______ 4. The quick reaction time that is crucial in some sports can be readily achieved with practice.

_______ 5. Despite the efforts of teachers and parents, most children with learning disabilities can expect their disabilities to persist and even worsen as they enter adulthood.

_______ 6. The best way for children to lose weight is through strenuous dieting.

_______ 7. Parental coldness toward infants is a primary cause of autism.

_______ 8. Most learning disabilities are caused by a difficult birth or other early trauma to the child.

_______ 9. ADHD is diagnosed more often in Great Britain than in the United States.

_______ 10. The drugs sometimes given to children to reduce hyperactive behaviors have a reverse effect on adults.

Progress Test 2

Progress Test 2 should be completed during a final chapter review. Answer the following questions after you thoroughly understand the correct answers for the Chapter Review and Progress Test 1.

Multiple-Choice Questions

1. During the years from 7 to 11, the average child:
   a. becomes slimmer.
   b. gains about 12 pounds a year.
   c. has decreased lung capacity.
   d. is more likely to become obese than at any other period in the lifespan.

2. Among the factors that are known to contribute to obesity are activity level, quantity and types of food eaten, and:
   a. a traumatic event.
   b. television-watching.
   c. attitudes toward food.
   d. all of the above.

3. A specific learning disability that becomes apparent when a child experiences unusual difficulty in learning to read is:
   a. dyslexia.
   b. dyscalcula.
   c. ADHD.
   d. ADHDA.

4. Problems in learning to write, read, and do math are collectively referred to as:
   a. learning disabilities.
   b. attention-deficit hyperactivity disorder.
   c. hyperactivity.
   d. dyscalcula.

5. A measure of obesity in which weight in kilograms is divided by the square of height in meters is the:
   a. basal metabolic rate (BMR)
   b. body mass index (BMI)
   c. body fat index (BFI)
   d. basal fat ratio (BFR)

6. Although primary enuresis is generally related to __________, secondary enuresis may be a sign of __________.
   a. sleep patterns; emotional troubles
   b. emotional troubles; sleep disturbances
   c. teratogen exposure; emotional troubles
   d. emotional troubles; teratogen exposure

7. The most effective form of help for children with ADHD is:
   a. medication.
   b. psychological therapy.
   c. environmental change.
   d. a combination of some or all of the above.

8. A key factor in reaction time is:
   a. whether the child is male or female.
   b. brain maturation.
   c. whether the stimulus to be reacted to is an auditory or visual one.
   d. all of the above.

9. The first noticeable symptom of autism is usually:
   a. the lack of spoken language.
   b. abnormal social responsiveness.
   c. both a. and b.
   d. unpredictable.

10. Which of the following is true of children with a diagnosed learning disability?
    a. They are, in most cases, average in intelligence.
    b. They often have a specific physical handicap, such as hearing loss.
    c. They often lack basic educational experiences.
    d. All of the above are true.

11. During the school years:
    a. boys are, on average, at least a year ahead of girls in the development of physical abilities.
    b. girls are, on average, at least a year ahead of boys in the development of physical abilities.
    c. boys and girls are about equal in physical abilities.
    d. motor-skill development proceeds at a slower pace, since children grow more rapidly at this age than at any other time.

12. Whether a particular child is considered obese depends on:
    a. the child's body type.
    b. the proportion of fat to muscle.
    c. cultural standards.
    d. all of the above.

13. Which approach to education may best meet the needs of learning-disabled children in terms of both skill remediation and social interaction with other children?
    a. mainstreaming
    b. special education
    c. inclusion
    d. resource rooms

14. Asperger syndrome is a disorder in which:
    a. body weight fluctuates dramatically over short periods of time.
    b. verbal skills seem normal, but social perceptions and skills are abnormal.
    c. an autistic child is extremely aggressive.
    d. a child of normal intelligence has difficulty In mastering a specific cognitive skill.

15. Which of the following is *not* a contributing factor in most cases of ADHD?
    a. genetic inheritance
    b. dietary sugar and caffeine
    c. prenatal damage
    d. postnatal damage

Matching Items

Match each term or concept with its corresponding description or definition.

Terms or Concepts

_______ 1. dyslexia
_______ 2. dyscalcula
_______ 3. mental retardation
_______ 4. attention-deficit hyperactivity disorder
_______ 5. asthma
_______ 6. echolalia
_______ 7. autism
_______ 8. developmental psychopathology
_______ 9. DSM-IV
_______ 10. learning disability
_______ 11. mainstreaming

Descriptions or Definitions

a. an unexpected difficulty with one or more academic skills
b. speech that repeats, word for word, what has just been heard
c. the diagnostic guide of the American Psychiatric Association
d. a pervasive delay in cognitive development
e. system in which learning-disabled children are taught in general education classrooms
f. disorder characterized by the absence of a theory of mind
g. difficulty in reading
h. chronic inflammation of the airways
i. behavior problem involving difficulty in concentrating, as well as excitability and impulsivity
j. difficulty in math
k. applies insights from studies of normal development to the study of childhood disorders

Thinking Critically About Chapter 11

Answer these questions the day before an exam as a final check on your understanding of the chapter's terms and concepts.

1. According to developmentalists, the best game for a typical group of 8-year-olds would be:
   a. football or baseball.
   b. basketball.
   c. one in which reaction time is not crucial.
   d. a game involving one-on-one competition.

2. Dr. Rutter, who believes that "we can learn more about an organism's normal functioning by studying its pathology and, likewise, more about its pathology by studying its normal condition," evidently is working from which of the following perspectives?
   a. clinical psychology
   b. developmental psychopathology
   c. behaviorism
   d. psychoanalysis

3. Nine-year-old Jack has difficulty concentrating on his classwork for more than a few moments, repeatedly asks his teacher irrelevant questions, and is constantly disrupting the class with loud noises. If his difficulties persist, Jack is likely to be diagnosed as suffering from:
   a. dyslexia.
   b. dyscalcula.
   c. autism.
   d. attention-deficit hyperactivity disorder.

4. Of the following 9-year-olds, who is likely to mature physically at the youngest age?
   a. Britta, who is of European descent
   b. Michael, who is of European descent
   c. Malcolm, who is of African descent
   d. Lee, who is of Asian descent

5. Ten-year-old Clarence is quick-tempered, easily frustrated, and is often disruptive in the classroom. Clarence may be suffering from:
   a. dyslexia.
   b. dyscalcula.
   c. attention-deficit disorder.
   d. attention-deficit hyperactivity disorder.

6. Because 11-year-old Wayne is obese, he runs a greater risk of developing:
   a. orthopedic problems.
   b. respiratory problems.
   c. psychological problems.
   d. all of the above.

7. Of the following individuals, who is likely to have the fastest reaction time?
   a. a 7-year-old
   b. a 9-year-old
   c. an 11-year-old
   d. an adult

8. Harold weighs about 20 pounds more than his friend Jay. During school recess, Jay can usually be found playing soccer with his classmates, while Harold sits on the sidelines by himself. Harold's rejection is likely due to his:
   a. being physically different.
   b. being dyslexic.
   c. intimidation of his schoolmates.
   d. being hyperactive.

9. In determining whether an 8-year-old has a learning disability, a teacher looks primarily for:
   a. exceptional performance in a subject area.
   b. the exclusion of other explanations.
   c. a family history of the learning disability.
   d. both a. and b.

10. When she moved her practice to England, Dr. Williams was struck by the fact that British doctors seemingly used the same criteria she used to diagnose ADHD to diagnose:
    a. dyslexia.
    b. dyscalcula.
    c. conduct disorder.
    d. antisocial personality.

11. If you were to ask an autistic child with echolalia, "what's your name?" the child would probably respond by saying:
    a. nothing.
    b. "what's your name?"
    c. "your name what's?"
    d. something that was unintelligible.

12. Although 12-year-old Brenda is quite intelligent, she has low self-esteem, few friends, and is often teased. Knowing nothing else about Brenda, you conclude that she may be:
    a. unusually aggressive.
    b. obese.
    c. arrogant.
    d. socially inept.

13. Danny has been diagnosed as having attention-deficit hyperactivity disorder. Every day his parents make sure that he takes the proper dose of Ritalin. His parents should:
    a. continue this behavior until Danny is an adult.
    b. try different medications when Danny seems to be reverting to his normal overactive behavior.
    c. make sure that Danny also has psychotherapy.
    d. not worry about Danny's condition; he will outgrow it.

14. In concluding her presentation entitled "Facts and falsehoods regarding childhood obesity," Cheryl states that, contrary to popular belief, _____ is *not* a common cause of childhood obesity.
    a. television-watching
    b. a traumatic event
    c. overeating of high-fat foods
    d. a prenatal teratogen

15. Curtis is 21 years old, 2 meters tall, and weighs 80 kilograms. His BMI equals _______________, making him statistically _______________.
    a. 40; obese
    b. 40; overweight
    c. 20; normal body weight
    d. 20; obese

Key Terms

Using your own words, write a brief definition or explanation of each of the following terms on a separate piece of paper.

1. body mass index
2. asthma
3. reaction time
4. children with special needs
5. developmental psychopathology
6. DSM-IV
7. autism
8. Asperger syndrome
9. mental retardation
10. learning disability
11. dyslexia
12. dyscalcula
13. attention-deficit hyperactivity disorder (ADHD)
14. mainstreaming
15. resource room
16. inclusion

ANSWERS

CHAPTER REVIEW

1. relatively smooth; rarer; minimal
2. more slowly; 5; 2 1/2

During the school years, children generally become slimmer, muscles become stronger, and lung capacity increases.

3. malnutrition; genes; maturation
4. quickly; quickly
5. body type; fat; muscle; cultural standards; 10
6. body mass Index (BMI); kilograms; height; 18
7. 20; 30
8. orthopedic; respiratory

Body type, including the amount and distribution of fat, as well as height and bone structure; individual differences in metabolic rate; and activity level are all influenced by heredity and can contribute to obesity.

9. fewer; more
10. is; slows down

While watching television, children (a) are bombarded with commercials for junk food, (b) consume many snacks, and (c) burn fewer calories than they would if they were actively playing.

11. more; attitudes toward food
12. is
13. lowers; more
14. is
15. physical activity; is
16. vision; near vision, muscle weakness, or steady scanning; school
17. sleep; sleep patterns; primary enuresis; once; secondary enuresis; emotional
18. asthma; developing; late adolescence; environmental

The rate of asthma has at least doubled since 1980 in virtually every developed nation. Asthma patients tend to be those least susceptible to other childhood illnesses. Asthma is at least 10 times more common in urban areas than in rural areas.

19. carpeted floors, more bedding, dogs and cats living inside the house, airtight windows, less outdoor play, crowded living conditions
20. grow slowly
21. reaction time; brain maturation
22. hand-eye coordination; movement
23. upper-arm; baseball; gymnastics
24. minimal; motivation; guidance; practice; culture; national policy

25. are not
26. genetic
27. hyperactivity, aggression, anxiety, autism, conduct disorders, depression, learning disabilities, and mental slowness
28. developmental psychopathology
29. social context; Diagnostic and Statistical Manual of Mental Disorders (DSM-IV)
30. autism; self-absorbed; is
31. Asperger syndrome
32. boys
33. communication ability; social skills; imaginative play; infancy
34. echolalia
35. rituals; imaginative
36. social understanding; theory of mind
37. emotional regulation
38. genetic; damage; prenatal; birth
39. 1; 4; language
40. individualized behavioral; skills
41. mental retardation; is not; learning disability
42. dyslexia; dyscalcula; spelling; handwriting
43. brain; auditory
44. attention-deficit hyperactivity disorder; attention
45. genetic inheritance; teratogens; lead poisoning or repeated blows to the head
46. aggression; attention-deficit hyperactivity disorder with aggression (ADHDA); oppositional; conduct
47. anxiety; depression
48. cultural; Great Britain; conduct disorder
49. do
50. medication; psychological; family and school environment
51. amphetamines; methylphenidate (Ritalin)
52. rigid; permissive
53. mainstreaming; resource room; inclusion

PROGRESS TEST 1

Multiple-Choice Questions

1. **d.** is the answer. (p. 341)
2. **c.** is the answer. (p. 348)

   a. Especially in forearm strength, boys are usually stronger than girls during middle childhood.

   b. During middle childhood, girls usually have greater overall flexibility than boys.

   d. Motor-skill development improves greatly during middle childhood.
3. **c.** is the answer. (p. 345)

   a. Strenuous dieting can be physically harmful and often makes children irritable, listless, and even sick—adding to the psychological problems of the obese child.

   b. The use of amphetamines to control weight is not recommended at any age.
4. **b.** Boys and girls are just about equal in physical abilities during the school years. (p. 348)
5. **b.** is the answer. (p. 356)

   a. This is dyscalcula.

   c. & d. The text does not give labels for learning disabilities in writing or speaking.
6. **d.** is the answer. (p. 345)
7. **a.** is the answer. (p. 351)

   b. & c. Because of its contextual approach, developmental psychopathology emphasizes *group* therapy and *all* domains of development.
8. **b.** is the answer. (p. 348)
9. **d.** is the answer. (p. 344)
10. **b.** is the answer. (pp. 357–358)
11. **c.** is the answer. (p. 361)
12. **c.** is the answer. (p. 341)

    a. The amount of daily exercise a child receives is an important factor in his or her tendency toward obesity; exercise does not, however, explain most of the variation in childhood physique.

    b. In some parts of the world malnutrition accounts for most of the variation in physique; this is not true of developed countries, where most children get enough food to grow as tall as their genes allow.
13. **c.** is the answer. Echolalia *is* a type of communication difficulty. (p. 353)
14. **d.** is the answer. (p. 354)
15. **d.** is the answer. (pp. 359–360)

True or False Items

1. F Physical variations in children from developed countries are caused primarily by heredity. (p. 341)
2. F If obesity is established in middle childhood, it tends to continue into adulthood. (p. 345)
3. T (p. 344)
4. F Reaction time depends on brain maturation and is not readily affected by practice. (p. 348)

5. F With the proper assistance, many learning-disabled children develop into adults who are virtually indistinguishable from other adults in their educational and occupational achievements. (p. 362)
6. F Strenuous dieting during childhood can be dangerous. The best way to get children to lose weight is by increasing their activity level. (p. 345)
7. F This was an early myth regarding the origins of autism. (p. 354)
8. F The causes of learning disabilities are difficult to pinpoint and cannot be specified with certainty. (p. 357)
9. F ADHD is more often diagnosed in the United States than in Great Britain. (p. 359)
10. T (p. 359)

PROGRESS TEST 2

Multiple-Choice Questions

1. **a.** is the answer. (p. 341)
   b. & c. During this period children gain about 5 pounds per year and experience increased lung capacity.
   d. Although childhood obesity is a common problem, the text does not indicate that a person is more likely to become obese at this age than at any other.
2. **d.** is the answer. (pp. 344–345)
3. **a.** is the answer. (p. 356)
   b. This learning disability involves math rather than reading.
   c. & d. These disorders do not manifest themselves in a particular academic skill but instead appear in psychological processes that affect learning in general.
4. **a.** is the answer. (p. 356)
   b. & c. ADHD is a general learning disability that usually does not manifest itself in specific subject areas. Hyperactivity is a facet of this disorder.
   d. Dyscalcula is a learning disability in math only.
5. **b.** is the answer. (p. 342)
6. **a.** is the answer. (p. 346)
   a. & d. Enuresis has not been linked to teratogen exposure.
7. **d.** is the answer. (pp. 359–361)
8. **b.** is the answer. (p. 348)
9. **c.** is the answer. (p. 353)
10. **a.** is the answer. (p. 355)
11. **c.** is the answer. (p. 348)
12. **d.** is the answer. (p. 342)
13. **c.** is the answer. (p. 360)
    a. Many general education teachers are unable to cope with the special needs of some children.
    b. & d. These approaches undermined the social integration of children with special needs.
14. **b.** is the answer. (p. 352)
15. **b.** is the answer. (p. 358)

Matching Items

1. g (p. 356)	**5.** h (p. 346)	**9.** c (p. 352)
2. j (p. 356)	**6.** b (p. 353)	**10.** a (p. 355)
3. d (p. 355)	**7.** f (p. 352)	**11.** e (p. 361)
4. i (p. 357)	**8.** k (p. 351)	

THINKING CRITICALLY ABOUT CHAPTER 11

1. **c.** is the answer. (p. 348)
   a. & b. Each of these games involves skills that are hardest for schoolchildren to master.
   d. Because one-on-one sports are likely to accentuate individual differences in ability, they may be especially discouraging to some children.
2. **b.** is the answer. (p. 351)
3. **d.** is the answer. (p. 357)
   a. & b. Jack's difficulty is in concentrating, not in reading (dyslexia) or math (dyscalcula).
   c. Autism is characterized by a lack of communication skills.
4. **c.** is the answer. (p. 342)
   a., b., & d. Among Americans, those of African descent tend to mature more quickly than those of European descent, who, in turn, tend to be maturationally ahead of those of Asian descent.
5. **d.** is the answer. (p. 358)
6. **d.** is the answer. (p. 343)
7. **d.** is the answer. (p. 348)
8. **a.** is the answer. (p. 343)
   b., c., & d. Obese children are no more likely to be dyslexic, physically intimidating, or hyperactive than other children.
9. **d.** is the answer. (p. 355)
10. **c.** is the answer. (p. 359)
11. **b.** is the answer. (p. 353)
12. **b.** is the answer. (p. 343)

13. c. is the answer. Medication alone cannot ameliorate all the problems of ADHD. (pp. 359–360)

14. d. is the answer. There is no evidence that teratogens have anything to do with obesity. (pp. 344–345)

15. c. is the answer. BMI = *weight/height squared.* Therefore, BMI for Curtis = 80/4, or 20. For adults, overweight begins at 25 BMI, and obesity begins at about 28 BMI (pp. 342–343)

KEY TERMS

1. **Body mass index (BMI)** is a measure of obesity in which a person's weight in kilograms is divided by his or her height squared in meters (p. 342)
2. **Asthma** is a disorder in which the airways are chronically inflamed. (p. 346)
3. **Reaction time** is the length of time it takes a person to respond to a particular stimulus. (p. 348)
4. **Children with special needs** require particular physical, intellectual, or social accommodations in order to learn. (p. 351)
5. **Developmental psychopathology** is a new field that applies the insights from studies of normal development to the study and treatment of childhood disorders, and vice versa. (p. 351)
6. **DSM-IV** is the fourth edition of the *Diagnostic and Statistical Manual of Mental Disorders*, developed by the American Psychiatric Association, the leading means of distinguishing various emotional and behavioral disorders. (p. 352)
7. **Autism** is a severe disturbance of early childhood characterized by inability or unwillingness to communicate, poor social skills, and diminished imagination. (p. 352)
8. **Asperger syndrome** is a disorder in which a person has many symptoms of autism, despite having near normal communication skills. (p. 352)
9. **Mental retardation** is a pervasive delay in cognitive development. (p. 355)
10. A **learning disability** is a difficulty in a particular cognitive skill that is not attributable to an overall intellectual slowness, a physical handicap, a severely stressful living condition, or a lack of basic education. (p. 355)
11. **Dyslexia** is a learning disability in reading. (p. 356)
12. **Dyscalcula** is a learning disability in math. (p. 356)
13. The **attention-deficit hyperactivity disorder (ADHD)** is a behavior problem in which the individual has great difficulty concentrating, is often excessively excitable and impulsive, and is sometimes aggressive. (p. 357)
14. **Mainstreaming** is an educational approach in which children with special needs are included in regular classrooms. (p. 361)
15. A **resource room** is a classroom in which children with special needs spend part of their day working with a trained specialist in order to learn basic skills. (p. 361)
16. **Inclusion** is an educational approach in which children with special needs receive individualized instruction within a regular classroom setting. (p. 361)

CHAPTER 12

The School Years: Cognitive Development

Chapter Overview

Chapter 12 looks at the development of cognitive abilities in children from age 7 to 11. The first section focuses on changes in the child's selective attention, processing speed and capacity, memory strategies, knowledge base, and problem-solving strategies. The second section discusses Piaget's view of the child's cognitive development, which involves a growing ability to use logic and reasoning.

The third section looks at language learning in the school years. During this time, children develop a more analytic understanding of words and show a marked improvement in pragmatic skills, such as changing from one form of speech to another when the situation so demands. The linguistic and cognitive advantages of bilingualism are discussed, as are educational and environmental conditions that are conducive to fluency in a second language.

The final section describes innovative new teaching methods, which emphasize active rather than passive learning and are derived from the developmental theories of Piaget, Vygotsky, and others. Studies that contrast these methods with more traditional methods have shown their effectiveness in reading and math education. A Changing Policy Report comparing education in the United States, Japan, and the Republic of China explores the reasons for the disparities. The chapter concludes by examining measures of cognitive growth and variations in cultural standards.

NOTE: Answer guidelines for all Chapter 12 questions begin on page 190.

Guided Study

The text chapter should be studied one section at a time. Before you read, preview each section by skimming it, noting headings and boldface items. Then read the appropriate section objectives from the following outline. Keep these objectives in mind and, as you read the chapter section, search for the information that will enable you to meet each objective. Once you have finished a section, write out answers for its objectives.

Remembering, Knowing, and Processing (pp. 365–372)

1. Describe the components of the information-processing system, noting how they interact.

2. Discuss advances in selective attention, processing speed and capacity, and memory skills during middle childhood.

3. (text and Research Report) Discuss advances in the knowledge base and metacognition during the school years.

Concrete Operational Thought (pp. 372–376)

4. Identify and discuss the logical operations of concrete operational thought and give examples of how these operations are demonstrated by schoolchildren.

5. Discuss limitations of Piaget's theory.

Language (pp. 376–384)

6. Describe language development during the school years, noting changing abilities in vocabulary, grammar, and code switching.

7. Identify several conditions that foster the learning of a second language, and describe the best approaches to bilingual education.

Thinking, Learning, and Schooling (pp. 384–395)

8. Discuss historical and cultural variations in the schooling of children, and explain why such variations have recently become troubling.

9. (Changing Policy) Compare the academic performance of children in Japan, the Republic of China, and the United States and identify differences in school and home life that may account for differences in academic performance.

10. Explain how achievement and aptitude tests are used in evaluating individual differences in cognitive growth, and discuss why use of such tests is controversial.

11. Discuss the influences of Piaget, the information-processing perspective, and Vygotsky on classroom education.

12. Discuss how cultural needs and standards direct cognitive growth.

Chapter Review

When you have finished reading the chapter, work through the material that follows to review it. Complete the sentences and answer the questions. As you proceed, evaluate your performance for each section by consulting the answers on page 190. Do not continue with the next section until you understand each answer. If you need to, review or reread the appropriate section in the textbook before continuing.

Remembering, Knowing, and Processing (pp. 365–372)

1. During middle childhood, children not only know more but also are more resourceful in ______________ and using their cognitive resources when solving a problem. In the words of John Flavell, they have acquired a sense of "the ______________ of thinking."

2. The idea that the advances in thinking that accompany middle childhood occur because of basic changes in how children ______________ and ______________ data is central to the ______________-______________ theory.

3. Incoming stimulus information is held for a split second in the ______________ ______________, after which most of it is lost.

4. Meaningful material is transferred into ______________ ______________, which is sometimes called ______________-______________ ______________. This part of memory handles mental activity that is ______________.

5. The part of memory that stores information for days, months, or years is ______________-______________ ______________.

6. The part of the information-processing system that regulates the analysis and flow of information is the ______________ ______________.

7. The ability to use ______________ ______________—to screen out distractors and concentrate on relevant information—improves steadily during the school years.

8. Children in the school years are better learners and problem solvers than younger children are, because they have faster ______________ ______________, and they have a larger ______________ ______________.

9. One reason for the cognitive advances of middle childhood is ______________ maturation, especially the ______________ of nerve pathways and maturation of the ______________ ______________.

   A more important reason is that processing becomes more efficient as children learn to use their ______________ ______________ better.

10. Processing capacity also becomes more efficient through ______________, as familiar mental activities become routine.

11. Memory ability improves during middle childhood in part because of the child's expanded ______________ ______________.

12. (Research Report) Research suggests that adults ________________ (are/are not) always more cognitively competent than children, and that many differences between schoolchildren's and adults' memory and reasoning may be due to children's more limited ________________ and ________________.

13. The ability to evaluate a cognitive task to determine what to do—and to monitor one's performance—is called ________________. When such efforts involve memory techniques, they are called ________________.

List some indicators of this developmental change during the school years.

14. During middle childhood, children's use of ________________ ________________ for retaining new information broadens significantly. For example, they begin to use ________________ to repeat information to be remembered and ________________ to improve the memorability of material through regrouping. Children's use of ________________ ________________ to access previously learned information also improves.

Concrete Operational Thought (pp. 372–376)

15. Another reason older children are more educable is that they are ________________ thinkers who seek explanations that are ________________, ________________, and ________________.

16. According to Piaget, between ages 7 and 11 children are in the stage of ________________ ________________.

17. The logical principle that certain characteristics of an object remain the same even when other characteristics change is ________________. The idea that a transformation process can be reversed to restore the original condition is ________________. The idea that a transformation in one dimension can be compensated for by one in another is ________________.

18. Many concrete operations underlie the basic ideas of elementary-school ________________ and ________________; they are also relevant to everyday ________________ problem solving.

19. In comparing Piaget and information-processing theorists, we note that the former emphasized ________________, whereas the latter emphasize ________________.

20. The concept that objects can be organized into categories according to some common property is ________________. The concept that a particular object or person may belong to more than one class is ________________ ________________.

21. Younger children have particular difficulty with the ________________ relations between ________________ and ________________. Eventually, however, they come to understand that categories or subcategories can be ________________, ________________ and ________________.

22. Recent studies have found that cognitive development is ________________ (less/more) erratic than Piaget's descriptions would suggest. Cognitive development seems to be more affected by ________________ factors than Piaget's descriptions imply.

Language (pp. 376–384)

23. During middle childhood, language development is much more ________________ (subtle/obvious) than in the preschool years. Children become more ________________ and ________________ in their processing of vocabulary and are better able to define words by

analyzing their ______________ to other words. Their love of words is evident in the ______________, secret ______________, and ______________ that they create.

24. In addition to improved understanding of logical relations, school-age children begin to understand other grammatical constructions, such as the correct use of ______________, the ______________, and ______________.

25. School-age children are more teachable than preschoolers, in part, because they are less ______________ in clinging to their grammatical mistakes. Their understanding of ______________ ______________ is also vastly improved.

26. Changing from one form of speech to another is called ______________ ______________. The ______________ ______________, which children use in situations such as the classroom, is characterized by extensive ______________, complex ______________, and lengthy ______________. With their friends, children tend to use the ______________ ______________, which has a more limited use of vocabulary and syntax and relies more on ______________ and ______________ to convey meaning.

27. Compared with the formal code, which is context-______________ (free/bound), the informal code is context-______________ (free/bound). While adults often stress the importance of mastery of the formal code, the informal code is also important in helping the child develop ______________ skills.

28. Cognitively and linguistically, it is a(n) ______________ (advantage/disadvantage) for children to learn more than one language.

29. The approach to bilingual education in which the child's instruction occurs entirely in the second language is called ______________. In ______________ ______________ programs, the child is taught first in his or her native language, until the second language is taught as a "foreign" language.

30. In ESL, or ______________ programs, children must master the basics of English before joining regular classes with other children. In contrast, ______________ ______________ requires that teachers instruct children in both their native language as well as in English. An approach to teaching a second language that recognizes the importance of nonnative cultural strategies in learning is called ______________-______________ ______________.

31. Immersion programs have been successful in ______________, with English-speaking children who were initially placed in French-only classrooms. Immersion tends to fail, however, if the child feels ______________, ______________, or ______________.

32. Ideally, children learn a first and second spoken language best under age ______________.

33. The best teachers of a second language are ______________.

Thinking, Learning, and Schooling (pp. 384–395)

34. There ______________ (is/is not) universal agreement on how best to educate schoolchildren.

35. Historically, ______________ (boys/girls) and wealthier children have been most likely to be formally taught and to have the greatest educational demands placed upon them.

36. Teaching techniques vary from the ______________ ______________ method to ______________ ______________, in which students are encouraged to interact and make use of all classroom resources.

37. (Changing Policy) Achievement scores show that American children are ________________ (ahead of/behind) their counterparts in most other industrialized countries, especially in the subjects of ________________ and ________________.

(Changing Policy) Give several examples of how schooling in the United States differs from that in Japan and the Republic of China.

38. (Changing Policy) Compared with American parents, parents in Japan and China tend to be ________________ (more/less) involved in their children's education.

39. (Changing Policy) The priorities of each culture are highly influential as well. As compared with ________________ (American/Japanese) teachers, ________________ (American/Japanese) teachers are better trained, and a much greater proportion are ________________ (women/men).

40. Tests that are designed to measure what a child has learned are called ________________ tests. Tests that are designed to measure learning potential are called ________________ tests.

41. The most commonly used aptitude tests are ________________ ________________.

In the original version of the most commonly used test of this type, a person's score was translated into a ________________ ________________, which was divided by the person's ________________ ________________ and multiplied by 100 to determine his or her ________________.

42. Two highly regarded IQ tests are the ________________-________________ and the ________________ tests; the latter test has special versions for ________________, ________________, and ________________.

43. (Figure 12.4) On current tests, two-thirds of all children score within a year or two of their age-mates, somewhere between ________________ and ________________. Children who score above ________________ are considered gifted, whereas those who score in the ________________-________________ range are considered to be slow learners.

44. Testing is controversial in part because a child's test performance can be affected by nonacademic factors, such as ________________ ________________.

45. IQ scores may seriously underestimate the intellectual potential of a ________________ child or overestimate that of a child from an ________________ background.

46. Robert Sternberg believes that there are three distinct types of intelligence: ________________, ________________, and ________________. Similarly, Howard Gardner describes ________________ (how many?) distinct intelligences.

47. Achievement tests can be ________________-________________, in which scores are compared to typical scores of children with the same background, or they can be ________________-________________, that is, measured against some objective benchmark. Most nationally used achievement tests are ________________-________________.

48. One danger of testing is that school systems may narrow their instructional goals to focus on ________________.

49. The tendency to view oneself as consistently above-average is called the ________________ ________________.

50. Passive learning ________________ (is/is not) the most appropriate form of instruction for most schoolchildren. Similarly, piecemeal learning ________________ (is/is not) a useful technique.

51. The information-processing perspective has led to a reemphasis on ______________-______________ ______________.

52. (text and Children Up Close) Teaching that is based on Vygotsky's perspective emphasizes the importance of ______________ ______________ in learning. An extensive experiment found that children taught according to this model had ______________ (higher/lower) reading achievement scores than those taught by more traditional methods.

53. (Children Up Close) A new approach in math replaces rote learning with ______________-______________ materials and active discussion, promoting a problem-solving approach to learning.

Progress Test 1

Multiple-Choice Questions

Circle your answers to the following questions and check them with the answers on page 190. If your answer is incorrect, read the explanation for why it is incorrect and then consult the appropriate pages of the text (in parentheses following the correct answer).

1. According to Piaget, the stage of cognitive development in which a person understands specific logical ideas and can apply them to concrete problems is called:
   a. preoperational thought.
   b. operational thought.
   c. concrete operational thought.
   d. formal operational thought.

2. Aptitude and achievement testing are controversial because:
   a. most tests are unreliable with respect to the individual scores they yield.
   b. test performance can be affected by many factors other than the child's intellectual potential or academic achievement.
   c. they often fail to identify serious learning problems.
   d. of all of the above reasons.

3. The idea that an object that has been transformed in some way can be restored to its original form by undoing the process is:
   a. identity.
   b. reversibility.
   c. reciprocity.
   d. automatization.

4. Information-processing theorists contend that major advances in cognitive development occur during the school years because:
   a. the child's mind becomes more like a computer as he or she matures.
   b. children become better able to process and analyze information.
   c. most mental activities become automatic by the time a child is about 13 years old.
   d. the major improvements in reasoning that occur during the school years involve increased long-term memory capacity.

5. The ability to filter out distractions and concentrate on relevant details is called:
   a. metacognition.
   b. information processing.
   c. selective attention.
   d. decentering.

6. The best example of a retrieval strategy is:
   a. reconstructing a lecture from notes.
   b. organizing terms to be learned in categories.
   c. studying in an environment that is free of distractions.
   d. repeating a multiplication table until it is automatic.

7. The term for the ability to monitor one's cognitive performance—to think about thinking—is:
   a. pragmatics.
   b. information processing.
   c. selective attention.
   d. metacognition.

8. Long-term memory is ______________ permanent and ______________ limited than working memory.
   a. more; less
   b. less; more
   c. more; more
   d. less; less

9. Tests that measure a child's potential to learn a new subject are called ______________ tests.
   a. aptitude
   b. achievement
   c. vocational
   d. intelligence

10. Class inclusion is the concept that:
    a. a particular object or person may belong to more than one category.
    b. objects can be organized in terms of classes.
    c. categories can be organized horizontally as well as vertically.
    d. categories need not overlap one another.

11. The formal code that children use in the classroom is characterized by:
    a. limited use of vocabulary and syntax.
    b. context-bound grammar.
    c. extensive use of gestures and intonation to convey meaning.
    d. extensive vocabulary, complex syntax, and lengthy sentences.

12. The educational emphasis on the importance of social interaction in the classroom is most directly derived from the developmental theory of:
    a. Vygotsky.
    b. Piaget.
    c. information processing.
    d. those who advocate immersion learning.

13. Critics of Piaget contend that:
    a. cognitive development is more homogeneous than Piaget predicted.
    b. children's progress through the cognitive stages is more uniform than Piaget thought.
    c. children demonstrate partial entrance into concrete operational thought earlier than Piaget predicted.
    d. individual differences in progress through the cognitive stages are minimal.

14. Historically, boys and wealthier children were more likely to be formally taught and to have greater educational demands placed upon them than girls or poor children. Today, this inequality:
    a. can be found only in developing countries.
    b. has largely disappeared.
    c. persists, even in developed countries.
    d. has been eliminated for girls, but not for poor children.

15. (Changing Policy) To what do cross-cultural researchers attribute the superior achievement test scores of Pacific-Rim students?
    a. genetics
    b. the high quality of home and classroom educational experiences
    c. a shorter school day and year
    d. classroom environments that emphasize passive learning

True or False Items

Write *true* or *false* on the line in front of each statement.

_______ 1. One major objection to Piagetian theory is that it describes the schoolchild as an active learner, a term appropriate only for preschoolers.

_______ 2. Learning a second language fosters children's overall linguistic and cognitive development.

_______ 3. Traditional aptitude and achievement tests emphasize verbal and reasoning skills.

_______ 4. Western classrooms today emphasize collaborative learning.

_______ 5. The process of telling a joke involves pragmatic language skills usually not mastered before age 7.

_______ 6. Code switching, especially the occasional use of slang, is a behavior characteristic primarily of children in the lower social strata.

_______ 7. (Changing Policy) American parents are more likely than Japanese parents to be dissatisfied with their children's academic performance.

_______ 8. Most information that comes into the sensory register is lost or discarded.

_______ 9. Most developmentalists agree that there should be a standard educational system for all children.

_______ 10. New standards of math education in many nations emphasize problem-solving skills rather than simple memorization of formulas.

Progress Test 2

Progress Test 2 should be completed during a final chapter review. Answer the following questions after you thoroughly understand the correct answers for the Chapter Review and Progress Test 1.

Multiple-Choice Questions

1. According to Piaget, 8- and 9-year-olds can reason only about concrete things in their lives. "Concrete" means:
    a. logical.
    b. abstract.
    c. tangible or specific.
    d. mathematical or classifiable.

2. In the earliest aptitude tests, a person's score was translated into a(n) _____ age that was divided by the person's _____ age to find the _____ quotient.
   a. mental; chronological; intelligence
   b. chronological; mental; intelligence
   c. intelligence; chronological; mental
   d. intelligence; mental; chronological

3. Tests that measure what a child has already learned are called _______________ tests.
   a. aptitude
   b. vocational
   c. achievement
   d. intelligence

4. When psychologists look at the ability of children to receive, store, and organize information, they are examining cognitive development from a view based on:
   a. the observations of Piaget.
   b. information processing.
   c. learning theory.
   d. the idea that the key to thinking is the sensory register.

5. The aptitude test that has special versions for preschoolers, schoolchildren, and adults is the:
   a. IQ test.
   b. Stanford-Binet.
   c. Wechsler test.
   d. WAIS-R.

6. The logical operations of concrete operational thought are particularly important to an understanding of the elementary-school subject(s) of:
   a. spelling.
   b. reading.
   c. math and science.
   d. social studies.

7. One storage strategy that develops toward the end of middle childhood is the regrouping of items to be remembered into categories. This technique is called:
   a. metacognition.
   b. selective attention.
   c. rehearsal.
   d. reorganization.

8. Which of the following Piagetian ideas is *not* widely accepted by developmentalists today?
   a. The thinking of school-age children is characterized by a more comprehensive logic than that of preschoolers.
   b. Children are active learners.
   c. How children think is as important as what they know.
   d. Once a certain type of reasoning ability emerges in children, it is evenly apparent in all domains of thinking.

9. Processing capacity refers to:
   a. the ability to selectively attend to more than one thought.
   b. the amount of information that a person is able to hold in working memory.
   c. the size of the child's knowledge base.
   d. all of the above.

10. Procedures for retaining new information are called:
    a. retrieval strategies.
    b. storage strategies.
    c. automatization.
    d. metacognition.

11. Which of the following is *not* a type of intelligence identified in Robert Sternberg's theory?
    a. academic
    b. practical
    c. achievement
    d. creative

12. Which aspect of the information-processing system assumes an executive role in regulating the analysis and transfer of information?
    a. sensory register
    b. working memory
    c. long-term memory
    d. control processes

13. An example of schoolchildren's growth in metacognition is their understanding that:
    a. transformed objects can be returned to their original state.
    b. rehearsal is a good strategy for memorizing, but outlining is better for understanding.
    c. objects may belong to more than one class.
    d. they can use different language styles in different situations.

14. A new approach to math education focuses on:
    a. rote memorization of formulas before problems are introduced.
    b. "hands-on" materials and active discussion of concepts.
    c. one-on-one tutorials.
    d. pretesting children and grouping them by ability.

15. Regarding bilingual education, many contemporary developmentalists believe that:
    a. the attempted learning of two languages is confusing to children and delays proficiency in either one or both languages.
    b. bilingual education is linguistically, culturally, and cognitively advantageous to children.
    c. second-language education is most effective when the child has not yet mastered the native language.
    d. bilingual education programs are too expensive to justify the few developmental advantages they confer.

Matching Items

Match each term or concept with its corresponding description or definition.

Terms or Concepts

_____ 1. automatization
_____ 2. reversibility
_____ 3. reciprocity
_____ 4. identity
_____ 5. information processing
_____ 6. selective attention
_____ 7. retrieval strategies
_____ 8. storage strategies
_____ 9. metacognition
_____ 10. immersion
_____ 11. norm-referenced
_____ 12. standards-based

Descriptions or Definitions

a. the ability to screen out distractions and concentrate on relevant information
b. the idea that a transformation process can be undone to restore the original conditions
c. the idea that certain characteristics of an object remain the same even when other characteristics change
d. developmental perspective that conceives of cognitive development as the result of changes in the processing and analysis of information
e. a test that is assessed relative to an objective benchmark
f. the idea that a transformation in one dimension is compensated for by a transformation in another
g. an educational technique in which instruction occurs entirely in the second language
h. procedures to access previously learned information
i. procedures for holding information in memory
j. a test that is assessed relative to a particular group average
k. process by which familiar mental activities become routine
l. the ability to evaluate a cognitive task and to monitor one's performance on it

Thinking Critically About Chapter 12

Answer these questions the day before an exam as a final check on your understanding of the chapter's terms and concepts.

1. Angela was born in 1984. In 1992, she scored 125 on an intelligence test. Using the original formula, what was Angela's mental age when she took the test?

a. 6
b. 8
c. 10
d. 12

2. Robert Sternberg and Howard Gardner would probably be *most* critical of traditional aptitude and achievement tests because they:

a. inadvertently reflect certain nonacademic competencies.
b. do not reflect knowledge of cultural ideas.
c. measure only a limited set of abilities.
d. underestimate the intellectual potential of disadvantaged children.

3. Compared to her 4-year-old sister, 9-year-old Andrea is more likely to seek explanations that are:

a. intuitive.
b. generalizable.
c. subjective.
d. all of the above.

4. Dr. Larsen believes that the cognitive advances of middle childhood occur because of basic changes in children's thinking speed, knowledge base, and memory retrieval skills. Dr. Larsen evidently is working from the _______________ perspective.

a. Piagetian
b. Vygotskian
c. information-processing
d. psychoanalytic

5. Some researchers believe that cognitive processing speed and capacity increase during middle childhood because of:

a. the myelination of nerve pathways.
b. the maturation of the frontal cortex.
c. better use of cognitive resources.
d. all of the above.

6. A child's ability to tell a joke that will amuse his or her audience always depends on:
   a. the child's mastery of reciprocity and reversibility.
   b. code switching.
   c. the child's ability to consider another's perspective.
   d. an expansion of the child's processing capacity.

7. For a 10-year-old, some mental activities have become so familiar or routine as to require little mental work. This development is called:
   a. selective attention.
   b. identity.
   c. metacognition.
   d. automatization.

8. A child who sings "*i* before *e* except after *c*" is making use of:
   a. rehearsal.
   b. automatization.
   c. a storage strategy.
   d. class inclusion.

9. In concluding her presentation, "Drawbacks to Standardized Testing," Alyssa notes that the Wobegon effect tends to occur most often with:
   a. aptitude tests.
   b. standards-based achievement tests.
   c. norm-referenced achievement tests.
   d. IQ tests.

10. A 9-year-old will typically cling less stubbornly to grammatical mistakes than a 4-year-old because the 9-year-old:
    a. has mastered the concept of conservation.
    b. is less egocentric in learning and applying rules.
    c. has more experience in humor and joke telling.
    d. understands the subjunctive.

11. Russian-speaking children do not master the subjunctive very much earlier than English-speaking children, even though the subjunctive is less complicated in the Russian language. The reason for this is that:
    a. cultural patterns make the subjunctive more difficult for Russian children to grasp.
    b. mastery of the subjunctive requires a particular level of cognitive development.
    c. the use of the subjunctive in Russian is very rare.
    d. Russian children score lower on language aptitude tests.

12. As compared with her 5-year-old brother, 7-year-old Althea has learned to adjust her vocabulary to her audience. This is known as:
    a. selective attention.
    b. a retrieval strategy.
    c. code switching.
    d. classification.

13. Compared with her mother, who attended elementary school in the 1950s, Bettina, who is now in the third grade, is likely to be in a class that places greater emphasis on:
    a. individualized learning.
    b. active learning.
    c. learning by discovery, discussion, and deduction.
    d. all of the above.

14. Six-year-old Samantha is taking a test of her ability to understand spatial relations. She is most likely taking the:
    a. Stanford-Binet.
    b. WPPSI.
    c. WISC-R.
    d. WAIS-R.

15. (Research Report) Concluding her class presentation on differences between the educational experiences of Japanese and American children, Nogumi states that:
    a. Japanese children devote more time to nonacademic activities than American children.
    b. American children spend less time in school than Japanese children.
    c. Japanese children appear to be less happy and less responsive in the classroom than American children.
    d. Japanese teachers are more likely to employ individual, as opposed to group, instruction.

Key Terms

Writing Definitions

Using your own words, write a brief definition or explanation of each of the following terms on a separate piece of paper.

1. information-processing theory
2. sensory register
3. working memory
4. long-term memory
5. control processes
6. selective attention
7. automatization
8. knowledge base
9. metacognition
10. storage strategies
11. retrieval strategies
12. concrete operational thought

13. identity
14. reversibility
15. reciprocity
16. classification
17. class inclusion
18. code-switching
19. formal code
20. informal code
21. immersion
22. English as a second language (ESL)
23. bilingual education
24. bilingual-bicultural education
25. aptitude tests
26. achievement tests
27. IQ tests
28. norm-referenced
29. standards-based
30. Wobegon effect

Cross Check

After you have written the definitions of the key terms in this chapter, you should complete the crossword puzzle to ensure that you can reverse the process—recognize the term, given the definition.

ACROSS

1. Form of speech used in casual situations, characterized by limited vocabulary and syntax.
4. Approach to bilingual education in which the child's instruction occurs entirely in the new language.
9. Approach to teaching English in which all instruction is in English, and the teacher does not speak the child's native tongue.
10. Tests that measure what a child has already learned in a particular academic subject or subjects.
11. Tests designed to measure potential, rather than actual, accomplishment.
13. Measure of intelligence, originally computed as mental age divided by chronological age times 100.
14. Strategy for placing and holding information in memory, such as rehearsal or reorganization.
15. Principle that a transformation in one dimension of an object can be compensated for by a transformation in another dimension.
16. Effect in which we tend to view ourselves, our children, and our culture as consistently above average.
17. Part of memory that stores unlimited amounts of information for days, months, or years.
18. Strategies for accessing previously learned information.

DOWN

2. Piaget's term for cognitive development during the school years.
3. The concept that an object or person may belong to more than one category or class.
5. Process by which familiar and well-rehearsed mental activities become routine and automatic.
6. Approach to teaching a second language that incorporates the child's native cultural symbols in the learning process.
7. The concept that objects can be organized into categories or classes according to some common properties.
8. The logical principles that a transformation process can be reversed to restore the original conditions.
12. Form of speech used in school and other formal situations, characterized by extensive vocabulary, complex syntax, and lengthy sentences.

ANSWERS

CHAPTER REVIEW

1. planning; game
2. process; analyze; information-processing
3. sensory register
4. working memory; short-term memory; conscious
5. long-term memory
6. control processes
7. selective attention
8. processing speed; processing capacity
9. neurological; myelination; frontal cortex; cognitive resources
10. automatization
11. knowledge base
12. are not; knowledge; experience
13. metacognition; metamemory

School-age children's better use of cognitive strategies derives from metacognitive growth. Furthermore, they know how to identify challenging tasks and devote greater effort to them; acquire a better grasp of which cognitive strategies are well-suited for which cognitive tasks; are more likely to spontaneously monitor and evaluate their progress than are preschoolers; and are more likely to use external aids to enhance memorization and problem solving.

14. storage strategies; rehearsal; reorganization; retrieval strategies
15. logical; rational; consistent; generalizable
16. concrete operations
17. identity; reversibility; reciprocity
18. math; science; social
19. maturation; experience
20. classification; class inclusion
21. hierarchical; categories; subcategories; hierarchical; overlapping; separate
22. more; sociocultural
23. subtle; analytic; logical; connections; poems; languages; jokes
24. comparatives; subjunctive; metaphors
25. stubborn; polite speech
26. code switching; formal code; vocabulary; syntax; sentences; informal code; gestures; intonation
27. free; bound; pragmatic
28. advantage
29. immersion; reverse immersion
30. English as a second language; bilingual education; bilingual-bicultural education
31. Canada; shy, stupid, or socially isolated
32. 5
33. peers
34. is not
35. boys
36. strict lecture; open education
37. behind; math; science

Japanese and Chinese children spend more hours per week in school than American children do, and they spend more time on homework. They also are more likely to attend supplemental classes at special schools if they fall behind and to have more of their classroom time devoted to academic activities. Teachers in Japan and the Republic of China tend to emphasize group instruction, whereas American teachers emphasize individual or small-group instruction.

38. more
39. American; Japanese; men
40. achievement; aptitude
41. intelligence tests; mental age; chronological age; IQ
42. Stanford-Binet; Wechsler; preschoolers; schoolchildren; adults
43. 85; 115; 130; 70–85
44. the capacity to pay attention and concentrate, emotional stress, health, language difficulties, and test-taking anxiety
45. disadvantaged; advantaged
46. academic; creative; practical; seven
47. norm-referenced; standards-based; norm-referenced
48. tasks measured by the tests
49. Wobegon effect
50. is not; is not
51. explicit teacher-centered instruction
52. social interaction; higher
53. hands-on

PROGRESS TEST 1

Multiple-Choice Questions

1. **c.** is the answer. (p. 372)

   a. Preoperational thought is "pre-logical" thinking.

   b. There is no such stage in Piaget's theory.

   d. Formal operational thought extends logical reasoning to abstract problems.

2. **b.** is the answer. (p. 389)

3. **b.** is the answer. (p. 372)

   a. This is the concept that certain characteristics of an object remain the same even when other characteristics change.

   c. This is the concept that a change in one dimension of an object can be compensated for by a change in another dimension.

   d. This is the process by which familiar mental activities become routine and automatic.

4. **b.** is the answer. (p. 367)

   a. Information-processing theorists use the mind-computer metaphor at every age.

   c. Although increasing automatization is an important aspect of development, the information-processing perspective does not suggest that most mental activities become automatic by age 13.

   d. Most of the important changes in reasoning that occur during the school years are due to the improved processing capacity of the person's *working memory.*

5. **c.** is the answer. (p. 367)

   a. This is the ability to evaluate a cognitive task and to monitor one's performance on it.

   b. Information processing is a perspective on cognitive development that focuses on how the mind analyzes, stores, retrieves, and reasons about information.

   d. Decentering, which refers to the school-age child's ability to consider more than one aspect of a problem simultaneously, is not discussed in this chapter.

6. **a.** is the answer. (pp. 367–368)

   b. & d. These are examples of storage strategies.

   c. This is a good idea, but it is not a retrieval strategy.

7. **d.** is the answer. (p. 370)

   a. Pragmatics refers to the practical use of language to communicate with others.

   b. The information-processing perspective views the mind as being like a computer.

   c. This is the ability to screen out distractions in order to focus on important information.

8. **a.** is the answer. (p. 366)

9. **a.** is the answer. (p. 385)

   b. Achievement tests measure what has already been learned.

   c. Vocational tests are achievement tests.

   d. Intelligence tests measure *general* aptitude, rather than aptitude for a specific subject.

10. **a.** is the answer. (p. 374)

    b. This describes classification.

    c. & d. Class inclusion is based on the hierarchical and overlapping nature of certain categories.

11. **d.** is the answer. (p. 379)

    a., b., & c. These are characteristic of the informal code that children use with friends in other settings.

12. **a.** is the answer. (p. 393)

13. **c.** is the answer. (p. 376)

    a., b., & d. Just the opposite is true.

14. **c.** is the answer. (p. 385)

15. **b.** is the answer. (pp. 386–387)

True or False Items

1. F Most educators agree that the school-age child, like the preschooler, is an active learner. (p. 372)
2. T (p. 379)
3. T (p. 390)
4. F Western classrooms tend to emphasize competition and individual achievement. (p. 390)
5. T (p. 376)
6. F Code switching (including occasional use of slang) is a behavior demonstrated by all children. (p. 378)
7. F Although the academic performance of American children lags behind that of Japanese children, American parents are more likely than Japanese (or Chinese) parents to express satisfaction with their children's academic performance. (p. 387)
8. T (p. 366)
9. F The complexity of the learning process, as described by information-processing researchers, indicates that there is no basic educational system that will work for everyone. (p. 393)
10. T (pp. 393–395)

PROGRESS TEST 2

Multiple-Choice Questions

1. **c.** is the answer. (p. 372)
2. **a.** is the answer. (p. 388)
3. **c.** is the answer. (p. 388)
4. **b.** is the answer. (p. 365)
5. **c.** is the answer. (p. 388)

   a. "IQ test" is too vague an answer. Both the Wechsler and the Stanford-Binet are IQ tests.

   d. The WAIS-R is the *adult* revision of the Wechsler test.

6. **c.** is the answer. (pp. 372–373)
7. **d.** is the answer. (p. 371)
   a. This is the ability to evaluate a cognitive task and to monitor one's performance on it.
   b. This is the ability to screen out distractions and focus on important information.
   c. This is the repeating of information in order to remember it.
8. **d.** is the answer. (p. 376)
9. **b.** is the answer. (p. 367)
10. **b.** is the answer. (p. 371)
   a. These are strategies for *accessing* already learned information.
   c. Automatization is the process by which well-learned activities become routine and automatic.
   d. This is the ability to evaluate a task and to monitor one's performance on it.
11. **c.** is the answer. (p. 389)
12. **d.** is the answer. (p. 366)
   a. The sensory register stores incoming Information for a split second.
   b. Working memory is the part of memory that handles current, conscious mental activity.
   c. Long-term memory stores information for days, months, or years.
13. **b.** is the answer. (p. 370)
14. **b.** is the answer. (pp. 393–395)
15. **b.** is the answer. (p. 379)

Matching Items

1. k (p. 368)	**5.** d (p. 365)	**9.** l (p. 370)
2. b (p. 372)	**6.** a (p. 367)	**10.** g (p. 380)
3. f (p. 372)	**7.** h (p. 371)	**11.** j (p. 390)
4. c (p. 372)	**8.** i (p. 371)	**12.** e (p. 390)

THINKING CRITICALLY ABOUT CHAPTER 12

1. **c.** is the answer. At the time she took the test, Angela's chronological age was 8. Knowing that her IQ was 125, we can solve the equation to yield a mental age value of 10. (p. 388)
2. **c.** is the answer. Both Sternberg and Gardner believe that there are multiple intelligences rather than the narrowly defined abilities measured by traditional aptitude and achievement tests. (p. 389)
   a., b., & d. Although these criticisms are certainly valid, they are not specifically associated with Sternberg or Gardner.
3. **b.** is the answer. (p. 372)
4. **c.** is the answer. (pp. 367–368)
   a. This perspective emphasizes the logical, active nature of thinking during middle childhood.
   b. This perspective emphasizes the importance of social interaction in learning.
   d. This perspective does not address the development of cognitive skills.
5. **d.** is the answer. (p. 368)
6. **c.** is the answer. Joke-telling is one of the clearest demonstrations of schoolchildren's improved pragmatic skills, including the ability to know what someone else will think is funny. (p. 379)
7. **d.** is the answer. (p. 368)
   a. Selective attention is the ability to focus on important information and screen out distractions.
   b. Identity is the logical principle that certain characteristics of an object remain the same even when other characteristics change.
   c. Metacognition is the ability to evaluate a task and to monitor one's performance on it.
8. **c.** is the answer. (p. 371)
   a. Rehearsal is the repetition of to-be-learned information.
   b. Automatization refers to the tendency of well-rehearsed mental activities to become routine and automatic.
   d. Class inclusion is the idea that a particular object may belong to more than one class.
9. **c.** is the answer. Tests that are designed with norms for average scores quickly become ways to prove that one is "above-average." (p. 391)
   a. & d. Aptitude and IQ tests measure potential for learning, rather than what has already been learned.
   b. Tests such as these have an independent, objective benchmark for success.
10. **b.** is the answer. (p. 377)
11. **b.** is the answer. (p. 377)
12. **c.** is the answer. (p. 378)
13. **d.** is the answer. (pp. 392–393)
14. **c.** is the answer. (p. 388)
15. **b.** is the answer. (p. 386)
   a. & d. In fact, the opposites are true.
   c. This is untrue.

KEY TERMS

Writing Definitions

1. According to **information-processing theory**, human thinking is analogous to a computer in sorting, categorizing, storing, and retrieving stimuli. (p. 365)
2. **Sensory register** is the memory system that stores incoming stimuli for a fraction of a second, after which it is passed into working memory, or discarded as unimportant; also called short-term memory. (p. 366)
3. **Working memory** is the part of memory that handles current, conscious mental activity. (p. 366)
4. **Long-term memory** is the part of memory that stores unlimited amounts of information for days, months, or years. (p. 366)
5. **Control processes** (such as selective attention and retrieval strategies) regulate the analysis and flow of information in memory. (p. 366)
6. **Selective attention** is the ability to screen out distractions and concentrate on relevant information. (p. 367)
7. **Automatization** is the process by which familiar and well-rehearsed mental activities become routine and automatic. (p. 368)
8. The **knowledge base** is a body of knowledge in a particular area that has been learned and on which additional learning can be based. (p. 368)
9. **Metacognition** is the ability to evaluate a cognitive task to determine what to do and to monitor one's performance on that task. (p. 370)
10. **Storage strategies** are procedures for placing and holding information in memory, such as rehearsal and reorganization. (p. 371)
11. **Retrieval strategies** are procedures for accessing previously learned information. (p. 371)
12. During Piaget's stage of **concrete operational thought**, lasting from ages 7 to 11, children can think logically about concrete events and objects but are not able to reason abstractly. (p. 372)
13. In Piaget's theory, **identity** is the logical principle that certain characteristics of an object remain the same even when other characteristics change. (p. 372)
14. **Reversibility** is the logical principle that a transformation process can be reversed to restore the original conditions. (p. 372)
15. **Reciprocity** is the logical principle that a transformation in one dimension of an object can be compensated for by a transformation in another. (p. 372)

    Example: A child who understands **reciprocity** realizes that rolling a ball of clay into a thin rope makes it longer, but also skinnier, than its original shape.
16. **Classification** is the concept that objects can be organized into categories or classes according to some common property. (p. 374)
17. **Class inclusion** is the concept that an object or person may belong to more than one category or class. (p. 374)
18. **Code switching** is a pragmatic communication skill involving changing from one form of speech to another. (p. 378)
19. The **formal code** is a form of speech used by children in school and other formal situations, characterized by extensive vocabulary, complex syntax, and lengthy sentences. (p. 379)
20. The **informal code** is a form of speech used by children in casual situations, characterized by limited vocabulary and syntax. (p. 379)
21. **Immersion** is an approach to bilingual education in which the child's instruction occurs entirely in the new language. (p. 380)
22. **English as a second language (ESL)** is an approach to teaching English in which all instruction is in English, and the teacher does not speak the child's native language. (p. 381)
23. **Bilingual education** is an approach to teaching a second language in which the teacher instructs the children in school subjects using their native language as well as the second language. (p. 381)
24. **Bilingual-bicultural education** is an approach to teaching a second language that incorporates the child's native cultural symbols in the learning process. (p. 381)
25. **Aptitude tests** are tests designed to measure potential, rather than actual, accomplishment. (p. 385)
26. **Achievement tests** are tests that measure what a child has already learned in a particular academic subject or subjects. (p. 388)
27. **IQ tests** are aptitude tests, which were originally designed to yield a measure of intelligence, calculated as mental age divided by chronological age, multiplied by 100. (p. 388)
28. **Norm-referenced** achievement tests compare a person's score with the average score of a group of people with the same amount of schooling or background. (p. 390)

29. **Standards-based** achievement tests compare an individual's score with a particular standard or criterion that is set in advance. (p. 390)

30. The **Wobegon effect** is the tendency to view oneself, one's children, and one's culture as consistently "above-average." (p. 391)

Cross Check

ACROSS

1. informal code
4. immersion
9. ESL
10. achievement
11. aptitude
13. IQ
14. storage
15. reciprocity
16. Wobegon
17. long term
18. retrieval

DOWN

2. concrete operations
3. class inclusions
5. automatization
6. bilingual-bicultural
7. classification
8. reversibility
12. formal code

CHAPTER 13

The School Years: Psychosocial Development

Chapter Overview

This chapter brings to a close the unit on the school years. We have seen that from ages 7 to 11, the child becomes stronger and more competent, mastering the biosocial and cognitive abilities that are important in his or her culture. Psychosocial accomplishments are equally impressive.

The first section of the chapter begins by exploring the growing social competence of children, as described by Freud, Erikson, learning, cognitive, sociocultural, and epigenetic systems theorists. The section continues with a discussion of the growth of social cognition and self-understanding.

Because the school years are a time of expanding moral reasoning, the chapter also examines Kohlberg's stage theory of moral development, as well as current reevaluations of his theory. Children's interaction with peers and others in their ever-widening social world is the subject of the next section.

The next section explores the problems and challenges often experienced by school-age children in our society, including the experience of parental divorce and remarriage and living in single-parent and blended families. The chapter closes with a discussion of the ways in which children cope with stressful situations.

NOTE: Answer guidelines for all Chapter 13 questions begin on page 207.

Guided Study

The text chapter should be studied one section at a time. Before you read, preview each section by skimming it, noting headings and boldface items. Then read the appropriate section objectives from the following outline. Keep these objectives in mind and, as you read the chapter section, search for the information that will enable you to meet each objective. Once you have finished a section, write out answers for its objectives.

An Expanding Social World (pp. 399–402)

1. Identify the common themes or emphases of different theoretical views of the psychosocial development of school-age children.

2. Define social cognition, and explain how children's theory of mind and emotional understanding evolve during middle childhood.

3. Describe the development of self-understanding during middle childhood and its implications for children's self-esteem.

Moral Development (pp. 402–407)

4. Outline Kohlberg's stage theory of moral development.

5. Identify and evaluate several criticisms of Kohlberg's theory.

The Peer Group (pp. 407–416)

6. Discuss the importance of peer groups, providing examples of how school-age children develop their own subculture and explaining the importance of this development.

7. Discuss how friendship circles change during the school years.

8. Discuss the distinction between appropriate and inappropriate aggression in schoolchildren's play, and note the plight of unpopular children.

9. (text and Research Report) Discuss the special problems of bullies and their victims, and describe possible ways of helping such children.

Families in School Years (pp. 416–427)

10. Identify five essential ways in which functional families nurture school-age children.

11. Contrast the styles of open and closed families, and differentiate four basic family structures.

12. (text and Changing Policy) Describe how American family structures have changed in recent decades, and discuss the benefits and some disadvantages of children living with both biological parents.

13. Discuss the impact of divorce and single-parent households on the psychosocial development of the school-age child.

14. Discuss the impact of blended families and other family structures on the psychosocial development of the school-age child.

Coping with Problems (pp. 427–432)

15. Identify the variables that influence the impact of stresses on schoolchildren, and discuss those factors that seem especially important in helping children to cope with stress.

16. (Changing Policy) Discuss the impact of poverty and homelessness on the development of school-age children.

Chapter Review

When you have finished reading the chapter, work through the material that follows to review it. Complete the sentences and answer the questions. As you proceed, evaluate your performance for each section by consulting the answers on page 207. Do not continue with the next section until you understand each answer. If you need to, review or reread the appropriate section in the textbook before continuing.

An Expanding Social World (pp. 399–402)

1. Freud describes middle childhood as the period of ______________, when emotional drives are ______________, psychosexual needs are ______________, and unconscious conflicts are ______________.
2. According to Erikson, the crisis of middle childhood is ______________ ______________ ______________.
3. Developmentalists influenced by learning theory are more concerned with children's ______________ of new cognitive abilities; those influenced by the cognitive perspective focus on ______________; and the sociocultural perspective emphasizes ______________ ______________.

Briefly describe the epigenetic systems perspective on the school-age child's new independence.

4. The rapid change in intellectual and social competence that many children experience at this time is known as the ______-______-______.

5. School-age children advance in their understanding of other people and groups; that is, they advance in ______ ______. At this time, the preschooler's one-step theory of mind begins to evolve into a complex, ______ view of others.

6. In experiments on children's social cognition, older children are more likely to focus on ______ (immediate behavior/possible consequences) when asked to predict another person's behavior in a situation.

7. Another example of children's advancing social cognition is that, as compared with younger children, older children are more likely to focus on ______ (physical characteristics/personality traits) when asked to describe other children.

8. In the beginning of the school years children often explain their actions by focusing on the immediate ______; a few years later they more readily relate their actions to their ______ and ______ ______.

9. During the school years, children begin to realize that people can experience several emotions ______ and that they can ______ their emotions to comply with social rules. As a result of their new social cognition, children can better manage their own ______.

10. As their self-understanding sharpens, children gradually become ______ (more/less) self-critical, and their self-esteem ______ (rises/dips). One reason is that they more often evaluate themselves through ______ ______. As they mature, children are also ______ (more/less) likely to feel personally to blame for their shortcomings.

Moral Development (pp. 402-407)

11. The theorist who has extensively studied moral development by presenting subjects with stories that pose ethical dilemmas is ______. According to his theory, the three levels of moral reasoning are ______, ______, and ______.

12. In preconventional reasoning, emphasis is on getting ______ and avoiding ______. "Might makes right" describes stage ______ (1/2), while "look out for number one" describes stage ______ (1/2).

13. In conventional reasoning, emphasis is on ______ ______, such as being a dutiful citizen, in stage ______ (3/4), or winning approval from others, in stage ______ (3/4).

14. In postconventional reasoning, emphasis is on ______ ______, such as ______ ______ (stage 5) and ______ ______ ______ (stage 6).

15. One criticism of Kohlberg's theory was that his dilemmas were too ______ and ______. A second is that the stages reflect values associated with ______, ______ cultures. Carol Gilligan believes that females develop a ______ ______ ______, based on concern for the well-being of others, more than a ______ ______ ______, based on depersonalized standards of right and wrong.

16. Acts of sharing, helping, and caring for other people without the expectations of reward are called ______ ______.

Lying to a teacher to cover for a friend _______________ (is/is not) generally considered to be _______________ by the society of children.

17. Because moral perception is also shaped by _______________ and _______________ values, what is merely conventional in one culture often takes on moral significance in another.

The Peer Group (pp. 407–416)

18. A peer group is defined as _______________ _______________.

19. Some social scientists call the peer group's subculture the _______________ _______________ _______________, highlighting the distinctions between children's groups and the general culture.

Identify several distinguishing features of this subculture.

20. Having a personal friend is _______________ (more/less) important to children than acceptance by the peer group. When asked what makes their best friends different from other acquaintances, older children are more likely than younger children to cite _______________ _______________. Older children also increasingly regard friendship as a forum for _______________.

21. Friendship groups typically become _______________ (larger/smaller) and _______________ (more/less) rigid during the school years.

22. A certain amount of defensive _______________ is expected in children's peer interactions. Variation in the norms for such behaviors _______________ (has/has not) been found to occur by age, by ethnic and economic group, by neighborhood, and by the specific _______________ _______________.

23. Children who are actively rejected tend to be either _______________-_______________ or _______________-_______________. Children in the latter group are typically _______________, anxious, and unhappy; low in _______________; and particularly vulnerable to _______________. Those in the former group tend to be _______________ and immature in their _______________ _______________. As rejected children get older, their problems _______________ (diminish/get worse).

Give an example of the immaturity of rejected children.

24. (Research Report) A key aspect in the definition of bullying is that harmful attacks are _______________. The effects of bullying _______________ (can be/usually are not) long-lasting.

Describe the effects of bullying on children.

25. Contrary to the public perception, bullies usually are not _______________ or _______________ at the peak of their bullying.

26. (text and Research Report) Bullying during middle childhood _______________ (is/is not) universal. An effective intervention in controlling bullying is to change the _______________ _______________ within the school so that bully-victim cycles are not allowed to persist.

Families in School Years (pp. 416-427)

27. A functional family nurtures school-age children by meeting their basic _______________, by encouraging _______________, fostering the development of _______________,

nurturing peer ______________, and by providing ______________ and ______________.

28. Families with an ______________ style encourage contributions from every family member; in those with a ______________ style, one parent, usually the ______________, sets strict guidelines and rules.

29. Family structures are defined as ______________.

30. Identify each of the following family structures:

a. ______________ A family that includes three or more generations, along with parents and children.

b. ______________ A family that consists of the father, the mother, and their biological children.

c. ______________ A family that consists of one parent with his or her biological children.

d. ______________ A family consisting of two parents, at least one with biological children from another union.

31. Longitudinal research studies demonstrate that children can thrive ______________ (only in certain family structures/in almost any family structure).

32. (Changing Policy) The preferred family structure in most developing countries in Asia and Latin America has been ______________, whereas in African and Arab nations, the ______________ household has flourished.

33. (Changing Policy) Although both ______________ families and ______________ families existed in the United States a hundred years ago, ______________ families were far more common.

34. (Changing Policy) The "traditional" family structure that dominated most of America's history is becoming ______________ (more/less) common.

35. (Changing Policy) If current trends continue, about ______________ percent of American children born in the 1990s will live with both biological parents from birth to age 18.

36. Children who have fewer physical, emotional, or learning difficulties are those who live with ______________.

Describe how children reared in this family structure fare at adolescence and early adulthood.

37. Give three reasons for the benefits of this family structure.

a. ______________

b. ______________

c. ______________

38. The advantages of traditional families are often ______________ (overstated/understated). Contributing to this is the fact that many studies do not take sufficient account of other factors that affect child development, the most obvious being ______________. Other factors that correlate with family structure and functioning include ______________.

39. In acknowledging that two-parent homes are generally best, the author notes two important qualifications.

a. ______________

b. ______________

40. Children raised in families with persistently high levels of conflict usually ______________ (do/do not) become impervious to the stress and tension.

41. The disruption surrounding divorce almost always adversely affects children for at least ______________.

Whether this distress is short-lived or long-lasting depends primarily on two post-divorce factors:

a. ______________________

b. ______________________

Cite several sources of instability that make it more difficult for children to adjust to divorce.

42. *Custody* means having ______________ responsibility for children. Although

______________ ______________

is theoretically the best decision following a divorce, in practice this often is not the case. Developmental research reveals that ______________ (mothers/fathers/neither parent) tend(s) to function better as the custodial parent.

Give several reasons that children whose fathers have custody may fare better than children whose mothers have custody.

43. The number of ______________-______________ households has increased markedly over the past two decades in virtually every major industrialized nation. Two reasons for this trend are:

a. ______________________

b. ______________________

44. When compared with others of the same ethnicity and socioeconomic status, children who live with one biological parent develop

____

(just as well as/more poorly than) those who live with two. This has been demonstrated in three areas of development:

a. ______________________

b. ______________________

c. ______________________

This generality ______________ (holds/does not hold) equally well for preschoolers, school-age children, and adolescents.

45. Children in single-parent households do tend to have more ______________ problems than other children. Two important factors in how well children in single-parent households fare are the emotional ______________ and ______________ resources of the single parent.

46. Most divorced parents ______________ (do/do not) remarry within a few years. The divorce rate for second marriages is ______________ (higher than/lower than/the same as) that for first marriages.

47. Children growing up in gay, lesbian, and other nontraditional families generally develop ______________ (poorly/quite well), depending on the particulars of

______________________.

As nontraditional families become more ______________ acceptable, the negative effects of nonnuclear families on children have ______________ (increased/decreased).

Coping with Problems (pp. 427–432)

48. (Changing Policy) On the whole, homeless children are even more disadvantaged than their peers of equal SES, with the result that many suffer from a loss of faith in life's possibilities and

______________ ______________.

49. Between ages 7 and 11 the overall frequency of various psychological problems ______________ (increases/decreases), while the number of evident competencies ______________ (increases/decreases).

50. Two factors that combine to buffer school-age children against the stresses they encounter are the development of ______________ ______________ and an expanding

______________________.

51. The impact of a given stress on a child depends on ____________________ ____________________ and the degree to which they affect ____________________ ____________________.

52. One reason that competence can compensate for life stresses is that if children feel confident, their ____________________ benefits, and they are better able to put the rest of their life in perspective. This explains why older children tend to be ____________________ (more/less) vulnerable to life stresses than are children who are just beginning middle childhood.

53. Another element that helps children deal with problems is the ____________________ ____________________ they receive. This can be obtained from grandparents or siblings, for example, or from ____________________ ____________________ and ____________________.

54. Most children ____________________ (do/do not) have an idyllic childhood. Such a childhood ____________________ (is/is not) necessary for healthy development.

Progress Test 1

Multiple-Choice Questions

Circle your answers to the following questions and check them with the answers on page 209. If your answer is incorrect, read the explanation for why it is incorrect and then consult the appropriate pages of the text (in parentheses following the correct answer).

1. The "5-to-7 shift" refers to the rapid change in ____________________ that children experience between ages 5 and 7.
   - **a.** intellectual and social competence
   - **b.** moral reasoning
   - **c.** friendship networks
   - **d.** self-esteem

2. In making moral choices, according to Gilligan, females are more likely than males to:
   - **a.** score at a higher level in Kohlberg's system.
   - **b.** emphasize the needs of others.
   - **c.** judge right and wrong in absolute terms.
   - **d.** formulate abstract principles.

3. The best strategy for helping children who are at risk of developing serious psychological problems because of multiple stresses would be to:
   - **a.** obtain assistance from a psychiatrist.
   - **b.** change the household situation.
   - **c.** increase the child's competencies or social supports.
   - **d.** reduce the peer group's influence.

4. Norms for aggression vary by:
   - **a.** age.
   - **b.** ethnic group.
   - **c.** socioeconomic group.
   - **d.** all of the above.

5. Compared with preschoolers, older children are more likely to blame:
   - **a.** failure on bad luck.
   - **b.** teachers and other authority figures.
   - **c.** their parents for their problems.
   - **d.** themselves for their shortcomings.

6. As rejected children get older:
   - **a.** their problems often get worse.
   - **b.** their problems usually decrease.
   - **c.** their friendship circles typically become larger.
   - **d.** the importance of the peer group to their self-esteem grows weaker.

7. Compared with average or popular children, rejected children tend to be:
   - **a.** brighter and more competitive.
   - **b.** affluent and "stuck-up."
   - **c.** economically disadvantaged.
   - **d.** socially immature.

8. A family that consists of two parents, at least one of whom has children from another union, is called a(n) ____________________ family.
   - **a.** nuclear
   - **b.** extended
   - **c.** blended
   - **d.** single-parent

9. Divorce and parental remarriage typically prove beneficial to children when they result in less financial stress and:
   - **a.** less loneliness for the parent.
   - **b.** greater role overload.
   - **c.** significant changes in lifestyle.
   - **d.** the inclusion of stepsiblings.

10. Older schoolchildren tend to be ________ vulnerable to the stresses of life than children who are just beginning middle childhood because they ________.
    a. more; tend to overpersonalize their problems
    b. less; have better developed skills for coping with problems
    c. more; are more likely to compare their well-being with that of their peers
    d. less; are less egocentric

11. Between the ages of 7 and 11, the overall frequency of various psychological problems:
    a. increases in both boys and girls.
    b. decreases in both boys and girls.
    c. increases in boys and decreases in girls.
    d. decreases in boys and increases in girls.

12. Studies of single-parent homes demonstrate that when compared with others of the same ethnicity and SES, children:
    a. fare better in mother-only homes.
    b. fare better in father-only homes, especially if the children are girls.
    c. develop quite similarly in both mother-only and father-only homes.
    d. fare better than children in two-parent homes.

13. During the school years, children become ________ selective about their friends, and their friendship groups become ________.
    a. less; larger
    b. less; smaller
    c. more; larger
    d. more; smaller

14. At mid-twentieth century, the "ideal" family structure:
    a. in most industrialized nations consisted of two biological parents living with their own two or three dependent children.
    b. in Asia and Latin America was the large extended family with grandparents, cousins, aunts, and uncles living within the same household.
    c. in many African and Arab nations included a greater variety of family structures, including the polygamous household.
    d. was all of the above.

15. Erikson sees the crisis of the school years as that of:
    a. industry versus inferiority.
    b. acceptance versus rejection.
    c. initiative versus guilt.
    d. male versus female.

True or False Items

Write *true* or *false* on the line in front of each statement.

________ 1. As they evaluate themselves according to increasingly complex self-theories, school-age children typically experience a rise in self-esteem.

________ 2. During middle childhood, acceptance by the peer group is valued more than having a close friend.

________ 3. Children from low-income homes often have lower self-esteem.

________ 4. In the majority of divorce cases in which the mother is the custodial parent, the father maintains a close, long-term relationship with the children.

________ 5. Divorce almost always adversely affects the children for at least a year or two.

________ 6. The quality of family interaction seems to be a more powerful predictor of children's development than the actual structure of the family.

________ 7. Prior to the federal welfare reform act of 1996, most single mothers received food stamps or some other form of government assistance.

________ 8. Children of low socioeconomic status are more likely than other children to have difficulty mastering the normal skills of middle childhood.

________ 9. The income of single-parent households is about the same as that of two-parent households in which only one parent works.

________ 10. School-age children are less able than younger children to cope with the chronic stresses that are troublesome at any age.

________ 11. The problems of most rejected children nearly always disappear by adolescence.

________ 12. Friendships become more selective and exclusive as children grow older.

Progress Test 2

Progress Test 2 should be completed during a final chapter review. Answer the following questions after you thoroughly understand the correct answers for the Chapter Review and Progress Test 1.

Multiple-Choice Questions

1. Children who are categorized as __________ are particularly vulnerable to bullying.
   a. aggressive-rejected
   b. passive-aggressive
   c. withdrawn-rejected
   d. passive-rejected

2. The main reason for the special vocabulary, dress codes, and behaviors that flourish within the society of children is that they:
   a. lead to clubs and gang behavior.
   b. are unknown to or unapproved by adults.
   c. imitate adult-organized society.
   d. provide an alternative to useful work in society.

3. In the area of social cognition, developmentalists are impressed by the school-age child's increasing ability to:
   a. identify and take into account other people's viewpoints.
   b. develop an increasingly wide network of friends.
   c. relate to the opposite sex.
   d. resist social models.

4. The school-age child's greater understanding of emotions is best illustrated by:
   a. an increased tendency to take everything personally.
   b. more widespread generosity and sharing.
   c. the ability to see through the insincere behavior of others.
   d. a refusal to express unfelt emotions.

5. Typically, children in middle childhood experience a decrease in self-esteem as a result of:
   a. a wavering self-theory.
   b. increased awareness of personal shortcomings and failures.
   c. rejection by peers.
   d. difficulties with members of the opposite sex.

6. A 10-year-old's sense of self-esteem is most strongly influenced by his or her:
   a. peers.
   b. siblings.
   c. mother.
   d. father.

7. Which of the following most accurately describes how friendships change during the school years?
   a. Friendships become more casual and less intense.
   b. Older children demand less of their friends.
   c. Older children change friends more often.
   d. Close friendships increasingly involve members of the same sex, ethnicity, and socioeconomic status.

8. Which of the following is an accurate statement about school-age bullies?
   a. They are unapologetic about their aggressive behavior.
   b. They usually have friends who abet, fear, and admire them.
   c. Their popularity fades over the years.
   d. All of the above are accurate statements.

9. If current trends continue, it is estimated that __________ of American children born in the 1990s will live with both biological parents from birth to age 18.
   a. less than 10 percent
   b. about 37 percent
   c. 53 percent
   d. 75 percent

10. Which of the following is true of children who live with both biological parents?
    a. They tend to have fewer physical and emotional problems.
    b. They tend to have fewer learning difficulties.
    c. They are less likely to abuse drugs.
    d. All of the above are true.

11. Two factors that most often help the child cope well with multiple stresses are social support and:
    a. social comparison.
    b. competence in a specific area.
    c. remedial education.
    d. referral to mental health professionals.

12. Some developmentalists believe that the advantage that traditional families confer on the psychosocial development of children is overstated because:
    a. many studies do not take sufficient account of other factors that affect child development, such as income.
    b. very little reliable research has been conducted on this issue.
    c. parents often are not honest in reporting their children's problems.
    d. of all of the above reasons.

13. Family ______ is more crucial to children's well-being than family ______ is.
   a. structure; SES
   b. SES; stability
   c. stability; SES
   d. functioning; structure

14. According to Freud, the period between ages 7 and 11 when a child's sexual drives are relatively quiet is the:
   a. phallic stage.
   b. genital stage.
   c. period of latency.
   d. period of industry versus inferiority.

15. Research studies have found that children who are forced to cope with one serious ongoing stress (for example, poverty or large family size) are:
   a. more likely to develop serious psychiatric problems than children with none of these stresses.
   b. no more likely to develop problems than other children.
   c. more likely to develop intense, destructive friendships than other children.
   d. less likely to be accepted by their peer group.

Matching Items

Match each term or concept with its corresponding description or definition.

Terms or Concepts

______ 1. prosocial
______ 2. preconventional
______ 3. conventional
______ 4. postconventional
______ 5. morality of care
______ 6. extended family
______ 7. blended family
______ 8. nuclear family
______ 9. industry vs. inferiority
______ 10. morality of justice

Descriptions or Definitions

a. moral thinking and behavior that are more common among boys and men
b. a family that includes other relatives in addition to parents and their children
c. moral reasoning in which the individual follows principles that supersede the standards of society
d. a family consisting of two parents, at least one of which is a stepparent
e. behavior that is performed to benefit other people without the expectations of reward
f. moral reasoning in which the individual focuses on his or her own welfare
g. a family consisting of two parents and their mutual offspring
h. according to Erikson, the psychosocial crisis of middle childhood
i. moral thinking and behavior that are more common among girls and women
j. moral reasoning in which the individual considers social standards and laws to be primary

Thinking Critically About Chapter 13

Answer these questions the day before an exam as a final check on your understanding of the chapter's terms and concepts.

1. As an advocate of the epigenetic systems perspective, Dr. Wayans is most likely to explain a 10-year-old child's new independence as the result of:
   a. the repression of psychosexual needs.
   b. the acquisition of new skills.
   c. greater self-understanding.
   d. the child's need to join the wider community and the parents' need to focus on younger children.

2. Dr. Ferris believes that skill mastery is particularly important because children develop views of themselves as either competent or incompetent in skills valued by their culture. Dr. Ferris is evidently working from the perspective of:
   a. behaviorism.
   b. social learning theory.
   c. Erik Erikson's theory of development.
   d. Freud's theory of development.

3. Bonnie, who is low achieving, shy, and withdrawn, is rejected by most of her peers. Her teacher, who wants to help Bonnie increase her self-esteem and social acceptance, encourages her parents to:
   a. transfer Bonnie to a different school.
   b. help their daughter improve her motor skills.
   c. help their daughter learn to accept more responsibility for her academic failures.
   d. help their daughter improve her skills in relating to peers.

4. Jorge, who has no children of his own, is worried about his 12-year-old niece because she wears unusual clothes and uses vocabulary unknown to him. What should Jorge do?
   a. Tell his niece's parents that they need to discipline their daughter more strictly.
   b. Convince his niece to find a new group of friends.
   c. Recommend that his niece's parents seek professional counseling for their daughter, because such behaviors often are the first signs of a lifelong pattern of antisocial behavior.
   d. Jorge need not necessarily be worried because children typically develop their own subculture of speech, dress, and behavior.

5. Compared with her 7-year-old brother Walter, 10-year-old Felicity is more likely to describe their cousin:
   a. in terms of physical attributes.
   b. as feeling exactly the same way she does when they are in the same social situation.
   c. in terms of personality traits.
   d. in terms of their cousin's outward behavior.

6. Seven-year-old Chantal fumes after a friend compliments her new dress, thinking that the comment was intended to be sarcastic. Chantal's reaction is an example of:
   a. egocentrism.
   b. feelings of inferiority.
   c. the distorted thought processes of an emotionally disturbed child.
   d. immature social cognition.

7. In discussing friendship, 9-year-old children, in contrast to younger children, will:
   a. deny that friends are important.
   b. state that they prefer same-sex playmates.
   c. stress the importance of help and emotional support in friendship.
   d. be less choosy about who they call a friend.

8. Children who have serious difficulties in peer relationships during elementary school:
   a. are at a greater risk of having emotional problems later in life.
   b. usually overcome their difficulties in a year or two.
   c. later are more likely to form an intense friendship with one person than children who did not have difficulties earlier on.
   d. do both b. and c.

9. After years of an unhappy marriage, Brad and Diane file for divorce and move 500 miles apart. In ruling on custody for their 7-year-old daughter, the wise judge decides:
   a. joint custody should be awarded, because this arrangement is nearly always the most beneficial for children.
   b. the mother should have custody, because this arrangement is nearly always the most beneficial for children in single-parent homes.
   c. the father should have custody, because this arrangement is nearly always the most beneficial for children in single-parent homes.
   d. to investigate the competency of each parent, because whoever was the more competent and more involved parent before the divorce should continue to be the primary caregiver.

10. Of the following children, who is likely to have the lowest overall self-esteem?
   a. Karen, age 5
   b. David, age 7
   c. Carl, age 9
   d. Cindy, age 10

11. Ten-year-old Benjamin is less optimistic and self-confident than his 5-year-old sister. This may be explained in part by the tendency of older children to:
   a. evaluate their abilities by comparing them with their own competencies a year or two earlier.
   b. evaluate their competencies by comparing them with those of others.
   c. be less realistic about their own abilities.
   d. do both b. and c.

12. Based on research on the norms for childhood aggression, which of the following schoolchildren is likely to be viewed most favorably by his or her peers?
   a. Eddie, the class bully
   b. Luwanda, who is not arrogant but doesn't shy away from defending herself whenever necessary
   c. Daniel, who often suffers attacks from his peers yet refuses to retaliate
   d. Hilary, who often suffers attacks from her peers yet refuses to retaliate

13. (Research Report) Of the following children, who is most likely to become a bully?
   a. Karen, who is taller than average
   b. David, who is above average in verbal assertiveness
   c. Carl, who is insecure and lonely
   d. Cindy, who is frequently subjected to physical punishment and verbal criticism at home

14. Which of the following was *not* listed as a reason that children living with both biological parents tend to fare best?
   a. Two adults can provide more complete caregiving than one.
   b. Married, biological parents are usually better able to provide financially for their children.
   c. Biological parents are generally more emotionally mature than other parents.
   d. All mammals, including humans, have a genetic impulse to protect and nurture their own children.

15. When it comes to moral reasoning, Guillermo believes that "might makes right." Kohlberg would say that Guillermo's emphasis on obedience to authority places him squarely in the ________________ stage.
   a. preconventional
   b. conventional
   c. postconventional
   d. ideological

Key Terms

Using your own words, write a brief definition or explanation of each of the following terms on a separate piece of paper.

1. industry versus inferiority
2. 5-to-7 shift
3. social cognition
4. social comparison
5. preconventional moral reasoning
6. conventional moral reasoning
7. postconventional moral reasoning
8. morality of care
9. morality of justice
10. prosocial behavior
11. peer group
12. society of children
13. aggressive-rejected children
14. withdrawn-rejected children
15. bullying
16. family structure
17. extended family
18. nuclear family
19. single-parent family
20. blended family

ANSWERS

CHAPTER REVIEW

1. latency; quieter; repressed; submerged
2. industry versus inferiority
3. acquisition; self-understanding; social awareness

From an epigenetic systems perspective, the school-age child's independence is the result of the species' need to free parental efforts so that they may be focused on younger children and to accustom school-age children to their peers and the adults in the community.

4. 5-to-7 shift
5. social cognition; multifaceted
6. possible consequences
7. personality traits
8. behavior; implications; possible consequences
9. simultaneously; disguise; emotions
10. more; dips; social comparison; more
11. Kohlberg; preconventional; conventional; postconventional
12. rewards; punishments; 1; 2
13. social rules; 4; 3
14. moral principles; social contracts; universal ethical principles
15. narrow; restricted; liberal Western; morality of care; morality of justice
16. prosocial behaviors; is; prosocial
17. cultural; religious
18. a group of individuals of similar age and social status who play, work, and learn together
19. society of children

The society of children typically has special norms, vocabulary, rituals, dress codes, and rules of behavior.

20. more; mutual help; self-disclosure
21. smaller; more
22. aggression; has; social situation
23. aggressive-rejected; withdrawn-rejected; lonely; self-esteem; bullying; impulsive; social cognition; get worse

Rejected children often misinterpret social situations—considering a compliment to be sarcastic, for example.

24. repeated; can be

Bullied children are anxious, depressed, underachieving, and have lower self-esteem and painful memories.

25. insecure; lonely
26. is; social climate
27. needs; learning; self-esteem; friendships; harmony; stability
28. open; closed; father
29. legal and genetic relationships between the adults and children in a household.
30. a. extended family
    b. nuclear family
    c. single-parent family
    d. blended family
31. in almost any family structure
32. a large extended family, with grandparents and great-grandparents, and often cousins, aunts, and uncles, living in the same household; polygamous
33. extended; polygamous; nuclear
34. less
35. 37
36. both biological parents

At adolescence, they are less likely to abuse drugs or be arrested and more likely to graduate from high school; in adulthood, they are more likely to graduate from college and to continue to develop with self-confidence, social acceptance, and career success.

37. a. Two adults generally provide more complete caregiving than one.
    b. All mammals have a genetic impulse to protect and nurture their own offspring.
    c. Two-parent homes usually have a financial advantage over other forms.
38. overstated; income; race, ethnic background, and religion
39. a. Not every biological parent is a fit parent.
    b. Not every marriage creates a nurturant household.
40. do not
41. a year or two
    a. the stability of the child's life
    b. the adequacy of the caregiving arrangement

One source of instability is the child's feeling abandoned by a trusted adult. Another is moving to a less desirable neighborhood and attending a different school. A third is a reduction in the household income, leading to reduced attention from parents.

42. caregiving; joint custody; neither parent

Children sometimes respond better to a man's authority than to a woman's. In addition, fathers who choose custody are those who are likely to be suited for it, whereas mothers typically have custody whether they prefer it or not. Father-only homes are, on average, more financially secure.

43. single-parent

a. Births to unmarried mothers are increasing

b. Divorce and death (especially due to homicide and AIDS) are increasing

44. just as well as

a. school achievement

b. emotional stability

c. protection from serious injury

holds

45. behavior; maturity; financial

46. do; higher than

47. quite well; how the family functions; socially; decreased

48. clinical depression

49. decreases; increases

50. social cognition; social world

51. the number of stresses the child is experiencing concurrently; the overall pattern of the child's daily life

52. self-esteem; less

53. social support; religious faith; practice

54. do not; is not

PROGRESS TEST 1

Multiple-Choice Questions

1. **a.** is the answer. (p. 400)
2. **b.** is the answer. (p. 404)
3. **c.** is the answer. (pp. 430–431)
4. **d.** is the answer. (p. 410)
5. **d.** is the answer. (p. 402)

   a., b., & c. Compared with preschool children, schoolchildren are more self-critical, and their self-esteem dips, so they blame themselves.
6. **a.** is the answer. (p. 411)
7. **d.** is the answer. (p. 411)
8. **c.** is the answer. (pp. 418)
9. **a.** is the answer. (p. 426)

   b., c., & d. These factors are likely to increase, rather than decrease, stress, and therefore to have an adverse effect on children.
10. **b.** is the answer. (p. 428)
11. **b.** is the answer. (p. 428)
12. **c.** is the answer. (p. 424)
13. **d.** is the answer. (p. 409)
14. **d.** is the answer. (p. 419)
15. **a.** is the answer. (p. 399)

True or False Items

1. **F** In fact, just the opposite is true. (p. 401)
2. **F** In fact, just the opposite is true. (p. 409)
3. **T** (p. 429)
4. **F** Only a minority of fathers who do not have custody continue to maintain a close relationship with their children. (p. 422)
5. **T** (p. 421)
6. **T** (p. 427)
7. **F** Even before the federal welfare reform act of 1996, fewer than half of all single mothers received government assistance of any kind. (p. 423)
8. **T** (p. 425)
9. **F** The income of single-parent households is substantially lower than that of two-parent households in which only one parent works. (p. 420)
10. **F** Because of the coping strategies that school-age children develop, they are better able than younger children to cope with stress. (p. 428)
11. **F** The problems of rejected children often get worse as they get older. (p. 411)
12. **T** (p. 409)

PROGRESS TEST 2

Multiple-Choice Questions

1. **c.** is the answer. (p. 411)

   a. These are usually bullies.

   b. & d. These are not subcategories of rejected children.
2. **b.** is the answer. (p. 408)
3. **a.** is the answer. (p. 400)

   b. Friendship circles typically become smaller during middle childhood, as children become more choosy about their friends.

   c. & d. These issues are not discussed in the chapter.
4. **c.** is the answer. (pp. 400–401)
5. **b.** is the answer. (p. 402)

   a. This tends to promote, rather than reduce, self-esteem.

   c. Only 10 percent of schoolchildren experience this.

   d. This issue becomes more important during adolescence.
6. **a.** is the answer. (p. 410)

7. **d.** is the answer. (pp. 409–410)

   a., b., & c. In fact, just the opposite is true of friendship during the school years.

8. **d.** is the answer. (pp. 412–413)
9. **b.** is the answer. (p. 419)
10. **d.** is the answer. (p. 418)
11. **b.** is the answer. (p. 430)
12. **a.** is the answer. (p. 420)

    b. In fact, a great deal of research has been conducted on this issue.

    c. There is no evidence that this is so.

13. **d.** is the answer. (p. 427)
14. **c.** is the answer. (p. 399)
15. **b.** is the answer. (p. 428)

    c. & d. The text did not discuss how stress influences friendship or peer acceptance.

Matching Items

1. e (p. 406)	**5.** i (p. 404)	**9.** h (p. 399)
2. f (p. 403)	**6.** b (p. 418)	**10.** a (p. 404)
3. j (p. 403)	**7.** d (p. 418)	
4. c (p. 403)	**8.** g (p. 418)	

THINKING CRITICALLY ABOUT CHAPTER 13

1. **d.** is the answer. (p. 400)

   a. This describes an advocate of Freud's theory of development.

   b. This is the viewpoint of a learning theorist.

   c. This is the viewpoint of a cognitive theorist.

2. **c.** is the answer. The question describes what is, for Erikson, the crisis of middle childhood: industry versus inferiority. (p. 399)

3. **d.** is the answer. (p. 431)

   a. Because it would seem to involve "running away" from her problems, this approach would likely be more harmful than helpful.

   b. Improving motor skills is not a factor considered in the text and probably has little value in raising self-esteem in such situations.

   c. If Bonnie is like most school-age children, she is quite self-critical and already accepts responsibility for her failures.

4. **d.** is the answer. (p. 408)
5. **c.** is the answer. (p. 401)

   a., b., & d. These are more typical of preschoolers.

6. **d.** is the answer. (p. 411)

   a. Egocentrism is self-centered thinking. In this example, Chantal is misinterpreting her friend's comment.

   b. & c. There is no reason to believe that Chantal is suffering from an emotional disturbance or that she is feeling inferior.

7. **c.** is the answer. (p. 409)
8. **a.** is the answer. (p. 411)
9. **d.** is the answer. (p. 422)
10. **d.** is the answer. Self-esteem decreases throughout middle childhood. (p. 401)
11. **b.** is the answer. (p. 402)

    a. & c. These are more typical of preschoolers than school-age children.

12. **b.** is the answer. (p. 410)

    a. Although a certain amount of aggression is the norm during childhood, children who are perceived as overly arrogant or aggressive are not viewed very favorably.

    c. & d. Both girls and boys are expected to defend themselves when appropriate and are viewed as weak if they do not.

13. **d.** is the answer. (pp. 414–415)

    a. & b. It is taller-than-average *boys* and verbally assertive *girls* who are more likely to bully others.

    c. This is a common myth.

14. **c.** is the answer. Although emotional maturity is an important factor in family functioning, the text does not suggest that biological parents are more mature than other parents. (pp. 418–419)
15. **a.** is the answer. (p. 403)

KEY TERMS

1. According to Erikson, the crisis of middle childhood is that of **industry versus inferiority**, in which children try to master many skills and develop views of themselves as either competent or incompetent and inferior. (p. 400)
2. The **5-to-7 shift** refers to the rapid change in intellectual and social competence that many children experience between ages 5 and 7. (p. 400)
3. **Social cognition** refers to a person's awareness and understanding of the personalities, motives, emotions, intentions, and interactions of other people and groups. (p. 400)
4. **Social comparison** is the tendency to assess one's abilities, achievements, and social status by measuring them against those of others, especially those of one's peers. (p. 401)

5. Kohlberg's first level of moral reasoning, **preconventional moral reasoning**, emphasizes obedience to authority in order to avoid punishment (stage 1) and being nice to other people so they will be nice to you (stage 2). (p. 403)
6. Kohlberg's second level of moral reasoning, **conventional moral reasoning**, emphasizes winning the approval of others (stage 3) and obeying the laws set down by those in power (stage 4). (p. 403)
7. Kohlberg's third level, **postconventional moral reasoning**, emphasizes the social and contractual nature of moral principles (stage 5) and the existence of universal ethical principles (stage 6). (p. 403)
8. Compared with boys and men, girls and women are more likely to develop a **morality of care** that is based on comparison, nurturance, and concern for the well-being of others. (p. 404)
9. Compared with girls and women, boys and men are more likely to develop a **morality of justice** based on depersonalized standards of right and wrong. (p. 404)
10. **Prosocial behavior** is any act, such as sharing or cooperating, performed to help other people without the expectations of reward or repayment. (p. 406)
11. A **peer group** is a group of individuals of roughly the same age and social status who play, work, or learn together. (p. 407)
12. Children in middle childhood develop and transmit their own subculture, called the **society of children**, which has its own games, vocabulary, dress codes, and rules of behavior. (p. 408)
13. The peer group shuns **aggressive-rejected children** because they are overly confrontational. (p. 411)
14. **Withdrawn-rejected children** are shunned by the peer group because of their withdrawn and anxious demeanor. (p. 411)
15. **Bullying** is the repeated, systematic effort to inflict harm on a child through physical, verbal, or social attack. (p. 412)
16. **Family structure** refers to the legal and genetic relationships that exist between members of a particular family. (p. 418)
17. An **extended family** is one that includes grandparents, aunts, cousins, or other relatives in addition to parents and their children. (p. 418)
18. A **nuclear family** consists of two parents and their mutual biological offspring. (p. 418)
19. A **single-parent family** consists of one parent and his or her (usually biological) children. (p. 418)
20. A **blended family** consists of two parents, at least one with biological children from another union. (p. 418)

CHAPTER 14

Adolescence: Biosocial Development

Chapter Overview

Between the ages of 10 and 20, young people cross the great divide between childhood and adulthood. This crossing encompasses all three domains of development—biosocial, cognitive, and psychosocial. Chapter 14 focuses on the dramatic changes that occur in the biosocial domain, beginning with puberty and the growth spurt. The biosocial metamorphosis of the adolescent is discussed in detail, with emphasis on sexual maturation, nutrition, and the effects of the timing of puberty, including possible problems arising from early or late maturation.

Although adolescence is, in many ways, a healthy time of life, the text addresses three health hazards that too often affect adolescence: sexual abuse, poor nutrition, and use of alcohol, tobacco, and other drugs.

NOTE: Answer guidelines for all Chapter 14 questions begin on page 223.

Guided Study

The text chapter should be studied one section at a time. Before you read, preview each section by skimming it, noting headings and boldface items. Then read the appropriate section objectives from the following outline. Keep these objectives in mind and, as you read the chapter section, search for the information that will enable you to meet each objective. Once you have finished a section, write out answers for its objectives.

Puberty Begins (pp. 439–445)

1. Outline the biological events of puberty.

2. Discuss the emotional and psychological impact of pubertal hormones.

3. Identify several factors that influence the onset of puberty.

4. Discuss the adjustment problems of boys and girls who develop earlier or later than their peers do.

The Growth Spurt (pp. 445–448)

5. Describe the growth spurt in both the male and the female adolescent, focusing on changes in body weight and height.

6. Describe the changes in the body's internal organ systems that accompany the growth spurt.

Sexual Characteristics (pp. 448–453)

7. Discuss the development of the primary sex characteristics in males and females during puberty.

8. (Children Up Close) Discuss how adolescents respond to the sexual changes of puberty and how these reactions have changed over the decades.

9. Discuss the development of the secondary sex characteristics in males and females during puberty.

10. (Research Report) Discuss the adolescent's preoccupation with body image and the problems that sometimes arise in the development of a healthy body image.

Health and Hazards (pp. 454–466)

11. Discuss sexual abuse, noting its prevalence and consequences for development.

12. Discuss the nutritional needs and problems of adolescents.

13. Compare and contrast the explanations of eating disorders offered by the major theories of development.

14. Discuss drug use among adolescents today, including its prevalence, its significance for development, and the best methods of prevention.

Chapter Review

When you have finished reading the chapter, work through the material that follows to review it. Complete the sentences and answer the questions. As you proceed, evaluate your performance for each section by consulting the answers on page 223. Do not continue with the next section until you understand each answer. If you need to, review or reread the appropriate section in the textbook before continuing.

Puberty Begins (pp. 439–445)

1. The period of adolescence extends roughly from age __________ to __________. The period of rapid physical growth and sexual maturation that ends childhood and brings the young person to adult size, shape, and sexual potential is called __________.

   List, in order, the major physical changes of puberty in

   Girls: __________

   Boys: __________

2. Puberty begins when a hormonal signal from the __________ triggers hormone production in the __________ __________, which in turn triggers increased hormone production by the __________ __________ and by the __________, which include the __________ in males and the __________ in females.

3. The hormone __________ causes the gonads to dramatically increase production of sex hormones, especially __________ in girls and __________ in boys. This, in turn, triggers the hypothalamus and pituitary to increase production of __________.

4. The increase in the hormone __________ is dramatic in boys and slight in girls, whereas the increase in the hormone __________ is marked in girls and slight in boys.

5. During puberty, hormonal levels have their greatest emotional impact __________ (directly/indirectly), via the __________ of __________.

6. Normal children begin to notice pubertal changes between the ages of __________ and __________.

7. The average American girl experiences her first menstrual period, called __________, between ages __________ and __________.

8. Genes are an important factor in the timing of menarche, as demonstrated by the fact that __________ and __________ reach menarche at very similar ages.

9. The average age of puberty __________ (varies/does not vary) from nation to nation and from ethnic group to ethnic group.

10. Stocky individuals tend to experience puberty __________ (earlier/later) than those with taller, thinner builds.

11. Menarche seems to be related to the accumulation of a certain amount of body __________. Consequently, female dancers, runners, and other athletes menstruate __________ (earlier/later) than the average girl, whereas females who are relatively inactive menstruate __________ (earlier/later).

12. The tendency of successive generations to develop in somewhat different ways as the result of improved nutrition and medical advances is called the __________. There is evidence that this trend has stopped in recent years in __________ countries.

13. Longitudinal research suggests that family emotional distance and stress may __________ (accelerate/delay) the onset of puberty.

14. Young people who experience puberty at the same time as their friends tend to view the experience more __________ (positively/

negatively) than those who experience it early or late.

15. For girls, ______________ (early/late) maturation may be especially troublesome.

Describe several common problems and developmental hazards experienced by early-maturing girls.

16. For boys, ______________ (early/late) maturation is usually more difficult.

17. Research on the timing of puberty in boys has found that the effects of early puberty are generally ______________ (positive/negative/mixed), while the effects of late puberty are ______________ (positive/negative/mixed).

Describe several characteristics and/or problems of late-maturing boys.

The Growth Spurt (pp. 445–448)

18. The first sign of the growth spurt is increased bone ______________ and ______________, beginning at the tips of the extremities and working toward the center of the body. At the same time, children begin to ______________ (gain/lose) weight at a relatively rapid rate.

19. The change in weight that typically occurs between 10 and 12 years of age is due primarily to the accumulation of body ______________. The amount of weight gain an individual experiences depends on several factors, including ______________, ______________, ______________, and ______________.

20. During the spurt in height, a greater percentage of fat is retained by ______________ (males/females), who naturally have a higher proportion of body fat in adulthood.

21. About a year after these height and weight changes occur, a period of ______________ increase occurs, causing the pudginess and clumsiness of an earlier age to disappear. In boys, this increase is particularly notable in the ______________ body.

22. Overall, between the ages of 10 and 14, the typical girl gains about ______________ in weight and ______________ in height; between the ages of 12 and 16, the typical boy gains about ______________ in height and about ______________ in weight.

23. The chronological age for the growth spurt ______________ (varies/does not vary) from child to child.

24. One of the last parts of the body to grow into final form is the ______________.

25. The two halves of the body ______________ (always/do not always) grow at the same rate.

26. Internal organs also grow during puberty. The ______________ increase in size and capacity, the ______________ doubles in size, heart rate ______________ (increases/decreases), and blood volume ______________ (increases/decreases). These changes increase the adolescent's physical ______________.

Explain why the physical demands placed on a teenager, as in athletic training, should not be the same as those for a young adult of similar height and weight.

27. During puberty, one organ system, the ______________ system, decreases in size, making teenagers ______________ (more/less) susceptible to respiratory ailments.

28. The hormones of puberty also cause many relatively minor physical changes that can have significant emotional impact. These include increased activity in ____________, ____________, and ____________ glands.

Sexual Characteristics (pp. 448–453)

29. Changes in ____________ ____________ ____________ involve the sex organs that are directly involved in reproduction. By the end of puberty, reproduction ____________ (is/is still not) possible.

Describe the major changes in primary sex characteristics that occur in both sexes during puberty.

30. In girls, the event that is usually taken to indicate sexual maturity is ____________. In boys, the indicator of reproductive potential is the first ejaculation of seminal fluid containing sperm, which is called ____________. In both sexes, full reproductive maturity occurs ____________ (at this time/several years later).

31. The first menstrual cycles are usually ____________, that is, they occur without ovulation.

32. (Children Up Close) Attitudes toward menarche, menstruation, and spermarche ____________ (have/have not) changed over the past two decades, so that most young people ____________ (do/do not) face these events with anxiety, embarrassment, or guilt.

33. Sexual features other than those associated with reproduction are referred to as ____________ ____________ ____________.

Describe the major pubertal changes in the secondary sex characteristics of both sexes.

34. Two secondary sex characteristics that are mistakenly considered signs of womanhood and manliness, respectively, are ____________ ____________ and ____________ and ____________ ____________.

35. (Research Report) Adolescents' mental conception of, and attitude toward, their physical appearance is referred to as their ____________ ____________.

(Research Report) Identify some common behaviors related to adolescents' preoccupation with their body image.

36. (Research Report) When asked what traits they look for in the other sex, adolescents list ____________.

37. (Research Report) Media images reinforce the cultural ideal that American men should be ____________ and ____________ and that women should be ____________ and ____________.

Health and Hazards (pp. 454–466)

38. The minor illnesses of childhood become ____________ (less/more) common during adolescence, because of increased ____________ at this age.

39. Any activity in which an adult uses a child for his or her own sexual stimulation or pleasure is considered ____________ ____________ ____________.

40. The damage done by sexual abuse depends on many factors, including how often it is ______________, how much it distorts ______________-______________ ______________, and how much it impairs normal ______________.

41. Sexualized adult-child interactions may escalate in late childhood or early adolescence, with onset typically between ages ______________ and ______________.

42. Adolescents may react to maltreatment in ways that younger children rarely do, with ______________ or by ______________.

43. Adolescent problems, such as pregnancy, often are tied to ______________ ______________ ______________.

44. Although ______________ (boys/girls) are more often the victims of sexual abuse, the other sex is also often sexually abused. Sexual molestation of ______________ (girls/boys) occurs at home by a parent or outside by someone from the ______________.

45. Although mothers and other female relatives seem to be ______________ (more/less) often the perpetrators of obvious sexual abuse, they ______________ (are/are not) sometimes guilty of sexual teasing and fondling.

46. Parents who ______________ with each other, or who are ______________, ______________ ______________, ______________, or ______________-______________ are much more likely to be sexually abusive. Income and education level ______________ (do/do not) predict who is likely to be sexually abusive.

47. Due to rapid physical growth, the adolescent needs a higher daily intake of ______________, ______________, and ______________. Specifically, the typical adolescent needs about 50 percent more of the minerals ______________, ______________, and ______________ during the growth spurt. Because of menstruation, adolescent females also need additional ______________ in their diets and are more likely to suffer ______________-______________ ______________ than any other subgroup of the population.

48. Adolescent nutrition may be adversely affected by childhood habits of ______________ and ______________, which often worsen in adolescence, especially if the person experiences increased ______________ ______________.

49. Another problem that often interferes with healthy eating is ______________ ______________, which alters the appetite and digestive processes. A third problem is ______________ ______________ and strange diets. Finally, severe ______________ can slow or even halt all of the changes of puberty.

50. The most hazardous periods for eating disorders are at about age ______________, and again at about age ______________.

51. The eating disorder in which a person undereats to the point of emaciation is ______________ ______________. Approximately ______________ percent of adolescent and young adult females suffer from this disorder.

52. A ______________ (rarer/more common) eating disorder that is characterized by binge-purge behavior is called ______________. Those who suffer from this disorder usually ______________ (are/are not) close to normal weight and may experience a range of serious health problems, including damage to the ______________ system and even ______________ failure. High school and college ______________ are more vulnerable to this disorder than other young women.

53. Evidence from twin studies suggests that the causes of eating disorders may be partly ______________. Those with eating disorders also tend to have a family history of ______________, ______________, and ______________ ______________.

54. Which major developmental theory explains eating disorders as the result of:

a. cultural pressure to be "slim and trim"? ______________

b. unresolved conflict with one's mother? ______________

c. the desire to project a strong, self-controlled, masculine image? ______________

d. low self-esteem and depression (stimulus) that precipitate extreme dieting (response)? ______________

e. The discovery that self-starvation reduces or remove the sexual pressures associated with normal maturation? ______________

55. Drug ______________ always harms physical and psychological development, whether or not it becomes ______________. Drug ______________ may or may not be harmful, depending in part on the ______________ of the person and the reason for and consequences of the drug's use.

56. After a long period of ______________ (decline/increase) during the 1980s, drug use by adolescents has begun to ______________ (increase/decrease) in the 1990s. This trend ______________ (also holds/does not hold) for regular use of tobacco.

57. Tobacco, alcohol, and marijuana may act as ______________ ______________, opening the door not only to regular use of multiple drugs but also to other destructive behaviors, such as risky ______________, ______________ from school, ______________ behavior, poor ______________ ______________, and ______________.

58. By decreasing food consumption and the absorption of nutrients, tobacco can limit the adolescent ______________ ______________.

59. Because alcohol loosens ______________ and impairs ______________, even moderate use can be destructive in adolescence. Teenagers who drink regularly are more likely to be ______________ active, to engage in ______________ behaviors, to be excessively absent from ______________, and more likely to ride in a car with a driver who has been ______________.

60. Marijuana ______________ (slows/accelerates) thinking processes, particularly those related to ______________ and ______________ reasoning.

Why do developmentalists urge teens to delay drug experimentation as long as possible?

61. (Changing Policy) A longitudinal study of adolescent drug use revealed that most "frequent users" ______________ (were/were not) "troubled adolescents." The typical frequent user was ______________.

List several measures that have proven to be at least partly effective in postponing and decreasing drug use.

62. Two social factors that tend to encourage drug use among younger adolescents are ______________ and lax ______________ attitudes.

63. Young people's likelihood of using drugs is directly related to their ______________ ______________ about the ______________ and ______________ of drug use.

64. Antidrug attitudes ______________ (have/have not) softened among adolescent Americans during the 1990s, perhaps because each cohort goes through ______________ ______________.

Progress Test 1

Multiple-Choice Questions

Circle your answers to the following questions and check them with the answers on page 225. If your answer is incorrect, read the explanation for why it is incorrect and then consult the appropriate pages of the text (in parentheses following the correct answer).

1. Which of the following most accurately describes the sequence of pubertal development in girls?
   a. breast buds and pubic hair; growth spurt in which fat is deposited on hips and buttocks; first menstrual period; ovulation
   b. growth spurt; breast buds and pubic hair; first menstrual period; ovulation
   c. first menstrual period; breast buds and pubic hair; growth spurt; ovulation
   d. breast buds and pubic hair; growth spurt; ovulation; first menstrual period

2. Although both sexes grow rapidly during adolescence, boys typically begin their accelerated growth about:
   a. a year or two later than girls.
   b. a year earlier than girls.
   c. the time they reach sexual maturity.
   d. the time facial hair appears.

3. The first readily observable sign of the onset of puberty is:
   a. the growth spurt.
   b. the appearance of facial, body, and pubic hair.
   c. a change in the shape of the eyes.
   d. a lengthening of the torso.

4. More than any other group in the population, adolescent girls are likely to have:
   a. asthma.
   b. acne.
   c. iron-deficiency anemia.
   d. testosterone deficiency.

5. For most young women, even a year after menarche, ovulation:
   a. cannot result in pregnancy.
   b. occurs regularly.
   c. is irregular.
   d. is in remission.

6. For males, the secondary sex characteristic that usually occurs last is:
   a. breast enlargement.
   b. the appearance of facial hair.
   c. growth of the testes.
   d. the appearance of pubic hair.

7. For girls, the specific event that is taken to indicate fertility is ______ ; for boys, it is ______ .
   a. the growth of breast buds; voice deepening
   b. menarche; spermarche
   c. anovulation; the testosterone surge
   d. the growth spurt; pubic hair

8. The most significant hormonal changes of puberty include an increase of ____________ in ____________ and an increase of ____________ in ____________ .
   a. progesterone; boys; estrogen; girls
   b. estrogen; boys; testosterone; girls
   c. progesterone; girls; estrogen; boys
   d. estrogen; girls; testosterone; boys

9. (Research Report) In general, most adolescents are:
   a. overweight.
   b. satisfied with their appearance.
   c. dissatisfied with their appearance.
   d. unaffected by cultural attitudes about beauty.

10. Of the following, who is most likely to suffer from anorexia nervosa?
    a. Bill, a 23-year-old professional football player
    b. Florence, a 30-year-old account executive
    c. Lynn, an 18-year-old college student
    d. Carl, a professional dancer

11. The damage caused by sexual abuse depends on all of the following factors *except*:
    a. repeated incidence.
    b. the gender of the perpetrator.
    c. distorted adult-child relationships.
    d. impairment of the child's ability to develop normally.

12. Early physical growth and sexual maturation:
    a. tend to be equally difficult for girls and boys.
    b. tend to be more difficult for boys than for girls.
    c. tend to be more difficult for girls than for boys.
    d. are easier for both girls and boys than late maturation.

13. (Research Report) After puberty, most adolescents have:
    a. a more positive body image.
    b. a more negative body image.
    c. the same body image they had prior to puberty.
    d. a body image that will not change significantly for the rest of their lives.

14. Drug use by adolescents:
    a. peaked in the 1970s.
    b. peaked in the 1980s.
    c. has begun to increase in the 1990s.
    d. continues to decline in the 1990s.

15. Parents who are __________ are much more likely to sexually abuse their adolescent children.
    a. immature
    b. socially isolated
    c. alcoholic
    d. all of the above

True or False Items

Write *true* or *false* on the line in front of each statement.

_______ 1. More calories are necessary during adolescence than at any other period during the life span.

_______ 2. Ovulation usually does not occur during a girl's first menstrual cycles.

_______ 3. The first indicator of reproductive potential in males is menarche.

_______ 4. Lung capacity, heart size, and total volume of blood increase significantly during adolescence.

_______ 5. Puberty generally begins sometime between ages 8 and 14.

_______ 6. Girls who mature late and are thinner than average tend to be satisfied with their weight.

_______ 7. (Research Report) The strong emphasis on physical appearance is unique to adolescents and finds little support from teachers, parents, and the larger culture.

_______ 8. Childhood habits of overeating and underexercising usually lessen during adolescence.

_______ 9. The problems of the early-maturing girl tend to be temporary.

_______ 10. Both the sequence and timing of pubertal events vary greatly from one young person to another.

Progress Test 2

Progress Test 2 should be completed during a final chapter review. Answer the following questions after you thoroughly understand the correct answers for the Chapter Review and Progress Test 1.

Multiple-Choice Questions

1. Which of the following is the correct sequence of pubertal events in boys?
    a. growth spurt; pubic hair; first ejaculation; lowering of voice
    b. pubic hair; first ejaculation; growth spurt; lowering of voice
    c. lowering of voice; pubic hair; growth spurt; first ejaculation
    d. growth spurt; lowering of voice; pubic hair; first ejaculation

2. Which of the following statements about adolescent physical development is *not* true?
    a. Hands and feet generally lengthen before arms and legs.
    b. Facial features usually grow before the head itself reaches adult size and shape.
    c. Oil, sweat, and odor glands become more active.
    d. The lymphoid system increases slightly in size, and the heart increases by nearly half.

3. In puberty, a hormone that increases markedly in girls (and only somewhat in boys) is:
    a. estrogen.
    b. testosterone.
    c. androgen.
    d. menarche.

4. Nutritional deficiencies in adolescence are frequently the result of:
    a. eating red meat.
    b. exotic diets or food fads.
    c. anovulatory menstruation.
    d. excessive exercise.

5. In females, puberty is typically marked by a(n):
    a. significant widening of the shoulders.
    b. significant widening of the hips.
    c. enlargement of the torso and upper chest.
    d. decrease in the size of the eyes and nose.

6. Nonreproductive sexual characteristics, such as the deepening of the voice and the development of breasts, are called:
    a. gender-typed traits.
    b. primary sex characteristics.
    c. secondary sex characteristics.
    d. pubertal prototypes.

7. Puberty is initiated when hormones are released from the __________, then from the __________, and then from the adrenal glands and the __________.
    a. hypothalamus; pituitary; gonads
    b. pituitary; gonads; hypothalamus
    c. gonads; pituitary; hypothalamus
    d. pituitary; hypothalamus; gonads

8. The typical bulimic patient is a:
   a. college-age woman.
   b. teenage girl who starves herself to the point of emaciation.
   c. woman in her late forties.
   d. teenager who suffers from life-threatening obesity.

9. With regard to appearance, adolescent girls are *most* commonly dissatisfied with:
   a. timing of maturation.
   b. eyes and other facial features.
   c. weight.
   d. legs.

10. Statistically speaking, to predict the age at which a girl first has sexual intercourse, it would be *most* useful to know her:
    a. socioeconomic level.
    b. race or ethnic group.
    c. religion.
    d. age at menarche.

11. Individuals who experiment with drugs early are:
    a. typically affluent teenagers who are experiencing an identity crisis.
    b. more likely to have multiple drug-abuse problems later on.
    c. less likely to have alcohol-abuse problems later on.
    d. usually able to resist later peer pressure leading to long-term addiction.

12. Compounding the problem of sexual abuse of boys, abused boys:
    a. feel shame at the idea of being weak.
    b. have fewer sources of emotional support.
    c. are more likely to be abused by fathers.
    d. have all of the above problems.

13. Puberty is *most accurately* defined as the period:
    a. of rapid physical growth that occurs during adolescence.
    b. during which sexual maturation is attained.
    c. of rapid physical growth and sexual maturation that ends childhood.
    d. during which adolescents establish identities separate from their parents.

14. Which of the following does *not* typically occur during puberty?
    a. The lungs increase in size and capacity.
    b. The heart's size and rate of beating increase.
    c. Blood volume increases.
    d. The lymphoid system decreases in size.

15. Teenagers' susceptibility to respiratory ailments typically ____________ during adolescence, due to a(n) ____________ in the size of the lymphoid system.
    a. increases; increase
    b. increases; decrease
    c. decreases; increase
    d. decreases; decrease

Matching Items

Match each term or concept with its corresponding description or definition.

Terms or Concepts

_______ 1. puberty
_______ 2. GH
_______ 3. testosterone
_______ 4. estrogen
_______ 5. growth spurt
_______ 6. primary sex characteristics
_______ 7. menarche
_______ 8. spermarche
_______ 9. secondary sex characteristics
_______ 10. body image
_______ 11. anorexia nervosa
_______ 12. bulimia nervosa

Descriptions or Definitions

a. onset of menstruation
b. period of rapid physical growth and sexual maturation that ends childhood
c. hormone that increases dramatically in boys during puberty
d. hormone that increases steadily during puberty in both sexes
e. an affliction characterized by binge-purge eating
f. hormone that increases dramatically in girls during puberty
g. first sign is increased bone length and density
h. attitude toward one's physical appearance
i. an affliction characterized by self-starvation
j. physical characteristics not involved in reproduction
k. the sex organs involved in reproduction
l. first ejaculation containing sperm

Thinking Critically About Chapter 14

Answer these questions the day before an exam as a final check on your understanding of the chapter's terms and concepts.

1. (Research Report) Fifteen-year-old Latoya is preoccupied with her "disgusting appearance" and seems depressed most of the time. The best thing her parents could do to help her through this difficult time would be to:
   a. ignore her self-preoccupation since their attention would only reinforce it.
   b. encourage her to "shape up" and not give in to self-pity.
   c. kid her about her appearance in the hope that she will see how silly she is acting.
   d. offer practical advice, such as clothing suggestions, to improve her body image.

2. Thirteen-year-old Rosa, an avid runner and dancer, is worried because most of her friends have begun to menstruate regularly. Her doctor tells her:
   a. that she should have a complete physical exam, because female athletes usually menstruate earlier than average.
   b. not to worry, since female athletes usually menstruate later than average.
   c. that she must stop running immediately, because the absence of menstruation is a sign of a serious health problem.
   d. that the likely cause of her delayed menarche is an inadequate diet.

3. Twelve-year-old Kwan is worried because his twin sister has suddenly grown taller and more physically mature than he. His parents should:
   a. reassure him that the average boy is one or two years behind the average girl in the onset of the growth spurt.
   b. tell him that within a year or less he will grow taller than his sister.
   c. tell him that one member of each fraternal twin pair is always shorter.
   d. encourage him to exercise more to accelerate the onset of his growth spurt.

4. Calvin, the class braggart, boasts that because his beard has begun to grow, he is more virile than his male classmates. Jacob informs him that:
   a. the tendency to grow facial and body hair has nothing to do with virility.
   b. beard growth is determined by heredity.
   c. girls also develop some facial hair and more noticeable hair on their arms and legs, so it is clearly not a sign of masculinity.
   d. all of the above are true.

5. The most likely source of status for a late-maturing, middle-SES boy would be:
   a. academic achievement or vocational goal.
   b. physical build.
   c. athletic prowess.
   d. success with the opposite sex.

6. Which of the following students is likely to be the most popular in a sixth-grade class?
   a. Vicki, the most sexually mature girl in the class
   b. Sandra, the tallest girl in the class
   c. Brad, who is at the top of the class scholastically
   d. Dan, the tallest boy in the class

7. Regarding the effects of early and late maturation on boys and girls, which of the following is *not* true?
   a. Early maturation is usually easier for boys to manage than it is for girls.
   b. Late maturation is usually easier for girls to manage than it is for boys.
   c. Late-maturing girls may be drawn into older peer groups and may exhibit problem behaviors such as early sexual activity.
   d. Late-maturing boys may not "catch up" physically, or in terms of their self-images, for many years.

8. Eleven-year-old Clarice, who matured early, is depressed because she is often teased about her well-developed figure. Her mother tells her that early-maturing girls:
   a. eventually have more close friends than those who are slower to mature.
   b. are more likely than late-maturing girls to be satisfied with the shape of their bodies.
   c. often become less popular as their counterparts begin to mature.
   d. enjoy the benefits of a. and b.

9. Twenty-four-year-old Connie, who has a distorted view of sexuality, has gone from one abusive relationship with a man to another. It is likely that Connie:
   a. has been abusing drugs all her life.
   b. was sexually abused as a child.
   c. will eventually become a normal, nurturing mother.
   d. had attention-deficit disorder as a child.

10. As a psychoanalyst, Dr. Mendoza is most likely to believe that eating disorders are caused by:
    a. contemporary pressure to be "slim and trim."
    b. low self-esteem and depression, which act as a stimulus for destructive patterns of eating.
    c. unresolved conflicts with parents.
    d. the desire of working women to project a strong, self-controlled image.

11. Which of the following adolescents is likely to begin puberty at the earliest age?
    a. Aretha, an African-American teenager who hates exercise
    b. Todd, a football player of European ancestry
    c. Kyu, an Asian-American honors student
    d. There is too little information to make a prediction.

12. Of the following teenagers, those most likely to be distressed about their physical development are:
    a. late-maturing girls.
    b. late-maturing boys.
    c. early-maturing boys.
    d. girls or boys who masturbate.

13. Thirteen-year-old Kristin seems apathetic and lazy to her parents. You tell them:
    a. that Kristin is showing signs of chronic depression.
    b. that Kristin may be experiencing psychosocial difficulties.
    c. that Kristin has a poor attitude and needs more discipline.
    d. to have Kristin's iron level checked.

14. I am a hormone that rises steadily during puberty in both males and females. What am I?
    a. estrogen
    b. testosterone
    c. GH
    d. menarche

15. Eleven-year-old Linda, who has just begun to experience the first signs of puberty, laments, "When will the agony of puberty be over?" You tell her that the major events of puberty typically end about ____________ after the first visible signs appear.
    a. 6 years
    b. 3 or 4 years
    c. 2 years
    d. 1 year

Key Terms

Using your own words, write a brief definition or explanation of each of the following terms on a separate piece of paper.

1. adolescence
2. puberty
3. gonads
4. menarche
5. secular trend
6. growth spurt
7. primary sex characteristics
8. spermarche
9. secondary sex characteristics
10. body image
11. childhood sexual abuse
12. anorexia nervosa
13. bulimia nervosa
14. drug abuse
15. addiction
16. drug use
17. gateway drugs
18. generational forgetting

ANSWERS

CHAPTER REVIEW

1. 11; 21; puberty

Girls: onset of breast growth, initial appearance of pubic hair, peak growth spurt, widening of the hips, first menstrual period, completion of pubic-hair growth, and final breast development

Boys: initial appearance of pubic hair, growth of the testes, growth of the penis, first ejaculation, peak growth spurt, voice changes, beard development, and completion of pubic-hair growth

2. hypothalamus; pituitary gland; adrenal glands; gonads (sex glands); testes; ovaries
3. GnRH (gonad releasing hormone); estrogen; testosterone; GH (growth hormone)
4. testosterone; estrogen
5. indirectly; psychological impact; visible changes
6. 8; 14
7. menarche; 9; 18
8. sisters; monozygotic twins
9. varies
10. earlier
11. fat; later; earlier
12. secular trend; developed
13. accelerate
14. positively

15. early

Early-maturing girls may be teased about their big feet or developing breasts. Those who date early may begin "adult" activities at an earlier age, may be pressured by their dates to be sexually active, and may suffer the decrease in self-esteem associated with being scrutinized by parents and criticized by friends.

16. late
17. positive; mixed

The effects of late maturation on boys are mixed, but late-maturing boys who are unusually short, who are not athletic, who appear physically weak or unattractive, and who are slow to be sexually active tend to have lower self-esteem. They also create more problems during adolescence.

18. length; density; gain
19. fat; gender; heredity; diet; exercise
20. females
21. muscle; upper
22. 38 pounds (17 kilograms); 9 5/8 inches (24 centimeters); 10 inches (25 centimeters); 42 pounds (19 kilograms)
23. varies
24. head
25. do not always
26. lungs; heart; decreases; increases; endurance

The fact that the more visible spurts of weight and height precede the less visible ones of the muscles and organs means that athletic training and weightlifting should match the young person's size of a year or so earlier.

27. lymphoid; less
28. oil; sweat; odor
29. primary sex characteristics; is

Girls: growth of uterus and thickening of the vaginal lining

Boys: growth of testes and lengthening of penis; also scrotum enlarges and becomes pendulous

30. menarche; spermarche; several years later
31. anovulatory
32. have; do not
33. secondary sex characteristics

Males grow taller than females and become wider at the shoulders than at the hips. Females take on more fat all over and become wider at the hips, and their breasts begin to develop. About 65 percent of boys experience some temporary breast enlargement. As the larynx grows, the adolescent's voice (especially in boys) becomes lower. Head and body hair become coarser and darker in both sexes. Facial hair (especially in boys) begins to grow.

34. breast development; facial and body hair
35. body image

Many adolescents spend hours examining themselves in front of the mirror; some exercise or diet with obsessive intensity.

36. good looking, sexy, fun, and kind and honest
37. tall; muscular; thin; shapely
38. less; immunity
39. childhood sexual abuse
40. repeated; adult-child relationships; development
41. 8; 12
42. self-destruction; counterattacking
43. childhood sexual abuse
44. girls; boys; community
45. less; are
46. fight; immature; socially isolated; alcoholic; drug-abusing; do not
47. calories; vitamins; minerals; calcium; iron; zinc; iron; iron-deficiency anemia
48. overeating; underexercising; social rejection
49. drug use; food fads; undernourishment
50. 13; 18
51. anorexia nervosa; 1
52. more common; bulimia nervosa; are; gastrointestinal; heart; athletes
53. genetic; depression, alcoholism, and drug addiction
54. **a.** sociocultural theory
    b. psychoanalytic theory
    c. cognitive theory
    d. learning theory
    e. epigenetic systems theory
55. abuse; addictive; use; maturation
56. decline; increase; also holds
57. gateway drugs; sex; alienation; antisocial; physical health; depression
58. growth rate
59. inhibitions; judgment; sexually; antisocial; school; drinking
60. slows; memory; abstract

Delaying experimentation increases the adolescent's chances of becoming realistically informed about the risks of drug use and of developing the reasoning ability to limit or avoid the use of destructive drugs in dangerous circumstances.

61. were; interpersonally alienated, emotionally withdrawn, and unhappy

The measures include health education classes that honestly portray the risk of drug use; increased punishment for store owners who sell alcohol or cigarettes to minors; raising the price of alcohol and cigarettes; enforcing drunk-driving laws; and teaching parents how to communicate with teenagers.

62. advertising; parental

63. peers' attitudes; acceptability; riskiness

64. have; generational forgetting

PROGRESS TEST 1

Multiple-Choice Questions

1. **a.** is the answer. (p. 439)

2. **a.** is the answer. (p. 442)

3. **a.** is the answer. (p. 445)

4. **c.** is the answer. This is because each menstrual period depletes some iron from the body. (p. 457)

5. **c.** is the answer. (p. 450)

a. & b. Even a year after menarche, when ovulation is irregular, pregnancy is possible.

d. Remission means a disappearance of symptoms, such as those of a particular disease; although at first ovulation is irregular, it certainly does not disappear.

6. **b.** is the answer. (p. 451)

7. **b.** is the answer. (p. 449)

8. **d.** is the answer. (p. 440)

9. **c.** is the answer. (pp. 452–453)

a. Although some adolescents become overweight, many diet and lose weight in an effort to attain a desired body image.

d. On the contrary, cultural attitudes about beauty are an extremely influential factor in the formation of a teenager's body image.

10. **c.** is the answer. (p. 457)

a. & d. Eating disorders are more common in women than in men.

b. Eating disorders are more common in younger women.

11. **b.** is the answer. (p. 454)

12. **c.** is the answer. (pp. 444–445)

13. **a.** is the answer. (p. 453)

14. **c.** is the answer. (p. 459)

15. **d.** is the answer. (p. 456)

True or False Items

1. T (p. 456)

2. T (p. 450)

3. F The first indicator of reproductive potential in males is ejaculation of seminal fluid containing sperm (spermarche). Menarche (the first menstrual period) is the first indication of reproductive potential in females. (p. 449)

4. T (p. 447)

5. T (p. 442)

6. F Studies show that the majority of adolescent girls, even those in the thinnest group, want to lose weight. (p. 457)

7. F The strong emphasis on appearance is reflected in the culture as a whole; for example, teachers (and, no doubt, prospective employers) tend to judge people who are physically attractive as being more competent than those who are less attractive. (pp. 452–453)

8. F These habits generally *worsen* during adolescence. (p. 457)

9. T (p. 444)

10. F Although there is great variation in the timing of pubertal events, the sequence is very similar for all young people. (p. 439)

PROGRESS TEST 2

Multiple-Choice Questions

1. **b.** is the answer. (p. 439)

2. **d.** is the answer. During adolescence, the lymphoid system *decreases* in size and the heart *doubles* in size. (p. 447)

3. **a.** is the answer. (p. 440)

b. Testosterone increases markedly in boys.

c. Androgen is another name for testosterone.

d. Menarche is the first menstrual period.

4. **b.** is the answer. (p. 456)

5. **b.** is the answer. (p. 446)

a. The shoulders of males tend to widen during puberty.

c. The torso typically lengthens during puberty.

d. The eyes and nose *increase* in size during puberty.

6. **c.** is the answer. (p. 450)

a. Although not a term used in the textbook, a gender-typed trait is one that is typical of one sex but not of the other.

b. Primary sex characteristics are those involving the reproductive organs.

d. This is not a term used by developmental psychologists.

7. a. is the answer. (p. 440)

8. a. is the answer. (pp. 458)

b. This describes an individual suffering from anorexia nervosa.

c. Eating disorders are much more common in younger women.

d. Most individuals with bulimia nervosa are usually close to normal in weight.

9. c. is the answer. (p. 457)

a. If the timing of maturation differs substantially from that of the peer group, dissatisfaction is likely; however, this is not the most common source of dissatisfaction in teenage girls.

b. & d. Although teenage girls are more likely than boys to be dissatisfied with certain features, which body parts are troubling varies from girl to girl.

10. d. is the answer. (p. 444)

11. b. is the answer. (p. 459)

12. a. is the answer. (p. 455)

b. This was not discussed in the text.

c. This is true of girls.

13. c. is the answer. (p. 439)

14. b. is the answer. Although the size of the heart increases during puberty, heart rate *decreases*. (p. 447)

15. d. is the answer. (p. 447)

Matching Items

1. b (p. 439)	**5.** g (p. 445)	**9.** j (p. 450)
2. d (p. 440)	**6.** k (p. 448)	**10.** h (p. 452)
3. c (p. 440)	**7.** a (p. 449)	**11.** i (p. 457)
4. f (p. 440)	**8.** l (p. 449)	**12.** e (p. 457)

THINKING CRITICALLY ABOUT CHAPTER 14

1. d. is the answer. (p. 453)

a., b., & c. These would likely make matters worse.

2. b. is the answer. (p. 442)

a. Because they typically have little body fat, female dancers and athletes menstruate *later* than average.

c. Delayed maturation in a young dancer or athlete is usually quite normal.

d. The text does not indicate that the age of menarche varies with diet.

3. a. is the answer. (p. 440)

b. It usually takes longer than one year for a prepubescent male to catch up with a female who has begun puberty.

c. This is not true.

d. The text does not suggest that exercise has an effect on the timing of the growth spurt.

4. d. is the answer. (p. 451)

5. a. is the answer. (p. 445)

b., c., & d. These are more typically sources of status for early-maturing boys.

6. d. is the answer. (p. 446)

a. & b. Early-maturing girls are often teased and criticized by their friends.

c. During adolescence, physical stature is typically a more prized attribute among peers than is scholastic achievement.

7. c. is the answer. It is *early*-maturing girls who are often drawn into older peer groups. (p. 444)

8. a. is the answer. (p. 444)

9. b. is the answer. (p. 454)

10. c. is the answer. (p. 458)

a. Those who emphasize sociocultural theory would more likely offer this explanation.

b. Those who emphasize learning theory would more likely offer this explanation.

d. Those who emphasize cognitive theory would more likely offer this explanation.

11. a. is the answer. African-Americans often begin puberty earlier than Asian-Americans or Americans of European ancestry. Furthermore, females who are inactive menstruate earlier than those who are more active. (p. 442)

12. b. is the answer. (p. 445)

a. Late maturation is typically more difficult for boys than for girls.

c. Early maturation is generally a positive experience for boys.

d. Adolescent masturbation is no longer the source of guilt or shame that it once was.

13. d. Kristin's symptoms are typical of iron-deficiency anemia, which is more common in teenage girls than in any other age group. (p. 457)

14. c. is the answer. (p. 440)

a. Only in girls do estrogen levels rise markedly during puberty.

b. Only in boys do testosterone levels rise markedly during puberty.

d. Menarche is the first menstrual period.

15. **b.** is the answer. (p. 440)

KEY TERMS

1. **Adolescence** is the period of biological, cognitive, and psychosocial transition from childhood to adulthood. (p. 439).
2. **Puberty** is the period of rapid physical growth and sexual maturation that ends childhood and brings the young person to adult size, shape, and sexual potential. (p. 439)
3. The **gonads** are the pair of sex glands in humans—the ovaries in girls and the testes or testicles in boys. (p. 440)
4. **Menarche**, which refers to the first menstrual period, is the specific event that is taken to indicate fertility in adolescent girls. (p. 442)
5. The **secular trend** is the tendency of successive cohorts to develop differently as a result of social changes, mainly improved nutrition and medical advances. (p. 442)
6. The **growth spurt**, which begins with an increase in bone length and density and includes rapid weight gain and organ growth, is one of the many observable signs of puberty. (p. 445)
7. During puberty, changes in the **primary sex characteristics** involve those sex organs that are directly involved in reproduction. (p. 448)
8. **Spermarche**, which refers to the first ejaculation of seminal fluid containing sperm, is the specific event that is taken to indicate fertility in adolescent boys. (p. 449)
9. During puberty, changes in the **secondary sex characteristics** involve parts of the body that are not directly involved in reproduction but that signify sexual development. (p. 450)
10. (Research Report) **Body image** refers to adolescents' mental conception of, and attitude toward, their physical appearance. (p. 452)
11. **Childhood sexual abuse** is any activity in which an adult uses a child for his or her own sexual stimulation or pleasure—even if the use does not involve physical contact. (p. 454)
12. **Anorexia nervosa** is a serious eating disorder in which a person restricts eating to the point of emaciation and possible starvation. (p. 457)
13. **Bulimia nervosa** is an eating disorder in which the person engages repeatedly in episodes of binge eating followed by purging through induced vomiting or the abuse of laxatives. (p. 457)
14. **Drug abuse** is the ingestion of a drug to the extent that it impairs the user's well-being. (p. 458)
15. **Addiction** is a person's dependence on a drug or a behavior in order to feel physically or psychologically at ease. (p. 458)
16. **Drug use** is the ingestion of a drug, regardless of the amount or affect of ingestion. (p. 459)
17. **Gateway drugs** are drugs—usually tobacco, alcohol, and marijuana—whose use increases the risk that a person will later use harder drugs. (p. 459)
18. **Generational forgetting** is the tendency of each new generation to ignore lessons (such as the hazards of drug use) learned by the previous cohort. (p. 465)

CHAPTER 15

Adolescence: Cognitive Development

Chapter Overview

Chapter 15 begins by describing the cognitive advances of adolescence. With the attainment of formal operational thought, the developing person becomes able to think in an adult way, that is, to be logical, to think in terms of possibilities, to reason scientifically and abstractly.

Not everyone reaches the stage of formal operational thought, however, and even those who do so spend much of their time thinking at less advanced levels. The discussion of adolescent egocentrism supports this generalization in showing that adolescents have difficulty thinking rationally about themselves and their immediate experiences. Adolescent egocentrism makes them see themselves as psychologically unique and more socially significant than they really are.

The second section addresses the question, "What kind of school best fosters adolescent intellectual growth?" Many adolescents enter secondary school feeling less motivated and more vulnerable to self-doubt than they did in elementary school. The rigid behavioral demands and intensified competition of most secondary schools do not, unfortunately, provide a supportive learning environment for adolescents. Schools can be more effectively organized by setting clear, attainable educational goals that are supported by the entire staff.

The chapter concludes with an example of adolescent cognition at work: decision making in the area of sexual behavior. The discussion relates choices made by adolescents to their cognitive abilities and typical shortcomings, and it suggests ways in which adolescents may be helped to make healthy choices.

NOTE: Answer guidelines for all Chapter 15 questions begin on page 238.

Guided Study

The text chapter should be studied one section at a time. Before you read, preview each section by skimming it, noting headings and boldface items. Then read the appropriate section objectives from the following outline. Keep these objectives in mind and, as you read the chapter section, search for the information that will enable you to meet each objective. Once you have finished a section, write out answers for its objectives.

Adolescent Thought (pp. 469–478)

1. Describe advances in thinking during adolescence.

2. Describe evidence of formal operational thinking during adolescence and provide examples of adolescents' emerging ability to reason deductively and inductively.

3. Discuss adolescent egocentrism and give three examples of egocentric fantasies or fables.

Schools, Learning, and the Adolescent Mind (pp. 478–486)

4. Evaluate the typical secondary school's ability to meet the cognitive needs of the typical adolescent.

5. Discuss the impact of ego- and task-involvement learning on the typical adolescent.

6. Explain how schools can be organized to more effectively meet adolescents' cognitive needs.

Adolescent Decision Making (pp. 487–488)

7. Briefly discuss the typical adolescent's inability to make major life decisions.

Thinking About Sex (pp. 488–498)

8. Explain how adolescent thinking contributes to adolescent pregnancy and sexually transmitted disease.

9. Discuss the role of parents as sex educators.

10. (Changing Policy) Explain and evaluate the new approach to sex education.

Chapter Review

When you have finished reading the chapter, work through the material that follows to review it. Complete the sentences and answer the questions. As you proceed, evaluate your performance for each section by consulting the answers on page 238. Do not continue with the next section until you understand each answer. If you need to, review or reread the appropriate section in the textbook before continuing.

Adolescent Thought (pp. 469–476)

1. The basic skills of thinking, learning, and remembering that advance during the school-age years ______________ (continue to progress/stabilize) during adolescence.

2. Advances in ______________ ______________ improve concentration, while a growing ______________ ______________ and memory skills allow teens to connect new ideas to old ones, and

strengthened _______________ and _______________ help them become better students.

3. Piaget's term for the fourth stage of cognitive development is _______________ _______________ thought. Other theorists may explain adolescent advances differently, but virtually all theorists agree that adolescent thought _______________ (is/is not) qualitatively different from children's thought. For many developmentalists, the single most distinguishing feature of adolescent thought is the capacity to think in terms of _______________. One specific example of this type of thinking is the development of _______________ thought.

4. Compared with younger individuals, adolescents have _______________ (more/less) difficulty arguing against their personal beliefs and self-interest.

5. During the school years, children make great strides in _______________ (inductive/deductive) reasoning.

6. During adolescence, they become more capable of _______________ reasoning—that is, they can begin with a general _______________ or _______________ and draw logical _______________ from it. This type of reasoning is a hallmark of formal operational thought.

7. Piaget devised a number of famous tasks involving _______________ principles to study how children of various ages reasoned hypothetically and deductively.

Briefly describe how children reason differently about the "balance-beam" problem at ages 7, 10, and 13.

8. More recent research has shown that the growth of formal reasoning abilities is far _______________ (faster/slower) and _______________ (more/less) complete than Piaget and others believed it to be. Each individual's intellect, experience, talents, and interests _______________ (do/do not) affect his or her thinking as much as the ability to reason formally.

9. The adolescent's belief that he or she is uniquely significant and that the social world revolves around him or her is a psychological phenomenon called _______________ _______________. David Elkind has argued that this form of thinking occurs because adolescents fail to differentiate between the _______________ and the _______________.

Give an example of this flawed thinking in adolescents.

10. An adolescent's tendency to feel that he or she is somehow immune to the consequences of dangerous or illegal behavior is expressed in the _______________ _______________.

11. An adolescent's tendency to imagine that her or his own life is unique, heroic, or even mythical, and that she or he is destined for great accomplishments, is expressed in the _______________ _______________.

12. Adolescents, who believe that they are under constant scrutiny from nearly everyone, create for themselves an _______________ _______________. Their acute self-consciousness reveals that young people are often not at ease with the broader _______________ _______________.

13. Adolescent egocentrism enables them to reflect more thoughtfully on their lives, but often at the cost of greater ______________ .

Schools, Learning, and the Adolescent Mind
(pp. 478–486)

14. The best setting for personal growth, called the optimum ______________-______________ ______________, depends on several factors, including ______________ ______________ ______________ .

15. The emergence of hypothetical, abstract thought makes adolescents ______________ (more/less) interested in the opinions of others. At the same time, they are ______________ (more/less) vulnerable to criticism than their behaviors imply. Instead of there being a good fit between adolescents' needs and the schools, there is often a ______________ ______________ .

Cite several ways in which educational settings tend *not* to be supportive of adolescents' self-confidence.

16. (Research Report) One outcome of the relatively common mismatch between student needs and the school environment is a widespread dip in academic ______________ as young people enter secondary school.

17. Educational goals ______________ (vary/do not vary) by culture. Similarly, the goals of the American education system ______________ (have/have not) changed much over the centuries.

18. The type of learning in which academic grades are based solely on individual test performance and students are ranked against each other is called ______________-______________ learning. In such situations, many students, especially ______________ and students from ______________ backgrounds, find it psychologically safer not to work very hard.

19. The type of learning in which grades are based on cooperatively acquiring certain competencies and knowledge that everyone is expected to attain is called ______________-______________ learning.

20. One benefit of cooperative learning is that it often provides students with their first exposure to people of different ______________, ______________, ______________, and ______________ backgrounds.

21. Cooperative learning is ______________ (more/less) likely to lead to rivalry among various ethnic, religious, and racial groups.

22. Schools that are most effective in educating students share the central characteristic of ______________ ______________ .

23. Attitudes regarding after-school jobs ______________ (vary/do not vary) from country to country.

24. In some nations, such as ______________, almost no adolescent is employed or even does significant chores at home. In many ______________ countries, many older adolescents have jobs as part of their school curriculum. Most parents in the United States ______________ (approve/do not approve) of youth employment.

25. Perhaps because many of today's jobs are not ______________, research finds that when adolescents are employed more than ______________ hours a week, their grades suffer. As adults, those who were employed extensively as teenagers are more likely to use ______________ and to feel ______________ (more/less) connected to their families.

Adolescent Decision Making (pp. 487–488)

26. For most of the big decisions, such as whether and where to go to college or find a job, adolescents ____________ (do/do not) play a major role in choosing.

Thinking About Sex (pp. 488–497)

27. Generally, research reveals that adolescent beliefs, values, and reasoning processes ____________ (do/do not) significantly affect their sexual behavior.

28. Diseases that are spread by sexual contact are called ____________ ____________ diseases. Among these are ____________. Sexually active adolescents also risk exposure to the ____________ virus.

29. Teenage pregnancy ____________ (is/is not) a worldwide problem. The country that is leading this trend is ____________ ____________.

Describe the likely consequences to all concerned of an American adolescent giving birth.

30. Most young people ____________ (believe/do not believe) sex should occur within the context of a committed, loving relationship. This attitude ____________ (varies/does not vary) from country to country.

31. Ignorance about sex and unavailability of contraception ____________ (do/do not) explain the high rates of adolescent pregnancy and STDs.

32. Knowing facts about sex has so little effect on adolescent sexual behavior, because they find it difficult to envision all the ____________ ____________; instead, they focus on ____________ considerations or difficulties.

33. Because of their sense of personal ____________, many adolescents seriously underestimate the chances of pregnancy or of contracting a disease.

34. The first step in encouraging adolescents to make more rational decisions about their sexuality requires adults to be more ____________ in *their* thinking about adolescent sexuality.

(Changing Policy) Briefly explain why traditional sex education is often irrelevant or ineffective.

35. (Changing Policy) A new form of sex education uses extensive ____________ ____________ and discussions to teach adolescents reasoning skills for dealing with sexual pressures.

36. (Changing Policy) Sex education is most effective with adolescents who ____________ (have/have not yet) become sexually active.

37. (Changing Policy) Traditionally, sex education was focused on ____________ (girls/boys). Today, sexual decision making is ____________ (more/less) likely to be shared by both parties.

38. One study found that mothers who were more religious, and more disapproving of teen sex, were ____________ (less/more) likely to know when their children were sexually active.

39. Many school systems are revising their sex education programs to make them more ____________ and focused on ____________ ____________.

40. In the United States, the teenage birth rate ____________ (increased/declined) between 1991 and 1996. At the same time, condom use among ____________ (males/females/both sexes) has ____________ (increased/decreased).

Progress Test 1

Multiple-Choice Questions

Circle your answers to the following questions and check them with the answers on page 239. If your answer is incorrect, read the explanation for why it is incorrect and then consult the appropriate pages of the text (in parentheses following the correct answer).

1. Many psychologists consider the distinguishing feature of adolescent thought to be the ability to think in terms of:
   a. moral issues.
   b. concrete operations.
   c. possibility, not just reality.
   d. logical principles.

2. Piaget's last stage of cognitive development is:
   a. formal operational thought.
   b. concrete operational thought.
   c. universal ethical principles.
   d. symbolic thought.

3. Advances in metamemory and metacognition deepen adolescents' abilities in:
   a. studying.
   b. the invincibility fable.
   c. the personal fable.
   d. adolescent egocentrism.

4. The adolescent who takes risks and feels immune to the laws of mortality is showing evidence of the:
   a. invincibility fable.
   b. personal fable.
   c. imaginary audience.
   d. death instinct.

5. Imaginary audiences, invincibility fables, and personal fables are expressions of adolescent:
   a. morality.
   b. thinking games.
   c. decision making.
   d. egocentrism.

6. The typical adolescent is:
   a. tough-minded.
   b. indifferent to public opinion.
   c. self-absorbed and hypersensitive to criticism.
   d. all of the above.

7. When adolescents enter secondary school, many:
   a. experience a drop in their academic self-confidence.
   b. are less motivated than they were in elementary school.
   c. are less conscientious than they were in elementary school.
   d. experience all of the above.

8. In ___________, academic grades are based solely on individual test performance, and students are ranked against each other.
   a. task-involvement learning
   b. ego-involvement learning
   c. academic tracking
   d. preconventional classroom environments

9. Thinking that begins with a general premise and then draws logical conclusions from it is called:
   a. inductive reasoning.
   b. deductive reasoning.
   c. "the game of thinking."
   d. hypothetical reasoning.

10. Serious reflection on important issues is a wrenching process for many adolescents because of their newfound ability to reason:
    a. inductively.
    b. deductively.
    c. hypothetically.
    d. symbolically.

11. The main reason for high rates of STDs and pregnancy during adolescence is cognitive immaturity, as evidenced by:
    a. the decline of the "good girl" morality.
    b. increased sexual activity.
    c. the inability to think logically about the consequences of sexual activity.
    d. a lack of information about sexual matters.

12. Many adolescents seem to believe that *their* lovemaking will not lead to pregnancy. This belief is an expression of the:
    a. personal fable.
    b. invincibility fable.
    c. imaginary audience.
    d. "game of thinking."

13. A parent in which of the following countries is *least* likely to approve of her daughter's request to take a part-time job after school?
    a. the United States
    b. Germany
    c. Great Britain
    d. Japan

14. In a new method of sex education, adolescents:
    a. develop reasoning skills to resist sexual pressures.
    b. are exposed to scare tactics designed to discourage sexual activity.
    c. are taught by teenagers who have contracted a sexually transmitted disease.
    d. experience all of the above.

15. To estimate the risk of a behavior, such as unprotected sexual intercourse, it is most important that the adolescent be able to think clearly about:
    a. universal ethical principles.
    b. personal beliefs and self-interest.
    c. probability.
    d. peer pressure.

True or False Items

Write *true* or *false* on the line in front of each statement.

_______ 1. Until young adulthood, most people do not make major decisions on their own.
_______ 2. Adolescents are generally better able than 8-year-olds to recognize the validity of arguments that clash with their own beliefs.
_______ 3. Everyone attains the stage of formal operational thought by adulthood.
_______ 4. Most adolescents who engage in risky behavior are unaware of the consequences, and potential costs, of their actions.
_______ 5. Adolescents often create an imaginary audience as they envision how others will react to their appearance and behavior.
_______ 6. Most developmentalists feel that competitive classroom environments are a healthy cognitive influence on adolescents.
_______ 7. Most teenagers believe that sex should occur only within the context of a committed, loving relationship.
_______ 8. Inductive reasoning is a hallmark of formal operational thought.
_______ 9. Adolescents are the group with the highest rates of the most prevalent sexually transmitted diseases (STDs).
_______ 10. The new wave of sex education tries to take into account adolescent thinking patterns, often involving role playing, discussions, and specific exercises designed to help adolescents weigh alternatives and analyze risks.

Progress Test 2

Progress Test 2 should be completed during a final chapter review. Answer the following questions after you thoroughly understand the correct answers for the Chapter Review and Progress Test 1.

Multiple-Choice Questions

1. Adolescents who fall prey to the invincibility fable may be more likely to:
    a. engage in risky behaviors.
    b. suffer from depression.
    c. have low self-esteem.
    d. drop out of school.

2. Thinking that extrapolates from a specific experience to form a general premise is called:
    a. inductive reasoning.
    b. deductive reasoning.
    c. "the game of thinking."
    d. hypothetical reasoning.

3. Recent research regarding Piaget's theory has found that:
    a. many adolescents arrive at formal operational thinking later than Piaget predicted.
    b. formal operational thinking is more likely to be demonstrated in certain domains than in others.
    c. whether formal operational thinking is demonstrated depends in part on an individual's experiences, talents, and interests.
    d. all of the above are true.

4. When young people overestimate their significance to others, they are displaying:
    a. concrete operational thought.
    b. adolescent egocentrism.
    c. a lack of cognitive growth.
    d. immoral development.

5. The personal fable refers to adolescents imagining that:
    a. they are immune to the dangers of risky behaviors.
    b. they are always being scrutinized by others.
    c. their own lives are unique, heroic, or even mythical.
    d. the world revolves around their actions.

6. The typical secondary school environment:
    a. has more rigid behavioral demands than the average elementary school.
    b. does not meet the cognitive needs of the typical adolescent.
    c. emphasizes ego-involvement learning.
    d. is described by all of the above.

7. As compared to elementary schools, most secondary schools exhibit all of the following *except*:
   a. a more flexible approach to education.
   b. intensified competition.
   c. more punitive grading practices.
   d. less individualized attention.

8. In ______________, grades are not assigned competitively but are based on acquiring competencies that *everyone* is expected to attain.
   a. ego-involvement learning
   b. task-involvement learning
   c. academic tracking
   d. preconventional classroom environments

9. Research has shown that adolescents who work at after-school jobs more than 20 hours per week:
   a. are more likely to use drugs as adults.
   b. have lower grades.
   c. tend to feel less connected to their families.
   d. have all of the above characteristics.

10. Educational settings that emphasize individual competition:
    a. may be destructive to adolescent development if not used properly.
    b. tend to be the most effective in educating students.
    c. are more effective in large schools than in small schools.
    d. have proven very effective in educating minority students.

11. One of the hallmarks of formal operational thought is:
    a. egocentrism.
    b. deductive thinking.
    c. symbolic thinking.
    d. all of the above.

12. In explaining adolescent advances in thinking, sociocultural theorists emphasize:
    a. the accumulated improvement in specific skills.
    b. mental advances resulting from the transition from primary school to secondary school.
    c. the completion of the myelination process in cortical neurons.
    d. advances in metacognition.

13. Although, on balance, teenagers display mature decision-making analysis and good choices in most areas, this is not the case in matters of sexual activity, especially if the teen:
    a. is well educated.
    b. has friends involved in similar activities.
    c. is under age 16.
    d. is able to draw support from caring adults.

14. Evidence that revised sex education programs are working comes from the fact that ______________ is (are) declining.
    a. the birth rate among teenagers
    b. the percentage of sexually active teenagers
    c. the use of condoms among teenagers
    d. all of the above

15. The most important characteristic of effective schools is:
    a. self-paced instruction.
    b. dividing classes into students with similar abilities.
    c. a standardized procedure for teaching each subject.
    d. high, clearly stated, and attainable goals.

Matching Items

Match each term or concept with its corresponding description or definition.

Terms or Concepts

_______ 1. invincibility fable
_______ 2. imaginary audience
_______ 3. person-environment fit
_______ 4. hypothetical thought
_______ 5. deductive reasoning
_______ 6. inductive reasoning
_______ 7. formal operational thought
_______ 8. ego-involvement learning
_______ 9. task-involvement learning
_______ 10. volatile mismatch
_______ 11. adolescent egocentrism

Descriptions or Definitions

a. the tendency of adolescents to focus on themselves to the exclusion of others
b. adolescents feel immune to the consequences of dangerous behavior
c. grading is based solely on individual test performance
d. a creation of adolescents, who are preoccupied with how others react to their appearance and behavior
e. the match or mismatch between an adolescent's needs and the educational setting
f. grading that does not foster competition among students
g. reasoning about propositions that may or may not reflect reality
h. the last stage of cognitive development, according to Piaget
i. thinking that moves from premise to conclusion
j. thinking that moves from a specific experience to a general premise
k. a clash between a teenager's needs and the structure and functioning of his or her school

Thinking Critically About Chapter 15

Answer these questions the day before an exam as a final check on your understanding of the chapter's terms and concepts.

1. A 13-year-old can create and solve logical problems on the computer but is not usually reasonable, mature, or consistent in his or her thinking when it comes to people and social relationships. This supports the finding that:
a. some children reach the stage of formal operational thought earlier than others.
b. the stage of formal operational thought is not attained by age 13.
c. formal operational thinking may be demonstrated in certain domains and not in other domains.
d. older adolescents and adults often do poorly on standard tests of formal operational thought.

2. An experimenter hides a ball in her hand and says, "Either the ball in my hand is red or it is not red." Most preadolescent children say:
a. the statement is true.
b. the statement is false.
c. they cannot tell if the statement is true or false.
d. they do not understand what the experimenter means.

3. Fourteen-year-old Monica is very idealistic and often develops crushes on people she doesn't even know. This reflects her newly developed cognitive ability to:
a. deal simultaneously with two sides of an issue.
b. take another person's viewpoint.
c. imagine possible worlds and people.
d. see herself as others see her.

4. Which of the following is the *best* example of a personal fable?
a. Adriana imagines that she is destined for a life of fame and fortune.
b. Ben makes up stories about his experiences to impress his friends.
c. Kalil questions his religious beliefs when they seem to offer little help for a problem he faces.
d. Julio believes that every girl he meets is attracted to him.

5. Which of the following is the *best* example of the adolescent's ability to think hypothetically?
   a. Twelve-year-old Stanley feels that people are always watching him.
   b. Fourteen-year-old Mindy engages in many risky behaviors, reasoning that, "nothing bad will happen to me."
   c. Fifteen-year-old Philip feels that no one understands his problems.
   d. Thirteen-year-old Josh delights in finding logical flaws in virtually everything his teachers and parents say.

6. Frustrated because of the dating curfew her parents have set, Melinda exclaims, "You just don't know how it feels to be in love!" Melinda's thinking demonstrates:
   a. the invincibility fable.
   b. the personal fable.
   c. the imaginary audience.
   d. adolescent egocentrism.

7. Compared to her 13-year-old brother, 17-year-old Yolanda is likely to:
   a. be more critical about herself.
   b. be more egocentric.
   c. have less confidence in her abilities.
   d. be more capable of reasoning hypothetically.

8. Nathan's fear that his friends will ridicule him because of a pimple that has appeared on his nose reflects a preoccupation with:
   a. his personal fable.
   b. the invincibility fable.
   c. an imaginary audience.
   d. preconventional reasoning.

9. Thirteen-year-old Malcolm, who lately is very sensitive to the criticism of others, feels significantly less motivated and capable than when he was in elementary school. Malcolm is probably:
   a. experiencing a sense of vulnerability that is common in adolescents.
   b. a lower-track student.
   c. a student in a task-involvement classroom.
   d. all of the above.

10. A high school principal who wished to increase the interest level and achievement of minority and female students would be well advised to:
    a. create classroom environments that are not based on competitive grading procedures.
    b. encourage greater use of standardized testing in the elementary schools that feed students to the high school.
    c. separate students into academic tracks based on achievement.
    d. do all of the above.

11. Seventy-year-old Artemis can't understand why his daughter doesn't want her teenage son to work after school. "In my day," he says, "we learned responsibility and a useful trade by working throughout high school." You wisely point out that:
    a. most after-school jobs for teens today are not very meaningful.
    b. after-school employment tends to have a more negative impact on boys than girls.
    c. attitudes are changing; today, most American parents see adolescent employment as a waste of time.
    d. teens in most European countries almost never work after school.

12. Who is the *least* likely to display mature decision making?
    a. Brenda, an outgoing 17-year-old art student
    b. Fifteen-year-old Kenny, who has few adults in whom he confides
    c. Monique, a well-educated 15-year-old
    d. Damon, an 18-year-old high school graduate who lives alone

13. After hearing that an unusually aggressive child has been in full-time day care since he was 1 year old, 16-year-old Keenan concludes that non-parental care leads to behavior problems. Keenan's conclusion is an example of:
    a. inductive reasoning.
    b. deductive reasoning.
    c. hypothetical thinking.
    d. adolescent egocentrism.

14. Cindy, a sexually active teenager who does not practice contraception, is likely to think that:
    a. having a child might not be so bad.
    b. it is unlikely that she will become pregnant after just one episode.
    c. she is less likely to become pregnant, or contract a STD, than others are.
    d. all of the above are true.

15. Dr. Malone, who wants to improve the effectiveness of her adolescent sex-education class, would be well advised to:
    a. focus on the biological facts of reproduction and disease, because teenage misinformation is largely responsible for the high rates of unwanted pregnancy and STDs.
    b. personalize the instruction, in order to make the possible consequences of sexual activity more immediate to students.
    c. teach boys and girls in separate classes, so that discussion can be more frank and open.
    d. use all of the above strategies.

Key Terms

Using your own words, write a brief definition or explanation of each of the following terms on a separate piece of paper.

1. formal operational thought
2. hypothetical thought
3. inductive reasoning
4. deductive reasoning
5. adolescent egocentrism
6. invincibility fable
7. personal fable
8. imaginary audience
9. person-environment fit
10. volatile mismatch
11. ego-involvement learning
12. task-involvement learning
13. sexually transmitted diseases (STDs)

ANSWERS

CHAPTER REVIEW

1. continue to progress
2. selective attention; knowledge base; metamemory; metacognition
3. formal operational; is; possibilities; hypothetical
4. less
5. inductive
6. deductive; premise; theory; conclusions
7. scientific

Preschoolers have no understanding of how to solve the problem. By age 7, children understand balancing the weights but don't know that distance from the center is also a factor. By age 10, they understand the concepts but are unable to coordinate them. By ages 13 or 14, they are able to solve the problem.

8. slower; less; do
9. adolescent egocentrism; unique; universal

One example of adolescent egocentrism is the young person who believes that no one else has ever had the particular emotional experiences he or she is having (feeling sad and lonely or being in love, for example).

10. invincibility fable
11. personal fable
12. imaginary audience; social world
13. self-criticism
14. person-environment fit; the individual's developmental stage, cognitive strengths, and learning style, as well as the traditions, educational objectives, and future needs of the society
15. more; more; volatile mismatch

Compared to elementary schools, most secondary schools have more rigid behavioral demands, intensified competition, more punitive grading practices, as well as less individualized attention and procedures.

16. self-confidence
17. vary; have
18. ego-involvement; girls; minority
19. task-involvement
20. economic; ethnic; religious; racial
21. less
22. having educational goals that are high, clearly stated, attainable, and supported by the entire staff
23. vary
24. Japan; European; approve
25. meaningful; 20; drugs; less
26. do not
27. do
28. sexually transmitted; gonorrhea, genital herpes, syphilis, and chlamydia; HIV
29. is; the United States

For the mother, the consequences include interference with education and social, personal, and vocational growth; for the couple if they marry, greater risk of abuse, abandonment, or divorce; for the child, greater risk of prenatal and birth complications, of lower academic achievement, and, at adolescence, of drug abuse, delinquency, dropping out of school, and early parenthood.

30. believe; does not vary

31. do not
32. possible alternatives (or consequences); immediate
33. invincibility
34. rational

Adolescents are often put off by traditional sex-education courses that focus on biological facts rather than on their actual sexual dilemmas and pressures.

35. role playing
36. have not yet
37. girls; more
38. less
39. practical; social interaction
40. declined; both sexes; increased

PROGRESS TEST 1

Multiple-Choice Questions

1. **c.** is the answer. (p. 470)

   a. Although moral reasoning becomes much deeper during adolescence, it is not limited to this stage of development.

   b. & d. Concrete operational thought, which *is* logical, is the distinguishing feature of childhood thinking.

2. **a.** is the answer. (p. 470)

   b. In Piaget's theory, this stage precedes formal operational thought.

   c. & d. These are not stages in Piaget's theory.

3. **a.** is the answer. (p. 469)

   b., c., & d. These are examples of limited reasoning ability during adolescence.

4. **a.** is the answer. (p. 476)

   b. This refers to adolescents' tendency to imagine their own lives as unique, heroic, or even mythical.

   c. This refers to adolescents' tendency to fantasize about how others will react to their appearance and behavior.

   d. This is a concept in Freud's theory.

5. **d.** is the answer. These thought processes are manifestations of adolescents' tendency to see themselves as being much more central and important to the social scene than they really are. (pp. 475–478)

6. **c.** is the answer. (p. 469)

7. **d.** is the answer. (pp. 478–479)

8. **b.** is the answer. (p. 481)

   a. In task-involvement learning, grades are based on acquiring certain competencies and knowledge that everyone, with enough time and effort, is expected to attain.

   c. Tracking, which is not discussed in this chapter, refers to the separation of students into distinct groups based on standardized tests of ability and achievement.

   d. This is not a type of classroom environment discussed in the text.

9. **b.** is the answer. (p. 472)

   a. Inductive reasoning moves from specific facts to a general conclusion.

   b. & c. The "game of thinking," which is an example of hypothetical reasoning, involves the ability to think creatively about possibilities.

10. **c.** is the answer. (p. 471)

11. **c.** is the answer. (p. 492)

    a. The text does not suggest that declining moral standards are responsible for the increased rate of STDs.

    b. Although this may be true, in itself it is not necessarily a result of adolescent cognitive immaturity.

    d. Various studies have found that merely understanding the facts of sexuality does not correlate with more responsible and cautious sexual behavior.

12. **b.** is the answer. (pp. 478, 492)

    a. This refers to adolescents' tendency to imagine their own lives as unique, heroic, or even mythical.

    c. This refers to adolescents' tendency to fantasize about how others will react to their appearance and behavior.

    d. This is the adolescent ability to suspend knowledge of reality in order to think playfully about possibilities.

13. **d.** is the answer. Japanese adolescents almost never work after school. (p. 485)

    a. American parents generally approve of adolescent employment.

    b. & c. Jobs are an important part of the school curriculum in many European countries.

14. **a.** is the answer. (p. 493)

15. **c.** is the answer. (p. 492)

True or False Items

1. T (p. 487)
2. T (p. 471)

3. F Some people never reach the stage of formal operational thought. (p. 474)
4. F According to William Gardner, adolescent behavior is guided by assumptions about costs and benefits. (pp. 491–492)
5. T (p. 478)
6. F In such competitive situations, many students find it easier and psychologically safer not to try, thereby avoiding the potential gains and pains of both success and failure. (pp. 481–482)
7. T (p. 490)
8. F Deductive reasoning is a hallmark of formal operational thought. (p. 472)
9. T (p. 488)
10. T (pp. 494–495)

PROGRESS TEST 2

Multiple-Choice Questions

1. **a.** is the answer. (p. 476)

   b., c., & d. The invincibility fable leads some teens to believe that they are immune to the dangers of risky behaviors; it is not necessarily linked to depression, low self-esteem, or the likelihood that an individual will drop out of school.
2. **a.** is the answer. (p. 472)

   b. Deductive reasoning begins with a general premise and then draws logical conclusions from it.

   c. & d. The "game of thinking," which is an example of hypothetical reasoning, involves the ability to think creatively about possibilities.
3. **d.** is the answer. (pp. 474–475)
4. **b.** is the answer. (p. 475)
5. **c.** is the answer. (p. 476)

   a. This describes the invincibility fable.

   b. This describes the imaginary audience.

   d. This describes adolescent egocentrism in general.
6. **d.** is the answer. (p. 479)
7. **a.** is the answer. (p. 479)
8. **b.** is the answer. (p. 482)

   a. In ego-involvement learning, grades *are* assigned competitively.

   c. Tracking, which is not discussed in this chapter, refers to the separation of students into distinct groups based on standardized tests of ability and achievement.

   d. This is not a type of classroom environment discussed in the text.
9. **d.** is the answer. (p. 486)
10. **a.** is the answer. (p. 481)
11. **b.** is the answer. (p. 472)
12. **b.** is the answer. (p. 470)

    a. & d. These are more likely to be emphasized by information-processing theorists.

    c. This reflects the biological perspective on development.
13. **c.** is the answer. (pp. 491–492)
14. **a.** is the answer. (p. 497)

    b. & c. These are on the rise.
15. **d.** is the answer. (p. 484)

Matching Items

1. b (p. 476)	**5.** i (p. 472)	**9.** f (p. 482)
2. d (p. 478)	**6.** j (p. 472)	**10.** k (p. 479)
3. e (p. 478)	**7.** h (p. 470)	**11.** a (p. 474)
4. g (p. 471)	**8.** c (p. 481)	

THINKING CRITICALLY ABOUT CHAPTER 15

1. **c.** is the answer. (p. 474)
2. **c.** is the answer. Although this statement is logically verifiable, preadolescents who lack formal operational thought cannot prove or disprove it. (p. 473)
3. **c.** is the answer. (pp. 470–471)
4. **a.** is the answer. (p. 476)

   b. & d. These behaviors are more indicative of a preoccupation with the imaginary audience.

   c. Kalil's questioning attitude is a normal adolescent tendency that helps foster moral reasoning.
5. **d.** is the answer. (p. 471)

   a. This is an example of the imaginary audience.

   b. This is an example of the invincibility fable.

   c. This is an example of adolescent egocentrism.
6. **d.** is the answer. (p. 475)
7. **d.** is the answer. (pp. 470–471)
8. **c.** is the answer. (p. 478)

   a. In this fable adolescents see themselves destined for fame and fortune.

   b. In this fable young people feel that they are somehow immune to the consequences of common dangers.

   d. This is a stage of moral reasoning in Kohlberg's theory.

9. **a.** is the answer. (pp. 478–479)
10. **a.** is the answer. (pp. 482–483)
11. **a.** is the answer. (p. 486)

    b. There is no evidence of a gender difference in the impact of employment on adolescents.

    c. & d. In fact, just the opposite are true.
12. **b.** is the answer. Mature decision making is least likely to be displayed by adolescents who are under age 16, who have less education, and who have few adults to talk with. (p. 491)
13. **a.** is the answer. (p. 472)

    b. Keenan is reasoning from the specific to the general, rather than vice versa.

    c. Keenan is thinking about an actual observation, rather than a hypothetical possibility.

    d. Keenan's reasoning is focused outside himself, rather than being self-centered.
14. **d.** is the answer. (pp. 491–492)
15. **b.** is the answer. (pp. 494–495)

KEY TERMS

1. In Piaget's theory, the last stage of cognitive development, which arises from a combination of maturation and experience, is called **formal operational thought**. A hallmark of formal operational thinking is the capacity for hypothetical, logical, and abstract thought. (p. 470)
2. **Hypothetical thought** involves reasoning about propositions and possibilities that may or may not reflect reality. (p. 471)
3. **Inductive reasoning** is thinking that moves from one or more specific experiences to a general conclusion. (p. 472)
4. **Deductive reasoning** is thinking that moves from the general to the specific, or from a premise to a logical conclusion. (p. 472)
5. **Adolescent egocentrism** refers to the tendency of adolescents to see themselves as much more socially significant than they actually are. (p. 475)
6. Adolescents who experience the **invincibility fable** feel that they are immune to the dangers of risky behaviors. (p. 476)
7. Another example of adolescent egocentrism is the **personal fable**, through which adolescents imagine their own lives as unique, heroic, or even mythical. (p. 476)

    Memory aid: A *fable* is a mythical story.
8. Adolescents often create an **imaginary audience** for themselves, as they assume that others are as intensely interested in them as they are. (p. 478)
9. The term **person-environment fit** refers to the best setting for personal growth, as in the optimum educational setting. (p. 478)
10. When teenagers' individual needs do not match the size, routine, and structure of their schools, a **volatile mismatch** may occur. (p. 479)
11. In **ego-involvement learning**, academic grading is based solely on individual test performance, and students are ranked against each other. (p. 481)

    Memory aid: In **ego-involvement learning**, one's ego is on the line as one is placed in competition with other students.
12. In **task-involvement learning**, grades are based on mastery of knowledge that everyone is expected to attain. (p. 482)
13. **Sexually transmitted diseases (STDs)** include all diseases that are spread by sexual contact. (p. 488)

CHAPTER 16

Adolescence: Psychosocial Development

Chapter Overview

Chapter 16 focuses on the psychosocial development, particularly the formation of identity, that is required for the attainment of adult status and maturity. The influences of family, friends, and society on this development are examined in some detail. Suicide—one of the most perplexing problems of adolescence—is then explored. The special problems posed by adolescent lawbreaking are discussed, and suggestions for alleviating or treating these problems are given. The chapter concludes with the message that, while no other period of life is characterized by so many changes in the three domains of development, for most young people the teenage years are happy ones. Furthermore, serious problems in adolescence do not necessarily lead to lifelong problems.

NOTE: Answer guidelines for all Chapter 16 questions begin on page 252.

Guided Study

The text chapter should be studied one section at a time. Before you read, preview each section by skimming it, noting headings and boldface items. Then read the appropriate section objectives from the following outline. Keep these objectives in mind and, as you read the chapter section, search for the information that will enable you to meet each objective. Once you have finished a section, write out answers for its objectives.

The Self and Identity (pp. 501–510)

1. Describe the development of identity during adolescence, including the emergence of "possible selves."

2. Describe the four major identity statuses, and give an example of each one.

3. (text and Children Up Close) Discuss the problems of identity formation encountered by minority adolescents.

Family and Friends (pp. 510–520)

4. Discuss parental influence on identity formation, including the effect of parent-child conflict and other aspects of family functioning.

5. Discuss the role of peers and friends in identity formation and in the development of male-female relationships.

Adolescent Suicide (pp. 520–525)

6. Discuss adolescent suicide, noting its incidence and prevalence, contributing factors, warning signs, and gender and national variations.

Breaking the Law (pp. 525–529)

7. Discuss delinquency among adolescents today, noting its prevalence, significance for later development, and best approaches for prevention or treatment.

Conclusion: A Life-Span View (pp. 528–530)

8. Discuss the theme of this text as demonstrated by adolescent development.

Chapter Review

When you have finished reading the chapter, work through the material that follows to review it. Complete the sentences and answer the questions. As you proceed, evaluate your performance for each section by consulting the answers on page 252. Do not continue with the next section until you understand each answer. If you need to, review or reread the appropriate section in the textbook before continuing.

The Self and Identity (pp. 501–510)

1. The momentous changes that occur during the teen years challenge adolescents to find their own ________________. In the process of trying to find their "true self," many adolescents experience the emergence of ________________ ________________.

2. Many adolescents take on a ________________ ________________, behaving in ways that are contrary to their true selves.

3. Identify and describe the purpose of three types of false selves.

   a. ________________________________

   b. ________________________________

   c. ________________________________

4. Adolescents who experiment with false selves report the highest levels of ________________ and ________________.

5. According to Erikson, the challenge of adolescence is ________________________________ ________________________________.

6. When the search for identify becomes overwhelming and confusing, adolescents may experience an ________________ ________________.

7. The ultimate goal of adolescence is to establish a new identity that involves both repudiation and assimilation of childhood values; this is called ________________ ________________.

8. The young person who prematurely accepts earlier roles and parental values without exploring alternatives or truly forging a unique identity is experiencing identity ________________.

9. An adolescent who adopts an identity that is the opposite of the one he or she is expected to adopt has taken on a ______________ ______________.

10. The young person who has few commitments to goals or values and is apathetic about defining his or her identity is experiencing ______________ ______________.

11. A time-out period during which a young person experiments with different identities, postponing important choices, is called an identity ______________.

12. The developmentalist who has extensively compared adolescents' identity statuses with various measures of their cognitive and psychological development is ______________.

13. In terms of their attitudes toward parents, the diffused adolescent is often ______________, the moratorium adolescent is more ______________, the forecloser shows more ______________ and ______________, and the achiever treats parents with more ______________.

14. Adolescents who have ______________ ______________ and those who have prematurely ______________ tend to have a strong sense of ethnic identification. Those who have ______________ tend to be high in prejudice, while those who are ______________ ______________ tend to be relatively low in prejudice.

15. The process of identity formation can take ______________ or longer.

16. Often, girls seek their new identities through their ______________ ______________, whereas boys tend to seek ______________ and even ______________ from others. However, ______________ differences seem to be more influential than ______________ in guiding the search for identity.

17. The surrounding culture can aid identity formation in two ways: by providing ______________, and by providing ______________ ______________ and ______________ that ease the transition from childhood to adulthood.

18. In a culture where most people hold the same moral, political, religious, and sexual values, identity is ______________ (easier/more difficult) to achieve.

19. For members of minority ethnic groups, identity achievement is often ______________ (more/less) stressful than it is for other adolescents. For minority ethnic groups, identity formation requires finding the right balance between transcending one's ______________ and immersing oneself in it.

20. (Children Up Close) For immigrants and minority-group members, identity achievement is often ______________ (more/less) difficult than it is for other adolescents. This may cause them to embrace a ______________ identity or, as is more often the case, to ______________ on identity prematurely.

21. (Children Up Close) Relationships with parents and other relatives ______________ (are/are not) particularly stressful for minority adolescents in the United States. Members of minority groups are often criticized by their ______________ if they make an effort to join the majority culture.

Family and Friends (pp. 510–520)

22. People who focus on differences between the younger and older generations speak of a ______________ ______________.
Numerous studies have shown that parents and adolescents substantially ______________ (agree/disagree) in their political, religious, educational, and vocational opinions. Indeed, virtually every aspect of adolescent behavior ______________ (is/is not) directly affected by the family.

23. The idea that family members in different developmental stages have a natural tendency to see the family in different ways is called the ______________ ______________.

24. In terms of the adolescent's achievement and self-esteem, ________________ parenting is better than either ________________ or ________________ parenting. Especially harmful are parents who are ________________-________________: Their teenagers are likely to lack ________________ and to be ________________, ________________-________________, and ________________.

25. Parent-child conflict is most common in ________________ (early/late) adolescence and is particularly notable with ________________ (mothers/fathers) and their ________________ (early/late)-maturing ________________ (sons/daughters).

26. Firstborns tend to have ________________ (more/fewer) conflicts with parents than later-borns do.

27. Among Chinese-, Korean-, and Mexican-American teens, conflict tends to arise in ________________ (early/late) adolescence due in part to their cultures' emphasis on family ________________.

28. The conflicts that arise in adolescence usually recede as family members revise their ________________ for one another in light of the child's growing ________________.

29. Four other elements of family functioning that have been heavily researched include ________________, ________________, ________________, and ________________.

30. Compared with European-American parents, ethnic-minority parents are more inclined toward ________________ parenting. One reason ethnic-minority children sometimes respond well to this is that they may perceive strict parenting as a sign of ________________ and support.

31. In terms of family control, a powerful deterrent to delinquency, risky sex, and drug abuse is ________________ ________________.

Too much interference, however, may contribute to adolescent ________________.

32. Overall, parent-child relations in all family types and nations, and among children of both sexes, are typically ________________. If there is conflict, it is more likely to center on details like the adolescent's ________________ ________________, rather than on ________________ ________________.

33. According to B. Bradford Brown, during adolescence the peer group serves four important functions.

a. ________________

b. ________________

c. ________________

d. ________________

34. The largely constructive role of peers runs counter to the notion of ________________ ________________. Social pressure to conform ________________ (falls/rises) dramatically in early adolescence, until about age ________________, when it begins to ________________ (fall/rise).

35. Research comparing school achievement and troubled behavior in Asian- and African-American teens reported that ________________ and ________________ were the deciding influence, rather than differences in ________________.

36. Usually, the first sign of heterosexual attraction is a seeming ________________ of members of the other sex. The pattern by which adolescents "warm up" to the other sex ________________ (is similar/varies greatly) from nation to nation.

Briefly outline the four-stage progression of heterosexual involvement.

37. For gay and lesbian adolescents, added complications usually ________ (slow down/speed up) romantic attachments. In cultures that are ________, many young men and women with homosexual or lesbian feelings may ________ their feelings, or try to ________ or ________ them.

Adolescent Suicide (pp. 520–525)

38. Adolescents under age 20 are ________ (more/less) likely to kill themselves than adults are.

39. Thinking about committing suicide, called ________ ________, is ________ (common/relatively rare) among high school students.

40. Most suicide attempts in adolescence ________ (do/do not) result in death. A deliberate act of self-destruction that does not result in death is called a ________.

41. List five factors that affect whether thinking about suicide leads to a self-destructive act or to death.

a. ________

b. ________

c. ________

d. ________

e. ________

42. The rate of suicide is higher for adolescent ________ (males/females). The rate of parasuicide is higher for ________ (males/females).

(Table 16.4) Briefly describe ethnic differences in suicide rates in the United States.

43. Suicide rates in North America have ________ (risen/fallen) since 1960. This is due in part to less parental ________ and greater adolescent access to ________, ________, and ________.

44. (Research Report) Suicide usually ________ (is/is not) a response to a specific and immediate psychological blow.

45. (Research Report) Suicide often occurs as a result of long-standing problems in the individual as well as in the person's ________ and ________ environment.

List several background elements that increase an individual's suicide risk.

46. (Research Report) Adolescents are susceptible to ________, in which one suicide leads to others.

47. (Research Report) List five warning signs of suicide.

a. ________

b. ________

c. ________

d. ________

e. ________

Breaking the Law (pp. 525–529)

48. Arrests are far more likely to occur during the ________ ________ of life than during any other time period. Although statistics indicate that the ________ (incidence/prevalence) of arrests is highest among this age group, they do not reveal how widespread, or ________, lawbreaking is among this age group.

49. If all acts of "juvenile delinquency" are included, the prevalence of adolescent crime is ______________ (less/greater) than official records report.

Briefly describe data on gender and ethnic differences in adolescent arrests.

50. (Changing Policy) Experts find it useful to distinguish ______________-______________ offenders, whose criminal activity stops by age 21, from ______________-______________ ______________ offenders, who become career criminals.

51. (Changing Policy) Developmentalists have found that it ______________ (is/is not) currently possible to distinguish children who actually will become career criminals.

52. Adolescents who later become career criminals are among the first of their cohort to ______________.

They also are among the least involved in ______________ activities, and tend to be ______________ in preschool and elementary school. At an even earlier age, they show signs of ______________ ______________, such as being slow in ______________ development, or being ______________, or having poor ______________ control.

53. For most delinquents, residential incarceration in a prison or reform school usually ______________ (is/is not) the best solution.

54. The victims of adolescent crime tend to be ______________ (teenagers/adults).

Conclusion: A Life-Span View (pp. 528-530)

55. For most young people, the teenage years overall are ______________ (happy/unhappy) ones.

56. Adolescents who have one serious problem ______________ (often have/do not usually have) others.

57. In most cases adolescent problems stem from earlier developmental events such as ______________ ______________.

Progress Test 1

Multiple-Choice Questions

Circle your answers to the following questions and check them with the answers on page 254. If your answer is incorrect, read the explanation for why it is incorrect and then consult the appropriate pages of the text (in parentheses following the correct answer).

1. According to Erikson, the primary task of adolescence is that of establishing:
   a. basic trust.
   b. an identity.
   c. intimacy.
   d. integrity.

2. According to developmentalists who study identity formation, foreclosure involves:
   a. accepting an identity prematurely, without exploration.
   b. taking time off from school, work, and other commitments.
   c. opposing parental values.
   d. failing to commit oneself to a vocational goal.

3. When adolescents adopt an identity that is the opposite of the one they are expected to adopt, they are considered to be taking on a:
   a. foreclosed identity.
   b. diffused identity.
   c. negative identity.
   d. reverse identity.

4. The main sources of emotional support for most young people who are establishing independence from their parents are:
   a. older adolescents of the opposite sex.
   b. older siblings.
   c. teachers.
   d. peer groups.

5. (Children Up Close) For members of minority ethnic groups, identity achievement may be particularly complicated because:
   a. their cultural ideal clashes with the Western emphasis on adolescent self-determination.
   b. democratic ideology espouses a color-blind, multiethnic society in which background is irrelevant.
   c. parents and other relatives tend to emphasize ethnicity and expect teens to honor their roots.
   d. of all of the above reasons.

6. In a crime-ridden neighborhood, parents can protect their adolescents by keeping close watch over activities, friends, and so on. This practice is called:
   a. generational stake.
   b. foreclosure.
   c. peer screening.
   d. parental monitoring.

7. Which of the following is *not* a common manifestation of the adolescent tendency to take on a false self?
   a. trying to impress or please others
   b. nonconformity resulting from anger toward society
   c. feeling that parents and peers have rejected one's "true self"
   d. experimenting with different behaviors "just to see how it feels"

8. If there is a "generation gap," it is likely to occur in ______________ adolescence and to center on issues of ______________.
   a. early; morality
   b. late; self-discipline
   c. early; self-control
   d. late; politics

9. (Children Up Close) Because of the conflict between their ethnic background and the larger culture, minority adolescents will *most often*:
   a. reject the traditional values of both their ethnic culture and the majority culture.
   b. foreclose on identity prematurely.
   c. declare a moratorium.
   d. experience identity diffusion.

10. In the long run, the most effective programs for preventing juvenile delinquency would include all of the following *except*:
    a. helping parents discipline in an authoritative manner.
    b. strengthening the schools.
    c. increasing the police presence in the area.
    d. shoring up neighborhood networks.

11. Compared to ethnic-majority children in the United States, ethnic-minority children are more likely to perceive ________ parenting as being ________.
    a. authoritarian; a sign of caring
    b. authoritarian; domineering
    c. authoritative; a sign of caring
    d. authoritative; domineering

12. Compared with normal adolescents, suicidal adolescents are:
    a. more concerned about the future.
    b. academically average students.
    c. likely to have few steady friends.
    d. less likely to have attempted suicide.

13. The early signs of life-course persistent offenders include all of the following *except*:
    a. signs of brain damage early in life.
    b. antisocial school behavior.
    c. delayed sexual intimacy.
    d. use of alcohol and tobacco at an early age.

14. Regarding gender differences in self-destructive acts, the rate of parasuicide is ________ and the rate of suicide is ________.
    a. higher in males; higher in females
    b. higher in females; higher in males
    c. the same in males and females; higher in males
    d. the same in males and females; higher in females

15. Conflict between parents and adolescent offspring is:
    a. most likely to involve fathers and their early-maturing offspring.
    b. more frequent in single-parent homes.
    c. more likely between firstborns and their parents than between later-borns and their parents.
    d. likely in all of the above situations.

True or False Items

Write *true* or *false* on the line in front of each statement.

________ 1. In cultures where everyone's values are similar and social change is slight, identity is relatively easy to achieve.

________ 2. Most adolescents have political views and educational values that are markedly different from those of their parents.

_______ 3. Peer pressure is inherently destructive to the adolescent seeking an identity.

_______ 4. For most adolescents, group socializing and dating precede the establishment of true intimacy with one member of the opposite sex.

_______ 5. Some adolescents who experiment with false selves tend to have low self-esteem.

_______ 6. Most adolescent self-destructive acts are a response to an immediate and specific psychological blow.

_______ 7. The majority of adolescents report that they have at some time engaged in law-breaking that might have led to arrest.

_______ 8. In finding themselves, teens try to find an identity that is stable, consistent, and mature.

_______ 9. Parents who are authoritative have the most destructive effect on their teenage offspring.

_______ 10. Warning signs of suicide include a sudden decline in school attendance and achievement and withdrawal from social relationships.

Progress Test 2

Progress Test 2 should be completed during a final chapter review. Answer the following questions after you thoroughly understand the correct answers for the Chapter Review and Progress Test 1.

Multiple-Choice Questions

1. The best way to limit adolescent law-breaking in general would be to:

a. strengthen the family, school, and community fabric.
b. increase the number of police officers in the community.
c. improve the criminal justice system.
d. establish rehabilitative facilities for law-breakers.

2. Which of the following was *not* identified as a warning sign of suicide in an adolescent?

a. a sudden decline in school achievement
b. an attempted suicide
c. running away
d. a sudden interest in friends and family

3. Parent-child conflict among Chinese-, Korean-, and Mexican-American families often surfaces late in adolescence because these cultures:

a. emphasize family closeness.
b. value authoritarian parenting.
c. encourage autonomy in children.
d. do all of the above.

4. Becoming a distinct self-determined individual is not always compatible with connections to one's heritage and peer group, causing some adolescents to experience a(n):

a. generational stake.
b. identity crisis.
c. foreclosure of identity.
d. rejecting-neglecting identity.

5. Which style of parenting do most psychologists recommend?

a. authoritarian
b. permissive
c. very strict
d. authoritative

6. Which of the following is *not* true regarding peer relationships among gay and lesbian adolescents?

a. Romantic attachments are usually slower to develop.
b. In homophobic cultures, many gay teens try to conceal their homosexual feelings by becoming heterosexually involved.
c. Many girls who will later identify themselves as lesbians are oblivious to these sexual urges as teens.
d. In many cases, a lesbian girl's best friend is a boy, who is more at ease with her sexuality than another girl might be.

7. The adolescent experiencing identity diffusion is typically:

a. very apathetic.
b. a risk-taker, anxious to experiment with alternative identities.
c. willing to accept parental values wholesale, without exploring alternatives.
d. one who rebels against all forms of authority.

8. Adolescents help each other in many ways, including:

a. identity formation.
b. independence.
c. social skills.
d. all of the above.

9. Crime statistics show that during adolescence:

a. males and females are equally likely to be arrested.
b. males are more likely to be arrested than females.
c. females are more likely to be arrested than males.
d. males commit more crimes than females but are less likely to be arrested.

10. Which of the following is the most common problem behavior among adolescents?

a. pregnancy
b. daily use of illegal drugs
c. minor law-breaking
d. attempts at suicide

11. A time-out period during which a young person experiments with different identities, postponing important choices, is called a(n):

a. identity foreclosure.
b. negative identity.
c. identity diffusion.
d. identity moratorium.

12. When adolescents' political, religious, educational, and vocational opinions are compared with their parents', the so-called "generation gap" is:

a. much smaller than when the younger and older generations are compared overall.
b. much wider than when the younger and older generations are compared overall.
c. wider between parents and sons than between parents and daughters.
d. wider between parents and daughters than between parents and sons.

13. Which of the following was *not* cited as a reason for teens with low self-esteem to take on a false self?

a. feelings of worthlessness
b. tendency to feel depressed
c. inability to perform well in school
d. feelings of hopelessness, that is, that life will not improve

14. Parent-teen conflict tends to center on issues related to:

a. politics and religion.
b. education.
c. vacations.
d. daily details, such as musical tastes.

15. According to a review of studies from various nations, suicidal ideation is:

a. not as common among high school students as is popularly believed.
b. more common among males than females.
c. more common among females than among males.
d. so common among high school students that it might be considered normal.

Matching Items

Match each term or concept with its corresponding description or definition.

Terms or Concepts

_____ 1. identity
_____ 2. identity achievement
_____ 3. foreclosure
_____ 4. negative identity
_____ 5. identity diffusion
_____ 6. identity moratorium
_____ 7. generation gap
_____ 8. generational stake
_____ 9. parental monitoring
_____ 10. suicidal ideation
_____ 11. parasuicide

Descriptions or Definitions

a. premature identity formation
b. contemplation of suicide
c. the adolescent has few commitments to goals or values
d. differences between the younger and older generations
e. self-destructive act that does not result in death
f. awareness of where children are and what they are doing
g. an individual's self-definition
h. a time-out period during which adolescents experiment with alternative identities
i. the adolescent establishes his or her own goals and values
j. family members in different developmental stages see the family in different ways
k. an identity opposite of the one an adolescent is expected to adopt

Thinking Critically About Chapter 16

Answer these questions the day before an exam as a final check on your understanding of the chapter's terms and concepts.

1. From childhood, Sharon thought she wanted to follow in her mother's footsteps and be a homemaker. Now, at age 40 with a home and family, she admits to herself that what she really wanted to be was a medical researcher. Erik Erikson would probably say that Sharon:
   a. adopted a negative identity when she was a child.
   b. experienced identity foreclosure at an early age.
   c. never progressed beyond the obvious identity diffusion she experienced as a child.
   d. took a moratorium from identity formation.

2. Fifteen-year-old David is rebelling against his devoutly religious parents by taking drugs, stealing, and engaging in other antisocial behaviors. Evidently, David has:
   a. foreclosed on his identity.
   b. declared an identity moratorium.
   c. adopted a negative identity.
   d. experienced identity diffusion.

3. Fourteen-year-old Sean, who is fiercely proud of his Irish heritage, is prejudiced against members of several other ethnic groups. It is likely that, in forming his identity, Sean:
   a. attained identity achievement.
   b. foreclosed on his identity.
   c. declared a lengthy moratorium.
   d. experienced identity diffusion.

4. (Children Up Close) In 1957, 6-year-old Raisel and her parents emigrated from Poland to the United States. Compared with her parents, who grew up in a culture in which virtually everyone held the same religious, moral, political, and sexual values, Raisel is likely to have:
   a. an easier time achieving her own unique identity.
   b. a more difficult time forging her identity.
   c. a greater span of time in which to forge her own identity.
   d. a shorter span of time in which to forge her identity.

5. An adolescent exaggerates the importance of differences in her values and those of her parents. Her parents see these differences as smaller and less important. This phenomenon is called the:
   a. generation gap.
   b. generational stake.
   c. family enigma.
   d. parental imperative.

6. In our society, the most obvious examples of institutionalized moratoria on identity formation are:
   a. the Boy Scouts and the Girl Scouts.
   b. college and the peacetime military.
   c. marriage and divorce.
   d. bar mitzvahs and baptisms.

7. First-time parents Norma and Norman are worried that, during adolescence, their healthy parental influence will be undone as their children are encouraged by peers to become sexually promiscuous, drug-addicted, or delinquent. Their wise neighbor, who is a developmental psychologist, tells them that:
   a. during adolescence, peers are generally more likely to complement the influence of parents than they are to pull their friends in the opposite direction.
   b. research suggests that peers provide a negative influence in every major task of adolescence.
   c. only through authoritarian parenting can parents give children the skills they need to resist peer pressure.
   d. unless their children show early signs of learning difficulties or antisocial behavior, parental monitoring is unnecessary.

8. Thirteen-year-old Cassandra is constantly experimenting with different behaviors and possible identities. It is likely that she:
   a. has low self-esteem.
   b. foreclosed prematurely on her identity.
   c. has great self-understanding.
   d. comes from a home environment in which there is considerable tension and conflict.

9. In forming an identity, the young person seeks to make meaningful connections with his or her past. This seeking is described by Erikson as an unconscious striving for:
   a. individual uniqueness.
   b. peer-group membership.
   c. continuity of experience.
   d. vocational identity.

10. A friend tells you that he doesn't want to live any more because his girlfriend has left him. The most helpful response would be:
   a. "Don't be ridiculous. You have plenty to live for."
   b. "Everyone has these experiences; you'll get over it."
   c. "She wasn't right for you. You're certain to find someone else."
   d. "When did this happen? Let's talk about it."

11. Statistically, the person *least* likely to commit a crime is a(n):
   a. African-American or Latino adolescent.
   b. middle-class white male.
   c. white adolescent of any socioeconomic background.
   d. Asian American.

12. Ray was among the first of his friends to have sex, drink alcohol, and smoke cigarettes. These attributes, together with his having been hyperactive and having poor emotional control, would suggest that Ray is at high risk of:
   a. becoming an adolescent-limited offender.
   b. becoming a life-course persistent offender.
   c. developing an antisocial personality.
   d. foreclosing his identity prematurely.

13. Carl is a typical 16-year-old adolescent who has no special problems. It is likely that Carl has:
   a. contemplated suicide.
   b. engaged in some minor illegal act.
   c. struggled with "who he is."
   d. done all of the above.

14. Statistically, who of the following is *most* likely to commit suicide?
   a. Micah, an African-American female
   b. Yan, an Asian-American male
   c. James, a Native American male
   d. Alison, a European-American female

15. Coming home from work, Malcolm hears a radio announcement warning parents to be alert for possible cluster suicide signs in their teenage children. What might have precipitated such an announcement?
   a. government statistics that suicide is on the rise in the 1990s
   b. the highly publicized suicide of a famous rock singer
   c. the recent crash of an airliner, killing all on board
   d. any of the above

Key Terms

Using your own words, write a brief definition or explanation of each of the following terms on a separate piece of paper.

1. identity
2. possible selves
3. false self
4. identity versus role confusion
5. identity crisis
6. identity achievement
7. foreclosure
8. negative identity
9. identity diffusion
10. identity moratorium
11. generation gap
12. generational stake
13. parental monitoring
14. peer pressure
15. suicidal ideation
16. parasuicide
17. cluster suicide
18. adolescent-limited offender
19. life-course persistent offender

ANSWERS

CHAPTER REVIEW

1. identity; possible (or multiple) selves
2. false self
3. a. The acceptable false self arises from the teen's perception that the real self is rejected by parents and peers.
   b. The pleasing false self tries to impress or please others.
   c. The experimental false self tries out different behaviors (or possible selves)
4. self-esteem; self-knowledge
5. identity versus role confusion
6. identity crisis
7. identity achievement
8. foreclosure
9. negative identity
10. identity diffusion
11. moratorium
12. James Marcia

13. withdrawn; independent; respect; deference; concern
14. achieved identity; foreclosed; foreclosed; identity achievers
15. ten years
16. social relationships; independence; isolation; personality; gender
17. values; social structures; customs
18. easier
19. more; background
20. more; negative; foreclose
21. are; peers
22. generation gap; agree; is
23. generational stake
24. authoritative; authoritarian; permissive; rejecting-neglecting; confidence; depressed; low-achieving; delinquent
25. early; mothers; early; daughters
26. more
27. late; closeness
28. expectations; maturity
29. communication; support; connectiveness; control
30. authoritarian; caring
31. parental monitoring; depression
32. supportive; musical tastes, domestic neatness, sleeping habits; world politics or moral issues
33. **a.** a source of information and a self-help group

    b. a source of support for the adolescent who is adjusting to changes in the social ecology of adolescence

    c. a kind of mirror in which to check one's reflection

    d. a sounding board for exploring and defining one's values and aspirations
34. peer pressure; rises; 14; fall
35. peers; community; race or ethnicity
36. dislike; is similar

The progression begins with groups of same-sex friends. Next, a loose, public association of a girl's group and a boy's group forms. Then, a smaller, heterosexual group forms from the more advanced members of the larger association. Finally, more intimate heterosexual couples peel off.

37. slow down; homophobic; deny; change; conceal
38. less
39. suicidal ideation; common
40. do not; parasuicide
41. **a.** the availability of lethal methods

    b. the extent of parental supervision

    c. the use of alcohol and other drugs

    d. gender

    e. the attitudes about suicide held by the adolescent's family, friends, and culture
42. males; females

Native American males have the highest rates, followed by European-American males, Asian-American males, African-American males, and Hispanic-American males.

43. risen; supervision; alcohol, drugs; guns
44. is not
45. family; social

Background elements that increase the risk of suicide include a temperamental inclination toward fits of rage or depression; having depressed, suicidal, or alcoholic parents; experiencing the early loss of a loved one; growing up with few steady friends; alcohol abuse and drug use; and experiencing unusual educational pressure.

46. cluster suicides
47. **a.** a sudden decline in school attendance and achievement

    b. talk of suicide

    c. withdrawal from social relationships

    d. an attempted suicide

    e. running away
48. second decade; incidence; prevalent
49. greater

Boys are three times as likely to be arrested as girls, and African-American youth are three times as likely to be arrested as European Americans, who are three times as likely to be arrested as Asian Americans.

50. adolescent-limited; life-course persistent
51. is
52. have sex, drink alcohol, and smoke cigarettes; school; antisocial; brain damage; language; hyperactive; emotional
53. is not
54. teenagers
55. happy
56. often have
57. genetic vulnerability, prenatal insults, family disruptions, childhood discord, learning difficulties, aggressive or withdrawn behavior in elementary school, inadequate community intervention

PROGRESS TEST 1

Multiple-Choice Questions

1. **b.** is the answer. (p. 501)

   a. According to Erikson, this is the crisis of infancy.

   c. & d. In Erikson's theory, these crises occur later in life.

2. **a.** is the answer. (p. 504)

   b. This describes an identity moratorium.

   c. This describes a negative identity.

   d. This describes identity diffusion.

3. **c.** is the answer. (p. 504)
4. **d.** is the answer. (p. 516)
5. **d.** is the answer. (pp. 508–509)
6. **d.** is the answer. (p. 514)

   a. The generational stake refers to differences in how family members from different generations view the family.

   b. Foreclosure refers to the premature establishment of identity.

   c. Peer screening is an aspect of parental monitoring, but it was not specifically discussed in the text.

7. **b.** is the answer. (p. 502)
8. **c.** is the answer. (p. 511)
9. **b.** is the answer. (pp. 508–509)

   a. This occurs in some cases, but not in *most* cases.

   c. Moratorium is a time-out in identity formation in order to allow the adolescent to try out alternative identities. It is generally not a solution in such cases.

   d. Young people who experience identity diffusion are often apathetic, which is not the case here.

10. **c.** is the answer. (pp. 528–529)
11. **a.** is the answer. (p. 514)

    b. This was not discussed in the text.

    c. This is true of girls.

12. **c.** is the answer. (p. 522)
13. **c.** is the answer. Most life-course persistent offenders are among the earliest of their cohort to have sex. (p. 528)
14. **b.** is the answer. (p. 524)
15. **c.** is the answer. (p. 512)

    a. In fact, parent-child conflict is more likely to involve mothers and their early-maturing offspring.

    b. The text did not compare the rate of conflict in two-parent and single-parent homes.

True or False Items

1. T (p. 507)
2. F Numerous studies have shown substantial agreement between parents and their adolescent children on political opinions and educational values. (p. 511)
3. F Just the opposite is true. (pp. 516–517)
4. T (pp. 518–519)
5. T (p. 502)
6. F Most self-destructive acts reflect long-standing problems. (p. 522)
7. T (p. 527)
8. T (p. 503)
9. F Authoritative parenting is the style most likely to *foster* the adolescent's achievement and self-esteem. (p. 512)
10. T (pp. 522–523)

PROGRESS TEST 2

Multiple-Choice Questions

1. **a.** is the answer. (p. 528)
2. **d.** is the answer. In fact, just the opposite is true: a sudden loss of interest in friends and family may be a warning sign of suicide. (p. 523)
3. **a.** is the answer. For this reason, autonomy in their offspring tends to be delayed. (p. 513)
4. **b.** is the answer. (p. 503)
5. **d.** is the answer. (p. 512)
6. **d.** is the answer. Lesbian adolescents find it easier to establish strong friendships with same-sex heterosexual peers than homosexual teenage boys do. (p. 520)
7. **a.** is the answer. (p. 504)

   b. This describes an adolescent undergoing an identity moratorium.

   c. This describes identity foreclosure.

   d. This describes an adolescent who is adopting a negative identity.

8. **d.** is the answer. (p. 516)
9. **b.** is the answer. (p. 526)
10. **c.** is the answer. (p. 527)
11. **d.** is the answer. (p. 504)

    a. Identity foreclosure occurs when the adolescent

prematurely adopts an identity, without fully exploring alternatives.

b. Adolescents who adopt an identity that is opposite to the one they are expected to develop have taken on a negative identity.

c. Identity diffusion occurs when the adolescent is apathetic and has few commitments to goals or values.

12. **a.** is the answer. (p. 511)

c. & d. The text does not suggest that the size of the generation gap varies with the offspring's sex.

13. **c.** is the answer. (p. 502)

14. **d.** is the answer. (p. 512)

a., b., & c. In fact, on these issues parents and teenagers tend to show substantial *agreement*.

15. **d.** is the answer. (p. 521)

Matching Items

1. g (p. 501)	**5.** c (p. 504)	**9.** f (p. 514)
2. i (pp. 503-504)	**6.** h (pp. 504-505)	**10.** b (p. 521)
3. a (p. 504)	**7.** d (p. 511)	**11.** e (p. 522)
4. k (p. 504)	**8.** j (p. 511)	

THINKING CRITICALLY ABOUT CHAPTER 16

1. **b.** is the answer. Apparently, Sharon never explored alternatives or truly forged a unique personal identity. (p. 504)

a. Individuals who rebel by adopting an identity that is the opposite of the one they are expected to adopt have taken on a negative identity.

c. Individuals who experience identity diffusion have few commitments to goals or values. This was not Sharon's problem.

d. Had she taken a moratorium on identity formation, Sharon would have experimented with alternative identities and perhaps would have chosen that of a medical researcher.

2. **c.** is the answer. (p. 504)

3. **b.** is the answer. (p. 505)

a. Identity achievers often have a strong sense of ethnic identification, but usually are low in prejudice.

c. & d. The text does not present research that links ethnic pride and prejudice with either identity diffusion or moratorium.

4. **b.** is the answer. Minority adolescents struggle with finding the right balance between transcending their background and becoming immersed in it. (pp. 508–509)

c. & d. The text does not suggest that the amount of time adolescents have to forge their identities varies from one ethnic group to another or has changed over historical time.

5. **b.** is the answer. (p. 511)

a. The generation gap refers to actual differences in attitudes and values between the younger and older generations. This example is concerned with how large these differences are perceived to be.

c. & d. These terms are not used in the text in discussing family conflict.

6. **b.** is the answer. (p. 505)

7. **a.** is the answer. (pp. 516–517)

b. In fact, just the opposite is true.

c. Developmentalists recommend authoritative, rather than authoritarian, parenting.

d. Parental monitoring is important for all adolescents.

8. **c.** is the answer. (p. 502)

a., b., & d. Experimenting with possible selves is a normal sign of adolescent identity formation.

9. **c.** is the answer. (p. 505)

10. **d.** is the answer. Talking about suicide is a clear warning sign of suicide. This attempt to communicate should be acted upon immediately; one way is to get the person to talk about it. (pp. 522–523)

11. **d.** is the answer. (p. 526)

12. **b.** is the answer. (p. 528)

13. **d.** is the answer. (pp. 501–502, 521, 527)

14. **c.** is the answer. (p. 525)

15. **b.** is the answer. (p. 522)

a., c., & d. Cluster suicides occur when the suicide of a well-known person leads others to attempt suicide.

KEY TERMS

1. **Identity**, as used by Erikson, refers to a person's self-definition as a separate individual in terms of roles, attitudes, beliefs, and aspirations. (p. 501).
2. In forming their identities, many adolescents try out various **possible selves**; that is, they imagine what the future might bring if one or another course of action is chosen. (p. 501).
3. A **false self** is a constellation of behaviors that is contrary to one's core being. (p. 502)
4. Erikson's term for the psychosocial crisis of ado-

lescence, **identity versus role confusion** refers to adolescents' need to combine their self-understanding and social roles into a coherent identity. (p. 503)

5. Some adolescents experience an **identity crisis**, in which their search for who they are becomes so overwhelming and confusing that self-definition is urgently sought. (p. 503)
6. In Erikson's theory, **identity achievement** occurs when adolescents attain their new identity by establishing their own goals and values and abandoning some of those set by their parents and culture and accepting others. (pp. 503–504)
7. In identity **foreclosure**, according to Erikson, the adolescent forms an identity prematurely, accepting earlier roles and parental values wholesale, without truly forging a unique personal identity. (p. 504)
8. Adolescents who take on a **negative identity**, according to Erikson, adopt an identity that is the opposite of the one they are expected to adopt. (p. 504)
9. Adolescents who experience **identity diffusion**, according to Erikson, have few commitments to goals or values and are often apathetic about trying to find an identity. (p. 504)
10. According to Erikson, in the process of finding a mature identity, many young people seem to declare an **identity moratorium**, a kind of time-out during which they experiment with alternative identities without trying to settle on any one. (pp. 504–504)
11. The **generation gap** refers to the alleged distance between generations in values, behaviors, and knowledge. (p. 511)
12. The **generational stake** refers to the tendency of each family member, because of that person's different developmental stage, to see the family in a certain way. (p. 511)
13. **Parental monitoring** is parental watchfulness about where one's child is and what he or she is doing, and with whom. (p. 514)
14. **Peer pressure** refers to the social pressure to conform to one's friends in behavior, dress, and attitude. It may be positive or negative in its effects. (p. 516)
15. **Suicidal ideation** refers to thinking about committing suicide, usually with some serious emotional and intellectual overtones. (p. 521)
16. **Parasuicide** is a deliberate act of self-destruction that does not result in death. (p. 522)
17. A **cluster suicide** refers to a series of suicides or suicide attempts that are precipitated by one initial suicide, usually that of a famous person or a well-known peer. (p. 522)
18. **Adolescent-limited offenders** are juveniles, whose criminal activity stops by age 21. (p. 528)
19. **Life-course persistent offenders** are adolescent lawbreakers who later become career criminals. (p. 528)